About the Author

An attorney and author who works as First Amendment Scholar for the First Amendment Center at Vanderbilt University, **David L. Hudson Jr.** writes regularly on the Supreme Court as a contributing editor to the American Bar Association's *Preview of U.S. Supreme Court Cases*. He also teaches classes at the Nashville School of Law, Vanderbilt Law School and Middle Tennessee State University. He is the author of more than 31 books, including *The Rehnquist Court: Understanding Its Impact and Legacy* (Praeger, 2006), and Visible Ink Press's *The Handy Supreme Court Answer Book* and *The Handy Law Answer Book*. He is a graduate of Duke University and Vanderbilt Law School.

Also from Visible Ink Press

The Handy Anatomy Answer Book
by James Bobick and Naomi Balaban
ISBN: 978-1-57859-190-9

The Handy Answer Book for Kids (and Parents),
    2nd edition
by Gina Misiroglu
ISBN: 978-1-57859-219-7

The Handy Astronomy Answer Book
by Charles Liu
ISBN: 978-1-57859-193-0

The Handy Dinosaur Answer Book, 2nd edition
by Patricia Barnes–Svarney and Thomas E.
Svarney
ISBN: 978-1-57859-218-0

The Handy Geography Answer Book, 2nd edition
by Paul A. Tucci
ISBN: 978-1-57859-215-9

The Handy Geology Answer Book
by Patricia Barnes–Svarney and Thomas E.
Svarney
ISBN: 978-1-57859-156-5

The Handy History Answer Book, 2nd edition
by Rebecca Nelson Ferguson
ISBN: 978-1-57859-170-1

The Handy Law Answer Book
by David L. Hudson Jr.
ISBN: 978-1-57859-217-3

The Handy Math Answer Book
by Patricia Barnes–Svarney and Thomas E.
Svarney
ISBN: 978-1-57859-171-8

The Handy Ocean Answer Book
by Patricia Barnes–Svarney and Thomas E.
Svarney
ISBN: 978-1-57859-063-6

The Handy Personal Finance Answer Book
by Paul Tucci
ISBN: 978-1-57859-322-4

The Handy Philosophy Answer Book
by Naomi Zack
ISBN: 978-1-57859-226-5

The Handy Physics Answer Book, 2nd edition
By Paul W. Zitzewitz, Ph.D.
ISBN: 978-1-57859-305-7

The Handy Politics Answer Book
by Gina Misiroglu
ISBN: 978-1-57859-139-8

The Handy Psychology Answer Book
by Lisa J. Cohen
ISBN: 978-1-57859-223-4

The Handy Religion Answer Book
by John Renard
ISBN: 978-1-57859-125-1

The Handy Science Answer Book®, 4th edition
by The Science and Technology Department Carnegie Library of Pittsburgh, James
E. Bobick, and Naomi E. Balaban
ISBN: 978-1-57859-140-4

The Handy Supreme Court Answer Book
by David L Hudson, Jr.
ISBN: 978-1-57859-196-1

The Handy Weather Answer Book, 2nd edition
by Kevin S. Hile
ISBN: 978-1-57859-221-0

Please visit the Handy series website at handyanswers.com

THE
HANDY
PRESIDENTS
ANSWER
BOOK

SECOND EDITION

David L. Hudson Jr., JD

VISIBLE
INK
PRESS

Detroit

THE HANDY PRESIDENTS ANSWER BOOK

Visible Ink Press®
43311 Joy Rd., #414
Canton, MI 48187-2075

Visible Ink Press is a registered trademark of Visible Ink Press LLC.

Most Visible Ink Press books are available at special quantity discounts when purchased in bulk by corporations, organizations, or groups. Customized printings, special imprints, messages, and excerpts can be produced to meet your needs. For more information, contact Special Markets Director, Visible Ink Press, www.visibleinkpress.com, or 734-667-3211.

Managing Editor: Kevin S. Hile
Art Director: Mary Claire Krzewinski
Typesetting: Marco Di Vita
Proofreaders: Sarah Hermsen and Sharon Malinowski
Cover images: Barack Obama courtesy of AP Images; all others, iStock.

Library of Congress Cataloguing-in-Publication Data

Hudson, David L., 1969–
The handy presidents answer book / David L. Hudson.
    p. cm.
Previous ed.: The handy presidents answer book / Roger Matuz with Gina Misiroglu and Lawrence W. Baker. ©2004.
Includes bibliographical references and index.
ISBN 978-1-57859-317-0
1. Presidents—United States—History—Miscellanea. 2. United States—Politics and government—Miscellanea. I. Matuz, Roger. Handy presidents answer book. II. Title.
E176.1.H843 2011
973.09'9—dc23   2011019771

Printed in the United States of America

10 9 8 7 6 5 4 3 2 1

Contents

Introduction

Commander in Chief, Leader of the Free World, the Most Powerful Person on the Globe —these monikers have been placed on the president—the head of the executive branch of the federal government of the United States of America. Simply stated, the president is the leader of the country.

Throughout American history, presidents have served as the driving forces behind the American government, lightning rods for praise and criticism and the head of the body politic. Forty-four men (no women, yet) have occupied this prestigious position with varying degrees of successes and failures. Some were born into prominent political families, while others grew up in abject poverty. Some were great communicators, while others relied on their subordinates to do much of their work. Many were former war heroes, while others were career politicians. A few were seemingly preordained by birth to become president, while others were accidents of history. A select few were neither and had relatively little public experience at all.

Many of the presidents were lawyers, others were military generals. Many had served as a U.S. senator, a state governor, or as a member in the U.S. House of Representatives. Some had interesting early careers, whether it be as a farmer or a Hollywood actor. Some lived to a ripe old age, becoming nonagenarians. Others died in office—sometimes by an assassin's bullet. A few achieved political or personal successes after leaving office such as becoming Chief Justice of the U.S. Supreme Court or returning to the U.S. House of Representatives. Still others drifted into oblivion, ostracized by the current tides of public opinion.

The second edition of the *Handy Presidents Answer Book* examines this special group of men—their early lives, jobs, political careers, their presidencies and their post-presidential years. The first edition of the *Handy Presidents Answer Book* organized the material by topic as opposed to by person. In the second edition, we have taken a different approach, focusing more on the people who occupied the Oval Office. We think this will make it easier for the student or researcher who wants to learn facts and material about a particular president or a particular point in American history.

Just like other books in the informative "Handy" series, the *Handy Presidents Answer Book* proceeds on the reader-friendly, question-and-answer format. You will learn not only matters of pressing political importance but also interesting matters of trivia and tidbits.

ACKNOWLEDGEMENTS

I would like to thank Roger Janecke of Visible Ink Press for his vision and for granting me another writing opportunity with the "Handy" series. I enjoyed writing the *Handy Presidents Answer Book,* second edition, as much as my two earlier works in the series: *The Handy Law Answer Book* and *The Handy Supreme Court Answer Book*. I would also like to thank Kevin Hile at Visible Ink for his superior editing abilities. I would like to thank my wife, Carla Hudson, for her excellent research skills. Thanks to all of my students at Middle Tennessee State University, Nashville School of Law, and Vanderbilt Law School, who enrich my experience with teaching various legal subjects on a daily basis.

PHOTO CREDITS

ORIGINS OF THE PRESIDENCY AND OFFICIAL DUTIES

What was the significance of the **Constitutional Convention of 1787** on the presidency?

The Constitutional Convention was the first time that the development of a strong national government, led by a chief executive who represented the will of the people, was seriously discussed. The Convention created the definition of the chief executive as it is found in the Constitution of the United States.

What were the **key debates** surrounding the presidency?

Three issues dominated the framers' discussion of the role the executive would play in the new government. First, the delegates discussed whether the executive should be a single individual or three individuals sharing the office. Second, they debated at length about the amount of power the executive should hold, including whether the chief executive should have the power to veto legislation and whether or not he should command the armed forces. Third, delegates debated the length of the executive's term (three-, six-, and seven-year terms were all considered) and discussed whether he should be eligible for reelection. In addition, they debated the best means by which to elect the executive—by state legislatures, both houses of Congress, by the Senate alone, by the governors, or by citizens.

How did the **topic of the presidency arise**, and what was the response?

When Pennsylvania delegate James Wilson suggested that the executive office should be held by one person, a lengthy silence followed. The delegates each had their own conceptions of executive power, and they were leery of granting too much control to a powerful executive who could usurp legislative authority and engage in tyrannical actions. The framers eventually decided upon a single executive, primarily because they felt conflicts would be more easily avoided if there were only one person in the nation's highest office. Also, they believed that Congress could more carefully watch and check a single executive.

What was the **result of the debates** regarding the presidency?

It was not until September 8, 1787, that the framers finally settled on the scope and definition of the executive office. A single leader, elected to a four-year term and eligible for reelection, with authority to veto bills enacted by Congress, would rule the nation. The president was also given command of the military and the power to appoint federal officials, subject to confirmation by the Senate. To ensure a balance of power, the legislative and judicial branches were given the ability to check presidential actions. The framers hoped this system of checks and balances would prevent the reign of a tyrannical executive. In addition to determining the executive's powers, the framers established the methods of selecting the president. Concerned about the people's ability to elect the president directly and cautious of giving full power to existing legislative bodies to select the president, they designed the electoral college, a group of presidential electors for each state who meet after the popular election to cast their ballots for the president and vice president.

DUTIES AND POWERS

What are the **duties of the president** of the United States?

The president's chief duty is to protect the U.S. Constitution and enforce the laws made by the Congress. However, he also has a host of other responsibilities tied to his job as the nation's leader. These include: recommending legislation to Congress, calling special sessions of Congress, delivering messages to Congress, signing or vetoing legislation, appointing federal judges, appointing heads of federal departments and agencies and other principal federal officials, appointing representatives to foreign countries, carrying on official business with foreign nations, acting as commander in chief of the armed forces, and granting pardons for offenses against the United States.

What are the executive and enumerated, or expressed, **constitutional powers** of the president?

Article II of the U.S. Constitution vests the "executive power" in the president. The president is commander in chief of the U.S. armed forces and, when called into action, the National Guard. The president may require the written opinion of military executive officers, and is empowered to grant reprieves and pardons, except in the case of impeachment. The president receives ambassadors and other public ministers,

Artist Robert Edge Pine's depiction of the Founding Fathers voting on the Declaration of Independence in what is now called Independence Hall in Philadelphia. Declaring a nation's independence is just the beginning. The hard work was ahead as these men had to determine a new form of government, including what powers its president would wield.

ensures that the laws are faithfully executed, and commissions all officers of the United States. The president has power, by and with the advice and consent of the U.S. Senate, to make treaties, provided that two-thirds of the senators present concur. The president also nominates and appoints ambassadors, other public ministers and consuls, justices of the Supreme Court, federal judges, and other federal officers, by and with the advice and consent of the Senate. The president has the power to temporarily fill all vacancies that occur during the recess of the Senate. In addition, the president may, under extraordinary circumstances, convene "emergency" sessions of Congress. Further, if the two houses disagree as to the time of adjournment, the president may adjourn the bodies. In addition to these powers, the president also has enumerated powers that allow him to directly influence legislation. The Constitution directs the president to periodically inform Congress on the State of the Union, and to recommend legislation that is considered necessary and expedient. Also, Article I, Section 7, of the Constitution grants the president the authority to veto acts of Congress.

What are the **implied constitutional powers** of the president?

The president possesses certain powers that are not enumerated in the U.S. Constitution. For example, although the Constitution does not grant the president the expressed power to remove administrators from their offices, as the chief executive the president holds power over executive branch officers, unless such removal power is limited by

3

public law. Another implied constitutional power is derived from the president's authority as commander in chief. Although Congress has the explicit power to declare war, the president holds the responsibility to protect the nation from sudden attack and has the ability to initiate military activities overseas without a formal declaration of war. Through the War Powers Resolution of 1973, Congress sought to define more clearly the conditions under which presidents unilaterally can authorize military action abroad.

What are the president's **various roles**?

Although the U.S. Constitution clearly assigns to the president only the roles of chief executive and commander of the country's armed forces, today the president of the United States assumes six basic roles: (1) chief executive; (2) chief of state/foreign relations; (3) commander in chief; (4) chief legislator; (5) chief of party; and (6) chief citizen, or popular leader.

What is the president's role as **chief executive**?

When wearing the hat of chief executive, sometimes called chief administrator, the president has four main duties: (1) enforcing federal laws and court rulings; (2) developing various federal policies; (3) appointing federal officials; and (4) preparing the national budget. Within the executive branch, the president has broad powers to manage national affairs and the workings of the federal government. The president can issue rules, regulations, and instructions called executive orders, which have the binding force of law upon federal agencies but do not require congressional approval. The president may also negotiate with foreign countries "executive agreements" that are not subject to Senate confirmation. The president nominates—and the Senate confirms—the heads of all executive departments and agencies, together with hundreds of other high-ranking federal officials. In addition, the president solely appoints other important public officials, including aides, advisors, and hundreds of other positions. Presidential nomination of federal judges, including members of the Supreme Court, is subject to confirmation by the Senate. Another significant executive power involves granting a full or conditional pardon to anyone convicted of breaking a federal law—except in a case of impeachment. In addition, as the nation's chief executive, the president prepares the national budget.

What **types of executive orders** does a president generally make?

From the founding of America, U.S. presidents have developed and used various types of presidential or executive directives. The best-known directives are executive orders and presidential proclamations—written instructions or declarations issued by the president that carry the full force of the law. These vary from formalities, such as the presidential proclamation of Earth Day or a National Day of Prayer, to orders that effect major policy changes, such as President Bill Clinton's executive orders calling for preferential treatment in federal contracting based on race or ethnicity.

What is the president's role as **chief of state**?

As the chief of state, the president is the ceremonial head of the United States. Under the Constitution, the president is the federal official primarily responsible for the relations of the United States with foreign nations. As chief of state, the president appoints ambassadors, ministers, and consuls, subject to confirmation by the Senate, and receives foreign ambassadors and other public officials. With the secretary of state, the president manages all official contacts with foreign governments. On occasion, the president may personally participate in summit conferences where chiefs of state meet for direct consultation.

Through the Department of State, the president is responsible for the protection of Americans abroad and of foreign nationals in the United States. The president decides whether to recognize new nations and new governments, and negotiates treaties with other nations, which become binding on the United States when approved by two-thirds of the Senate.

What is the president's role as **commander in chief**?

Article II, Section 2, of the U.S. Constitution states that the president is the commander in chief of the U.S. Army, Navy, and, when it is called into federal service, state militias (now called the National Guard). Historically, presidents have used this authority to commit U.S. troops without a formal declaration of war. However, Article I, Section 8, of the Constitution reserves to Congress the power to raise and support the armed forces as well as the sole authority to declare war. These competing powers have been the source of controversy between the legislative and executive branches over war making, so much so that in 1973 Congress enacted the War Powers Resolution, which limits the president's authority to use the armed forces without specific congressional authorization, in an attempt to increase and clarify Congress's control over the use of the military. In addition, the armed forces operate under the doctrine of civilian control, which means that only the president or statutory deputies—such as the secretary and deputy secretary of defense—can order the use of force. The chain of command is structured to ensure that the military cannot undertake actions without civilian approval or knowledge.

How is the president the **chief legislator**?

Despite the constitutional provision that "all legislative powers" shall be vested in the Congress, the president, as the chief formulator of public policy, plays a major legislative role. The president can veto any bill passed by Congress and, unless two-thirds of the members of each house vote to override the veto, the bill does not become law. Much of the legislation dealt with by Congress is drafted at the initiative of the executive branch. In his annual and special messages to Congress, the president may propose legislation he believes is necessary. If Congress should adjourn without acting on

The president's power to veto legislation can sometimes make the chief executive a target of criticism. President Andrew Jackson was lampooned in this cartoon as being a despotic monarch after he vetoed a bill to recharter the Bank of the United States.

those proposals, the president has the power to call it into special session. But beyond this official role, the president, as head of a political party and as principal executive officer of the U.S. government, is in a position to influence public opinion and thereby the course of legislation in Congress.

To improve their working relationships with Congress in recent years, presidents have set up a Congressional Liaison Office in the White House. Presidential aides keep abreast of all-important legislative activities and try to persuade senators and representatives of both parties to support administration policies.

What is the president's **"veto power"**?

There are two types of vetoes available to the president. The regular veto, called a "qualified negative veto," is limited by the ability of Congress to gather the necessary two-thirds vote of each house for constitutional override. The other type of veto is not explicitly outlined in the U.S. Constitution, but is traditionally called a "pocket veto." As an "absolute veto" that cannot be overridden, it becomes effective when the president fails to sign a bill after Congress has adjourned and is unable to override the veto. The president's veto authority is a significant tool in legislative dealings with Congress. It is not only effective in directly preventing the passage of legislation undesirable to the president, but serves as a threat, thereby bringing about changes in the content of legislation long before the bill is ever presented to the president.

When can a president **call a special session** with Congress?

Article II, Section 3, of the U.S. Constitution gives the president power to convene Congress, or either house, "on extraordinary occasions." Usually, when the president calls for an extra session he indicates the exact matter that needs the attention of Congress. However, once convened, Congress cannot be limited in the subject matter that it will consider. The president is also empowered by the Constitution to adjourn Congress "at such time as he may think proper" when the House and Senate disagree with

> ## In what ways is the president the chief citizen?
>
> **P**resident Franklin D. Roosevelt probably summed up the duties of this role best when he called the presidency "preeminently a place of moral leadership." As a representative of the nation's people, the president automatically assumes the role of its chief citizen, or popular leader. The nature of this role mandates a certain trust between the president and the people, since it is the president's duty to work for the public interest amidst competing private interests, and to place the nation's best interests above the interests of any one group or citizen. In turn, the president relies on public support to help pass his legislative agenda through Congress—gaining the trust of the public with regard to these issues through exposure, straightforwardness, and strong leadership.

respect to the time for adjournment; however, to date no president has exercised this power. Many constitutional experts believe the provision applies only in the case of extraordinary sessions.

What is the president's **power to pardon**?

Article II, Section 2, of the U.S. Constitution states that "the president shall have the power to grant reprieves and pardons for offenses against the United States, except in cases of impeachment." The pardon power is exclusive to the executive branch, with no requirement for consent from any other branch of government. Of all of the president's responsibilities, the pardon power is perhaps the most delicate and political, in that it is meant to be an instrument that rights the wrongs of those who have violated federal laws, and is purely subjective on the part of the president. Presidents may exercise this power on behalf of a particular person or a group of people.

REQUIREMENTS

What are the **qualifications** for becoming president?

According to Article II, Section 1, of the U.S. Constitution, any person seeking the presidency must be a natural-born citizen, at least thirty-five years old, and a resident of the United States for at least fourteen years. Constitutional scholars have debated whether a child born abroad of an American parent constitutes "a natural-born citizen." While most maintain that such a person should qualify as a natural-born citizen, no definitive consensus has been reached.

How **many terms** can a president serve?

Article II, Section 1, of the U.S. Constitution mandates that the president serve a four-year term. This time period was chosen because the framers agreed that four years was enough time for a president to have learned the ropes, demonstrated his leadership abilities, and established sound policies. The Constitution placed no limit on the number of terms that a president might serve until 1951, with the adoption of the Twenty-second Amendment, which states that "no person shall be elected to the office of the President more than twice, and no person who has held the office of President, or acted as President, for more than two years of a term to which some other person was elected President shall be elected to the office of the President more than once." Congress passed this law after Franklin D. Roosevelt was elected president four times.

Have **other term limits** been suggested?

Since the Twenty-second Amendment was passed in 1951, several presidents—including Harry S. Truman, Dwight D. Eisenhower, and Ronald Reagan—have called for its repeal. Their main argument has centered on the fact that the amendment places an arbitrary time limit on the office, and that the ultimate will of the people should be regarded when electing their chief officer, despite the amount of time that he has already served. Critics of the amendment concur, saying the time limit undercuts the authority of a two-term president, especially in the latter half of his second term. Still other presidents, most recently Jimmy Carter, have lobbied for a single, nonrenewable six-year term, arguing that this time period would allow the president to more feasibly focus on implementing long-term policies that would benefit the nation and release him from the pressure of campaigning for a second term—a cumbersome task that ultimately distracts him from the day-to-day responsibilities of the office.

When does the president **begin his term**?

When the Constitution was ratified, Congress was given power to determine the date for beginning the operations of the new presidential administration. Congress set the date as March 4, 1789. Although George Washington did not take the oath of office until April 30 of that year, his term officially began on March 4. Later, the Twentieth (or so-called "lame duck") Amendment, which was ratified in 1933, established January 20 as the date on which presidents would be inaugurated. In 1937, Franklin D. Roosevelt became the first president to take the oath on January 20.

The change of date eliminated the often-awkward "lame duck" period of four months, during which an outgoing president's power was realistically diminished. There was no longer the need for a longer time frame between election and inauguration, which was necessitated earlier in history by the more modest means of travel and communication.

What is the **presidential oath**?

The oath of the office for the president is outlined in Article II, Section 1, of the U.S. Constitution, and reads as follows: "I do solemnly swear (or affirm) that I will faithfully execute the office of President of the United States, and will, to the best of my ability, preserve, protect, and defend the Constitution of the United States." Usually, the chief justice of the Supreme Court administers the oath, although there is no provision made for this within the Constitution. In fact, throughout American history other judges have administered the oath at times of unexpected presidential succession.

President Ulysses S. Grant takes the presidential oath of office in 1873. Chief Justice Salmon P. Chase swears in the new chief executive.

What are the president's **salary** and **benefits**?

As of the term that began on January 20, 2001, the president's salary is $400,000 per year. Congress sets the president's salary, which cannot be increased or decreased during a presidential term. In addition, the president is allocated a $50,000-per-year taxable expense allowance to be spent however he chooses. During his term in office, the president also enjoys many perks, including living in the White House, orchestrating office suites and a large staff, sailing on the presidential yacht, flying in his private jet (Air Force One), holding meetings at the Camp David resort in Maryland, and enjoying abundant travel and entertainment funds, among other benefits. In addition, since 1959, each former president has received a lifetime pension.

Can a president be **removed from office**?

Yes. Presidential power is not absolute. It is limited and kept in check by both constitutional and political constraints. The ultimate limit on presidential power is removal from office by Congress through "Impeachment for, and Conviction of, Treason, Bribery, or other high Crimes and Misdemeanors," as outlined in Article II, Section 4, of the U.S. Constitution.

What is **impeachment**?

Impeachment is the process by which the president, vice president, federal judges and justices, and all civil officials of the United States may be removed from office. Officials may be impeached for treason, bribery, and other high crimes and misdemeanors. The

House of Representatives has sole authority to bring charges of impeachment, by a simple majority vote, and the Senate has sole authority to try impeachment charges. An official may be removed from office only upon conviction, which requires a two-thirds vote of the Senate. The Constitution provides that the chief justice shall preside when the president is tried for impeachment.

In cases of impeachment, resignation, or death, who **succeeds the president**?

According to the Twenty-fifth Amendment, adopted in 1967, the vice president succeeds to the office if the president dies, resigns, or is removed from office by impeachment.

THE WHITE HOUSE

Where does the president **reside**?

The president of the United States lives and works in the White House in Washington, D.C., located at 1600 Pennsylvania Avenue. The White House is three stories high, with offices, public rooms, guest rooms, and the family's living space taking up most of the fifty-five thousand square feet of the building. All told, there are 132 rooms (including 16 family guest rooms, 1 main kitchen, 1 diet kitchen, 1 family kitchen, and 31 bathrooms) in the residence. There are 412 doors, 147 windows, 28 fireplaces, 8 staircases, and 3 elevators. In addition, the property houses a tennis court, a jogging track, a swimming pool, a gym, a movie theater, and a bowling lane. It is surrounded by approximately eighteen acres of lawns and gardens.

What was the **White House like originally**?

The original White House was designed by Irish-American architect James Hoban, and built between 1792 and 1800. The presidential home, made of gray stone, was called the "Executive Mansion." The building was first made white with lime-based whitewash in 1798, when its walls were finished, primarily as a means of protecting the porous stone from freezing. John and Abigail Adams moved into a house that was still unfinished; in fact, many of the plaster walls were still wet and about half of the thirty-six rooms had not been plastered at all. The largest room in the house, the East Room, was also unfinished. Because Abigail Adams thought that the president's laundry should not be hung to dry outside on the lawn for the public to see, she set up drying lines in the East Room.

When was the president's residence **officially called the White House**?

Although the term "White House" was used to describe the building as early as 1809, President Theodore Roosevelt officially adopted the moniker in 1901, when he engraved it on his stationery. Before then, the building was referred to as the Executive Mansion, the Presidential Palace, or the Presidential Mansion. First Lady Dolley Madison called it the President's Castle.

When did the **White House burn down**?

In 1814, during the War of 1812, the British burned down the White House. President James Madison immediately ordered the rebuilding of the destroyed mansion, insisting that it be restored to its original condition. To ensure authenticity, Madison enlisted the help of the White House's original architect, James Hoban. Workers used the stone slabs that had survived the fire to rebuild the White House, and afterward gave it a fresh coat of white paint. The rebuilding took a total of three years, and was reopened by President James Monroe for a New Year's party in 1818. Today, approximately three hundred gallons of white paint are used to cover the exterior of just the center section of the White House, excluding the East and West Wings. Only one other fire tinged the building in its history; in 1929, the West Wing caught on fire during Herbert Hoover's administration.

During which administrations did the White House receive **significant updates and remodeling**?

Before major restoration began in the late 1940s, the White House had already undergone many changes. In the 1820s, workers added extra pavilions and porticos (ornamental, decklike structures with columns supporting a roof), after the design of archi-

A drawing of the original White House around 1807, five years before the War of 1812, when British forces burned it down.

tect Benjamin Latrobe, who also designed the U.S. Capitol. In 1833, water pipes were added; in the 1850s, a stove was added; in 1881, an elevator was added. The first telephone was wired into the White House during Rutherford B. Hayes's administration (1877–1881); during Benjamin Harrison's administration, in 1891, the White House was wired for electricity. The first-story West Wing offices were constructed in 1901-02 during the term of Theodore Roosevelt, because he needed the second-floor office area for living space for his large family. A new east entrance was also built to allow groups of carriages to enter the property. And in 1909, President William Howard Taft remodeled the president's office, creating the Oval Office in the center of the West Wing. In 1927, President Calvin Coolidge and his wife relocated to nearby Dupont Circle while the White House roof was raised and replaced, and a third floor was added to allow for guest bedrooms and additional storage. In 1933, engineers installed air conditioning in the private quarters of the White House.

When was the **White House renovated**?

During President Harry S. Truman's administration, the White House was found to be structurally unsound. Under Truman's recommendation, the residence underwent major renovation. From 1948 to 1952, construction workers tore down the entire interior, retaining only the third floor and the original outer walls that architect James Hoban built. Using steel instead of wood, workers reinforced the building, adding several rooms, and restoring the existing rooms to their original appearance.

Where did President **Truman live** while the White House was being **restored**?

Throughout much of Truman's presidency, the interior of the White House was completely gutted and renovated while the Trumans lived at Blair House, right across Pennsylvania Avenue.

What are some of the White House's **famous rooms**?

One of the most famous rooms in the White House is the Lincoln Room, named for President Abraham Lincoln. In Lincoln's administration, it was his cabinet room and the room in which he signed the 1863 Emancipation Proclamation. Today, the president's guests often sleep in the Lincoln Room and the Rose Room.

The White House as it appeared in 1814, not long after it was rebuilt.

The East Wing (which houses offices for executive branch workers) and the West Wing (where the president and the president's staff work) are on either side of the main building. The Oval Office, located in the West Wing, is familiar to most Americans because this is the location from which president's speeches are often broadcast. The East Room, the largest public room, is where the president often hosts receptions, dances, and concerts. Also used for receptions are three rooms named for the color of their decorations: the Blue Room (which received its name in 1837), the Green Room (which received its original name, the "Green Drawing Room," from John Quincy Adams sometime between 1825 and 1829), and the Red Room (which received its name in 1840). The State Dining Room accommodates more than one hundred guests. The China Room, originally called the "Presidential Collection Room," was designated by First Lady Edith Wilson in 1917 to display the growing collection of White House china. Although more than one million visitors tour the White House every year, the public is not allowed on the second or third floors; the second floor is where the president and his family reside.

What **changes** have been made to the **White House post–September 11**?

For two years following the terrorist attacks of September 11, 2001, the public had limited access to the White House as work was done to strengthen security and redecorate several areas. In January 2002, President George W. Bush unveiled a redecorated Oval Office, featuring bronze silk damask draperies, an oval custom-made rug featuring the presidential seal, cream-colored sofas, and Texas landscape paintings. Upstairs in the

13

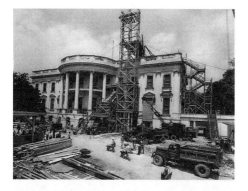

By the late 1940s, the White House was literally falling apart. President Truman had no choice but to completely rebuild the president's home.

president's private quarters, longtime Bush family decorator Ken Blasingame remade several of the president's rooms. Although White House curator William Allman said, "To the naked eye, nothing much has changed," several rooms have been redecorated, including the East Room, which has had a $200,000 update. Some historic paintings in the Red, Green, and Blue Rooms have been reframed, and gardeners planted a new row of crab apple trees in the Rose Garden.

PARTIES AND PLATFORMS

How did the **first two political parties evolve**?

The first two parties, the Federalists and the Democratic-Republicans, were shaped during the administration of the country's first president, George Washington. The Federalist Party was a creation of Alexander Hamilton, secretary of the treasury under Washington. Hamilton believed that the success of the new government would depend on its economic stability, and as such favored full funding of the entire federal debt and the assumption of the states' debts by the federal government. The opposition party, the Jeffersonian (or Democratic) Republicans, was organized by Congressman James Madison and Thomas Jefferson, who served as secretary of state during Washington's first term. The Democratic-Republicans formed in opposition to many of Washington's economic policies, denouncing many of Hamilton's decisions, such as the ratification of Jay's Treaty with Great Britain.

Is it true that **George Washington** was elected **without** the help of a **political party**?

Yes. Believing that political parties were complicated, if not outright detrimental to society, America's Founding Fathers were set on developing a system for electing presidents without the aid of political parties and national campaigns. When George Washington was elected president in early 1789, he was the first and last president to do so without the support of a political party. When the Constitution of the United States was ratified, the electoral college unanimously elected Washington president, an act they repeated in 1792. Although this method worked fine for Washington, its weaknesses were revealed with the development of political parties, and ultimately the original design of the electoral college system lasted only through four presidential elections.

15

What did **George Washington** have to **say about political parties**?

George Washington detested the concept of parties, or factions, because he did not want any political group in the nation to become too powerful. In his Farewell Address to the nation, first published in Philadelphia's *American Daily Advertiser* on September 19, 1796, Washington warned against the party system in America. Cautioning the public "in the most solemn manner" against the "baneful effects of the spirit of Party," Washington said the party system "serves to distract the Public Councils, and enfeeble the Public Administration ... agitates the Community with ill founded Jealousies and false alarms; kindles the animosity of one ... against another ... opens the door to foreign influence and corruption."

What were the key **differences** between the **Federalists** and the **Democratic-Republicans**?

The Federalists were a powerful and wealthy party, made up mostly of lawyers, big businessmen, bankers, merchants, and professionals who were influential in New England and the northern part of the United States, where big business thrived. In terms of political thought, the Federalists believed in strong government leadership and a loose constructionist interpretation of the Constitution. They also supported improved relations with England over France.

By contrast, the Democratic-Republicans, known as the "party of the common man," were a party made up of farmers, small businessmen, and laborers, and influenced the southern and western parts of the United States, where agriculture was strong. The Democratic-Republicans adopted a strict constructionist interpretation of the Constitution.

What **role** did political **parties play** in the elections of **1796** and **1800**?

The development of political parties accidentally resulted in the election outcomes of 1796 and 1800. Under the framers' method of electing a president (described in Article II, Section 1, of the Constitution), each elector cast two votes without indicating which vote was for the president and which vote was for the vice president. As a result, a number of mishaps could occur. For example, in the election of 1796, this system produced a president from one party (Federalist John Adams) and a vice president from another party (Thomas Jefferson of the Democratic-Republicans). In the presidential election of 1800, the electors of the Democratic-Republican Party gave Thomas Jefferson and Aaron Burr, who were both of that same party, an equal number (seventy-three) of electoral votes. Because the votes were tied, the election was thrown to the House of Representatives, where each state voted as a unit to decide the outcome of the election. Since the Federalist-dominated House consistently divided its votes between the two men, the deadlock wasn't broken until the thirty-sixth ballot, when

Jefferson gained the majority of necessary votes to claim presidential victory. The final results were ten states in favor of Jefferson, and four in favor of Burr. To prevent tie votes in the electoral college that were made probable by the rise of political parties, in 1804 Congress and the states adopted the Twelfth Amendment to the Constitution, which provides that electors "name in their ballots the person voted for as president, and in distinct ballots the person voted for as vice president."

What were the **major contributions** of this **first party system**?

The first party system ushered in the concept of modern political parties. During the late 1700s, American parties became an important, integrated part of the national government. Distinctly different from any other entity that existed before, parties allowed leaders to legitimately oppose government policies without opposing the concept of government itself. The leaders of the Democratic-Republicans, especially, learned how to become sensitive to the will of the people and how to respond to changing social conditions, something that the Federalists never fully grasped and which quickly brought about their demise. With a distinct national ideology, the Democratic-Republicans became an enduring organization through several administrations, learning how to rally support for their causes from like-minded leaders. Parties used the congressional caucus as a means of nominating candidates, and they recruited candidates for all offices, developing a party structure that would continue to be shaped into the nineteenth century.

What **other parties** were in existence **until 1832**?

Though the first American party system is generally discussed in terms of the Federalists and the Democratic-Republicans, there were other political parties that existed in the 1820s and early 1830s, including the National Republicans and the Anti-Masonics.

Who were the **National Republicans**?

The National Republicans were the administration party during John Quincy Adams's presidency (1825–1829). Adams's supporters adopted the name National Republicans because they favored strong economic nationalism, much like the defunct Federalist Party. The National Republicans stood in opposition to Andrew Jackson's Democratic-Republican Party, which favored a limited national government and opposed economic aristocracy. As the National Republicans dissolved in the mid-1830s, the Whigs emerged.

Who were the **Anti-Masonics**?

Formed in New York in 1828, the Anti-Masonic Party was the first third party to appear in American national politics. It was formed primarily in response to America's suspicion of secret societies like the Masons and in reaction to the perceived Masonic threat to public institutions during that time in American history. The Anti-Masonic Party

One of the most prominent members of the Whig Party was Henry Clay. Clay, who was greatly admired by Abraham Lincoln, ran unsuccessfully for the office of president, but served as Speaker of the House from 1823 to 1825 and was Secretary of State during the John Quincy Adams' administration.

was the first party to hold a nominating convention and the first to announce a platform—nominating William Wirt of Maryland for president and Amos Ellmaker of Pennsylvania as his running mate in September 1831.

Who were the **Whigs**?

The Whig Party emerged during the second quarter of the nineteenth century, formed to oppose President Andrew Jackson and the Democratic Party. The term "Whig" came into popular parlance in 1834 and continued until the party disbanded after the presidential election of 1856. The anti-Jackson group drew upon the political history of two revolutions for their name: the American Revolution and the opposition to the king in seventeenth-century England.

Why did the **Whig Party disappear**?

When Vice President John Tyler, a defender of slavery, succeeded to the presidency in 1841 after the death of President William Henry Harrison, he rejected the Whig's political platform. Tyler's attempt to annex Texas made the slavery-extension controversy a heated political issue, and soon the Whigs abandoned Tyler and expelled him from the party. When Millard Fillmore succeeded his fellow Whig President Zachary Taylor, following the latter's death in 1850, the Whigs were already showing deep signs of fracture. Key members had joined alternative parties, such as the Free-Soil Party, which opposed the extension of slavery in the western territories. In the election of 1852, the Whigs supported the antislavery presidential candidate, General Winfield Scott, instead of states' rights candidate Fillmore. Scott lost the presidential race, winning only forty-two electoral votes, and the antislavery faction, mostly comprised of northern Whigs, joined the newly formed Republican Party in 1854. The election of 1856 was the last time a Whig ran for president.

What **other political parties** dominated the political scene **between 1844 and 1856**?

During the mid-1800s, several political parties rose up, mainly in response to the slavery issue that had divided the nation. Three parties garnered headlines at this point in

America's history: the Liberty Party; the Free-Soil Party; and the American Party, colloquially referred to as the Know-Nothings.

What was the **Liberty Party**?

The Liberty Party was a short-lived mid-nineteenth-century political party that supported abolitionism. Formed by members who broke away from William Lloyd Garrison's American Anti-Slavery Society (1833–70), the Liberty Party nominated James G. Birney for president in 1840 and 1844. The party never quite got off the ground, and in 1848 members joined with other like-minded leaders to form the Free-Soil Party.

Who were the **Free-Soilers**?

Another short-lived political party, the Free-Soil Party was in existence for only about four years, from 1848 to 1852. Formed to oppose the extension of slavery into the territories, the Free-Soil Party was a melding of abolitionists from the Democratic Party, the Whig Party, the Liberty Party, and a group known as the Barnburners, a radical antislavery arm of the New York Democrats. The party held its first convention in 1848. Free-Soilers nominated a ticket of former U.S. president Martin Van Buren and former Massachusetts state senator Charles Francis Adams (son of former U.S. president John Quincy Adams).

Who were the **Know-Nothings**?

More formally known as the American Party, the Know-Nothing Party was founded in New York City in 1849. It was organized to oppose the large influx of immigrants who entered the United States after 1846. Because Know-Nothings believed that these primarily Irish and Roman Catholic immigrants threatened to destroy America, the party strove to use government power to uphold its vision of an Anglo-Saxon Protestant society. Their platform outlined a limited immigration policy, proposed that only native-born Americans could hold public office, and advocated a twenty-one-year

19

mandatory waiting period for immigrants before they were granted citizenship and voting rights. Despite their strength during the election of 1856, in which they supported former president Millard Fillmore, the Know-Nothings declined as a national party when many members defected to the Republican Party. Although their numbers remained strong in several northern states in the late 1850s, the party had eroded as a national presence before the presidential election of 1860.

What is the **origin** of the **Republican Party**?

The Republican Party was born in the early 1850s by antislavery activists and individuals who believed that government should grant western lands to settlers free of charge. The first official Republican meeting took place on July 6, 1854, in Jackson, Michigan, during which the name "Republican" was chosen because it alluded to equality and reminded individuals of Thomas Jefferson's Democratic-Republican Party. At the Jackson convention, the new party adopted a platform and nominated candidates for office in Michigan. In 1856, the Republicans became a national party when former U.S. senator John C. Frémont of California was nominated for president. Even though the Republican Party was considered a "third party" because the Democrats and Whigs constituted the two-party system at the time, it wasn't long before Republicans passed the Whigs. In the 1860 election, Abraham Lincoln became the first Republican to win the White House.

What were some of the political **parties** that **dominated the landscape** during the **1880s and 1890s**?

Two parties were popular during this time frame: the Greenbacks, who were active between 1874 and 1884, and the Populists, who nominated a presidential candidate in 1892. The Greenbacks took their name from the paper money called "greenbacks" that was issued during the Civil War (1861–65). Made up of farmers who had been financially devastated by the Panic of 1873, the Greenbacks believed the government should issue larger amounts of money in an effort to help people, especially farmers, by raising prices and making their debts easier to pay. In the presidential election of 1876, the Greenbacks nominated inventor Peter Cooper; in 1880, they nominated former U.S. representative James B. Weaver of Iowa, who advocated a pro-agriculture agenda and the prohibition of alcohol.

Who were the **Populists**?

Also known as the People's Party, the Populist Party was formed by a group of small farmers and sharecroppers to oppose large-scale commercial agriculture that they feared would put them out of work. The national party was officially founded in 1892 through a merger of the Farmers' Alliance and the Knights of Labor. That year, the Populist presidential candidate, James B. Weaver, won over one million votes. The populists also elected ten representatives, five senators, three governors, and approximately fifteen hundred members of state legislatures. Between 1892 and 1896, however, the party was intimidated by southern Democrats, and after 1896 the party began to decline.

Populists advocated federally regulated communication, transportation, and banking systems to offset the economic depression and prevent poverty among working-class families. Progressive Republican Theodore Roosevelt resurrected many Populist ideas and recast them in new forms as he expanded the federal regulation of business corporations, and addressed many People's Party concerns in his Progressive policies. Other Populist ideas—particularly those calling for aid to farmers and employment on public works projects in times of economic depression—became reality during the 1930s with the New Deal programs of Democratic president Franklin D. Roosevelt.

President Teddy Roosevelt was the leader of the Progressive Party, also known as the "Bull Moose" Party, after leaving the Republican Party.

What was Teddy Roosevelt's Progressive **"Bull Moose"** Party?

Also known as the Bull Moose Party, the Progressive Party was formed in 1912 by

21

former President Theodore Roosevelt (served 1901–1909). Progressives supported women's suffrage, environmental conservation, tariff reform, stricter regulation of industrial combinations, and prohibition of child labor. Unhappy with the conservative policies of William Howard Taft and dominant Republicans, Roosevelt and many liberal Republicans transferred their allegiance to the Progressives. The Progressives nominated Roosevelt for president and California governor Hiram W. Johnson for vice president in the campaign of 1912. Roosevelt bested his former close Republican colleague, incumbent president Taft, in the popular vote and by a margin of eighty-eight to eight in the electoral vote, but the split in the Republican vote resulted in a victory for the Democratic candidate, New Jersey governor Woodrow Wilson. Progressive candidates for state and local offices did poorly, and the party disappeared in 1916 when Roosevelt returned to the Republican Party.

Who were the **Dixiecrats**?

The Dixiecrats were a small group of southern Democrats in the election of 1948 who opposed President Harry S. Truman's civil rights program and revolted against the civil rights plank adopted at the Democratic National Convention. A group of states' rights leaders met in Birmingham, Alabama, and nominated South Carolina governor Strom Thurmond for president. However, Thurmond garnered only thirty-nine electoral votes and 1.1 million popular votes. Many Dixiecrats switched their allegiance to the Republican Party or remained a Democratic voting bloc that supported conservative policies.

What are the **two dominant political parties** in the United States **today**?

In the United States today, two parties dominate the political landscape: the Democrats and the Republicans. The Democratic Party tends to draw its base of support from the poor and lower-middle-class, ethnic and religious minorities, women, and union members. Generally, their platform deals with such issues as support for government programs; support for the public sector; and support for affirmative action, reproductive rights, gay rights, and gun control. Conversely, the Republican Party tends to draw its support from the upper-middle-class and elite, business owners, and Protestant Anglo-Saxon men. The party tends to support a strong private sector, business and military interests, gun rights, and tax cuts. As a rule, Republicans are hesitant to embrace rights-based policies like affirmative action, and have a history of opposing welfare and government-spending programs.

Which **presidents** are known for **switching parties**?

Most presidents remained associated with a certain political party from early in their careers until the ends of their lives, though a few changed their affiliations. Before he was elected to the vice presidency in 1840, John Tyler switched his political allegiance from the Jackson Democrats to the newly formed Whig Party. Once Tyler succeeded to

Alabama Governor George Wallace, seen in this 1963 photo (standing in the doorway), attemped to keep authorities from integrating the University of Alabama. The pro-segregation governor ran for president under the American Independent Party ticket. Wallace much later publicly apologized for his racist stance.

the presidency after President William Henry Harrison died in office, he abandoned many Whig principles, lost the support of his Whig cabinet, and was ejected by the party. In the 1930s and 1940s, Ronald Reagan was a Democrat; however, he gradually adopted a more conservative political ideology and officially changed his political affiliation to Republican in 1962. Reagan served as Republican governor of California from 1967 to 1975 and as the Republican president for two terms, from 1981 to 1989.

Three presidents changed their party affiliation after their presidency: Martin Van Buren, a Democrat, became a candidate for the Free Soil Party; Millard Fillmore, a Whig, became a candidate for the American, or Know-Nothing, Party; and Theodore Roosevelt, a Republican, founded the Progressive—or Bull Moose—Party.

What are some **third parties** that are **active today**?

Any political party that is not Republican or Democratic receives a base of support, and plays a role in influencing the outcome of an election is considered a minor party or "third party." There are many third parties in today's political playground, including the American Independent Party, the American Reform Party, the Communist Party USA, the Green Party, the Independence Party, the Libertarian Party, the Natural Law Party, the Peace and Freedom Party, the Reform Party, and the Socialist Party USA. Third parties often voice a protest vote against one or both of the major parties, and often enter a political race to deflect votes from one of the major candidates.

23

Which **third-party presidential bids** have been noteworthy in the **post–World War II** era?

No third-party candidate has ever come close to winning the presidency, and only eight minor parties have managed to win a single state's electoral votes. However, historians agree that there have been four noteworthy third-party presidential bids since World War II, when third-party or independent candidates have garnered more than 7 percent of the popular vote. In 1948, two independent candidates for president challenged the Republican candidate, Thomas E. Dewey, and the Democratic and then-President Harry S. Truman. On the right, Strom Thurmond—then a Democratic governor from South Carolina—ran as the nominee of the Dixiecrats or States' Rights Party, a group of dissident Democrats in favor of racial segregation. On the left, Henry Wallace, a former vice president under Franklin D. Roosevelt, ran as the nominee of the Progressive Party. Thurmond won twenty-two percent of the vote in the South, the only area of the country in which he campaigned; Wallace garnered slightly more than 2 percent of the vote.

In 1968, George Wallace, the pro-segregation governor of Alabama, ran as the presidential nominee of the American Independent Party. Wallace, who won 13.8 percent of the vote, was thought to have taken votes away from both major-party candidates, Democrat Hubert Humphrey and Republican Richard Nixon. In 1980, U.S. representative John Anderson of Illinois ran as the presidential nominee of the National Unity Movement. It was assumed that Anderson, a moderate, would take votes away from both the Democratic nominee, President Jimmy Carter, and the Republican nominee, Ronald Reagan. In the end, Anderson won seven percent of the vote, which hardly dampened Reagan's landslide victory. Recent examples of significant third-party candidates include H. Ross Perot, who in 1992 ran as the presidential nominee of United We Stand America, the precursor of the Reform Party. Political commentators argue that Perot's strong garnering of nineteen percent of the vote probably hurt the Republican candidate, President George Bush, while helping elect Democratic nominee Bill Clinton. And some could argue that Ralph Nader's presence in the 2000 presidential race—small as it was, with only a little under three percent of the popular vote—siphoned key votes from Democratic candidate Al Gore, who despite gaining the majority of popular votes lost the electoral vote to Republican George W. Bush.

CAMPAIGNS AND NOMINATIONS

How are **political parties** and **political campaigns related**?

While political parties perform a variety of functions, they are mainly involved in nominating candidates for office and organizing their elections. Their major responsibilities include recruiting candidates for local, state, and national office; nominating candidates through caucuses, conventions, and the primary election; "getting out the vote" for their candidates and providing voters with information about candidates and their parties; and facilitating mass electoral choice—that is, helping voters recognize their options and encouraging electoral competition. In addition, they influence the institutions of national government and the policy-making process. For example, Congress is organized around the two-party system, and the Speaker of the House position is a party office. Parties determine the makeup of congressional committees, including those who chair the committees, whose positions are no longer based solely on seniority.

What is a **primary**?

A primary is a state-run election for the purpose of nominating party candidates to run in the general election. Presidential primaries perform this function indirectly, because voters elect delegates to a national convention rather than directly seeking presidential candidates. Most states restrict voting in a primary to party members; such states are called closed primary states. Open primary states allow the voter to choose either party's ballot in the voting booth on primary day, and none of the open primary states require voter registration by party. Today, more than three-fourths of the states use presidential primaries; in the 2000 presidential election, approximately 84 percent of the Democratic delegates and 89 percent of the Republican delegates were chosen in the primaries.

When was the **primary introduced**?

The primary was introduced in 1904, when Florida became the first state to adopt the primary as a way of choosing delegates to nominating conventions. By 1912, fifteen states provided some type of primary election, and that year was also the first in which a candidate sought to use primaries as a way to obtain the presidential nomination (former president Theodore Roosevelt challenged incumbent William Howard Taft; Roosevelt won nine primaries to Taft's one, but lost the nomination). By 1916, twenty state Democratic and Republican parties selected their delegates in primaries. The introduction of the primary is significant to election history because it expanded democratization of the nominating process by enabling party members to choose delegates. However, in its infancy stage, the primary failed to attract many voters, and some states even abandoned it. It didn't fully recapture the electorate's attention until 1969, when the Democratic National Committee formed the McGovern-Fraser Commission to reform and revive the delegate selection process.

What are **caucuses** and **state conventions**?

A caucus is a meeting of party members or leaders to select nominees for public office and to conduct other party business. In the presidential nominating process, it is often used in combination with a state convention to elect delegates to the national nomi-

What is Super Tuesday?

"Super Tuesday" is the term used to describe a Tuesday in early March of a presidential election year when the most states simultaneously hold their primary elections, and the single day when the largest number of nominating delegates can be won. This day is key for presidential candidates, who must do well if they hope to secure their party's nomination. The phrase "Super Tuesday" was first used during the slate of primary elections that took place in Alabama, Georgia, Kentucky, Texas, Florida, Tennessee, Oklahoma, Louisiana, and Mississippi on March 8, 1988. Since then, the particular states holding primaries on Super Tuesday has varied from year to year. The 2004 "Super Tuesday" was held on March 2, during which California, Connecticut, Georgia, Maryland, Massachusetts, New York, Ohio, Rhode Island, and Vermont held Democratic primaries, while a caucus was conducted in Minnesota.

nating convention. Approximately twelve states use a caucus or convention system (or both) for choosing delegates, and each state's parties and legislature regulate the methods used. The caucus or convention is the oldest method of choosing delegates, and it differs from the primary system because its focus is on party organization.

Why are the **Iowa caucus** and the **New Hampshire primary** important?

Iowa and New Hampshire are important because they hold the nation's first caucus and primary, respectively, of the campaign season. The voting in these states has become critical to presidential candidates because candidates who do well in these states garner early media attention and are instantly dubbed their parties' front-runners. Although victories in these states often set the tone for the presidential race, success isn't automatic, as evidenced by two late twentieth-century examples: In 1980, George Bush beat Ronald Reagan in the Republican Iowa caucuses, but Reagan won the party's nomination for president; in 1996, journalist Patrick Buchanan won the New Hampshire primary in a victory over former U.S. senator Bob Dole of Kansas, but Dole received the Republican nomination. In an effort to gain more control over the nomination process, a number of states have moved their primaries ahead on the campaign calendar.

What happens at the **national party convention**?

The delegates elected in primaries, caucuses, or state conventions meet at their national party convention in the summer before the November election to choose the party's presidential and vice presidential candidates, ratify the party platform, elect officers, and adopt rules. Up until the mid-twentieth century, delegates arrived at national nominating conventions with differing levels of commitments to presidential candidates, and thus the convention was an event of excitement and fervor. However, today the nominee is usually known well in advance of the convention, based on the accumulation of a majority of delegate votes. As a result, the convention characteristically serves to ratify a choice already arrived at by party primaries, caucuses, and state conventions. Sometimes the nominee reveals his choice for running mate during the convention. In almost every national convention since 1956, one candidate has gone to each party's convention with a clear, strong lead in delegate totals.

When did national **party conventions arise**?

The election of 1824 brought an end to the congressional caucus as a nominating device, after which state legislative caucuses, conventions, and other methods were used to nominate presidential candidates. However, 1831 marked the first year that the national convention was used. The Anti-Masonic Party met in Baltimore in September of that year to choose William Wirt as its presidential candidate; in 1832, both the Democrats and National Republicans followed suit. Because the national convention was made up of delegates chosen by party holders, activists, and office holders in each state, it was a natural extension on the national level of the way party conventions worked at the state level.

What is the concept of **political bosses and smoked-filled rooms**?

In their early incarnation, national conventions were often unruly, strongly contested meetings, and frequently many ballots and extensive political maneuvering were

required before a presidential candidate could be nominated. A political party's nominee for president was often selected by influential party members and leaders (called "party bosses") at the party's national convention, after a lot of negotiation in "smoked-filled rooms"—where the air was filled with intrigue, not to mention cigar and cigarette smoke.

The term came into use at the 1920 Republican National Convention in Chicago, when Republicans met to select a front-runner for the presidential nomination. After the first day of balloting, the convention adjourned without a nominee from among the eleven candidates, forcing party leaders and U.S. senators to meet in a smoke-filled room at the Fair-

The nomination process that resulted in the Republicans naming Herbert Hoover as their candidate was so chaotic that it inspired changes that helped greatly democratize the process at the next Republican National Convention.

27

banks Hotel to choose a candidate. The result was U.S. senator Warren G. Harding of Ohio, a candidate acceptable to both the conservative and progressive wings of the party. Realizing that this was not a democratic method of choosing a major-party presidential candidate, the Democratic and Republican parties began opening up the process to voters through the primary and caucus system.

What is a **"dark horse" candidate**?

The term "dark horse candidate" is used to describe a minor candidate or party figure who was not originally considered but who steps in as a compromise choice. A dark horse, in betting parlance, is not among the betting favorites. The first dark horse candidate to win nomination was Tennessee politician James K. Polk, who emerged from the Democratic Convention of 1844 and went on to win the presidency. The opposition Whig Party had used the slogan, "Who is James K. Polk?"

Other dark horse candidates in history include: New Hampshire politician Franklin Pierce, New York politician Horatio Seymour, Ohio governor Rutherford B. Hayes, U.S. representative James A. Garfield of Ohio, U.S. senator Warren G. Harding of Ohio, and former U.S. representative John W. Davis of West Virginia. Of these, Pierce, Hayes, Garfield, and Harding were elected president.

What **different campaign styles** have made history?

Throughout the nineteenth and early twentieth centuries, presidential campaigns were conducted at the grassroots level, often by party leaders and office holders, but seldom by the candidate himself. One notable exception is William Jennings Bryan's 1896 tour of the country by rail in order to deliver his Democratic message to the American people. Other nominees held "front porch" campaigns, during which candidates didn't leave the privacy of their own homes. Introduced by Benjamin Harrison, the front porch campaign became notable in 1896 when 750,000 voters flocked to William McKinley's Canton, Ohio, home to hear the candidate speak. A modern example of the front-porch campaign is the "Rose Garden" campaign, whereby sitting presidents seeking reelection minimize their travel schedule and instead deliver announcements from the White House, in an effort to simultaneously campaign and maintain their demanding executive agenda. The term "front porch" campaign has come to denote any campaign conducted close to home without extensive travel or one-on-one interaction with the populace.

Active campaigning became more prominent with Franklin D. Roosevelt, who in 1932 conducted the first modern "whistle stop" campaign, traveling thirteen thousand miles by train and visiting thirty-six states in an effort to reach voters. The "whistle stop" campaign—during which candidates toured the country by train and delivered speeches from the rear platform—became a tried and true campaigning method. Historians generally cite Harry S. Truman as the candidate who holds the record for the most stops, covering thirty-two thousand miles and delivering an average of ten

Do modern candidates go back to campaign methods of previous eras?

Interestingly so, yes. Although air travel is by far the most expedient way of reaching the voting populace, several recent candidates tried a more grass-roots approach. In both 1992 and 1996, for example, Democrat Bill Clinton and his running mate, Al Gore, launched their campaign with an extensive bus tour across several states. The public seemed refreshed by this method of campaigning, and supporters cheered them on at bus stops and along the highways. In 1992, Republican nominee George Bush reenacted the "whistle stop" campaign era, as he traveled by train to several cities, delivering his message from the rear platform of the train.

speeches per day in his successful 1948 election campaign. Roosevelt is also known for another groundbreaking act: in 1932, he flew from New York to Chicago to accept the Democratic nomination, ushering in an era of campaign travel by air. A thoroughly modern campaigning device, air travel allows candidates to touch base in media markets across the country and gain media exposure. According to media reports, George W. Bush paid about $3 million to charter his own private plane during his twenty-month bid for the presidency in 2000.

How have **candidates used the media** to their advantage during the campaigning process?

Today, the media covers early campaign strategy, presidential primaries, party conventions, presidential debates, and dozens of other campaign happenings up until the November election. Presidential candidates use the media to showcase their platform issues and personalities, playing to a host of radio, television, and Internet opportunities. In the early days of campaigning, this precedent was set by Theodore Roosevelt, who encouraged media coverage of his family, and was greatly expanded upon by Warren G. Harding and his wife, Florence, during his 1920 campaign. In the 1930s and 1940s, radio and then film emerged as a major campaign communications tool, and candidates took advantage of radio and newsreels in an effort to reach a mass audience at unprecedented levels. Notwithstanding the large circulation rates of the daily newspapers, from 1920 to 1950, radio continued to be the major political information source for most Americans. Television surpassed radio's dominance during the presidential election of 1952, when an estimated fifty-three percent of the population watched television programs on the Dwight Eisenhower–Adlai Stevenson race.

Since 1952, when full-scale television coverage of the national conventions began, the media took on a new dimension for the presidential candidate. That year Dwight

President Carter used television to try and convey a more neighborly atmosphere in national addresses that he called "fireside chats."

D. Eisenhower spent almost two million dollars on television advertising. Since that time, television has been used to project the candidate's image and stance on various issues. Paid advertising, news coverage, and presidential debates have thrived on television. In fact, *New York Times* columnist Russell Baker wrote that after the high-profile 1960 televised debates between Richard Nixon and John F. Kennedy, "television replaced newspapers as the most important communications medium in American politics." In 1992, television reached new heights in the campaigning process when billionaire H. Ross Perot bought air time to produce infomercials and made the rounds on the morning and late-night talk-show circuits. The 1990s also saw the dramatic rise of the candidates' use of e-mail, fax, direct-mail, videos, and other alternate media formats. Blogs, website forums for communication among supporters of a candidate, became popular in the 2004 presidential campaign. Pioneered by Democratic dark horse candidate Howard Dean, blogs were quickly created for nominees George W. Bush and John Kerry.

What were some of the **first historically notable debates**?

Historians cite the 1858 Illinois senatorial debate between Republican Abraham Lincoln and incumbent Democratic senator Stephen Douglas as the most significant early debate. Douglas agreed to the joint appearances only after Lincoln followed him around the state and questioned him from the audience. Finally, seven separate debates were held, one in each of the state's congressional districts. Without the aid of a moderator or a press panel, Lincoln and Douglas debated the hot issue of the day, slavery. Then relatively unknown, Lincoln received nationwide attention for his now-famous "House Divided" speech, during which he maintained that the "government cannot endure, permanently half slave and half free." The Lincoln-Douglas debates were controversial because they occurred in front of the voting public, even though state legislatures elected U.S. senators at that time in history. The debates were followed by newspaper and telegraph synopses, but did not ignite a trend in candidate debates. Lincoln lost the Senate race, but beat Douglas in the 1860 race for the U.S. presidency, during which there were no debates.

The 1960 presidential debate was the first general election debate held in U.S. history, and it ushered in a new era of debating in the twentieth century. As part of a larger movement to reform presidential campaigns, Congress suspended the equal time provision of the Communications Act of 1934 to permit a two-man televised debate. Before an audience of seventy million, in four debates over the course of September and October, the Republican contender, Vice President Richard Nixon, and the Democratic hopeful, U.S. senator John F. Kennedy of Massachusetts, debated both domestic issues—including health care, education, and taxes—and foreign affairs. Television provided the first real opportunity for millions of voters to see their candidates in competition, and political commentators often cite Kennedy's good looks and honed oratory skills as key to his winning favor with the voting public.

What are some **notable debates** of the **late twentieth century**?

For a variety of reasons, including candidates' reluctance and the equal-time provision of the Communications Act, no presidential debates took place between 1960 and 1976. By 1976, both the law and candidates' attitudes had changed, and the 1976 debates between incumbent Gerald Ford and challenger Jimmy Carter were significant: it was the first time a sitting president participated in televised presidential debates, and the first time that vice presidents were included in debates.

The 1980s and 1990s marked an era where presidential debates became the most talked-about aspect of a candidate's campaign. The September 1980 Ronald Reagan–John Anderson debate marked the first time only one major party candidate (Reagan) participated in a general election debate (Democrat Jimmy Carter did not want to debate independent Anderson and refused to participate). In 1992, presidential debates were at an unprecedented high; ninety-seven million viewers tuned in for the presidential debate between incumbent president George Bush, Democratic contender Bill Clinton, and independent H. Ross Perot. This debate marked the first time a third-party candidate participated in general election debates with both major party candidates. Later in 1992, in Richmond, Virginia, the three candidates debated the issues in front of some two hundred average Americans who questioned them for approximately ninety minutes. The debate's "town meeting" format garnered unprecedented attention because it featured the candidates meeting face-to-face with the populace.

How did **twentieth-century campaigns** capitalize on a **candidate's image**?

The growth of radio, television, and the Internet, coupled with the late twentieth-century predominance of political consultants and image makers, has transformed the modern political campaign into one based on candidate image. A key turning point in the importance of a candidate's image took place during the 1960 presidential debates. Many listening to the debates on radio declared Richard Nixon the winner, while those watching the debates on television were certain that John F. Kennedy would claim the presidency. Kennedy, a tanned, good-looking and well-rested orator, appeared relaxed and assured, and stood in stark contrast to an ill, gaunt, and sweating Nixon. More than thirty years later, Democrat Bill Clinton pioneered the "talk-show campaign" when he appeared in 1992 on the late-night Arsenio Hall Show playing his saxophone. As the "candidate for a new generation," Clinton aimed to reach a younger audience and perpetuate his image of a maverick who could change a stale Republican government. In 2000, both candidates Al Gore and George W. Bush were interviewed on the Oprah Winfrey Show in an effort to attract women voters. And in 2004 Democratic presidential candidate, John Kerry, announced his candidacy in front of an aircraft carrier to underscore his military credentials as a decorated Vietnam veteran.

What were some **notable campaign slogans**?

Many memorable presidential campaign slogans can be found in political history. Slogans often express something of the character or platform of the candidate, or they may just be catchy phrases crafted to attract voters. In 1840, presidential hopeful William Henry Harrison and his running mate John Tyler ran for election under one of the catchiest campaign slogans in history, "Tippecanoe and Tyler Too!" In 1844, James K. Polk ran under the slogan "54 degrees, 40 minutes or Fight!" The slogan referred to the latitude parallel of 54 degrees, 40 minutes—the area of the Oregon Territory subject to dispute with Great Britain. This slogan was adopted by those who stood by Polk's desire to have the United States own this territory, or go to war for it. In 1856, western explorer and national hero John Frémont won the first Republican presidential nomination with the slogan, "Free Soil, Free Men, Frémont," which referred to the antislavery platform of Frémont and the Republicans.

During his reelection campaign of 1864, when the country was divided by war and party, Lincoln encouraged voters, "Don't swap horses in the middle of the stream." In 1869, during the era of Reconstruction, Ulysses S. Grant ran on the slogan "Let Us Have Peace." In 1896, "Patriotism, Protection, and Prosperity" were the key words for William McKinley. In 1924, Calvin Coolidge and his supporters touted "Keep Cool with Coolidge," a slogan that reflected the public's sense of optimism over the economy. In 1928, Herbert Hoover promised "A Chicken in Every Pot, and a Car in Every Garage." Harry S. Truman ran under the slogan "Give 'em Hell, Harry!" for his 1948 campaign, a phrase with which he was forever associated. In 1952, voters liked the catchy "I Like Ike" slogan that Dwight D. Eisenhower adopted.

How much money is spent on presidential campaigns?

The amount of money spent on presidential campaigns has skyrocketed since the mid-twentieth century. In 1952, presidential candidates spent a combined $16 million on their campaigns. By 1972, this amount rose to $90 million. And in 1996, the amount had totaled $120 million. These figures represent an increase of 750 percent from 1952 to 1996.

Late twentieth-century slogans have tended to discuss the concept of a new America. In 1980, Ronald Reagan implored voters, "Let's Make America Great Again." In 1988, George Bush promised "A Kinder, Gentler Nation." In 1996, Bill Clinton promised he was, "Building a Bridge to the 21st Century." George W. Bush's campaign slogan of "Compassionate Conservatism" also became a catchphrase for his first administration.

Was **religion** an **issue** in certain campaigns?

In early political campaigns, no issue was beyond scrutiny, including a candidate's religion. In 1856, the American Party expressed its hostility to the Irish Catholics that were immigrating to the United States. In that year's presidential election, the American Party charged that Republican candidate John C. Frémont was a Catholic, a claim that Frémont refused to publicly deny because he maintained it was not a legitimate issue. In 1928, the Democratic candidate for president, New York governor Alfred E. Smith, was criticized for being a Catholic. Also a proponent of the repeal of Prohibition, Smith was the butt of slurs and jokes by opponents of a Catholic voice in American politics. The periodical *Fellowship Forum* stated, "The real issue in this campaign is Protestant Americanism versus rum and Romanism." Smith lost the election by a wide margin to his Protestant opponent, Republican Herbert Hoover.

In 1960, Democratic candidate John F. Kennedy encountered anti-Catholic bias emanating from a suspicion that a Catholic president would submit his presidential decision-making authority to the pope in Rome. Kennedy responded with a televised speech, in which he refuted claims that Catholicism was incompatible with the secular office of president and proclaimed his allegiance to the separation of church and state. The speech was edited into a commercial broadcast frequently throughout the campaign, and Kennedy won by a thin margin of the popular and electoral votes.

As a sign of a more religiously tolerant populace, 2000 vice presidential candidate Joseph Lieberman experienced wide support among Democrats of all religions for his candidacy. Political analysts agree that Lieberman's Orthodox Judaism—which holds strictly to traditional Jewish beliefs and practices—only helped the image of presidential running mate Al Gore.

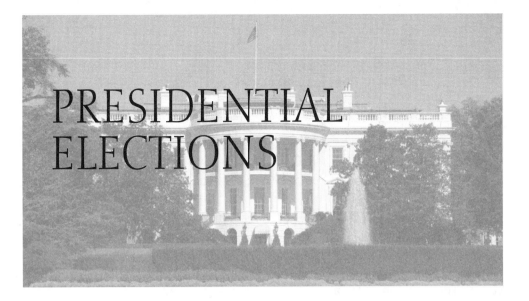

PRESIDENTIAL ELECTIONS

THE ELECTORAL COLLEGE

Is the presidential **candidate** who gets the **highest number of popular votes** the **winner**?

No. The president and vice president of the United States are not elected directly by the popular vote, but rather are elected by electors, individuals who are chosen in the November general election in presidential election years. Known collectively as the electoral college, it is this entity that votes directly for the president and vice president.

What is the **electoral college**?

When Americans vote for a president and vice president, they are actually voting for presidential electors, known collectively as the electoral college. It is these electors, chosen by the people, who elect the chief executive. The Constitution assigns each state a number of electors equal to the combined total of the state's Senate (always two) and House of Representatives delegation (which may change each decade according to the size of each state's population as determined in the U.S. Census); at the time of the 2004 presidential election, the number of electors per state ranged from 3 to 55, for a total of 538.

In each presidential election year, a group (called a ticket or slate) of candidates for elector is nominated by political parties and other groupings in each state, usually at a state party convention, or by the party state committee. In most states, voters cast a single vote for the slate of electors pledged to the party presidential and vice presidential candidates of their choice. The slate winning the most popular votes is elected; this is known as the winner-take-all, or general ticket, system. Maine and Nebraska use the district system, under which two electors are chosen on a statewide, at-large basis, and one is elected in each congressional district. Electors assemble in their respective states on the Monday after the second Wednesday in December. They are pledged and expected, but not required, to vote for the candidates they represent. Separate ballots are cast for president and vice president, after which the electoral college ceases to exist for another four years.

How are the **electoral votes tabulated**?

The electoral vote results are counted and certified by a joint session of Congress, held on January 6 of the year succeeding the election. A majority of electoral votes is required to win. In the 2008 presidential election, this number was 270 of the 538 electors. If no candidate receives a majority, then the president is elected by the House of Representatives, and the vice president is elected by the Senate, a process known as a contingent election.

How are **electors chosen**?

The U.S. Constitution left the method of selecting electors up the states, so methods vary. Generally, the political parties nominate electors at their state party conventions (in thirty-six states) or by a vote of the party's central committee in each state (in ten states). Aside from members of Congress and employees of the federal government, who are prohibited from serving as an elector in order to maintain the balance between the legislative and executive branches of the federal government, anyone may serve as an elector. Since electors are often selected in recognition of their service and dedication to their political party, they are often state-elected officials, party leaders, or persons who have a personal or political affiliation with the presidential candidate. Today, all states choose their electors by direct statewide election, except for Maine and Nebraska.

Were the **electors always chosen** by **popular election**?

No. While today all presidential electors are chosen by eligible voters, in the early republic more than half the states chose electors in their legislatures, thus eliminating any direct involvement of the voting public in the election. After 1800, this practice changed, as voting rights expanded to include a larger section of the population. By 1836, all the

A young African American woman casts her vote at a Washington, D.C., high school in the 1964 presidential election. This simple act represents hard-won triumphs in civil rights that took hundreds of years to accomplish. Her vote, however, actually goes toward selecting a representative in the electoral college and not directly for her personal choice for president.

states except South Carolina selected their electors by a statewide popular vote. South Carolina continued to choose its electors through the state legislature until 1868.

What is **electoral reapportionment**?

Each state's electoral votes are equal to the combined numerical total of its House of Representatives delegation (currently ranging from one to fifty-three, depending on population) and Senate membership (two for each state). The number of electoral votes per state, based on the 2000 census, ranges from three to fifty-five. These totals are adjusted following each census, taken every ten years, in a process called reapportionment. This process reallocates the number of members of the House of Representatives to reflect changing rates of population growth or decline among the states. Thus, a state may gain or lose electors following census reapportionment. The 2000 census allocations will be in effect for the presidential elections of 2004 and 2008. The electoral votes will be reallocated following the 2010 census, and the changes will be in effect for the first time for the 2012 presidential election.

How does the **electoral college relate** to the **popular vote**?

Civil rights leader Martin Luther King Jr. once said, "The most important step that a person can take is a short walk to the ballot box." Within his or her state, a person's vote is significant. Under the electoral college system, the people do not elect the president and vice president through a direct nationwide vote, but a person's vote helps

37

decide which candidate receives that state's electoral votes. It is possible that an elector could ignore the results of the popular vote, but that occurs very rarely.

The Founding Fathers devised the electoral college system as part of their plan to share power between the states and the national government. Under the federal system adopted in the U.S. Constitution, the nationwide popular vote has no legal significance. As a result, it is possible that the electoral votes awarded on the basis of state elections could produce a different result than the nationwide popular vote. The electoral vote totals determine the winner, not the statistical plurality or majority a candidate may have in the nationwide vote totals. Forty-eight out of the fifty states award electoral votes on a "winner-takes-all" basis (as does the District of Columbia), whereby the candidate who receives the most popular votes in a state wins all that state's electoral votes.

What is a **"faithless elector"**?

A faithless elector is the term used to describe an elector in the electoral college who does not follow the will expressed by the popular vote in a presidential election. Instead, he or she casts an electoral vote for another candidate. For example, in the presidential election of 1976, Republicans carried the state of Washington; however, one Republican elector from that state refused to vote for Republican presidential nominee Gerald Ford. The most recent example occurred in 1988, when a Democratic elector for West Virginia voted for Lloyd Bentsen for president and Michael Dukakis for vice president—instead of the other way around. However, the vote of a faithless elector has never influenced the results of a presidential election. Although most states legally require electors to vote for the candidates to whom they are pledged, the U.S. Constitution allows electors discretion in the voting process.

Why was the **electoral college created**?

The Founding Fathers established the electoral college as a compromise between election of the president by Congress and election by popular vote. They were attempting to create a blueprint that would allow for the election of the president without political parties, without national campaigns, and without disturbing the carefully designed balance between the presidency and the Congress, and between the states and the federal government. It sought to meet a number of democratic needs: to provide a degree of popular participation in the election process, give the less populous states some additional leverage in the election process, and generally insulate the election process from political manipulation.

What were some **early flaws** in the **electoral college**?

Though the electoral college system worked in theory, it was flawed in practice. It did not take into account the fact that political parties and their distinct ideologies would enter into politics at the national level. Under the original system, each elector cast two votes for president (and they had to be for different candidates) and no vote for vice president. The candidate who received the most votes was elected president, provided it was a majority of the number of electors, and the runner-up automatically became vice president. While this early voting method worked for the elections of 1789 and 1792, problems arose with the election of 1800.

What happened in the **election of 1800**?

By 1800, the fledgling Federalist and Democratic-Republican parties had begun to take shape. The Democratic-Republican Party ran incumbent vice president Thomas Jefferson as its presidential candidate and Aaron Burr as its vice presidential candidate. The Federalist Party ran incumbent president John Adams and diplomat Charles C. Pinckney. However, an equal number of electors voted for both Jefferson and Burr (Adams received sixty-five votes and Pinckney got sixty-four votes). While their intention was to elect Jefferson as president and Burr as vice president, the vote showed that both men were tied for the presidency with seventy-three electoral votes each. Burr seized the opportunity to become president, and the Federalist Party seized the opportunity to help defeat Jefferson and claim the presidency. Amid bitter infighting, the election was thus thrown into the House of Representatives—where each of the states then in existence had one vote—to decide the fate of the election. Before Jefferson finally received a majority of the votes, the House voted thirty-six times, casting ballots over a period of six days. In the end, ten states voted for Jefferson and four states voted for Burr. As the runner-up, Burr became vice president.

The election of 1800 exposed the flaws of the early electoral college system and led to the adoption of the Twelfth Amendment, which was ratified by the states in September 1804. According to this amendment, electors cast separate ballots for president and vice president. The amendment also says that if no candidate receives an absolute majority of electoral votes, then the House of Representatives selects the president among the top three contenders—with each state casting only one vote and an absolute majority needed to claim the presidency.

How did the **electors finally choose Jefferson**?

When the election of 1800 was thrown into the House of Representatives, a num-

Aaron Burr was a strong contender in the 1800 presidential election against rival Thomas Jefferson. Federalist Alexander Hamilton, however, schemed to get Jefferson elected, and Burr was so offended by this that he killed Hamilton in their now-famous duel.

ber of Federalists schemed to elect Aaron Burr as president. In order to do this, they had to defeat Democratic-Republican Thomas Jefferson with a majority of votes. To beat Jefferson, a number of Federalists planned to vote for Burr, even though he was a Democratic-Republican. In the end, one man was responsible for Jefferson's victory: his old political rival, Federalist Alexander Hamilton. Because Hamilton thought that Burr would make a poor ruler and thus could not support his party's choice due to principle, he persuaded enough Federalists to cast their votes for Jefferson. Never one to forgive an offense, in 1804 Vice President Burr shot and killed his rival Hamilton in a duel. Scholars cite the election of 1800 as one of the most colorful in American history—especially given its ultimate conclusion.

What are the **criticisms** of the **electoral college**?

Detractors of the electoral college tend to be proponents of the popular vote, and often mention the fact that the electoral college can result in a president being elected, as in the election of 1824, with fewer popular and electoral votes than his opponent. Opponents also point to the risk of faithless electors, although there has never been an instance of a faithless elector changing the outcome of a presidential election. Depressed voter turnout is another result critics cite when mentioning the institution of the electoral college; they maintain, for example, that because each state is entitled to the same number of electoral votes regardless of voter turnout, there is no incentive for states to encourage their citizens to go to the polls at election time. Another argument is that the results of the electoral-college election can fail to accurately reflect the national popular will. This can happen because of the "winner-takes-all" system, whereby the presidential candidate with the most popular votes in the states wins all of that state's electoral votes (this is true for forty-eight of the fifty states, as well as for Washington, D.C.). Even if a third-party candidate were to win as many as twenty-five percent of the voters nationwide, it is possible that he or she could still end up without any electoral college votes. According to the National Archives and Records Administration, the American Bar Association has criticized the electoral college, calling it "archaic" and "ambiguous," and its polling showed sixty-nine percent of lawyers favored abolishing it in 1987.

What are the arguments in **favor** of the **electoral college**?

Mandated by the U.S. Constitution and modified by the Twelfth and Twenty-third Amendments, the "College of Electors," as the Founders called it, has served as the nation's method for selecting its highest official for over two hundred years. Besides its durability and longevity as an election method, proponents argue the electoral college contributes to the cohesiveness of the United States because it requires that candidates receive a distribution of popular support in order to be elected president. In the twentieth-first century, no one region of the country contains the absolute majority (270) of electoral votes required to elect a president. Therefore, there is an incentive for presidential candidates to pull together coalitions of states. Proponents also mention that the electoral college contributes to democracy by encouraging a healthy, two-party system. It is extremely difficult for third-party candidates to secure enough popular votes in enough states to win a presidential election. In addition to protecting the executive office from fleeting third parties, the electoral college system forces third-party movements to converge into either the Republican or Democratic Party. The result is two large political parties that tend to fall within the center of public opinion, rather than multiple third parties with divergent fringe views. Surveys of political scientists have supported continuation of the electoral college.

DISPUTES, ANOMALIES, AND CLOSE-CALLS

Which are the **most disputed elections** in American history?

Historians generally rank the elections of 1824, 1876, and 2000 as the most controversial elections in American history. In the 1824 election, Andrew Jackson won the popular vote in a four-way race, but lost the presidency to John Quincy Adams after the election was thrown into the House of Representatives. Jackson supporters maintained there was a "corrupt bargain" between Adams and the fourth-place finisher, Speaker of the House Henry Clay. There were claims that Adams's appointment of Clay to the post of secretary of state—a position then viewed as a stepping-stone to the presidency—was part of a deal struck in return for Clay persuading his House supporters to select Adams over Jackson. The 1876 election, conducted in the tense decade following the Civil War (1861–1965), also failed to determine a winner in the electoral college. Democrat Samuel Tilden won the popular vote but ultimately lost to Republican Rutherford B. Hayes in a vote of a Republican-majority election commission. Like the 2000 election, Florida also played a key role in the election of 1876, as one of the hotly contested states. The election of 2000 between Al Gore and George W. Bush has unquestionably been the most disputed election of modern times—raising issues of balloting problems, including high rates of spoiled, unmarked, or uncounted ballots in Florida and other states; the vote-counting and certification process; the legal validity of absentee ballots; and the legal parameters of vote counts, an issue that reached the U.S. Supreme Court. In fact, some have drawn parallels to the election of 1876, claiming that Bush "stole" Florida, much like Hayes "stole" the southern states more than 120 years ago.

Which are the **closest elections**?

The two closest elections, if measured by popular-vote totals, were in 1796 and 1800. In both cases, John Adams and Thomas Jefferson won the election with a few hundred   41

Which presidents were elected to the office with a national popular vote of less than 50 percent?

Fourteen presidential candidates became president with a popular vote of less than 50 percent of the total ballots cast nationwide. They are: John Quincy Adams (32 percent in 1824); Zachary Taylor (47 percent in 1848); James Buchanan (45 percent in 1856); Abraham Lincoln (40 percent in 1860); Rutherford B. Hayes (48 percent in 1876); James A. Garfield (48.3 percent in 1880); Grover Cleveland (49 percent in 1884 and 46 percent in 1892); Benjamin Harrison (48 percent in 1888); Woodrow Wilson (42 percent in 1912 and 49 percent in 1916); Harry S. Truman (49 percent in 1948); John F. Kennedy (49.7 percent in 1960); Richard Nixon (43.4 percent in 1968); Bill Clinton (43 percent in 1992 and 49 percent in 1996), and George W. Bush (48 percent in 2000). In fact, only three successful presidential candidates since 1960—Lyndon B. Johnson in 1964, Richard Nixon in 1972, and Ronald Reagan in 1984—have captured more than 55 percent of the popular vote.

popular votes. However, at that time in America's history, the electorate was composed solely of property-owning white males. With only one electoral vote separating the two candidates, the election of 1876 was the closest electoral-vote election in all of history. The following election, of 1880, was also close, as Republican James A. Garfield received just ten thousand more popular votes than Democrat Winfield Hancock. The election of 1884 was another close election, as Democrat Grover Cleveland broke his party's almost-thirty-year hiatus when he won the election by twenty-nine thousand popular votes. In 1888, Cleveland won the popular vote by a narrow 1 percent, but his opponent, Benjamin Harrison, picked up more electoral votes and eventually claimed the election. Cleveland returned victorious in 1892, and thus became the only president to win two nonconsecutive terms.

Which elections make up the **twentieth century's close-call list**?

In the twentieth century, five elections stand out as true close calls: 1916, 1948, 1960, 1976, and 2000. In 1916, Democratic incumbent Woodrow Wilson beat his Republican challenger, former governor of New York Charles Evans Hughes, by more than a half a million popular votes. However, Wilson nearly lost the presidency because of the close race in California, where early returns indicated Hughes had won the state. Wilson eventually took California by approximately three thousand votes—bringing him an electoral vote victory of 277 to Hughes's 254.

In 1948, all eyes were focused on Republican Thomas Dewey of New York, who seemed assured of beating incumbent Democrat Harry S. Truman, whose election was threatened by the insurgent candidacies of Dixiecrat Strom Thurmond of South Carolina and Progressive Henry Wallace of Iowa. After embarking on a thirty-thousand-mile "whistle-stop" campaign—in which he delivered some three hundred speeches to six million voters—Truman defeated Dewey by some two million votes—despite pollsters and newspaper headlines incorrectly calling Dewey the victor on election night.

In the 1960 presidential election, some 119,000 votes ended up separating incumbent Republican vice president Richard Nixon and Democrat John F. Kennedy, making it one of the closest elections of the twentieth century. When it became clear that Kennedy, a U.S. senator from Massachusetts, had won the state of Illinois by approximately eight thousand popular votes—thus picking up that state's electoral votes—Nixon conceded the election. The 1976 election between sitting Republican president Gerald Ford and Democratic challenger Jimmy Carter was close in the electoral

Charles Evans Hughes (pictured with his wife, Antoinette) was a former New York governor who became Chief Justice of the U.S. Supreme Court. He was almost elected president of the United States when he ran against Woodrow Wilson in 1916.

college, but Carter won by almost two million votes in the national popular vote totals. Despite these close races, no election in history has come down to such a margin as the 537-popular-vote difference in Florida that ultimately decided the 2000 presidential contest between Democrat Al Gore and Republican George W. Bush.

What were the **circumstances** surrounding the closeness of the 1960 election?

After a campaign in which the major issues of the national economy and the communist challenge were batted back and forth, in October 1960 pollster George Gallup predicted a close race, which he refused to forecast in exact numbers. In fact, Democrat John F. Kennedy ended up winning the presidency by a plurality of 119,450 votes—the closest popular-vote contest since the Harrison–Cleveland race of 1888. Although Republican Richard Nixon won more individual states than Kennedy, Kennedy eventually prevailed by winning key states with many electoral votes, such as Illinois, New York, Pennsylvania, and Texas—despite the fact that former president Dwight D.

Eisenhower lobbied on Nixon's behalf in those closely contested states. The key state was Illinois, worth twenty-seven electoral votes, which Kennedy won amidst serious allegations of fraud in that state and Texas. Although the news media launched a series of investigative articles on voting fraud on the part of the Democrats, Nixon did not pursue a vote recount and quietly conceded the election. Like other notable losers of presidential elections before him, Nixon ran again. In 1968, he defeated Democratic contender Hubert Humphrey by a clear majority of electoral votes.

Which **eighteenth- and nineteenth-century** elections were **landslides**?

America's very first election, in 1789, was America's first landslide election, where all sixty-nine electors of the electoral college voted unanimously for George Washington. In 1792, Washington again won the vote of every elector, making him the only president in history to be elected unanimously. During 1820's "Era of Good Feelings," incumbent president James Monroe stood unopposed for reelection. His victory was near-unanimous: one of the 231 electors voted instead for Secretary of State John Quincy Adams, a noncandidate—supposedly to preserve Washington's record as the only unanimously elected president in history. Andrew Jackson's 1828 victory was another landslide election; "Old Hickory" claimed the electoral vote victory by garnering 178 votes while incumbent president John Quincy Adams won 83 votes. In addition, a greatly expanded electorate gave Jackson some 648,000 votes to Adams's 507,000. Further, most historians rank the election of Abraham Lincoln to a second term in 1864 as one of the nineteenth-century's most interesting landslide elections.

Was the election of **1864** considered a **landslide**?

Historians mention the election of 1864 as unparalleled in American history. It was a landslide victory for sitting president Abraham Lincoln, who remained in office while America was in the midst of its only civil war. Lincoln won the election, despite criticisms over his handling of the war and the odds against him: no president had won a second term since Andrew Jackson more than thirty years prior. While some people voted to replace Lincoln, the Union Army successes (including General William Sherman's capture of Atlanta), Lincoln's release of Union soldiers to go home on furlough (and vote), and Lincoln's campaign slogan, "Don't swap horses in the middle of the stream," won out over Democratic challenger George B. McClellan. Lincoln received 212 electoral votes to McClellan's 21. Lincoln's most vocal critics were in Southern states that seceded from the Union.

Which **twentieth-century elections** were **landslides**?

The 1920 presidential election was the first landslide victory in the twentieth century. The Republican contender, U.S. senator Warren Harding of Ohio, beat his Democratic opponent, Ohio governor James Cox, by a whopping 26 percent of the popular vote.

ABRAHAM LINCOLN,

REPUBLICAN CANDIDATE FOR PRESIDENT OF THE UNITED STATES.

Abraham Lincoln's campaign poster for the 1860 election. When he ran for reelection in 1864, Lincoln won in a landslide against General George B. McClellan.

Also notable is the election of 1924, during which Republican incumbent Calvin Coolidge beat Democratic opponent John W. Davis of West Virginia. Coolidge campaigned little because of his teenage son's sudden death during the summer, but the country was prosperous, the nation was at peace, and his catchy Republican campaign slogan, "Keep Cool with Coolidge," attracted voters. Franklin D. Roosevelt was one of America's most popular presidents, and is often cited in historian polls as the best of the twentieth-century presidents. Roosevelt won his second-term election in 1936, garnering 61 percent of the popular vote to the 37 percent received by his Republican contender, Kansas governor Alf M. Landon. In the election of 1948, when most of the nation had prophesied a Harry S. Truman defeat, the incumbent Democrat beat his Republican contender, New York governor Thomas E. Dewey, in a landslide election. Truman won more than twenty-four million popular votes, 49 percent of the national total, to Dewey's twenty-two million, and won 303 electoral votes.

The only late-twentieth-century president to win with a landslide was Republican Ronald Reagan, who beat incumbent Democratic president Jimmy Carter in 1980. The former California governor's platform of steep tax cuts, a balanced budget, decontrol of oil and gas prices, and a greater reliance on nuclear power resonated with a nation riddled with a host of problems: rising unemployment, runaway inflation, a severe gasoline shortage, and the lingering American hostage crisis in Iran. Amidst America's growing discontent with Carter, Reagan's sense of humor and personal appeal scored high with the one hundred million viewers who watched the presidential debates and—despite periodic language slip-ups throughout his campaign—Reagan conveyed confidence and strength. He won the presidency with forty-three million votes to Carter's thirty-five million. Reagan also gained the electoral votes of forty-four states—making Carter's defeat the most lopsided of any sitting president since Herbert Hoover's loss to Franklin D. Roosevelt in 1932.

Why was the **1992 election unique**?

Independent candidate and Texas billionaire H. Ross Perot won 19 percent of the popular vote in the 1992 presidential election, although he received no electoral votes because he was not particularly strong in any one state. Perot received the most popular votes of any third-party candidate since Theodore Roosevelt in 1912. While history has shown that any candidate who wins a majority or plurality of the popular vote stands a good chance of winning in the electoral college, one only has to consider the results of the elections of 1824, 1876, 1888, and 2000 to know there are no guarantees. Sheer tenacity, millions of dollars with which to finance his own campaign, and a unique campaign appeal made Perot successful. In addition, Perot propelled his campaign by debating the two major-party candidates, Republican George Bush and Democrat Bill Clinton, and presented his platform through infomercials, a new form of political media advertising he single-handedly pioneered. Although Perot ran again under his newly formed Reform Party in 1996—even claiming nine percent of the popular vote—his second campaign was not equal to his first.

How many **incumbent presidents** were **defeated** in their bid for another term?

Ten incumbent presidents were defeated in their bids for reelection: John Adams (1800), John Quincy Adams (1828), Martin Van Buren (1840), Grover Cleveland (1888), Benjamin Harrison (1892), William Howard Taft (1912), Herbert Hoover (1932), Gerald Ford (1976), Jimmy Carter (1980), and George Bush (1992). Five sitting presidents—John Tyler (1844), Millard Fillmore (1852), Franklin Pierce (1856), Andrew Johnson (1868), and Chester Alan Arthur (1884)—wanted to run but did not win their party's nomination.

INAUGURATIONS AND THE
FIRST ONE HUNDRED DAYS

What is **Inauguration Day**?

Inauguration Day marks the beginning of a president's new term. The Oath of Office is the main focus of the day, and the only activity required by law. As mandated by Article II, Section 1, of the U.S. Constitution, the president-elect recites the oath, "I do solemnly swear (or affirm) that I will faithfully execute the office of President of the

United States, and will to the best of my ability, preserve, protect, and defend the Constitution of the United States." George Washington added the words, "so help me God," and most presidents have followed suit. President Washington also set the precedent of kissing the Bible after taking the oath, although not all presidents have followed this custom (most notably Franklin Pierce, who preferred simply to place his left hand on it, and Theodore Roosevelt, who didn't use a Bible at all but an upraised hand). Washington also followed his swearing-in with the nation's first inaugural address, a tradition most presidents have adopted. Since the early days of Washington, each president has added his own stamp on the day's events, so Inauguration Day reflects the personality and tastes of the incoming chief executive.

Is **Inauguration Day** always held on the **same day**?

Yes. Inauguration Day originally took place on March 4, giving electors from each state nearly four months after Election Day to cast their ballots for president. In 1933, the Constitution's Twentieth Amendment officially changed the date to January 20, in an effort to expedite the change in presidential administrations. Franklin D. Roosevelt's second inauguration in 1937 was the first to take place on the new date.

What are some **Inauguration Day firsts** and **little-known facts**?

George Washington delivered the shortest inaugural address in history—just 135 words—during his second inauguration in 1793. John Adams began the tradition of having the oath of office administered by the chief justice of the Supreme Court. During his first inauguration in 1801, Thomas Jefferson became the first, and probably only, president to walk to and from his inaugural. In 1828, Andrew Jackson became the first president to take the oath of office on the East Portico of the Capitol in Washington, D.C., a tradition many presidents have since followed. While most presidents have read their inaugural addresses from written notes, Franklin Pierce broke tradition in 1853 when he recited his address. In 1945, Franklin D. Roosevelt took the presidential oath on the White House South Portico to spare himself an exhausting day, as America was engaged in World War II. In 1977, Jimmy Carter was the first president to walk from the Capitol to the White House with his family after the ceremony. In 1981, Ronald Reagan became the first president to take the presidential oath on the West Front of the U.S. Capitol (facing west in honor of his tenure as California's governor), and every president after him has followed suit. In 1985, Reagan participated in two inaugural addresses—a private ceremony on January 20 and a public ceremony the next day—so as not to conflict with the festivities of Super Bowl Sunday.

What were the most **memorable inaugural addresses**?

To inspire Americans, inaugural addresses have been carefully composed and edited by presidents and their trusted advisors. Abraham Lincoln's first inaugural address made

47

The first president of the United States of America, George Washington, took the oath of office in Philadelphia, Pennsylvania, adding the ending words, "So help me, God," himself.

no mention of the Republican Party platform, which clearly condemned slavery. Against a backdrop of succession and strife, Lincoln instead admonished listeners, "In your hands, my dissatisfied fellow-countrymen, and not in mine, is the momentous issue of civil war." Until the final draft, Lincoln's address had ended with a question for the South: "Shall it be peace or sword?" However, the famous concluding paragraph ended instead on the less contentious note: "We are not enemies, but friends." Lincoln's Second Inaugural Address, in which he pled for peace and reconciliation, is considered among his best speeches. President Lincoln called on Americans to "finish the work we are in, to bind up the nation's wounds."

John F. Kennedy's 1961 inaugural address challenged Americans to live up to the nation's ideals and outlined his ideas on foreign policy. Kennedy's conclusion, "Ask not what your country can do for you—ask what you can do for your country," is among the most famous lines from an inaugural address. The inauguration also featured Robert Frost, who read his poem "The Gift Outright" in front of an audience of thousands. Nearly thirty years later, Bill Clinton paid homage to Kennedy when he asked asked poet Maya Angelou to read her poem "The Rock Cries Out to Us Today" at his 1993 inauguration.

The words of inaugural addresses not only usher in a new leader and set the country on its course, they encourage and calm Americans during uncertain times. In 1933, Franklin D. Roosevelt assured those discouraged by the Great Depression by promising, "This great nation will endure as it has endured, will revive and will prosper." He added, "The only thing we have to fear is fear itself."

What is noteworthy about Abraham **Lincoln's first Inauguration Day**?

The celebratory happenings of most Inauguration Days contrast sharply with the day of President Abraham Lincoln's first inauguration. He arrived in Washington, D.C., in March 1861 amidst the dampened national mood of the secession of seven southern states from the Union. Fearing violence, Lincoln arrived at his inauguration via a secret route, carefully guarded by General Winfield Scott's soldiers. Lincoln and outgoing president James Buchanan arrived safely at the Capitol, where Lincoln took the oath of office on the East Portico. In his inaugural address, Lincoln appealed for the preservation of the Union, vowing not to use force to maintain the Union or interfere with slavery in the states in which it existed. Despite his appeal, a little more than a month later, the Confederates launched the first attack of the Civil War.

What was unique about Calvin **Coolidge's "inauguration"**?

Historians call Calvin Coolidge's swearing-in "the lamplit inaugural." At 2:47 A.M. on August 3, 1923, Vice President Calvin Coolidge was sworn into office by his father, John C. Coolidge, a Vermont notary public, in his father's Vermont farmhouse, where the vice president had been vacationing with his wife. President Warren G. Harding had died just hours before in a San Francisco hotel, but it took four hours for a telegram announcing the news to reach the East Coast. The Plymouth Notch home had no electricity, so by the light of a kerosene lamp, Coolidge became the thirtieth president of the United States. Coolidge was the only president to be sworn in by his father and in his family's home.

What were the circumstances surrounding Gerald **Ford's speech** upon becoming president?

On August 9, 1974, Gerald Ford was sworn in as president of the United States after Richard Nixon resigned amidst the Watergate scandal. After taking the oath, Ford delivered a straightforward speech that beseeched the confidence of the American people. Acknowledging that "our long national nightmare is over," Ford admitted, "The oath that I have taken is the same oath that was taken by George Washington and by every President under the Constitution. But I assume the presidency under extraordinary circumstances never before experienced by Americans. This is an hour of history that troubles our minds and hurts our hearts." Ford had been nominated and then approved as vice president in late 1973 after his predecessor, Spiro Agnew, had resigned due to his own personal scandal. Former New York governor Nelson Rockefeller succeeded Ford as a non-elected vice president in December 1974. Ford and Rockefeller were the first and only, thus far, to reach office under the provisions of the Twenty-fifth Amendment.

Why is President **George W. Bush's inaugural address** notable?

President George W. Bush delivered his inaugural address among a sea of supporters and detractors, some of who protested the November 2000 election outcome with signs that read, "Not My President." The ceremony took place at the Capitol's West Front in Washington, D.C., where Bush delivered a speech laden with acknowledgment of the days behind and promises of the days ahead: "While many of our citizens prosper, others doubt the promise—even the justice—of our own country," Bush said. "The ambitions of some Americans are limited by failing schools, and hidden prejudice, and the circumstances of their birth. And sometimes our differences run so deep, it seems we share a continent, but not a country. We do not accept this, and will not allow it.... Everyone belongs, everyone deserves a chance." Despite an optimistic and timely message, shouts of protesters intermittently drowned out the marching bands and cheers, reflecting Americans' divisiveness over the election results and their hesitancy toward the new president.

When was the **first inaugural ball** held?

Although George Washington hosted an informal ball after his inauguration in 1789, the first official inaugural ball was held in honor of James Madison who, along with his wife, Dolley, danced the night away at Long's Hotel in Washington, D.C. As time went on, the balls became more elaborate: Martin Van Buren's inauguration featured two inaugural gala balls, and President William Henry Harrison held three to meet his supporters' demand for tickets. Later inaugurations have featured specially built pavilions for dancing, multiple ball sites throughout the capital, and even inaugural parties in other cities. Nine inaugural balls were held in honor of President George W. Bush in 2001.

Which **inaugural parties** go down in history?

Andrew Jackson's first inauguration in 1829 is famous for its public reception. For the first time in history, Jackson invited the public to attend an inaugural party—an invitation that attracted thousands of newly enfranchised supporters, including old soldiers, backwoodsmen, and immigrants, to the White House. Their enthusiasm over the day's events and downright rowdiness caused thousands of dollars of property damage and forced the new president to narrowly escape out a window. A fourteen-hundred-pound wheel of cheese was consumed in two hours. Meanwhile, White House staff members placed tubs of punch on the lawn in an effort to draw the crowd out of the White House, and then carefully locked the doors behind them. Though one eyewitness compared the event to the "inundation of the northern barbarians into Rome," Amos Kendall, an editor from Kentucky, heralded, "It was a proud day for the people. General Jackson is their own president." Four years later, Jackson delivered his second inaugural address to a more subdued crowd in the Capitol's Hall of Representatives.

Jackson's bash laid the groundwork for most twentieth-century presidents, who have enjoyed glitz and glamour consistently since Warner Bros. Studios sent a trainload of Hollywood stars to Franklin D. Roosevelt's inauguration in 1932. In 1961, John F. Kennedy turned inaugural events into a nationwide happening when he televised his gala, which was hosted by Frank Sinatra and attended by the movie stars of the day. Bill Clinton, determined to outdo those presidents before him, reportedly spent as much on the inauguration events of 1993 as he did on his campaign for president a year earlier. The central event of his inaugural celebration was a Call for Reunion concert at the Lincoln Memorial in Washington, where artists such as Aretha Franklin, Michael Bolton, Tony Bennett, Bob Dylan, Diana Ross, and LL Cool J performed. At a televised party, the rock group Fleetwood Mac reunited to sing "Don't Stop Thinking about Tomorrow," Clinton's campaign theme song.

Why are the **first one hundred days** a significant benchmark for the president?

Since the election of Franklin D. Roosevelt in 1932, historians and political commentators have used a president's first one hundred days in office as a first benchmark for judging his performance. When Roosevelt delivered his first inaugural address, America was in the depths of the Great Depression, with an unemployment rate of twenty-five percent, a severe banking crisis, and a populace that was fearful of its future. President Roosevelt took immediate action with Congress on his New Deal program. By the end of his first one hundred days, Congress had passed fifteen bills, and Roosevelt was well on his way to enacting his program of social recovery. Although the first one hundred days is a contrived timeline, observers use this time frame not only to discuss how a president has performed out of the starting gate, but also as a gauge of how he will do for the rest of his administration.

What is the president's **State of the Union address**?

As outlined by Article II, Section 3, of the U.S. Constitution, the president's State of the Union address is an annual message from the president of the United States to Congress and the nation. During the address, the chief executive reports on conditions in the United States and abroad; recommends a legislative program for the coming session of Congress; and frequently presents his views of, and vision for, the present and future. The message was generally known as "the President's Annual Message to Congress" until well into the twentieth century. Although some historians suggest that the phrase "State of the Union" emerged after World War II, Franklin D. Roosevelt actually coined the phrase: his 1934 message is identified in his papers as his "Annual Message to Congress on the State of the Union."

Who delivered the **first State of the Union** address?

On January 8, 1790, President George Washington delivered the first message before a joint session of Congress in New York. During Washington's administration, and that of John Adams, it was customary for the president to appear before a joint session of Congress and deliver the address personally. Each House subsequently debated and approved official replies to the president's message, which were then delivered personally to the president by delegations of senators and representatives. America's third president, Thomas Jefferson, began the precedent of sending written reports, which continued until Woodrow Wilson convened Congress in 1913 and delivered his message verbally.

Is there a **State of the Union** address **every year**?

Since World War II, there have occasionally been times when a president has not delivered an annual address. Several recent presidents—Ronald Reagan in 1981, George Bush in 1989, and Bill Clinton in 1993—have chosen not to give an official State of the Union address the year they were first inaugurated as president. Other presidents, such as Reagan and Bush, have chosen not to deliver a message immediately prior to their departure from office (although President Reagan delivered a televised farewell address from the Oval Office on January 8, 1989). And both incoming and outgoing presidents have occasionally given State of the Union messages within weeks of each other. President Dwight D. Eisenhower's first message, delivered to Congress on February 7, 1953, followed on the heels of President Harry S. Truman's final message, delivered to Congress just a month earlier.

What are some of the **most notable speeches** and **documents** made by presidents?

In carrying out his roles of popular leader and chief executive, the president often makes compelling speeches in order to rally the American people around a national goal or reassure them during a time of crisis. While it can be argued that each president has made a memorable speech or proffered key words of wisdom, some of the more timeless and poignant orations include George Washington's farewell address (1796); James Monroe's State of the Union address proclaiming the Monroe Doctrine (1823); Abraham Lincoln's Gettysburg Address (1863) and his Second Inaugural Address (1865); Woodrow Wilson's war message, advising Congress to declare war on Germany (1917); Franklin D. Roosevelt's first inaugural address and first fireside chat (1933) and his war message (1941); John F. Kennedy's inaugural address (1961); Lyndon B. Johnson's State of the Union address proposing his "Great Society" program (1965); Richard Nixon's resignation speech (1974); and Ronald Reagan speaking in Germany near the Berlin Wall, imploring Soviet premier Mikhail Gorbachev to "tear down this wall" (1987).

GEORGE WASHINGTON

(1732–1799)
1st President (1789–1797)
Party Affiliation: None, though some historians list him as a "Federalist"
Opponents: None

EARLY LIFE AND FAMILY

Where and when was George Washington **born**?

George Washington was born in Westmoreland County, Virginia, to Augustine Washington and Mary Ball Washington on February 22, 1732.

Did George Washington have any **siblings**?

Yes, George had several siblings. He was the oldest of five children. George had three brothers and one sister.

He also had two older half-brothers, Lawrence and Augustine, who were the product of his father's first marriage. George was particularly close to his older half-brother, Lawrence, who watched over George after his father died when he was only eleven years old.

What did George Washington's **father do** for a living?

Augustine Washington was a tobacco planter who owned a sizeable portion of land of more than 1,000 acres. He served as a justice of the peace and sheriff of Westmoreland County for a time, too.

A portrait of George Washington in full uniform painted by Charles Willson Peale.

> ## Did George Washington actually chop down a cherry tree?
>
> No, the George Washington cherry tree was a story made up by Washington biographer Mason Locke ("Parson") Weems in his book *The Life of Washington* (1800). In the tale, Washington chopped down a tree and when his father confronted him, Washington replied: "Father, I cannot tell a lie."

Who was the **leader** of the **Washington family**?

The leader of the Washington family was John Washington, who came to the American continent in the late sixteenth century. Washington apparently used the law to take land from the Indians.

Where did **Lawrence Washington live**?

Lawrence, Washington's half brother, lived on his estate named Mount Vernon. Washington later inherited this estate in 1761, when Lawrence's wife died. Mount Vernon not only became Washington's home, but it remains a popular tourist attraction for those interested in the history of the United States.

What was Washington's **schooling**?

Washington received schooling from tutors at his home and from local schoolhouses. His favorite subject was mathematics. Washington's formal education never went beyond that of a grade-school equivalence.

Did he **marry**?

Yes, George Washington had one wife, Martha Dandridge Custis Washington, whom he married in 1759.

Did he have any **children**?

George and Martha had no children together, but Martha had two children—John and Martha—by a previous marriage. Sadly, both of Washington's stepchildren died at a relatively young age—John in his twenties and Martha in her teens. Washington outlived both of his stepchildren.

Who was **Sally Fairfax**?

Sally Fairfax was the wife of Washington's friend George William Fairfax. Washington liked Sally and some have speculated that this may have led to an affair. Others say that Sally remained the love of his life but that there was no physical affair.

Washington returning to his Mt. Vernon home after a hunt in a painting by Jean Leon Gerome Ferris.

EARLY CAREER

What **career** did **Lawrence suggest** to his younger brother, George?

Lawrence suggested that young George enlist in the Navy, an idea Washington's mother did not favor.

What was Washington's **first career**?

Washington first earned a living as a surveyor, obtaining a job through his brother Lawrence's connections. Lawrence had married Ann Fairfax of the wealthy Fairfax family. The head of the Fairfax family, William Fairfax, took a liking to young George and employed him as an assistant to his son George William Fairfax to help survey in the Shenandoah Valley.

Washington later worked as the surveyor for Culpepper County, Washington, and also worked on projects for Lord Fairfax.

How did Washington enter the **military**?

Washington's brother Lawrence held the title of adjutant general for the colony of Virginia. When Lawrence died, Washington asked Robert Dinwiddie—the colony's lieutenant governor—for his brother's former position. Lord Fairfax assured Dinwiddie that young George was the best person for the position. Dinwiddie acquiesced and twenty-one-year-old George Washington became a major.

How did Washington first attract **public attention**?

Washington first earned public acclaim for his work as a major under Governor Dinwiddie. In 1753, the governor assigned Washington the task of traveling to the Ohio Valley for the purpose of telling the French to leave the region. Washington led several other men on a trip that required them to cross the Blue Ridge Mountains, the Allegheny Mountains and up into the area near Lake Erie to deliver the King of England's message to the French to leave the land. During his trip, Washington also met up with an important Seneca chief whose name was Tanacharison.

By what Native American **name did Tanacharison call Washington?**

Historian Joseph Ellis reports that Tanacharison called Washington "Conotocarius," which means "town taker." The chief relayed that this same name had been bestowed upon Washington's great-grandfather John Washington.

How did the French receive **Washington's letter**?

The French treated Washington with respect and sent him back with a politely written letter in which they made it clear that they—not the English—had the proper claim to the lands in the Ohio Valley.

What account do we have of **Washington's trip**?

Governor Dinwiddie encouraged Washington to write of his exploits. The result was Washington's *The Journal of George Washington,* which was published in several colonial newspapers. The account was republished in England and Scotland.

What **pre-Revolutionary War experience** did Washington obtain?

In 1754, Governor Dinwiddie promoted Washington to the position of lieutenant colonel and sent him out to defend Virginia's land interests in the Ohio region in a conflict that became known as the French and Indian War. Early in the conflict, he defeated French and Indian forces in Pennsylvania and built a refuge called Fort Necessity. However, he later had to surrender the area to the French and Indians. Even worse, he had to sign a terms of surrender in French.

The next year he was promoted to colonel and continued leading troops in the French and Indian War. In 1758, Washington led Virginia's forces, which joined British forces to a great victory at Fort Duquesne. However, he could not obtain a commission from the British army. He then turned his attention to politics.

What was his **military position** during the **Revolutionary War**?

On June 15, 1775, the Second Continental Congress unanimously approved John Adams's nomination of Washington as commander of the Continental army. He served as leader of the colonial forces from the beginning of the war until the siege of Yorktown from Lord Charles Cornwallis in 1781. Washington often commanded troops who were besieged by superior armed forces and plagued with inadequate resources. He achieved a few victories, such as leading his troops across the Delaware River to surprise British forces in Trenton, New Jersey in 1776. But, he also suffered several notable defeats, including in New York and Pennsylvania. He and his troops suffered mightily during the winter at Valley Forge, Pennsylvania from 1777 to 1778.

POLITICAL OFFICES

What **political positions** did Washington achieve **before** his **presidency**?

After learning that he would not obtain a commission from the British army, Washington turned his focus to politics. He won a seat to the Virginia House of Burgesses, serving the people of Frederick County and later Fairfax County. He served continuously in the House of Burgesses until 1774.

What other **notable governmental positions** did he hold?

Washington served as a delegate from his home state of Virginia at the First Continental Congress, held in Philadelphia in 1774. He also served as a delegate for the Second Continental Congress the next year.

More importantly, Washington presided over the Constitutional Convention of 1787 when leaders from various states met to "revise" the existing governmental charter—the Articles of Confederation. The Articles failed to provide for a powerful central government with the net result that states acted out of their own self-interest. The members of the Philadelphia Convention went far beyond their stated task of revising the Articles of Confederation. Instead, they created an entirely new government through the United States Constitution. Washington did not participate in the debates, but his presence gave the proceeding much more legitimacy.

PRESIDENCY

Where did Washington **serve as president**?

Washington served as President during his first year in office in New York, which was the nation's capital at that time. In 1790, Congress passed the Residence Act, which called for the creation of a new capital in what became known as the District of Columbia, where the new governmental buildings could be constructed. Philadelphia served as the temporary location of the capital until 1800, when the District of Columbia was ready for the president. Thus, Washington was the only president who did not reside in the District of Columbia.

A portrait of Washington taking the oath of office.

How was George Washington **elected president**?

In the Constitution, the original method of electing the president called for no popular vote among the people at all. The election was determined by the votes of the members of the electoral college. The electors at that time selected two people. The person with the highest number of electoral votes would serve as president, while the person with the second highest number of votes would serve as vice president. There were sixty-nine electors for the presidential election of 1789. All sixty-nine cast votes for George Washington.

How was George Washington **reelected president**?

The presidential election of 1792 was conducted in the same manner as the election in 1789. This time there were 132 electors and they unanimously elected George Washington.

Who was Washington's **vice president**?

John Adams of Massachusetts served as Washington's vice president during both of his terms. Adams received thirty-four electoral votes in the 1789 election and seventy-seven electoral votes in the 1792 election. He would later become the country's second president after Washington declined to run for a third term.

Who were the original members of **Washington's cabinet**?

Washington sought to form a group of key advisors to assist him in leading the new federal government. He chose Alexander Hamilton as secretary of the treasury, Thomas Jefferson as secretary of state, Henry Knox as secretary of war, Edmund Ran-

59

What two members of Washington's cabinet disagreed mightily over many issues?

Hamilton and Jefferson disagreed mightily over many issues. Their disagreements in part contributed to the rise of the two-party political system in the United States. Hamilton was a Federalist, the party that generally favored a very strong central government and tended to ally with Great Britain. Jefferson became a Democratic-Republican, which favored a less powerful central government and tended to ally with France. Hamilton favored a strong fiscal policy, including the creation of the National Bank. Jefferson viewed the measure as an unconstitutional grab of power by the federal government. The only thing Hamilton and Jefferson seemingly could agree on was that they both liked Washington.

dolph as attorney general, and Samuel Osgood as postmaster general. Hamilton, Jefferson, Knox, and Randolph regularly counseled Washington on a wide range of matters. As postmaster general, Osgood did not participate in those discussions.

Hamilton led the Department of the Treasury, Jefferson led the Department of State, Randolph led the Department of Justice and Knox led the Department of War (now called the Department of Defense). Congress approved of these executive branch agencies.

What was **Hamilton's expertise**?

Hamilton was an expert in fiscal matters and he created the fiscal program for the Washington administration. Most notably, he created the proposal for a national bank called the First Bank of the United States, which would operate for a twenty-year term. Congress approved the national bank in 1791 and Washington signed it into law in February 1791.

What did **Washington think** of **political parties**?

Washington disfavored political parties, believing they would create discord in the country. In his farewell address upon leaving office, he warned the country that political parties "are likely, in the course of time and things, to become potent engines, by which cunning, ambitious, and unprincipled men will be enabled to subvert the power of the people, and to usurp for themselves the reins of government." He warned that partisan politics and different political factions could create a "frightful despotism" for the country.

Who were Washington's U.S. **Supreme Court appointees**?

Washington's first six appointments to the U.S. Supreme Court were: Chief Justice John Jay and Justices James Wilson, William Cushing, John Blair, John Rutledge, and

James Iredell. The U.S. Constitution does not provide for a specific number of justices. Rather, Congress originally set the number at six justices.

Washington later appointed Thomas Johnson, William Paterson, Samuel Chase, and Oliver Ellsworth. Washington's nephew Bushrod Washington became the next Supreme Court justice, though he was appointed by the next president, John Adams.

What was the **Neutrality Proclamation**?

The Neutrality Proclamation was a policy announced by President Washington that the United States would not interfere in the frayed relationship between Great Britain and France. The proclamation ensured that the United States would not enter into a war on President Washington's watch, as he believed such an entry would threaten the well-being of the fledging nation.

The French felt a sense of betrayal by Washington's decision, as the French had served as a key ally during the War for Independence. However, Washington was devoted to the betterment of the United States, not what was best for France. But there were critics who maintained that Washington was too subservient at times to Great Britain.

What was the **Whiskey Rebellion**?

The Whiskey Rebellion was an uprising among many grain farmers in western Pennsylvania, who objected to the Whiskey Act of 1791, a tax that had been imposed by the federal government on whiskey. The farmers believed that the federal government had overstepped its bounds by imposing too great a tax burden on farmers. The protest was seen by some as reminiscent of the colonists' protest of the British government's Stamp Act tax on the colonists.

Washington eventually considered the resistance movement serious enough that he led a formidable force of more than thirteen thousand troops to suppress the rebellion. It was the only time that a sitting president actually led troops toward a battle. Washington led the troops to Carlisle, Pennsylvania, but not all the way to face the farmers who were just outside Pittsburgh. The farmers kowtowed to the federal authority and Washington pardoned those in the uprising who swore allegiance to the federal government.

What was the **Jay Treaty**?

The Jay Treaty was a treaty with Great Britain that the United States signed in 1794 during Washington's second term. At the time, British troops remained stationed in the American northwest in defiance of the Treaty of Paris, the treaty that ended the Revolutionary War. Great Britain claimed that the Americans had not paid back all pre-revolutionary debts. Also, British ships were blocking American merchant vessels in the Caribbean in an attempt to stem American trade with France.

Washington sent Chief Justice John Jay to negotiate a treaty with British officials. The resulting agreement was known as the Jay Treaty. The British agreed to remove their troops from the Ohio frontier. America's debts would be settled by arbitration. The British received most favored nation status for trading. Though criticized, the treaty—which was in effect for ten years—prevented an American-British conflict for many years, until the War of 1812.

How did Washington **contribute** to the tradition of **executive privilege**?

In 1796, the House of Representatives demanded to see administration documents concerning the Jay Treaty. Washington refused to hand over the documents, reasoning that only the Senate—not the House—is responsible for the ratification of treaties. Washington's act of refusing to comply with the House's demands is seen as a precursor to the concept of executive privilege.

Did Washington **veto** any bills from Congress?

Yes, George Washington vetoed two bills during his two terms in office. In 1792, he vetoed the Apportionment Act that would have set the number of members of the U.S. House of Representatives based on the U.S. Census of 1790. Key members of Washington's cabinet advised Washington that the measure was unconstitutional. Washington took their advice and vetoed the measure. Congress attempted to override the veto, but could not obtain the necessary two-thirds majority.

In his second term Washington vetoed a bill that would have eliminated the light dragoons—the mounted infantry of the U.S. military. Washington felt the measure was unwise, writing that it "is generally agreed that some Cavalry either Militia or regular will be necessary."

What **future president** did **Washington remove** from a **government appointment**?

Washington removed future president James Monroe from his position as minister to France in 1796. Monroe had resigned from the U.S. Senate in 1794 to accept the appointment. Initially, Monroe seemed to succeed in his position, even obtaining the release of famed writer Thomas Paine from a prison in France. However, Monroe ran afoul of Washington for his ardent opposition to the Jay Treaty.

What other **future president** did Washington **appoint** as **minister** to a **foreign country**?

Washington appointed the future sixth president of the United States, John Quincy Adams, as minister to the Netherlands in 1794 and later minister to Portugal in 1796.

> ### What famous holiday did Washington officially proclaim?
>
> **W**ashington established the first celebration of Thanksgiving on a national level in November 1789. Washington's proclamation called for a day of "Publick [sic] Thanksgiving and Prayer." Many years later, President Abraham Lincoln officially made Thanksgiving a permanent national holiday.

POST PRESIDENCY

What did Washington do in **retirement**?

Washington and his wife, Martha, returned to Mount Vernon, where he stayed busy on his estate. He became involved in discussions with Alexander Hamilton and other members of President Adams's cabinet about possibly coming out of retirement to lead the U.S. military again in case of a French invasion. But, for the most part, Washington lived a relatively quiet life at Mount Vernon for the few years that he had left.

When did George Washington **die**?

Washington died on December 14, 1799, at his estate at Mount Vernon. His wife, Martha, lived only a few more years, passing in 1802.

As a tribute, what **future president named his son** George Washington?

In 1801, John Quincy Adams named his son George Washington after the country's first president. Unfortunately, George Washington Adams committed suicide in his late twenties.

When did George Washington's **birthday** become a **federal holiday**?

In 1879, Washington's birthday became a federal holiday. It is designated as the third Monday in February and sometimes is known as Presidents' Day instead.

When was the **Washington Monument** built?

The Washington Monument, the tallest building in the nation's capital, was built beginning in 1848 and ending in 1884. It remains a popular tourist attraction in the United States.

JOHN ADAMS

(1735–1826)
2nd President, 1797–1801
Party Affiliation: Federalist
Chief 1800 Opponent: Thomas Jefferson (Democratic-Republican)

EARLY LIFE AND FAMILY

Where and when was John Adams **born**?

John Adams was born in Braintree, Massachusetts, to John and Susanna Boylston Adams on October 30, 1735.

Did John Adams have any **siblings**?

Yes, John Adams had two younger brothers—Peter Boylston Adams and Elihu Adams. Both Peter and Elihu served in the Revolutionary War. Peter lived into his mid eighties, passing away in 1823. Elihu died from dysentery while fighting in the Revolutionary War as a captain of the militia in 1775.

What was John Adams's **father's occupation**?

John Adams Sr. worked as a farmer and at various civic offices in Braintree, Massachusetts, including as a tax collector and selectman. He also served as a church deacon. He impressed upon his son John the importance of working hard on his studies. If young John failed to perform his studies, his father would give him extra duties on the farm.

A portrait by John Singleton Copley of John Adams when he was Washington's vice president.

What famous cousin of John Adams was a prominent leader during the Revolutionary War period?

Adams's famous second cousin was Samuel Adams, a prominent politician in Massachusetts, where he first served in the state assembly in 1765. He strongly advocated against British taxation and other policies he deemed harmful to colonial interests. Samuel Adams later became a member of the Continental Congress and signed the Declaration of Independence.

What was Adams's **schooling**?

His father, John—a farmer, constable and deacon—tutored his son in his early years. Young John then attended area schools until he entered Harvard at age fifteen in 1751. His favorite instructor at Harvard was astronomer John Winthrop.

Did he **marry**?

Adams married Abigail Smith in October 1764, in Weymouth, Massachusetts. She was an extremely intelligent person who handled the job of first lady with aplomb and grace. She often accompanied her husband on diplomatic missions. She was an early advocate for women's rights.

Did he have any **children**?

Adams had five children: Abigail Amelia, John Quincy, Susanna, Charles, and Thomas Boylston. Susanna died at only two years of age and Charles only lived to age thirty. His other three children lived much longer. His second child, John Quincy Adams, later became the sixth president of the United States.

EARLY CAREER

Upon **college graduation**, what did Adams do?

Adams taught school in Worcester after graduating from Harvard. In August 1756, Adams signed a contract to learn law under attorney James Putnam in Worcester. He was admitted to the Massachusetts bar in November 1759.

What **types of law cases** did Adams take?

He handled all types of cases, ranging from property law to criminal law to admiralty law. He became well known for some of his criminal defense work. In 1769 he successfully defended several American sailors who were charging with murdering a British naval officer who had come upon their ship. Pleading that his clients acted out of self-defense, Adams obtained a not guilty verdict from the jury.

In a more famous case, in 1770 Adams defended several British soldiers who fired upon a growing mob of people on a Boston street. The tragic event became known as the Boston Massacre. Adams successfully defended the British captain, Thomas Prescott, who was in charge of the troops who fired upon the crowd. Adams earned a not guilty verdict for Prescott. Adams also defended eight other British soldiers tried for their alleged role in the Boston Massacre. He earned six not guilty verdicts and reduced charges of manslaughter for the other two.

Who were some of **Adams's mentors and heroes** in his early legal career?

Adams studied law under the tutelage of Jeremiah Gridley. He also looked up to James Otis, a lawyer and writer, who was a magnificent advocate in the courtroom. Otis is best known for fighting against the use of writs of assistance, search warrants that allowed British naval officials to conduct roving searches without any semblance of probable cause.

What writings did **Adams publish** during his early career?

Adams wrote an essay entitled "A Dissertation on the Canon and the Federal Law." It spoke about the rights of Americans and how these rights should be respected by British law. He also drafted "The Braintree Instructions," which talked about the unfairness of taxes imposed on Americans without their consent.

POLITICAL OFFICES

What **political offices** did Adams hold **before the presidency**?

Adams was elected in 1770 to the Massachusetts legislature, where he served for four years. He served as a member of the Continental Congress in 1774. He also served as a member of the Second Continental Congress from 1775 to 1778. He then served as ambassador to the Netherlands in 1782. Three years later, in 1785, Congress appointed Adams to become the country's first ambassador to Great Britain. In 1789, he began his two terms as the nation's first vice president under President George Washington.

What **famous document** did Adams **help create** and sign as a member of the Continental Congress?

The Continental Congress formed a committee of five men to draft what became known as the Declaration of Independence. These men were John Adams, Benjamin

Franklin, Thomas Jefferson, Robert R. Livingston, and Roger Sherman. The committee eventually selected Thomas Jefferson to write the Declaration. Adams and Jefferson were the only presidents to sign the Declaration.

What **other famous document** did Adams draft in 1776?

Adams published a short essay on the proper form of government for colonial governments entitled *Thoughts on Government*. He advocated for a bicameral legislative body, writing that "a people cannot be long free, nor ever happy, whose government is in one assembly." He also wrote that the judicial branch must be independent from the legislative and executive branches: "[The] judicial power ought to be distinct from both the legislative and executive, and independent upon both, that so it may be a check upon both."

What did Adams accomplish when he served as U.S. **ambassador** to the **Dutch Republic**?

He managed to convince the Dutch to recognize the United States and he helped to create the first American embassy in any foreign country in 1782 in the Dutch Republic. He negotiated a treaty of commerce with the Dutch later that year. Adams also managed to convince Dutch leaders to lend considerable sums of money to his new country.

Did Adams enjoy the **vice presidency**?

Adams did not think much of the office of vice president. He referred to it as "the most insignificant office that ever the imagination of man contrived." Part of this was due to the fact that Adams and Washington were not particularly close. Washington rarely consulted Adams on questions of policy or political importance. Adams did cast numerous deciding votes, as the vice president casts the deciding vote when the Senate is tied. Adams cast the deciding vote against a bill that would have given the Senate the power to remove officials from the presidential cabinet.

PRESIDENCY

Whom did **Washington endorse** as his **successor**?

President George Washington endorsed his vice president, John Adams. Washington had had a falling out a few years earlier with Thomas Jefferson, his former secretary of state, so he did not choose him.

Whom did **Adams defeat** to win the **presidency**?

Adams captured the presidency by only three electoral votes, defeating Thomas Jefferson by a vote of seventy-one to sixty-eight. Because the vice president went to the person with the second most number of electoral votes, Jefferson ironically became Adams's vice president even though Jefferson was a member of a different political party. Adams ran as a Federalist, while Jefferson was a Democratic-Republican. It was the only time in American history that a president and vice president came from two different parties, because Congress changed the voting procedure in the Twelfth Amendment to the U.S. Constitution.

Who **finished third** in the election?

Thomas Pinckney of South Carolina finished third in the election with fifty-nine electoral votes. Alexander Hamilton used his political influence to try to get many Federalists to support Adams instead of Pinckney.

Which member of **Adams's cabinet** served in **multiple positions**?

Samuel Dexter served as Adams's secretary of war from May 1800 to January 1801. Upon Oliver Wolcott's resignation as secretary of treasury, Dexter assumed that position for the remainder of President Adams's term as president. Like Adams, Dexter came from Massachusetts, where he served in both the U.S. House of Representatives and later the Senate. He also graduated from Harvard like President Adams.

Where did **Adams reside** as president?

Adams initially resided in Philadelphia, Pennsylvania. However, in November 1800, Adams moved to the White House, becoming the first president to live in the new capital of Washington, D.C. He only lived there for four months, however, as he lost in his reelection bid to his vice president, Jefferson.

What **branch** of the **armed forces** was created during Adams's presidency?

Congress passed a law in May 1798 that created the Department of the Navy. Con-

A lithograph by Gilbert Stuart portraying President John Adams.

What famous man swore in Adams as president?

The Chief Justice of the U.S. Supreme Court, Oliver Ellsworth, swore in John Adams as president in March 1797. This began a tradition that has existed ever since in American history.

gress and Adams wanted this branch of the armed forces to deal with the serious threat of French vessels on the seas.

What **series of laws** passed by Congress and signed by President Adams caused **great controversy**?

The Alien and Seditions Act, passed in 1798, caused great controversy. This legislation consisted of four laws: (1) the Naturalization Act, which increased the required period of residence for would-be citizens from five to fourteen years; (2) the Alien Friends Act, which gave the president the power to remove from the country outsiders he deemed "dangerous"; (3) the Alien Enemies Act, which gave the president the power to deport those aliens who were from countries at war with the United States; and (4) the Sedition Act, which made it a crime to make "false, scandalous and malicious" writings against the government. Many—including Vice President Thomas Jefferson—opposed these laws as an invasion of state rights and a violation of individual freedoms. For example, many believed that the Sedition Act of 1798 violated the First Amendment rights of freedom of speech and press.

Who was **prosecuted** under the **Sedition Act**?

For the most part, the Sedition Act was used to prosecute editors of Democratic-Republican newspapers. These editors published newspapers that criticized President Adams and his foreign policy towards France. Men such as Benjamin Franklin Bache, editor of the *General Advertiser* in Philadelphia (also known as the *Aurora*), and Anthony Haswell, editor of the *Vermont Gazette,* were arrested for their sharp criticism of Federalists.

Who were Adams's U.S. **Supreme Court appointees**?

Adams nominated three men to the U.S. Supreme Court during his tenure: Bushrod Washington, Alfred Moore and John Marshall. Washington, a nephew of former President George Washington, served for nearly thirty years on the court. Moore, the shortest man ever to serve on the court, only served four years. Marshall became the court's fourth chief justice in the history of the U.S. Supreme Court, where he served for thirty-four years. Many consider John Marshall to be the greatest jurist in Supreme Court history.

What other **role** did **John Marshall play** in Adams's presidency?

John Marshall served as President Adams's secretary of state for most of Adams's last year in office. Marshall replaced Timothy Pickering, who had been working more for Federalist Party leader Alexander Hamilton than Adams. Part of the problem was that Adams did not appoint many of his own people to serve in his cabinet. Instead, he kept four people from Washington's cabinet, including Pickering as secretary of state, Oliver Wolcott as secretary of the treasury, James McHenry as secretary of war, and Charles Lee as attorney general.

What was the **Quasi-War**?

The Quasi-War was the name given to the conflict between France and the United States between 1798 and 1800. French and American vessels fought at sea for much of that time, though there never was a formal declaration of war.

What was the **XYZ Affair**?

The XYZ Affair refers to a failed peace mission between three American envoys (Charles Cotesworth Pinckney, John Marshall, and Elbridge Gerry) and three agents of the French foreign minister Talleyrand (Jean Conrad Hottinger, Pierre Bellamy, and Lucien Hauteval). Talleyrand instructed his three envoys to refuse negotiations with the American envoys unless Talleyrand received a personal payment (in actuality, a bribe) of $25,000 and a loan of $10 million to France. The three Americans refused and negotiations ended, exacerbating tensions between the two countries. Adams later referred to the three French agents as X, Y, and Z.

Did Adams **seek** a **second term**?

Yes, President Adams sought a second term as the Federalist Party leader. However, Jefferson once again ran as the Democratic-Republican nominee. This time Jefferson obtained more electoral votes, defeating Adams seventy-three to sixty-five. More of the country had supported Democratic-Republicans than the Federalists. Democratic-Republicans had more seats in both Houses of Congress for the first time in American history.

POST PRESIDENCY

Where did Adams **reside after leaving office**?

Adams returned to his native Massachusetts, living on his farm in Quincy, Massachusetts. He spent much of his time reading and writing.

When did **Adams** and **Jefferson reconcile**?

The two former political rivals reconciled in 1812 after exchanging friendly letters. A mutual friend, Dr. Benjamin Rush—also a signer of the Declaration of Independence—prevailed upon his two friends to make peace. Adams and Jefferson exchanged regular correspondence after that time.

When did Adams **die**?

Adams died on July 4, 1826—ironically the same day as rival and friend Thomas Jefferson. Legend has it that on his deathbed he uttered the words: "Thomas Jefferson still lives." However, unknown to Adams, Jefferson had died a few hours earlier. Only four presidents lived to be nonagenarians—Adams, Herbert Hoover, Gerald Ford, and Ronald Reagan.

THOMAS JEFFERSON

(1743–1826)
3rd President, 1801–1809
Party Affiliation: Democratic-Republican
Chief 1800 Opponent: John Adams (Federalist)
Chief 1804 Opponent: Charles Cotesworth Pinckney (Federalist)

EARLY LIFE AND FAMILY

Where and when was Thomas Jefferson **born**?

Thomas Jefferson was born in Shadwell, Virginia, to Peter and Jane Randolph Jefferson on April 13, 1743.

What did **Jefferson's father** do for a living?

Peter Jefferson worked as a farmer and surveyor. He also became a judge and militia leader in Albemarle County, Virginia.

How many **siblings** did Thomas Jefferson have?

Thomas Jefferson had nine siblings. He was the third oldest of ten and the eldest son.

What was his **education**?

Jefferson began his schooling at Shadwell, but his parents sent him away to a school run by a Scottish minister named William Douglas. He then studied at another school

Portrait of President Thomas Jefferson by Henry R. Robinson.

run by a minister named James Maury. At the age of sixteen, Jefferson entered The College of William & Mary, where he graduated with high honors in 1762.

Did he **marry**?

Jefferson married widower Martha Jefferson on January 1, 1772.

Did he have any **children**?

Jefferson had six children: Martha, Jane Randolph, an infant son who died at birth, Mary, Lucy Elizabeth, and another daughter named Lucy Elizabeth. Only one of his children lived past seven years old: Martha "Patsy" Jefferson.

EARLY CAREER

What was **Jefferson's first profession** after graduating college?

Jefferson read law under attorney George Wythe for five years. In 1767, he passed the bar and began handling cases on his own. He handled many property law disputes during his legal career.

Who was **George Wythe**?

George Wythe was a prominent attorney from Virginia who also served as mayor of the city of Williamsburg, signed the Declaration of Independence and served as a member of the Continental Congress. Wythe was an older attorney who served as a mentor of sorts for Thomas Jefferson, who read law under him for several years. Wythe later became the country's first law professor at William & Mary.

What **famous document** did Jefferson **draft** in 1776?

Jefferson was the principal author of the Declaration of Independence. He drafted the document in several days. He showed it to John Adams and Benjamin Franklin, who made some minor revisions. Later the Continental Congress examined the wording of the document and made more substantial changes. But, the bulk of the document remained as Jefferson wrote it. Congress approved the Declaration on July 4, though members of Congress signed the copy from the printers in early August.

Who was Sally Hemings?

Sally Hemings was a slave owned by Thomas Jefferson. It has been alleged that Jefferson had a sexual relationship with Hemings and that she bore his children. In 1802 James T. Callendar wrote about Jefferson's affair with a "slave named Sally" in the *Richmond Recorder*. Debate still rages among historians as to the veracity of the Jefferson-Hemings relationship. Some suggest that Jefferson's younger brother Randolph may have fathered children with Sally Hemings. DNA testing of Jefferson and Hemings descendants in 1998 showed a definite genetic link between the two families.

From which **philosopher and political theorist** did Jefferson draw heavily in writing the **Declaration of Independence**?

Jefferson drew from the works of John Locke, an English writer of the seventeenth century who wrote such classics as *Two Treatises of Government* (1689) and *Essay Concerning Human Understanding* (1690). Locke argued against the divine right of kings and believed in natural law—that power should reside ultimately in the people.

What **other famous document** about religious freedom did Jefferson draft?

In 1777 Jefferson drafted the Virginia Statute for Religious Freedom, which the Virginia legislature enacted into law in 1786. The document called for government to respect the religious preferences of individuals and forbade government from establishing a particular religion. For example, a passage in the law provided: "Be it enacted by General Assembly that no man shall be compelled to frequent or support any religious worship, place, or ministry whatsoever, nor shall be enforced, restrained, molested, or burdened in his body or goods, nor shall otherwise suffer on account of his religious opinions or belief."

Which **book** of Jefferson's achieved **international attention**?

In 1781, Jefferson published *Notes on the State of Virginia,* which included data on his home state of Virginia and his philosophies on good government. He also discussed the subject of slavery in two chapters of the book. He originally conceived of the book while drafting questions about his home state of Virginia from François Barbe-Marbois, the leader of a French delegation in Philadelphia. Jefferson realized that his answers to the French leader would make a fine book.

What was the name of **Jefferson's famous estate**?

In 1769, Jefferson began work on his estate, which he called Monticello, "small mountain" in Italian. Monticello remains a historical treasure and top tourist site in the

United States. It is known for its fabulous architecture and its incredible landscape, featuring many different types of trees.

What were some of Jefferson's **inventions**?

Jefferson invented a plow that could delve deeper into the soil than standard plows of the time and could be used on hillsides. The French Agricultural Society bestowed an award to Jefferson for his plow invention. He developed a macaroni machine, after acquiring a taste for many fine foods during his long stay in Europe. He also developed a swivel chair, a dumbwaiter, and a wheel cipher.

POLITICAL OFFICES

What were the various **political positions** that Jefferson held **before the presidency**?

Jefferson served as a member of the Virginia House of Burgesses, a delegate to the Continental Congress, governor of Virginia, minister to France, secretary of state, and vice president.

When did Jefferson **enter the political arena**?

Jefferson became elected to the Virginia House of Burgesses at age twenty-five in 1768. He often voted in favor of the interests of the middle class rather than the wealthiest landowners.

How long did Jefferson **serve as governor**?

Jefferson became Virginia's governor in 1779, when the colonies were battling the British in the Revolutionary War. He was reelected in 1780, but during his second term Virginia fell victim to British invasion. Jefferson narrowly escaped when his estate, Monticello, was besieged by enemy troops. He did not seek a third term in

A political cartoon depicts President Jefferson trying to defend his policies on foreign commerce.

1781. He was succeeded by William Fleming, a physician and soldier who served as governor little more than week, and then Thomas Nelson, Jr., a fellow signer of the Declaration of Independence.

With whom did Jefferson **clash as secretary of state**?

Jefferson served as President George Washington's secretary of state. During that time, he often clashed with the secretary of the treasury, Alexander Hamilton. Hamilton favored a strong central government, a national bank, and federal taxes. Jefferson favored a limited federal government, opposed the national bank, and generally opposed the expansion of federal power. More often than not, Washington took Hamilton's advice on such matters.

Did Jefferson have an active role in government as **vice president**?

No, he and President Adams parted company on many political issues of the day. Jefferson did not take an active part in the administration. He actively opposed the administration on many matters. For example, he campaigned and wrote against the Sedition Act of 1798 that President Adams had signed into law.

Jefferson did preside over the Senate—the main constitutional duty of vice presidents. He wrote *The Manual of Parliamentary Practice,* which became the leading rulebook for members of both houses of Congress.

79

PRESIDENCY

Whom did **Jefferson defeat** to win the **presidency**?

Jefferson defeated incumbent John Adams to win the presidency in the election of 1800. That reversed the result four years earlier when Adams had narrowly defeated Jefferson to capture the presidency.

What **complication** resulted from the **election of 1800**?

The problem in the election of 1800 was that Jefferson received the same number of votes as his presumed vice presidential candidate, Aaron Burr. Both Jefferson and Burr received seventy-three votes. Because the two received the same number of votes, the House of Representatives voted to determine who would serve as President. This problem led to the relatively quick passage of the Twelfth Amendment a few years later in 1804.

Who **resolved the tie** between Jefferson and Burr?

The U.S. House of Representatives eventually broke the electoral vote tie between Jefferson and Burr. However, it took thirty-six ballots to resolve the controversy. The rules required that the winner receive an electoral margin in nine of the then-existing sixteen states. In the first thirty-five ballots, Jefferson was the winner in eight states—one short of the necessary nine. Finally, on the thirty-sixth ballot, the states of Maryland and Vermont shifted support to Jefferson, which gave him victory in ten states.

Which **former political foe** actively **lobbied for Jefferson** and against Burr?

Alexander Hamilton—Jefferson's rival in President Washington's administration—was not a supporter of Thomas Jefferson. But Hamilton absolutely despised Burr. Hamilton used his considerable influence among the Federalist members of the House of Representatives to swing the election in the House to Jefferson.

Who served as Jefferson's **secretary of state**?

Jefferson selected his friend and fellow Virginian James Madison to serve as his secretary of state. Madison served in this capacity for Jefferson's full two terms. He later became Jefferson's successor and the country's fourth president.

Who served as Jefferson's **secretary of the treasury**?

Albert Gallatin served as Jefferson's secretary of the treasury. Born in Switzerland, Gallatin served in the Pennsylvania legislature beginning in 1790. He was elected to the U.S. Senate in 1793, but many members of the Federalist Party objected to him and alleged that he had not been a citizen of the United States long enough to serve as

Where did Jefferson send American troops to fight on foreign soil?

Jefferson became the first president to send soldiers to fight on foreign soil when he sent troops to engage Tripoli, which had declared war on the United States. In the First Barbary War, America faced the so-called Barbary States, which included the Sultanate of Morocco and the regencies of Algiers, Tunis, and Tripoli. Tripoli managed to capture the USS Philadelphia during the conflict, but a Marine unit secured the vessel and burned it, preventing its use by the enemy. Marines later defeated Tripoli forces in the city of Derna.

a senator. He later served several terms in the U.S. House of Representatives before become secretary of the treasury. In the House of Representatives, he opposed the Alien and Sedition Acts of 1798. He later served in the same position for James Madison. No individual has ever served as secretary of treasury longer than Gallatin.

Who served as Jefferson's **secretary of war**?

Henry Dearborn, a physician and a veteran of the Revolutionary War, served as Jefferson's secretary of war for both terms. British forces captured Dearborn at the Battle of Quebec and he was imprisoned for a year. He later served his country in the War of 1812.

What **famous jurist did not get along** with Jefferson?

John Marshall, a fellow Virginian, did not get along well with Jefferson, even though the two were distant cousins. Marshall was a Federalist and a supporter of President Adams. Adams later nominated Marshall as the fourth Chief Justice of the U.S. Supreme Court. During one of his last acts as president, Adams created more than two hundred new judicial posts and attempted to fill them with Federalists.

Upon taking office, Jefferson ordered his secretary of state, James Madison, to withhold the commissions. William Marbury, one of those would-be federal judges, sued to have Madison deliver his commission. The celebrated case of *Marbury v. Madison* (1803) came before the U.S. Supreme Court. Marshall technically ruled for Jefferson, disallowing Marbury's commission, but criticized the actions of Jefferson and Madison and exclaimed that the judicial branch had the power to review actions of the executive and legislative branches—a power known as judicial review.

Whom did **Jefferson defeat** to win **reelection in 1804**?

Jefferson routed Federalist candidate Charles Cotesworth Pinckney of South Carolina to win the election of 1804. Jefferson garnered 162 electoral votes to only 14 for Pinckney.

What famous land expedition did Jefferson order?

Jefferson ordered Meriwether Lewis and William Clark to explore the western part of North America. This famous trip became known as The Lewis and Clark Expedition. Like Jefferson, Meriwether Lewis was born in Albemarle County in Virginia, and served as Jefferson's trusted White House secretary. When Jefferson discussed the idea of a western expedition, Lewis agreed to take the lead in the matter. Lewis asked Clark, a man whom he met while defending federal interests during the Whiskey Rebellion, to accompany him on the trip.

Who was Jefferson's **vice president** for his **second term** as president?

George Clinton served as Jefferson's vice president during his second term. Clinton was the former Governor of New York. He later served as James Madison's first vice-president. He became the first individual—of only two men in American history—to serve as vice president under two different presidents.

What **famous land deal** greatly expanded the United States during Jefferson's presidency?

Jefferson approved and ordered the Louisiana Purchase with Napoleon Bonaparte, the Emperor of France. Jefferson desired to acquire the French colony of Louisiana mainly to acquire the port city of New Orleans for commerce and defense purposes. James Monroe and Robert R. Livingston negotiated the purchase with French authorities. The $15 million purchase included more than 800,000 square miles, and roughly doubled the size of the United States. Congress approved the purchase—completed in the form of a treaty—by a vote of twenty-four to seven.

Upon the agreement, Livingston said: "From this day the United States take their place among the powers of the first rank."

What **unpopular legislation** did Jefferson sign to avoid entering the English–French conflict?

Jefferson signed an embargo act—known as the Embargo Act of 1807—to keep America completely out of the conflict between Great Britain and France. Each side prohibited any of its allies from trading with its enemy. Jefferson refused to become involved in the war and responded with the Embargo Act, which was an attempt to show the United States' neutrality in the English-French conflict. The measure prohibited for-

The Jefferson Memorial in Washington, D.C.

eign trade with either nation. The banning of trade with either nation was unpopular, but it did lead to the creation of more textile mills and other industries in the United States. Jefferson lifted the embargo shortly before leaving office.

Who were Jefferson's U.S. **Supreme Court appointees**?

Jefferson appointed William Johnson, Brockholst Livingston, and Thomas Todd to the Supreme Court. Johnson served thirty years on the Court and helped develop the tradition of dissents. Johnson sometimes openly disagreed with Chief Justice John Marshall's rulings. Livingston served nearly sixteen years on the Court, while Todd served nearly nineteen years on the high court.

POST PRESIDENCY

What **great achievement** did Jefferson accomplish in his retirement that was significant enough that he wanted it on his **epitaph**?

Jefferson founded the University of Virginia in Charlottesville in 1819. He designed the architectural layout of the campus, recruited faculty to the university, and helped design the curriculum.

83

What **message** did Jefferson ask to be inscribed on his **tombstone**?

Here was buried Thomas Jefferson
Author of the Declaration of American Independence
Of the Statute of Virginia for Religious Freedom
And Father of the University of Virginia.

What famous **quote** by a **future president** showed great regard for the incredible **intellect of Jefferson**?

President John F. Kennedy told a group of forty-nine Nobel Peace Prize winners at the White House in 1962: "I think this is the most extraordinary collection of talent and of human knowledge that has ever been gathered together at the White House—with the possible exception of when Thomas Jefferson dined alone."

Where does **Jefferson's visage commonly appear** in the United States?

Jefferson is one of four presidents to have their images displayed at Mount Rushmore in the Black Hills of South Dakota. The other three are George Washington, Abraham Lincoln, and Theodore Roosevelt. Jefferson also appears on the nickel coin and the two dollar bill.

When did Jefferson **die**?

Jefferson died on July 4, 1826, the same day as his sometimes friend and rival John Adams. He was eighty-three years old.

JAMES MADISON

(1751–1836)
4th President, 1809–1817
Party Affiliation: Democratic-Republican
Chief 1808 Opponent: Charles Cotesworth Pinckney (Federalist)
Chief 1812 Opponent: DeWitt Clinton (Federalist)

EARLY LIFE AND FAMILY

Where and when was James Madison **born**?

James Madison was born in Port Conway, Virginia, to James and Eleanor Rose Conway Madison on March 16, 1751. He lived on the family's estate, Montpelier.

What was unusual about **Madison's mother**?

James Madison's mother lived an extremely long life. She was born in January 1731 and passed away in February 1829, at the age of 98.

What did Madison's **father do** for a living?

As with George Washington's father, Augustine, James Madison Sr. was a prominent tobacco planter. He owned a large plantation named Montpelier. He also served as a colonel in the Virginia militia.

Did James Madison have any **siblings**?

Yes, Madison was the oldest of twelve siblings, though three died in infancy. One of his brothers, William Madison, fought in the Revolutionary War and served as a lawyer.

What was his **education**?

Madison learned at home for many of his early years. At age eleven, he studied under the tutelage of Donald Robertson of the Innes plantation. Madison studied mathematics, geography, languages, and history from Robertson, whom Madison credited later in life with developing his love of learning. At age sixteen, Madison studied for two years under the Reverend Thomas Martin. Madison then entered the College of New Jersey

Portrait of President James Madison by John Sully.

(later renamed Princeton University) where he studied history, government, and law. He graduated from college in two years.

Did he **marry**?

Madison married Dolley Dandridge Payne Todd in 1794. Madison was forty-three, while Todd was a twenty-six-year-old widow.

Did he have any **children**?

Dolley had a son, John Payne Todd, from her first marriage to Philadelphia lawyer John Todd, who died in 1792. Madison later adopted John Payne as his own son.

Whom did Madison **nearly marry** years before he met Dolley?

In Philadelphia, Madison became smitten with a fifteen-year-old girl named Catherine "Kitty" Floyd. In those times, women often married at a very early age. New York delegate

> ## Who was John Witherspoon?
>
> John Witherspoon was the president of the College of New Jersey during Madison's time there. Madison took courses under Witherspoon and became inspired by some of his teacher's positions with regard to natural rights and religious freedom.

William Floyd, Kitty's father, approved and encouraged her relationship with the thirty-two-year-old Madison. The two became engaged, but Kitty later broke off the engagement.

What was unusual about **Madison's size**?

Madison was a very diminutive man, standing five feet, four inches tall and weighing approximately one hundred pounds. He is the shortest of all the presidents. Perhaps that is why one of his nicknames was "Little Jemmy."

EARLY CAREER

What did Madison do **after graduation**?

Madison returned home to Montpelier after graduation in ill health, partly because of his excessive studying. He continued his insatiable quest for learning more about politics and government. He joined the Committee of Safety, a local Virginia defense organization. Later, he was commissioned as a colonel in the Orange County militia.

Did Madison fight in the **Revolutionary War**?

No, Madison's poor health precluded him from fighting in combat. He did serve in various positions during the Revolutionary War, however, including as a colonel in the Orange County militia and as a member of a local group known as the Committee of Safety. He also tirelessly advocated on behalf of independence.

POLITICAL OFFICES

What was Madison's **first political position**?

Madison earned a seat in the Virginia House of Delegates in 1776 where he helped in the creation of his state's constitution. It was in this position that he met his lifelong friend and colleague Thomas Jefferson.

What political **race** did **Madison lose**?

Madison ran for reelection in the Virginia House of Delegates in 1777 under the new constitution. During this election, Madison learned a valuable lesson about popular support when he refused to follow the practice of providing alcohol to voters. He lost the election to a tavern owner who had no such qualms.

When did Madison **join** the **Continental Congress**?

Madison joined the Continental Congress in 1779 at the age of twenty-nine. He argued for a stronger central government in much of his legislative work. He proposed that representatives from different states meet in Annapolis, Maryland, to discuss how to improve the existing constitution of the United States—the Articles of Confederation.

The Articles of Confederation provided much power to the states but provided for a weak central government that could not regulate commerce between the states. Madison later supported the call for a new convention in Philadelphia to discuss how to improve the Articles of Confederation.

What was Madison's **role** in the **Philadelphia Convention**?

Madison played a key role in the Philadelphia Convention. He arrived early and had prepared well for the convention. A month before the convention opened, Madison published a document called "Vices of the Political Systems of the United States." He criticized many aspects of the Articles of Confederation.

At the convention he introduced several resolutions to provide for a stronger central government. His most famous contribution in terms of resolutions was the so-called Virginia Plan. Though sometimes referred to as the Randolph Plan because Edmund Randolph formally introduced it, Madison wrote the essence of the measure. Madison's plan consisted of a bicameral legislature—a U.S. House of Representatives and a Senate. The number of representatives in each house would be determined by the state's population. Under this plan, the people would elect members to the U.S. House of Representatives, but then members of the House would elect and vote on membership to the Senate. The Virginia Plan also included plans for a national (or federal) judiciary.

He also took a detailed set of notes about the proceedings of the Convention. Historians emphasize that without Madison's notes, we would know little about the historic meetings in Philadelphia that eventually led to the U.S. Constitution. Madison instructed that his detailed notes of the Convention were not to be released until the last delegate at the Convention died. Ironically, that last delegate was Madison, who died in 1836 at the age of eighty-five.

Madison also played a key role in persuading fellow Virginian George Washington to attend the proceedings. The delegates elected Washington as chairman of the meeting. Washington's presence was important given his leadership and popularity after the Revolutionary War.

What did Madison do to **help** with the **ratification** of the **Constitution**?

Madison knew that the delegates' work was not complete simply because they had finished and signed the new Constitution. They had to convince the different states of the need and importance of this new constitution. They had to convince the states to ratify this new constitution, which radically changed the power of the central government.

Using pseudonyms, Madison—along with Alexander Hamilton and John Jay—drafted a series of essays called The Federalist Papers, which advanced forceful arguments for the necessity of the new Constitution. Madison also argued in the Virginia legislature for the need for Virginia to ratify the Constitution. Madison argued directly against Virginia governor Patrick Henry.

From what position did **Madison push** for the **Bill of Rights**?

Madison won election to the newly created U.S. House of Representatives, where he served for eight years beginning in 1789. In the House of Representatives, Madison spearheaded the adoption of the Bill of Rights—a series of amendments to the U.S. Constitution that would secure individual freedom and popular support for the new Constitution. For his role in the ratification of the U.S. Constitution and Bill of Rights, Madison is referred to as "the Father of the Constitution" and "the Father of the Bill of Rights."

What were, in Madison's words, **"the great rights of mankind"**?

Madison's "great rights of mankind" were the Bill of Rights. On June 8, 1789, Madison made an impassioned plea in the U.S. House of Representatives, arguing for the adoption of the Bill of Rights to the U.S. Constitution. Madison argued in part that many of the people would support the newly enacted Constitution if only they could be assured that their individual freedoms would be protected.

As Madison stated it: "[There is a] great body of the people falling under this description, who at present feel much inclined to join their support to the cause of federalism, if they were satisfied in this one point: We ought not to disregard their inclination, but, on principles of amity and moderation, conform to their wishes, and expressly declare the great rights of mankind secured under this constitution."

Where did Madison look in **proposing his amendments** to the Constitution?

Madison looked largely to existing state constitutions, which contained guarantees of individual freedom in the form of declarations of rights. For example, many existing state declarations of rights protected freedom of speech and religion, trial by jury and the right to due process.

What **famous document** did Madison draft in **opposition** to the **Alien and Sedition Acts**?

Madison—and his friend Thomas Jefferson—adamantly opposed the Alien and Sedition Acts of 1798, adopted by the Federalist-controlled Congress and signed by President John Adams. In response, Madison and Jefferson drafted the Virginia and Kentucky resolutions, documents approved by the states' respective state legislatures, declaring the new federal laws null and void. Madison drafted the Virginia Resolution, while Jefferson wrote the Kentucky Resolutions.

What **role** did Madison serve in **Jefferson's presidency**?

Madison served as Jefferson's secretary of state for two terms. He served as Jefferson's key advisor on political matters.

As secretary of state, how did Madison become involved in a **famous Supreme Court decision**?

When Jefferson became president, he sought to thwart former President John Adams's last-minute attempt to stock the federal judiciary with Federalist appointees. Jefferson ordered Madison, his secretary of state, not to deliver the commissions of some of the new midnight justices. One of these individuals was William Marbury, who later sued to have his commission delivered.

That led to the famous constitutional case of *Marbury v. Madison* (1803) in which Chief Justice John Marshall ruled that the federal law allowing the appointment of Marbury was unconstitutional. However, Marshall also took time to criticize Madison and Jefferson and to declare that the judicial branch had the power to declare legislative and executive branch acts unconstitutional under judicial review.

What famous political word derived from Elbridge Gerry?

The term gerrymander came from Elbridge Gerry's name. When he served as governor of Massachusetts, Gerry signed a bill that redrew several congressional districts in a manner that appeared to favor Democratic-Republicans. A newspaper editor coined the term gerrymandering to refer to this process of redrawing voting district lines for political purposes.

PRESIDENCY

Whom did **Madison defeat** to win his **first term** as president?

Madison defeated Federalist candidate Charles Cotesworth Pinckney in the election of 1808. Madison won 122 electoral votes to Pinckney's 87. It was the second consecutive presidential election that Pinckney lost.

Who were James Madison's **vice presidents**?

Madison's first vice president was George Clinton, who had been Jefferson's vice president. However, Clinton died in 1812, before the end of Madison's first term. Madison's second vice president was Elbridge Gerry, who also had been a member of the Constitutional Convention of 1787. Gerry also died in office in 1814. No one served as Madison's vice president after Gerry died.

Which **future president** served in **Madison's administration**?

James Monroe, the country's fifth president, served as James Madison's secretary of state for Madison's full two terms in office. For a brief time, Monroe also served as Madison's secretary of war after the resignation of John Armstrong.

What **war did Madison declare** that defined his presidency?

Madison asked Congress to declare war on Great Britain, leading to the so-called War of 1812. English ships continually stopped American ships on the high seas, seizing cargoes and even abducting sailors. The British also supported attacks by various Indian tribes in the Northwest.

Which **two future presidents were war heroes** during the War of 1812?

Andrew Jackson and William Henry Harrison, the future seventh and ninth presidents respectively, achieved great acclaim during the War of 1812 for military successes.

This cartoon portrays President Madison's flight from the capital before the British invasion during the War of 1812.

Jackson led a group of militia and others against British forces in the Battle of New Orleans, which took place between December 1814 and January 1815. Jackson led American forces to a stunning victory over the British.

General William Henry Harrison won the Battle of the Thames over the Shawnee Indian leader Tecumseh in 1813. Harrison originally achieved acclaim when, as the governor of the Indiana territory, he led a successful campaign against a group of Indians at the Battle of Tippecanoe.

What happened to the **nation's capital** during the **War of 1812**?

British forces overran Washington, D.C. and burned both the White House and the U.S. Capitol. General William Winder, whom Madison had appointed as commander in charge of defending the capital, did an inadequate job in preparing the area's defenses. Madison had to flee the city after hearing from General Wilder of the oncoming British invasion.

Which **member** of Madison's **cabinet lost his job** as a result of the burning of the Capitol?

Secretary of War John Armstrong received blame for the poor defense of the Capitol during the War of 1812. Armstrong resigned under pressure in September 1814,

> ### What battle in the War of 1812 led to the "Star-Spangled Banner"?
>
> A young lawyer named Francis Scott Key became inspired to write a ballad—later known as the "Star Spangled Banner"—after seeing an American flag still flying after the British attack on Fort McHenry in the Battle of Baltimore. His initial title was the "Defence of Fort McHenry." President Woodrow Wilson declared the "Star Spangled Banner" the country's national anthem in 1916.

essentially as the scapegoat for the British burning of the capitol city. Future fifth president of the United States James Monroe served as secretary of war along with his secretary of state duties.

What **treaty** ended the **War of 1812**?

The Treaty of Ghent effectively ended the War of 1812. The treaty was signed in the Netherlands (modern-day Belgium) in December 1814, though it was not ratified until February 1815 after the intervening Battle of New Orleans. Under the treaty, which the U.S. Senate ratified unanimously, the United States received its territories near the Great Lakes and Maine but renounced any lands they had acquired in Canada.

What did Madison do with regard to a **national bank**?

Madison supported the chartering of the Second National Bank of the United States. He recognized that the country was struggling with debt as a result of the War of 1812. The bank's charter lasted for twenty years.

Who were Madison's U.S. **Supreme Court appointees**?

Madison appointed two men to the U.S. Supreme Court—Joseph Story and Gabriel Duvall. Madison appointed the thirty-two-year-old Story to the Court in 1811, making him the youngest person ever to serve on the high court. Story was a highly respected legal scholar and attorney who later helped found Harvard Law School. He served more than thirty-two years on the Court. Duvall served twenty-three years on the Court, though he authored few opinions and nearly always agreed with Chief Justice John Marshall.

POST PRESIDENCY

Did Madison have any **contact with James Monroe** after stepping down?

Yes, James Monroe would consult with Madison about many political matters. Madison often served as an informal advisor to his friend and successor.

What **position** did Madison accept during his **post presidency**?

Madison agreed to become the new rector of the University of Virginia after his friend and mentor Thomas Jefferson died. Madison had worked on the development and creation of the university with Jefferson over many years.

What important **political event** in **Virginia** occupied Madison for some of 1829 and 1830?

Madison participated as a delegate to the Virginia Constitutional Convention of 1829 to 1830, which resulted in changes to Virginia's existing state constitution of 1776. Madison helped to bridge a compromise between the wealthy landowners in the eastern part of the state with the less wealthy western region of the state. The net result was a constitution that loosened the restrictions on suffrage—the right to vote—and changed the membership of the Virginia General Assembly.

When did Madison **die**?

Madison died at the age of eighty-five on June 28, 1836.

JAMES MONROE

(1758–1831)
5th President, 1817–1825
Party Affiliation: Democratic-Republican
Chief 1816 Opponent: Rufus King (Federalist)
Chief 1820 Opponent: None

EARLY LIFE AND FAMILY

Where and when was James Monroe **born**?

James Monroe was born in Westmoreland County, Virginia, to Spence Monroe and Elizabeth James Monroe on April 28, 1758.

What was his **father's occupation**?

Spence Monroe was a carpenter and a farmer.

Who were James Monroe's **siblings**?

He had four siblings—a sister named Elizabeth Monroe Buckner and three brothers named Spence Jr., Andrew, and Joseph. Spence died at age one, while Andrew and Joseph lived longer lives.

Where did James receive his **early education**?

James received home schooling until age eleven. After that, he studied at Campbelltown Academy, a prestigious school headed by Reverend Archibald Campbell. John

Portrait of President James Monroe.

> ## What family member assisted Monroe in his education and upbringing?
>
> **M**onroe's father died in 1774, when James was only sixteen years old. James, as the eldest son, had the responsibility of providing for the education and care of his younger siblings. James turned for help to his uncle, Joseph Jones. Jones was a judge in Fredericksburg who had no children of his own at the time. Judge Jones had a special bond with his young nephew and provided him with key guidance for many years. Judge Jones later served on the Virginia Supreme Court and enjoyed the friendship of George Washington, Thomas Jefferson, and James Madison. Jones's connections proved vital to his young nephew's later political successes.

Marshall, the future fourth Chief Justice of the U.S. Supreme Court, was one of his young classmates at the academy. At age sixteen, Monroe entered The College of William & Mary. He dropped out of college to fight in the Revolutionary War.

Who was his **wife**?

Monroe married Elizabeth Kortright on February 16, 1786, in New York, New York. Elizabeth was the product of a wealthy family, as her father, Captain Lawrence Kortright made a sizeable fortune during the French and Indian War.

Did he have any **children**?

Yes, James and Elizabeth had three children: Eliza, James, and Maria. James died at age two, while the two daughters lived into adulthood.

EARLY CAREER

What **incident in college** was a precursor to Monroe's **military career**?

Monroe joined a group of twenty-four young men led by Theodorick Bland Jr. that marched on the governor's palace, protesting his connection to the British government. The young men removed two hundred muskets and three hundred swords from the palace and gave them to the local militia.

When did Monroe **turn to** a **military career**?

Monroe and his college roommate John F. Mercer left William & Mary in the spring of 1776 and joined the Third Virginia Infantry. Monroe and Mercer were commissioned as lieutenants.

Who was the **first general** under whom Monroe received **training**?

Monroe received training under General Andrew Lewis, who had served under George Washington at Fort Necessity during the French and Indian War. He later led expeditions against the Shawnee Indians and was considered a first-rate military commander.

What was Monroe's **war experience**?

Monroe served in the Virginia regiment and later in the Continental Army. The Third Virginia Infantry later met up with General George Washington. Monroe was serving under Washington during the Battle of Trenton. In this battle, Monroe suffered a gunshot wound after leading the troops into battle. Fortunately, a Dr. Riker saved Monroe and stopped the severe bleeding. After his bravery at the battle, Monroe was promoted to the rank of captain. He had to take three months off to heal.

He returned to camp as a major, under the command of William Alexander, a brigade commander for George Washington. Monroe served during the rough winter of Valley Forge. For his service, Washington sent a positive letter of recommendation to Virginia officials, who named Monroe a lieutenant-colonel in the Virginia Regiment. However, he had no cadre of soldiers to lead, and later transitioned to a career in politics.

Monroe remained very proud of his military service throughout his life. Even while he was president, he preferred the title "colonel." He even donned a blue tunic like the one worn by General Washington during the time of the Revolutionary War.

What did Monroe do **after the war** but **before** he entered **politics**?

Monroe studied law under Thomas Jefferson for three years from 1780 until 1783. Jefferson was quite fond of Monroe and spoke of his protégé in glowing terms: "Turn his soul wrong side outwards and there is not a speck on it."

He then practiced law in Fredericksburg, Virginia.

POLITICAL OFFICES

What was Monroe's **first political position**?

Monroe served in the Virginia House of Delegates in 1782 after being elected at age twenty-four.

What **experiences** did Monroe have during his time with the **Confederation Congress**?

Monroe served the Confederation Congress—the congress set forth by the Articles of Confederation—for three years beginning in 1783. During this time, Monroe traveled out west toward the Great Lakes area. He learned a great deal during this trip and later developed a plan for adding territories to the United States. Some of his ideas later culminated in the Northwest Ordinance of 1787.

Who defeated Monroe in a run for a seat in the U.S. House of Representatives?

Monroe lost to fellow Virginian and friend James Madison in 1789 for a House of Representative position. Monroe lost to Madison by 330 votes. However, Monroe rebounded to win a seat to the U.S. Senate in 1790.

Why did Monroe leave the Senate?

Monroe left the Senate after President George Washington appointed him as a minister to France in 1794. During his time as minister to France, Monroe negotiated the release of Thomas Paine, the American writer who authored *Common Sense*. Monroe also obtained the release of other American prisoners in France. However, Monroe objected to U.S. foreign policy and the Jay Treaty, which he felt too closely aligned American interests with Great Britain as opposed to France. Washington discharged him from his position.

What was Monroe's next political position?

After leaving the minister to France position, Monroe practiced law until he was elected governor of Virginia in 1799. Monroe quelled the slave rebellion led by Gabriel during his time as governor.

What was Monroe's role during the Jefferson presidency?

In 1803, Jefferson appointed Monroe minister plenipotentiary to France and instructed him to negotiate with French leaders for the purchase of New Orleans. Along with Robert Livingstone, Monroe negotiated what became known as the Louisiana Purchase.

What were James Monroe's positions during the Madison administration?

James Monroe served as James Madison's trusted secretary of state but also filled in as secretary of war after the resignation of John Armstrong. He is the only person in history to serve as both secretary of state and secretary of war simultaneously.

PRESIDENCY

Whom did Monroe defeat in the election of 1816?

Monroe trounced Federalist Rufus King during the election of 1816. King was a former signer of the U.S. Constitution, a former U.S. senator from New York and a former Federalist candidate for vice president before running for president in 1816. Monroe soundly defeated King by an electoral vote landslide of 183 to 34.

What **treaty** helped soothe relations between the **U.S.** and **Britain** in Monroe's first year of office?

The two countries signed the Rush-Bagot treaty in 1817, which demilitarized the Great Lakes area by the northern border of the U.S. This had been a hotly contested area of military conflict during the War of 1812. Under the treaty, each side would remove military posts and a border was established between the U.S. and British territory (later Canada). The treaty was named after U.S. Secretary of State Richard Rush and British minister Sir Charles Bagot.

What members of **Monroe's cabinet** later **ran** for **president**?

Monroe's secretary of state, John Quincy Adams, later became his successor and the sixth president of the United States. His secretary of the treasury, William H. Crawford, ran against Quincy Adams and others during the election of 1824. Monroe's attorney general, William Wirt, ran as a minor third-party candidate during the election of 1832.

What was **"The Era of Good Feelings"**?

"The Era of Good Feelings" was a time period of relative domestic and political calm, often used to describe the time period of much of the Monroe presidency. Benjamin Russell, a journalist with the Boston newspaper the *Columbian Centinel*, coined the term after President Monroe visited the New England area to quell any sectional differences.

What was the **Panic of 1819**?

The Panic of 1819 was a major financial crisis marked by mortgage foreclosures, inflation, and banks recalling loans. The federal government and Monroe responded with the Land Act of 1820, which helped alleviate some of the financial pressure.

What **treaty** at least **temporarily averted** national **problems** over the **slavery** question?

The Missouri Compromise of 1820 at least temporarily averted a national battle between pro-slave and anti-slave states. The controversy arose in 1819 when the territory of Missouri applied for statehood. Representative James Tallmadge Jr. of New York introduced an amendment that would prohibit slavery in Missouri. The Missouri Compromise allowed slavery in Missouri and land south of Missouri, but prohibited slavery in lands in the northern half of the U.S., roughly the latitude of Missouri.

Whom did Monroe **defeat** to win his **second term** as president?

Monroe had no opposition in his second term. He received a near-unanimous vote in the electoral college. One elector, William Plumer of New Hampshire, cast a vote for John Quincy Adams—without the approval of Adams.

What **state** did Monroe acquire **from Spain**?

President Monroe obtained what is now the state of Florida from Spain in February 1819 under the Adams-Onis Treaty. The treaty was named after U.S. Secretary of State John Quincy Adams and Spanish foreign minister Luis de Onis. Under the treaty, Spain ceded Florida to the United States and the two countries set the southern borders of the United States and established that U.S. territory extended out to the Pacific Ocean.

Whom did Monroe send to **deal** with the **Seminole Indians** on the Georgia–Florida border?

Monroe sent General Andrew Jackson down to the border to deal with the Seminole Indians, who had conducted a series of raids in southern Georgia. Jackson exceeded Monroe's orders and traveled into Florida, going so far as to order the hanging of two British subjects who Jackson claimed were inciting the Seminole attacks.

What **countries to the south** of the United States did President Monroe and the United States **recognize**?

The United States recognized Mexico as an independent country in December 1822 and Argentina in January 1823. Both were former Spanish colonies.

What was the **Monroe Doctrine**?

The Monroe Doctrine was a foreign policy statement announced by President Monroe during his seventh annual address to Congress delivered in December 1823. The doctrine established that the United States would not interfere with developments on the

European continent, but that the United States would oppose vigorously any attempt by European countries with suspicion and "as dangerous to our peace and safety." Historians have lauded the doctrine as one of the most significant statements in the history of American foreign policy.

What **foreign capital city** is **named after** James Monroe?

Monrovia, the capital city of the West African country Liberia, is named after President James Monroe. The president had favored the colonization of the area and had been a supporter of the American Colonization Society, which advocated resettling freed blacks from the United States in West Africa.

What was Monroe's **policy toward Native Americans**?

Monroe supported a policy that would protect the rights of Native Americans to land. In his first inaugural address he said: "With the Indian tribes it is our duty to cultivate friendly relations and to act with kindness and liberality in all our transactions." He advocated a policy that would set aside land for the Native Americans—a policy some of his successors did not follow.

Who were Monroe's U.S. **Supreme Court appointees**?

Monroe had the opportunity to nominate only one person to the U.S. Supreme Court even though he was a two-term president. He nominated Smith Thompson, who had served on the New York State Supreme Court and as United States secretary of the navy under Monroe. Thompson served on the high Court for twenty years until his death in 1843.

POST PRESIDENCY

After the presidency what did Monroe do?

President Monroe spent much of time at his estate, Oak Hill. He spent a great deal of time with his friend James Madison. He also spent a great deal of time reading in his

President Monroe's tomb in Richmond, Virginia.

library, which contained more than three thousand books. Unfortunately, Monroe's financial situation had deteriorated over the years and he had to sell off some of his land to pay off debts. He applied to recover monies from the federal government for his years of service, finally receiving a congressional grant of $30,000—less than half the sum recommended by a congressional committee.

President Monroe also provided service to the University of Virginia, where he worked with Presidents Jefferson and Madison. He committed himself to writing, including *The Political Writings of James Monroe.*

When did President Monroe **die**?

President Monroe died in New York, New York, on July 4, 1831. Ironically, he died on the same day—July fourth—as Presidents John Adams and Thomas Jefferson.

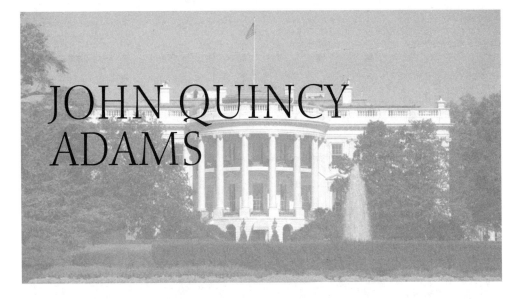

JOHN QUINCY ADAMS

(1767–1848)
6th President, 1825–1829
Party Affiliation: Democratic-Republican
(though he was a member of several political parties during his career)
Chief 1824 Opponents: Andrew Jackson (Democratic-Republican), William Crawford
(Democratic-Republican), Henry Clay (Democratic-Republican),
and John C. Calhoun (Democratic-Republican)

EARLY LIFE AND FAMILY

Where and when was John Quincy Adams **born**?

John Quincy Adams was born in Braintree, Massachusetts, to John and Abigail Adams on July 11, 1767.

What was his **father's profession**?

John Quincy Adams was the oldest son of John Adams, the second president of the United States. They were the first father and son to serve as commanders in chief of the United States of America. It was not until George W. Bush became the forty-third president, following in the footsteps of his father, George H. W. Bush, that there was another father and son who both won the presidency. John Adams was a politician and a lawyer—just as John Quincy Adams would become.

Portrait of President John Quincy Adams by Thomas Sully.

What famous battle did young Adams witness as a child?

His mother, Abigail, took him to watch the Battle of Bunker Hill in June 1775. In later years, he would recall that he and his mother both wept. They witnessed the death of a family friend during the conflict, Dr. Joseph Warren.

Did John Quincy Adams have any **siblings**?

Yes, he had four siblings: an older sister named Abigail and nicknamed "Nabby," a younger sister named Susanna (who died as an infant), and two younger brothers named Charles and Thomas.

Did Adams have a **religious upbringing**?

Yes, his parents instilled in him at an early age the practice of regular reading of the Bible. He read the Bible for an hour a day as a youngster in different languages. He was reared as a Congregationalist, though in later years he joined the Unitarian Church.

What was his **early education**?

He received education at home, then accompanied his father to France in 1778, when the elder Adams was selected to serve as a special envoy to France. He entered a private school in Paris with other young American boys, including Benjamin Franklin Bache, the grandson of Benjamin Franklin who later became a famous newspaper editor.

In 1780, his father worked as a diplomat in the Netherlands. Young John and his brother Charles entered the Latin School there to continue their studies. However, they didn't like the school and their father removed them. He sent young John to the University of Leyden, where he studied under Benjamin Waterhouse.

Later, John Quincy Adams accompanied his father to Russia when he was only fourteen years old. There, he studied largely on his own. A few years later, he returned to the United States and attended Harvard University. Initially, he was rejected by Harvard; Joseph Willard, president of the college, said Adams needed more instruction in Latin and Greek. John Quincy Adams studied feverishly and entered Harvard in the spring of 1786 as a junior. He graduated in less than two years, ranking second in a class of fifty-one.

Who was his **first love**?

A twenty-three-year-old Adams fell in love with sixteen-year-old Mary Frazier of Newburyport, Massachusetts. He wanted to ask for her hand in marriage but did not do so, partly at the insistence of his mother, Abigail. She warned her son about the dangers of marrying too young and how it might negatively impact his career. It took Adams many years to recover from the loss of this relationship.

Did he **marry**?

He married Louisa Catherine Johnson in 1797. She was the daughter of a British mother and an American father; her father, Joshua, served as the U.S. consul in Great Britain. Louisa was born in London and remains the only First Lady to ever be born outside the United States. Adams received criticism in some American newspapers for marrying a foreign-born woman from England, and some referred to him as "the American Prince of Wales."

Did he have any **children**?

Adams and his wife, Louisa, had four children—a daughter Louisa, who died as an infant at age one—and three sons: George Washington, John, and Charles Francis. George—whom John Quincy Adams named after President Washington—committed suicide.

EARLY CAREER

After graduation from Harvard, what did Adams do?

He studied law for several years under Newburyport lawyer Theophilus Parsons, who would later become chief justice of the Massachusetts Supreme Judicial Court. Adams practiced law in Massachusetts, but he lost his first case and never did like the practice of law very much. He preferred reading, writing political essays, and getting involved in politics.

What **letters** did Adams **publish** that attracted attention?

He wrote a series of essays entitled "Letters of Publicola" that were published in a Boston newspaper. The essays defended the American system of government and dis-

> ## What later essays that Adams wrote attracted the attention of George Washington?
>
> Adams wrote a series of essays in 1793 and 1794 that defended President Washington's proclamation of neutrality that Washington had issued when Great Britain and France began fighting. The French minister to the United States, Edmond Genet, had attacked Washington's position. Adams—writing under the pen names "Marcellus," "Columbus," and "Barneveld"—supported the president and showed a keen understanding of international law.

agreed with some of Thomas Paine's theories in his *The Rights of Man* (1791). The essays attracted the attention of prominent Federalists and led many conservatives to support Adams in his early political career.

What **position** did Adams hold at **Harvard University**?

While he served as a politician in his pre-presidency days, Adams doubled as a professor of rhetoric at his alma mater. In 1804, he was appointed the first Boylston Professor of Rhetoric and Oratory at Harvard. He began teaching at the university in 1806 while he was a U.S. senator.

What **major U.S. Supreme Court case** did Adams **argue** in 1809?

Adams argued on behalf of Massachusetts native John Peck in the famous case of *Fletcher v. Peck* (1810). The case involved a Georgia state law that invalidated the sale of more than thirty million acres of land to several Northern companies. It was alleged that several Georgia legislators received bribes for their votes approving the land deals.

The law invalidating the land sales presented problems for innocent third parties who purchased the land without knowledge of the shady origins of how the land was first acquired. In what some historians think was a contrived lawsuit—many believe the plaintiff and defendant planned the lawsuit together—Robert Fletcher of New Hampshire sued John Peck of Massachusetts in 1803 to establish his valid claim to the land.

The Court ruled that the Georgia law invalidating the original land sales was unconstitutional because it violated the Constitution's Contract Clause, preventing states from impairing the obligations of contracts. Chief Justice Marshall reasoned that the new law could negatively impact innocent, third-party purchasers like Fletcher.

POLITICAL OFFICES

Who **appointed Adams** to his **first** official **political positions**?

President George Washington appointed Adams as minister to the Netherlands in 1794 and as minister to Portugal in 1796. Adams thought so highly of President Washington that he later named one of his sons George Washington Adams.

What **position** did his **father appoint him** to?

President John Adams appointed his son John Quincy to become minister of Prussia in 1797. John Quincy Adams expressed reluctance to his father about accepting the position because he feared it would be derided as a nepotistic appointment. However, his father sternly told him that he was the best person for the job. At the end of his presidency, John Adams terminated John Quincy's diplomatic career, fearing that incoming President Thomas Jefferson might dismiss his son and cause him some humiliation.

What was Adams's **first nondiplomatic political office**?

Adams won election to the Massachusetts state Senate in 1802 as a Federalist candidate. He did not expect to win the race, as some Federalists felt betrayed by his father during his presidency. Adams showed his independent streak in his first political office, voting against a bank charter favored by Federalists.

What political **race did Adams lose** in 1802?

Adams then decided to run for a seat in the U.S. House of Representatives. However, he lost the election to the Democratic-Republican incumbent, Dr. William Eustis. Adams lost the election by a mere fifty-nine votes. Eustis himself had a fine political career, later serving as U.S. secretary of war and then as governor of Massachusetts.

What was Adams's **next political position**?

Adams then ran for a seat in the U.S. Senate, which he won in 1803 as a Federalist. As a U.S. senator, Adams once again showed his independent streak by supporting some major political moves by Democratic-Republican President Thomas Jefferson. Adams supported both the Louisiana Purchase and the Embargo Act of 1807. The support of the Embargo Act, which harmed shipping interests in New England, caused the Massachusetts legislature to call for his dismissal. Adams resigned his position in June 1808.

To what position did **President Madison appoint** Adams?

President Madison appointed Adams as minister to Russia in 1809. The Senate confirmed him a by a vote of nineteen to seven. Adams got along exceedingly well with Russian czar

Alexander I. In fact, Adams enjoyed his position in Russia so much that he even turned down an appointment to the U.S. Supreme Court—something unimaginable in modern-day America. Another reason for Adams's decision might be that his position as minister to Russia paid considerably more than the salary of a justice on the Court.

What **famous treaty** did **Adams help** bring about?

Adams was part of the team that helped bring about the Treaty of Ghent, which brought an end to the War of 1812. Signed in late December 1914, the treaty did not officially end the hostilities until it reached Washington, D.C., in February 1915.

What **diplomatic position** did Adams hold next, a job that **his father had held previously**?

President Madison then appointed Adams to be minister to England, something his father had done years earlier. Adams served in that capacity for two years until President James Monroe appointed him secretary of state.

How did Adams perform as **secretary of state**?

Adams performed well as secretary of state under President Monroe. He crafted the foreign policy doctrine that later bore the president's name—the Monroe Doctrine. Historian Robert V. Remini writes in his 2002 biography of Adams, *John Quincy Adams*: "John Quincy Adams is arguably the greatest secretary of state to serve that office." He helped negotiate the Adams-Onis, or Transcontinental Treaty of 1819, which established the western boundaries of the Louisiana purchase and solidified relations between the United States and Spain.

PRESIDENCY

Who were the **candidates** in the election of **1824**?

The candidates were John Quincy Adams, Andrew Jackson from Tennessee, William H. Crawford from Georgia, and Henry Clay from Kentucky. Adams and Crawford had both served in the cabinet of President James Monroe—Adams as secretary of state and Crawford as secretary of the treasury. Jackson was a U.S. senator and former war hero, while Clay was the Speaker of the U.S. House of Representatives.

Who won the **popular vote** in the presidential election of **1824**?

Jackson captured the popular vote with more than 150,000 votes, while Adams captured just over 100,000. Jackson also won more electoral votes (99) than Adams (84).

However, Jackson failed to capture the required majority of 131 electoral votes, as Crawford tallied 41 electoral votes and Clay 37. When no candidate receives a majority of the electoral votes, the decision falls to the House of Representatives. The representatives from each state vote for a candidate. Adams ended up capturing 13 states (Jackson 7 and Crawford 4). Thus, Adams became president as he captured more than a majority of the states (13 out of 24) to win the electoral vote and the presidency.

What was the **"corrupt bargain"**?

The corrupt bargain referred to a claim asserted by Jacksonians—supporters of Andrew Jackson—that John Quincy Adams and Henry Clay engaged in a corrupt bargain to get votes for Adams. They maintained that Clay encouraged others in the House to vote for Adams because Adams agreed to name Clay as his secretary of state if he won the presidency. While Clay did encourage members of the House to vote for Adams rather than Jackson and later became Adams's secretary of state, the two contended that there never was any "corrupt bargain." Clay maintained that he thought Adams would be better equipped to handle the presidency than Jackson.

What was Adams's **policy** toward **Native Americans**?

Adams favored treating the Native Americans fairly, something that his opponents used against him in his reelection campaign in 1828. In his inaugural address, he called on his country "to promote the civilization of the Indian tribes." However, his administration did not protect the Creek Indians in Georgia.

Many Americans—including Adams's opponent, Andrew Jackson—supported the trampling of the Native Americans' rights. Adams later admitted his country had harmed the Native Americans greatly: "These are crying sins for which we are answerable before a higher jurisdiction."

What **sport or recreation** did John Quincy Adams engage in regularly while president?

He loved to swim in the Potomac River, which he often did as early as 5:00 A.M. Sometimes he even skinny-dipped in the river. One story—which may or may not be true—was that female journalist Anne Royell successfully obtained an exclusive interview with Adams by refusing to give him his clothes when he finished his swim unless the spoke to her on the record.

First Lady Louisa Catherine Adams as portrayed by artist Charles Robert Leslie.

What were some of Adams's **proposals as president**?

He favored the creation of a system of roads, canals, and highways that would make travel across the United States easier. He managed to pass a law that allowed the Cumberland Road to pass into Ohio and he funded a project that would create a canal from the Chesapeake Bay to the Ohio River. He also advocated the establishment of a uniform system of weights and measures—something akin to the metric system—which failed, even though Adams wrote a detailed report to Congress on the issue. In addition, he advocated for a national university and the creation of a naval academy.

Unfortunately, Adams had little success with most of his proposals. His presidency was doomed in part by the presence of so many Jacksonian Democrats in Congress, who adamantly believed that Jackson deserved the presidency.

What happened in **Adams's reelection attempt**?

Adams could never overcome the allegations that he did not deserve to win the election of 1824, as the Jacksonians fanned the flames of public discontent. Furthermore, many members of Congress were allied with Jackson and continually thwarted Adams's proposals. In 1828, Jackson supporters effectively convinced enough voters that he deserved the election four years earlier and he deserved it now. Jackson won 178 electoral votes to only 83 for Adams.

What did John Quincy Adams have **in common with his father** with respect to **reelection**?

John Quincy Adams and his father were the only two of the first seven presidents to not win reelection. Presidents George Washington, Thomas Jefferson, James Madison,

113

James Monroe, and Andrew Jackson all served two full terms in office. John Quincy Adams also did not attend the inauguration of his successor, Andrew Jackson, just as his father declined to attend the inauguration of his successor, Thomas Jefferson.

POST PRESIDENCY

What **political position** did Adams hold **after the presidency**?

Two years after his defeat in his reelection attempt, Adams ran for a seat in the U.S. House of Representatives in 1830. He won reelection eight times, serving nearly twenty years.

What was **different** about Adams's **politics** as a **representative**?

Adams opposed the policies of President Andrew Jackson and the newly called Democratic Party. Instead, Adams joined the Whig Party, where he continually advocated abolitionist views. For much of his political career, Adams maintained a streak of independence that often upset members of his own political party.

What **rule** in the House did Adams consistently **oppose**?

He consistently opposed a congressional gag rule on antislavery petitions in Congress. In 1836, Representative Charles Pinckney from South Carolina introduced a measure that would bar discussion of antislavery petitions. The House approved the measure and continually reaffirmed the measure year after year. John Quincy Adams adamantly opposed the measure and fought to have it rescinded. Finally, in 1844, the House voted down the measure by a 108 to 80 vote. In his diary, Adams wrote: "Blessed, forever blessed be the name of God!"

What famous **case** did Adams **argue** before the **U.S. Supreme Court**?

Adams argued before the Supreme Court in the *Amistad* case, which involved the
mutiny of Africans who had been kidnapped into slavery aboard the Spanish ship

Amistad. The Africans argued that they were not slaves and should not be returned to Connecticut, where they had been placed by the U.S. commander who had found the ship. They also argued that they should not be returned to Spain since they were free Africans. Adams and Roger Sherman Baldwin argued the case on behalf of the Africans before the U.S. Supreme Court. The Court ruled in favor of Adams's clients.

How did Adams **die**?

Adams suffered a stroke on the House floor in February 1848. Two days later he died. Several of his colleagues remarked that it was fitting that Adams worked until his death given his devotion to the House.

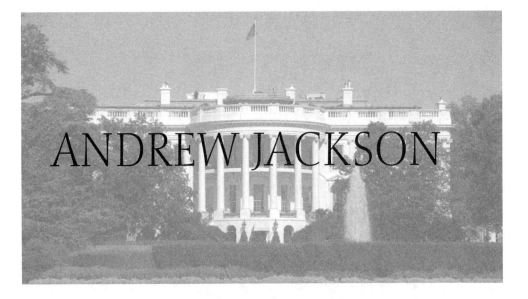

ANDREW JACKSON

(1767–1845)
7th President, 1829–1837
Party Affiliation: Democrat
Chief 1828 Opponent: John Quincy Adams (National Republican)
Chief 1832 Opponent: Henry Clay (National Republican)

EARLY LIFE AND FAMILY

Where and when was Jackson **born**?

Andrew Jackson was born in the Waxhaws, an area located between the future states of North and South Carolina, to Irish immigrants Andrew and Elizabeth Hutchinson Jackson on March 15, 1767.

What **happened** to **his parents**?

His father, Andrew Sr., was a farmer, though he died at age twenty-nine, three weeks before Andrew was born. His mother died of cholera when Andrew was only fourteen years old.

Did Andrew Jackson have any **siblings**?

Yes, Andrew Jackson had two older brothers, Hugh and Robert. His oldest brother, Hugh, died in the Revolutionary War in 1779 at the Battle of Stono Ferry near Charleston, South Carolina. Robert died of smallpox in 1781 shortly after he and Andrew were freed from captivity at the hands of British forces.

Portrait of President Andrew Jackson by artist Thomas Sully.

How did Jackson receive the scars on his face?

Andrew and his older brother, Robert, were captured by the British during the Revolutionary War. When a British officer ordered Andrew to shine his boots, Andrew refused, claiming that he wanted to be treated as a prisoner of war. The officer then slashed Andrew with his weapon. After this incident, Andrew and his brother were taken to a prison camp in Camden before Jackson's mother managed to secure their release.

What **sport** did young Andrew **enjoy**?

He enjoyed wrestling with his friends. Though not a large kid, he had wiry strength and an unquenchable desire to compete and win. One of his friends said: "I could throw him three times out of four, but he would never stay throwed."

What **other sport** did Jackson acquire a taste for that he carried over into adulthood?

Jackson loved horse racing and betting on racehorses. He first acquired this interest in Charleston after he inherited some money from either his grandfather or mother. He remained an ardent aficionado of horse racing his entire life.

What happened to **Jackson's mother**?

She died in 1781 shortly after securing the release of Andrew and Robert, who died only two days after his release. His mother nursed Andrew back to health and then left for Charleston to take care of two of her nephews. She died in Charleston.

What did his **mother want him to do** as an adult?

Elizabeth wanted Andrew to become a Presbyterian minister. She was a devout person and instilled in Andrew the need for regular church attendance. Every Sunday, she took Andrew to services that lasted three to four hours. Later in life, Jackson said that he read several chapters of the Bible each day.

What was his **education**?

He received a limited education, learning a bit at home during his early years. He studied law in Salisbury, North Carolina, though he didn't receive a modern legal education. Jackson learned on the job as a country lawyer studying under lawyer Spruce Macay.

Who was **Jackson's wife**?

Jackson married Rachel Donelson, the youngest child of prominent native of Nashville, Tennessee, John Donelson. Jackson became interested in Rachel while he rented a home from Donelson's widow. When he first met Rachel, she was married to Lewis Robards. Jackson did not like how Robards treated Rachel and confronted him about it.

Andrew Jackson's wife, born Rachel Donelson, in an engraving by John Chester Buttre.

Robards returned to the state of Kentucky and filed for divorce—or so Rachel and Andrew thought. Andrew and Rachel married in 1791, but apparently Robards had not obtained a divorce. Robards obtained a divorce in 1793 on the grounds that Rachel had committed adultery (with Jackson). Jackson and Rachel then officially married again in January 1794.

Did he have any **children**?

No, Jackson and his wife never had any children, but they did adopt a nephew of Rachel's when they were in their early forties, named him Andrew Jackson Donelson, and reared him as their own.

EARLY CAREER

What was Jackson's **first job**?

As a young teenager, he served in the Revolutionary War. It was during this time that he was captured with his brother. He became the second president to be a prisoner at war; George Washington was captured during the French and Indian War. Jackson then worked in a shop that made saddles for equestrians.

How did Jackson **progress in the law**?

Jackson first learned the law under Spruce Macay in Salisbury, North Carolina. He later traveled to McLeanville, North Carolina, where he set up his own law practice. In 1788, he and friend John McNairy traveled to what later became Tennessee and practiced what was sometimes known as "frontier law." They also prospered with land speculating.

Who was Spruce Macay?

Spruce Macay was a lawyer and judge in Salisbury, North Carolina, who had gone to college at Princeton (then The College of New Jersey). He had the largest law practice in the city and had been a mentor to many young lawyers. Jackson learned under Macay with another young lawyer named William Cupples.

McNairy became a judge and he appointed his friend Jackson as Solicitor of the Western District and later Solicitor of the Territory of Tennessee. In 1798, he was appointed to the Tennessee Supreme Court, where he served until 1804.

What other lawyer was a mentor to Jackson in those North Carolina days?

John Stokes, a former Revolutionary War veteran, also served as a mentor to Jackson in those early days of his legal career. Jackson often accompanied Stokes as the latter traveled throughout Montgomery County, North Carolina, practicing law.

What was Jackson's life like in Salisbury?

Jackson practiced law with a passion. His first case ended with a dueling challenge from Jackson to the opposing attorney, although the two worked out their differences before actually dueling. Exhibiting the same energy he showed in his work, Jackson was known for partying very hard. Legend has it that he even arranged for a group of prostitutes to attend a society Christmas party.

After leaving Salisbury, where did Jackson go?

Jackson moved to Nashville, Tennessee, when he was twenty-one. He stayed at a boarding house operated by Mrs. John Donelson, the widow of one of the most famous men in Tennessee and one of Nashville's founding fathers.

What other jobs did Jackson have in his legal career?

He served as a prosecutor for the western district of North Carolina (what would become the state of Tennessee) and then later as a judge on the Tennessee Superior Court from December 1798 until July 1804. He left the court to focus on his life as a planter and merchant.

121

Whom did Jackson kill in a duel?

Jackson killed a man named Charles Dickinson in May 1806, following a dispute between Jackson and Joseph Erwin over a horse race. Apparently, Erwin owed Jackson some money after losing a bet. When there was difficulty collecting the money, Jackson or one of his friends made a negative comment about Erwin.

Erwin's son-in-law, Dickinson, intervened and challenged Jackson to a duel. Dickinson, apparently quite handy with a pistol, fired first and hit Jackson. Jackson then returned fire and killed Dickinson. Jackson carried Dickinson's bullet in his body the rest of his life.

Besides law, what **other occupations** did Jackson engage in?

He became a successful merchant, farmer, and soldier. He opened a general store in Gallatin, Tennessee, that made him a good amount of money. He also was a successful farmer, relying on the working manpower of his slaves.

However, what made Jackson famous was his rise through the military. In 1801, Tennessee officials made him commander of the Tennessee militia. He achieved lasting fame for his efforts during the War of 1812 against both Indian and British forces.

How did Jackson **almost** come to a **deadly fight** with **Tennessee's governor**?

In 1803, Jackson entered into a quarrel with John Sevier, the governor of Tennessee; both men felt they should become the leader of the state's militia. Jackson made a comment about Sevier's past service to the state, which caused Sevier to reply that Jackson's only contribution had been to take a trip "with another man's wife." Upon hearing this insult of Rachel, Jackson became enraged and the two shot at each other.

Which **other famous politician** did Jackson have a **quarrel** with in the early 1800s?

Jackson had a quarrel with future U.S. Senator Thomas Hart Benton and his brother Jesse. In September 1813, Jackson saw the brothers and words were exchanged. Jesse Benton shot and wounded Jackson, who survived.

POLITICAL AND MILITARY CAREER

What were Jackson's **first political positions**?

In 1796, he was selected as a delegate to the Tennessee Constitutional Convention, the body that created the Tennessee Constitution and established Tennessee as the six-

Currier & Ives created this artistic rendition of General Jackson leading troops in the Battle of New Orleans, which actually occurred after the end of the War of 1812.

teenth state in the United States. Later that year, he became a member of the U.S. House of Representatives, and in 1797 was elected to the U.S. Senate. He left the Senate after only one year and successfully ran for a position on the Tennessee Superior Court.

What **famous battles** did Jackson prevail in during the **War of 1812** and the **Creek War**?

He led a successful campaign against the Creek Indians at the Battle of Horseshoe Bend in 1814 during the Creek War (which is sometimes considered to be part of the War of 1812). Most famously, Jackson led outnumbered American forces in the Battle of New Orleans in January 1815. The defeat of the British made Jackson a national hero.

What **war brought Jackson** into potential **conflict** with the **presidency**?

President James Monroe asked Jackson to lead a campaign against the Seminole and Creek Indians in December 1817. Jackson ruthlessly carried out his task—and then arguably exceeded it. He ordered the execution of two British officers suspected of plotting against the United States by supplying weapons to the Indians. He also invaded the area known as Florida, a Spanish territory at the time. President James Monroe—against the advice of some of his cabinet members—declined to punish or even censor Jackson for his actions.

123

When was **Jackson nominated** for president?

The Tennessee legislature nominated Jackson for president in 1822. He was also elected to the U.S. Senate again in 1824. He lost a disputed election to John Quincy Adams even though Jackson garnered more popular and electoral votes. However, Jackson did not tally a majority of electoral votes, as there were multiple candidates. He then lost the election in the House of Representatives.

PRESIDENCY

What did Jackson **think** of the **electoral college**?

He despised it, perhaps largely because of the outcome of the election of 1824, an election he ultimately lost. Jackson favored reliance on the popular vote; he felt it expressed the will of the people better than the electoral college.

Whom did **Jackson defeat** in the election of **1828**?

Jackson defeated incumbent John Quincy Adams in the election of 1828. Jackson garnered 178 electoral votes to Adams's 83. John Quincy Adams carried several northeastern states, such as Massachusetts, Connecticut, and Rhode Island—but Jackson carried fifteen states, including New York and Pennsylvania.

What **charges** were leveled **against Jackson** during the **campaign**?

Some called him a wife stealer because he began a relationship with Rachel before she was officially divorced from Lewis Robards. Other charges focused on his affinity for dueling and his alleged barbarism in killing Indians during various conflicts, and some detractors made awful comments about his deceased mother.

What **tragedy befell Jackson after** his **election victory** but before his inauguration?

His wife, Rachel, died on December 22, and did not live to see her husband inaugurated as president. She suffered a heart attack, though Jackson believed that the cause of

> ## What was unusual about Jackson's inauguration celebration?
>
> Jackson's inauguration in March 1829 was attended by masses of people. A virtual mob of people flocked to the White House to shake hands with Jackson, who was considered a president for the people, rather than an East Coast elitist. By some accounts, Jackson was nearly trampled by the rush of people and had to retreat from the White House grounds.

her death was directly related to the stress caused by newspaper attacks on her character related to the adultery charges from years earlier. Jackson never forgave anyone who said a cross word about his wife—when she was alive or after her death.

Who served as the **presidential hostess**?

Ordinarily, the First Lady serves as the presidential hostess, but Andrew Jackson was a widower when he entered the White House. His niece Emily—the wife of his nephew Andrew Jackson Donelson—served as the hostess.

Who was Jackson's **first vice president**?

Jackson's first vice president was John C. Calhoun, a Yale-educated man from South Carolina. It was an uneasy alliance, as the two were not friends. Calhoun resigned from the vice presidency in December 1832, as his home state of South Carolina chafed under federal tariffs. The South Carolina state legislature had elected him senator and it was from that perch that Calhoun would battle Jackson politically.

What **famous exchange of toasts** did Jackson and Calhoun engage in?

In April 1830, political leaders held an annual dinner in honor of Thomas Jefferson's birthday at the Indian Queen's Hotel. President Jackson believed that too many of the politicians agreed with the nullification doctrine sometimes associated with Jefferson's Kentucky Resolutions. Calhoun, for example, had been a proponent of nullification when a federal law infringed too much on a state's power.

Jackson gave the toast: "Our Union—it must be preserved." Calhoun then spoke after Jackson with the following toast in a trembling voice: "The Union—next to our liberty the most dear."

What was Jackson's position on the **National Bank**?

He opposed the National Bank of the United States in part because it favored the rich and the northeastern states over those in the south and west. He also believed that it

125

created too much power in a single institution. He vetoed the re-chartering of the bank in 1832 and withdrew U.S. funds from it 1833, effectively destroying the bank.

What was the **Nullification Crisis**?

The nullification crisis arose around the claims by some political leaders in South Carolina— including Jackson's first vice president John C. Calhoun—that a state could nullify federal laws that it found unconstitutional and not worthy of respect. South Carolina advocated the nullification doctrine after the U.S. Congress passed a tariff bill that state leaders found unwise and unfair.

What was the **Eaton Affair**?

The Eaton Affair involved how the wives of Jackson's cabinet members treated Peggy Eaton, the wife of Secretary of War John Eaton. Many women, including Floride Calhoun—the wife of vice president John C. Calhoun—believed that Peggy Eaton did not comport herself properly and married John Eaton far too soon after the death of her first husband.

Andrew Jackson sided with Peggy Eaton and it led to great tension among his cabinet. It led to the effective dissolution of Jackson's original cabinet. Jackson came to rely on a group of informal advisors known as his "Kitchen Cabinet."

Who composed Jackson's **unofficial "Kitchen Cabinet?"**

Jackson's "Kitchen Cabinet" consisted of Martin Van Buren—his former secretary of state who would become his vice president in his second term; Francis Preston Blair, the editor of the Washington *Globe*; Amos Kendell, the editor of two newspapers and later Jackson's postmaster general; William B. Lewis, who formerly served as quartermaster under General Jackson; Andrew Jackson Donelson, his nephew; John Overton, his longtime friend and business partner; and Roger B. Taney, his attorney general whom he later nominated as Chief Justice of the U.S. Supreme Court.

Whom did **Jackson defeat** in the election of **1832**?

Andrew Jackson defeated Henry Clay, the National Republican or Whig Party candidate, by a sizeable margin in the election of 1832. Jackson received 219 electoral votes to only 49 for Clay. He also had a sizeable lead in the popular election results.

What **law** led to the forced **removal** of many Native American?

In 1830, Congress passed the Indian Removal Act, a measure that President Jackson supported and signed into law in May. Technically, the law called for the voluntary removal of various native tribes from the southeastern part of the United States in states such as Georgia. In practice, the law led to the forced removal of the Native Americans from their lands. The most famous of these removals was by the Cherokees from Georgia to what later became Oklahoma. This arduous journey became immortalized in history as the "Trail of Tears."

Who were Jackson's U.S. **Supreme Court appointees**?

Jackson appointed six men to the U.S. Supreme Court: John McLean in 1830, Henry Baldwin in 1830, James Moore Wayne in 1835, Roger Brooke Taney in 1836, Philip Pendleton Barbour in 1836, and John Catron in 1837.

McLean served more than thirty years on the Court and provided one of two dissenting votes years later in *Dred Scot v. Sanford* when the majority of the Court upheld slavery. Baldwin served fourteen years but suffered from mental illness later in his judicial career. James Moore Wayne also served more than thirty years on the Court. Roger Brooke Taney served twenty-eight years on the Court as Chief Justice. Barbour, a former Speaker of the House, served less than five years. Catron served more than twenty-eight years and was the only justice from Jackson's home state of Tennessee.

What **former president** called **Jackson** a **"barbarian"** in 1833?

John Quincy Adams, a Harvard graduate, recoiled at the idea that his alma mater was going to give President Jackson an honorary degree. Adams, who did not attend Jackson's inauguration, wrote Harvard's president: "I would not be present to witness her disgrace in conferring her highest literary honors upon a barbarian who could not write a sentence of grammar and hardly could spell his own name."

Who tried to **assassinate President Jackson**?

An unemployed house painter named Richard Lawrence fired two guns at Jackson in Washington, D.C. in February 1835, as Jackson was leaving the funeral service of former U.S. Congressman Warren R. Davis. Jackson chased his assailant with his cane and made sure that Lawrence was apprehended.

Lawrence was a mentally ill man who sometimes believed that he was the King of England. He had tried to kill his sister before and had threatened others. Lawrence was deemed insane and never brought to trial.

POST PRESIDENCY

Whom did **Jackson support** as his **successor**?

Jackson supported his vice president, Martin Van Buren. as his successor rather than another Tennessean, Judge Hugh Lawson White. He later actively campaigned for Van Buren.

Which fellow **Tennessean** did Jackson **help elevate** to the **presidency** in his last years?

Jackson supported fellow Tennessean James K. Polk for presidency during the election of 1844. Polk ran as the Democratic Party candidate but only emerged after the eighth ballot at the party's convention. Martin Van Buren held the early lead in the first few ballots but couldn't achieve enough votes, partly because he did not favor the annexation of Texas—an issue upon which Jackson and Polk agreed.

Where did **Jackson reside** after leaving the presidency?

He returned to his estate, The Hermitage, near Nashville, Tennessee, the residence he first inhabited in 1804.

When did Jackson **die**?

Jackson died on June 8, 1845, at The Hermitage, at the age of seventy-eight, of tuberculosis and heart failure.

MARTIN VAN BUREN

(1782–1862)
8th President, 1837–1841
Party Affiliation: Democrat
Chief 1836 Opponents: William Henry Harrison (Whig), Hugh Lawson White (Whig),
Daniel Webster (Whig), and Willie Person Mangum (Democrat)

EARLY LIFE AND FAMILY

Where and when was Van Buren **born**?

Van Buren was born in Kinderhook, New York, to Abraham and Maria Hoes Alen Van Buren on December 5, 1862. Kinderhook was located about twenty miles from Albany.

What did his **parents do** for a living?

His father was a farmer and innkeeper. The inn that Abraham owned was often frequented by politicians, including John Jay, Aaron Burr, and Alexander Hamilton. One rumor that circulated during Martin Van Buren's lifetime was that Burr—a frequent guest of the inn—was Van Buren's actual father. While this rumor has never been confirmed, what was incontrovertible was that at an early age young Martin Van Buren was exposed to political discussions. He later said that these talks left an indelible impression on him.

Did Martin Van Buren have any **siblings**?

Yes, Martin Van Buren had seven brothers and sisters—three half-siblings and four full siblings. His mother had three children by her first marriage before she married Martin

Portrait of President Van Buren by artist John Sartain.

Van Buren's father. One of these half-siblings was James Isaac Van Buren. Abraham and Maria then had five children together, including young Martin. The other Van Buren children were: Dircke, Hannan, Lawrence, and Abraham.

Which of Van Buren's **siblings** also had a distinguished **political career**?

Van Buren's half-brother James Isaac Van Buren served in the U.S. House of Representatives from 1807 to 1809.

What was Martin's **early education**?

He attended a one-room schoolhouse in Kinderhook in his early years. Later, he attended the Kinderhook Academy where he studied Latin. He had to leave school at the age of thirteen because of his family's financial burdens.

Did he **marry**?

Yes, Martin Van Buren married his distant cousin Hannah Hoes, who was also a childhood friend. She died in 1819 and Van Buren never remarried.

Did he have any **children**?

Yes, Martin and Hannah had five children: Abraham, John, Martin, Winfield Scott, and Smith Thompson. Abraham later served as Van Buren's secretary when he was president. He also distinguished himself during military action in the Mexican War.

His son John became a lawyer and later served as New York attorney general, as did his famous father. John also served in the U.S. House of Representatives.

EARLY CAREER

What was Van Buren's **initial occupation**?

Van Buren worked in the law office of Kinderhook lawyer Francis Silvester when he was only fourteen years old. He worked at Silvester's office for five years and did everything from sweeping floors and running errands to helping with more substantive legal matters. One story said that when Van Buren was only fifteen years old, he impressed a local judge with his note-taking in court. The judge asked the young teenager to sum up the case for the jurors.

Portrait of Hannah Hoes Van Buren by engraver John Chester Buttre.

Which future **president did Van Buren campaign for** when he was eighteen?

Van Buren campaigned for Thomas Jefferson when he ran for president.

What other **lawyer** did **Van Buren work for** in his early years?

In 1802 Martin spent a year with young lawyer William Van Ness, a well-connected lawyer in New York City.

When did he **begin practicing law**?

Martin Van Buren was admitted to the bar in 1803 and began practicing law with his half-brother James in Kinderhook. He handled many types of cases, advocating the interests of bankers, business owners, and farmers. He later was named the attorney for Columbia County, New York, a position he held for several years.

POLITICAL OFFICES

What was Van Buren's **first political position**?

In 1812, Van Buren ran for a seat in the New York Senate against Edward Livingston. The twenty-nine-year-old Van Buren ran as a Democratic-Republican and defeated the favored Livingston, who was a Federalist from a well-connected political family. A newspaper inaccurately reported that Livingston had won. Actually, Van Buren narrowly prevailed by a few hundred votes.

The Albany Regency was a group of politicians from the Albany, New York, area who formed what was essentially a political machine. The group, led by Van Buren, held similar political beliefs and controlled New York politics for about eighteen years. Thurlow Weed, a New York political figure, who favored Clinton more than Van Buren, coined the term to refer to Van Buren and his political allies. Van Buren was considered to be one of the fathers of so-called machine politics and the Albany Regency was, in many senses, his machine.

What **cause** did **Van Buren fight for** as a state senator?

Van Buren opposed the idea of imprisoning people, including farmers, for their debt. His efforts would eventually help lead to legislation years later that banned the practice.

What **political party** was Van Buren a member of while a **state senator**?

Van Buren was a Bucktail, a political party in New York opposed to prominent politician and Van Buren rival DeWitt Clinton. The Bucktails derived their interesting name from the fact many members of the party wore a deer's tail in their hats at political conventions.

What **position** did Van Buren work in **addition to** being a **state senator**?

In 1815, Van Buren served as the New York attorney general while still serving as a state senator. He also was named judge advocate and handled several prosecutions for the state.

What **famous prosecution** did Van Buren handle as **state attorney general**?

Van Buren successfully prosecuted Brigadier General William Hull for treason. Hull had surrendered the city of Detroit to the British in 1812 without any significant resistance. Van Buren secured a conviction and Hull was sentenced to death by firing squad. However, President James Madison intervened and pardoned Hull.

Who was Van Buren's **political enemy** in New York?

Van Buren's chief rival was DeWitt Clinton, who became governor of New York in 1817 and earlier had served in the U.S. Senate. Clinton referred to Van Buren as "the prince of villains." Clinton is best known for running for President in 1812 against James Madison. The two battled for control of the Democratic-Republican party for years.

> ## Why was Van Buren's tenure as governor so short?
>
> **V**an Buren served only forty-three days as New York's governor. He had made it clear to members of the Albany Regency that if Andrew Jackson became president, he might leave New York for a position in Washington, D.C. in Jackson's cabinet. That is exactly what happened, as Jackson asked Van Buren to be his secretary of state.

When he was governor of New York, Clinton removed Van Buren as attorney general and replaced him with Thomas J. Oakley. Van Buren also tried for a seat on the bench, but Governor Clinton vetoed such an idea.

When did Van Buren become a **national politician**?

This process began when Van Buren defeated incumbent Nathan Sanford in February 1821, to gain a seat in the U.S. Senate. It was during his time in the Senate that he worked with John C. Calhoun and Andrew Jackson, making political contacts that would ensure his rise up the ladder. He later became the Senate majority leader in 1827.

What **lifetime position** did Van Buren **decline** while a member of the Senate?

Van Buren initially agreed with Secretary of the Navy Smith Thompson's suggestion that President James Monroe appoint Van Buren to the U.S. Supreme Court. However, President Monroe did not move very quickly and Van Buren made it known that he did not want the appointment.

After serving in the Senate, what was Van Buren's **next political position**?

Van Buren was elected governor of New York in 1829. In 1828, his political rival DeWitt Clinton had died. Lieutenant Governor Nathaniel Pitcher assumed the position of governor. While Pitcher was a Bucktail, he did not have widespread support. Members of the Albany Regency convinced Van Buren that he needed to run and become governor.

What did Van Buren **accomplish** as **secretary of state**?

Van Buren managed to convince the British to open their ports in the Caribbean to American ships. This treaty with the British opened the West Indies to American merchants. He also oversaw a treaty with France that settled the question of the amount of compensation that American citizens could obtain for damages caused by the French while seizing American ships; some of these claims dated back to the Napoleonic era.

> ## What hobby did Van Buren share with President Jackson?
>
> They both loved horses and horse racing and gambling on horse racing. They often rode horses together, and during those rides they would discuss national political issues.

He initiated positive diplomatic communications with Russia and oversaw a successful treaty with Turkey that gave U.S. ships the right to sail in the Black Sea.

What was Van Buren's **role** in **Jackson's cabinet**?

Van Buren played a key role in Jackson's cabinet, as he and Jackson were on good terms. Van Buren was the only member of Jackson's cabinet that was a member of Jackson's unofficial "Kitchen Cabinet"—a group of Jackson allies and close political circle of advisors. Historians believe that Van Buren helped convince Jackson to get rid of his entire cabinet, including his vice president John C. Calhoun. Van Buren resigned his position but worked behind the scenes to help Jackson's successful reelection.

How did the **Eaton Affair** help Van Buren?

The Eaton affair was a major source of controversy during the first term of the Jackson presidency. Many wives of cabinet members shunned Peggy Eaton, the wife of John Eaton, the secretary of war. This enraged President Jackson, who may have identified with Eaton because his deceased wife, Rachel, had been the victim of scurrilous verbal assaults in newspapers. Van Buren cagily befriended Peggy Eaton and gained Jackson's greater trust. Van Buren was able to convince Jackson that he, not the others in his cabinet, was the president's true supporter and ally.

What was **supposed to be** Van Buren's **next position** after **secretary of state**?

Van Buren's next position was supposed to be minister to England. Jackson nominated him to the position but the Senate refused to confirm his nomination. Prominent senators such as John C. Calhoun—Jackson's former vice president—Henry Clay and Daniel Webster actively voted against him and galvanized opposition against the nomination. The nomination was tied and the tie-breaking vote went to Calhoun, as leader of the Senate.

How did the **rejection** actually **benefit Van Buren**?

It was said that Calhoun's actions had broken a minister but elected a vice president. Van Buren was viewed in some circles as a political martyr and President Andrew Jackson selected him as his vice president for his second term.

This political cartoon shows President Van Buren greeting Senator Henry Clay, a presidential hopeful critical of some of the president's fiscal policies. Note the men in the background with long hair and beards. They are Clay supporters who vowed not to shave or cut their hair until Clay became president.

PRESIDENCY

Whom did Van Buren **defeat** in the election of **1836**?

Van Buren defeated a host of Whig candidates, including William Henry Harrison, Hugh Lawson White, Daniel Webster, and Willie Person Mangum. Van Buren received 170 electoral votes; 70 went to Harrison, 26 to White, 14 to Webster, and 11 to Mangum.

Who was Van Buren's **vice president**?

Van Buren's vice president was Richard Minter Johnson, a former war hero during the War of 1812 and a former U.S. senator from Kentucky. Johnson had an open interracial relationship with one of his former slaves whom he actually regarded as his common law wife. Opposition to Johnson was strong enough that he did not get a sufficient number of electoral votes while running with Van Buren. The Senate had to elect Johnson as vice president.

What was the **Panic of 1837**?

The Panic of 1837 was a severe economic crisis that doomed Van Buren to becoming a one-term president. President Jackson had issued an executive order called the Specie

135

Circular, or Coinage Act, which required that all payment for government lands be paid in gold and silver. Jackson issued the order because of perceived rampant land speculation.

Jackson also refused to reissue a charter for the Second National Bank. Van Buren carried out these financial policies when he became president. Many banks began to fail and a period of inflation engulfed the economy. The Panic led to roughly five years of economic depression. The net effect politically was that Van Buren and the Democratic Party suffered, while the Whig Party rose in popularity.

Who served as the **hostess** at the **White House**?

Peggy Eaton served as the hostess at the White House during Van Buren's first term in office. Dolley Madison, the widow of former President James Madison also sometimes served as White House hostess during the Van Buren presidency.

What diplomatic **crisis** arose with **Canada** during the Van Buren presidency?

Some Canadians began moving for independence from Great Britain. Some Americans helped the Canadians in their effort, which exacerbated tensions in the U.S.–Great Britain relationship. Canadian loyalists, with support from Great Britain, then seized an American ship named the *Caroline,* which contained supplies for Canadian rebels. During this seizure, American Amos Durfree was killed.

Van Buren ordered General Winfield Scott to the area to prevent further hostilities. He also issued a proclamation of neutrality, stating that the United States would remain neutral in the Canadian–British struggle.

What was the **"Aroostook War"**?

The Aroostook War was not really a war. It was a tense conflict between Maine and New Brunswick about the proper border between the United States and Canada in the area along the Aroostook River. In 1839, the Maine legislature sent militia to the river to remove what it perceived to be Canadian interlopers. The New Brunswick lieutenant governor, Sir John Harvey, issued an order to remove Americans from what he believed to be Canadian, and thus British, land.

Van Buren dispatched General Winfield Scott to work out a compromise. Eventually, both countries signed the Ashburton-Webster treaty of 1842 that set out the exact borders between Maine and Canada.

Who were Van Buren's U.S. **Supreme Court appointees**?

Van Buren nominated two men to the U.S. Supreme Court: John McKinley in 1837 and Peter V. Daniel in 1841, shortly before he left office. McKinley, a U.S. Senator from Alabama, served fourteen years on the Court. He was actually a recess appointment to the court, as Congress had expanded the number of justices on the Court. Daniel was a Virginian politician and a federal district court judge appointed by Jackson in 1836. He served on the Court for approximately nineteen years.

To whom did Van Buren **lose** the **election of 1840**?

Van Buren lost his bid for reelection to William Henry Harrison, the Whig candidate that he had defeated in 1836. This time Harrison won 236 electoral votes to only 60 for Van Buren.

POST PRESIDENCY

Did Van Buren **try to regain** the **presidency**?

Yes, he sought the presidency in both 1844 and 1848. He toured much of the country in 1842, attempting to build support for another run for office. He expected to carry the Democratic Party nomination in 1844. At the party convention, Van Buren was in the lead after numerous votes but he could not garner the necessary two-thirds vote. Eventually, James K. Polk became the party's nominee and then the president.

Polk served only one term and Van Buren still held his presidential ambitions. In 1848, he ran as a third-party candidate for the Free Soil Party. He garnered 10 percent of the popular vote, but received no electoral votes. It was, however, the first real third-party in American political history.

What **books** did Van Buren **write**?

Van Buren wrote his autobiography and then also wrote a book on political parties entitled *An Inquiry into the Origin and Course of Political Parties in the United States,* which was published five years after his death.

When did Van Buren **die**?

Van Buren died on July 24, 1862, in Kinderhook, New York.

WILLIAM HENRY HARRISON

(1773–1841)
9th President, 1841
Party Affiliation: Whig Party
Chief 1840 Opponent: Martin Van Buren (Democrat)

EARLY LIFE AND FAMILY

Where and when was Harrison **born**?

Harrison was born on the Berkeley Plantation in Charles City County, Virginia, to Benjamin Harrison V and Elizabeth Bassett Harrison on February 9, 1773.

What did his **father do** for a living?

Benjamin Harrison V was a planter, farmer, and politician. He is best known as being a member of the First and Second Continental Congresses. As a member of the Second Continental Congress, he signed the Declaration of Independence. He also later served as governor of Virginia.

What was his **educational background**?

He learned under private tutors at Berkeley Plantation and then at Richmond, Virginia, after his father became governor. He then attended Hampden-Sydney College, focusing his studies on history and literature. However, since a young age he had aspired to a

Presidential portrait of William Henry Harrison by artist James Reid Lambden.

career in medicine. With his father's blessing, he went to Richmond to study medicine and then moved to Pennsylvania to study under Dr. Benjamin Rush, a prominent physician and, like Harrison's father, a signer of the Declaration of Independence.

Did William Henry Harrison have any **siblings**?

Yes, Harrison was the youngest child of seven.

Who was his **wife**?

William Henry Harrison married Anna Tuthill Symmes on November 25, 1795. He married Anna against her father's wishes. Her father was John Cleves Symmes, a lawyer, judge, and politician. He believed that Harrison did not have enough money and prominence for his daughter. William and Anna married while Mr. Symmes was out of town.

Did he have any **children**?

Yes, William and Anna had ten children: Elizabeth Bassett, John Cleves Symmes, Lucy Singleton, William Henry, John Scott, Benjamin, Mary Symmes, Carter Bassett, Anna Tuthill, and James Findlay.

Which of Harrison's **sons** became a **politician**?

His son John Scott Harrison became a member of the U.S. House of Representatives, where he served two terms. John Scott's son Benjamin—one of William Henry's grandsons—became the twenty-third president of the United States. Thus, John Scott Harrison is the only person in American history whose father and son were both presidents of the United States.

MILITARY CAREER

What **tragic event** caused Harrison to **leave** the **pursuit of a medical career**?

His father passed away when William Henry was eighteen years old. He chose to return home from Pennsylvania and begin a military career. With assistance from Senator Richard Henry Lee, he enlisted in the First Infantry Regiment as an ensign. He soon became a lieutenant.

When did he **first engage in combat**?

He engaged in combat under the command of General "Mad" Anthony Wayne at the Battle of Fallen Timbers near Toledo, Ohio, against a group of Indian tribes. Harrison's bravery during battle impressed General Wayne.

Where did Harrison **build his home**?

He built a home on a large farm that he called Grouseland a few miles from Cincinnati. He modeled his home after the Virginia estate where he was reared.

With which two **Native American leaders** did Harrison famously **battle**?

Harrison, while governor of the Indiana territory, tried to negotiate with, and then battled, Shawnee chief Tecumseh and his brother Tenskwatawa. Harrison engaged Tecumseh in negotiations, but those negotiations failed. In November 1811, Harrison and his forces defeated Indian forces at the Battle of Tippecanoe. Harrison and his forces destroyed the Indiana town known as Prophetstown, named after Tenskwatawa, who was called "The Prophet." Harrison later became known as "Old Tippecanoe" for winning this battle.

What was Harrison's **role** during the **War of 1812**?

Harrison was promoted to major general and given authority over all military forces in the Northwest Territory. He battled both Indian forces, including Tecumseh and Tenskwatawa, and the British. In October 1813, he won the Battle of the Thames over Indian forces. This battle increased Harrison's fame and made him a national figure even more than the Battle of Tippecanoe.

What was **The Prophet's curse**?

Legend has it that Tenskwatawa placed a curse upon Harrison in 1836, saying that Harrison would not win the presidency, or, if he did win the presidency, he would die. The curse was placed upon Harrison by "The Prophet" for the death of his brother Tecumseh at the Battle of the Thames.

Allegedly, the curse was supposed to apply to American leaders every twenty years. As strange it sounds, for many decades, there was a disturbing pattern of American presidents dying every twenty years. Harrison died in 1841 after winning the election of 1840; Lincoln died in 1865, having been elected in 1860; James Garfield died in 1881 from an assassin's bullet after winning the election of 1880; President William McKinley died in 1901 after winning the election of 1900; President Warren G. Harding died in 1923 after winning the election of 1920; Franklin Roosevelt died in 1945 and he had won the election of 1940; and President John F. Kennedy died in 1963 after winning the election of 1960.

POLITICAL OFFICES

Who **appointed Harrison** to his **first political position**?

President John Adams appointed Harrison to the position of secretary of the Northwest Territory. He also acted as a delegate from the area to Congress. While he couldn't vote, he could attend sessions of Congress and advise representatives on different matters. He also could introduce measures for consideration.

What **other position** did **President Adams appoint Harrison** to?

President Adams, impressed by Harrison's performance as secretary of the Northwest Territory, appointed him governor of the territory of Indiana. This territory was a massive land area that consists of modern day Indiana, Illinois, and Wisconsin. He served in this capacity under several presidents for a dozen years.

When did Harrison **serve in Congress**?

Harrison served in the U.S. House of Representatives for the state of Ohio from 1816 to 1819. He then served as a U.S. senator from Ohio from 1825 to 1828. He also served as an Ohio state senator from 1825 to 1829.

Who appointed Harrison to his **first overseas political position**?

President John Quincy Adams appointed Harrison as minister to Columbia in 1828. However, President Andrew Jackson recalled him from this position in 1829.

What did Harrison do **after he left** the position in **Columbia**?

Harrison returned to Ohio and worked on his farm. He later worked as a courtroom clerk for the court of common pleas in Hamilton County. He also began a campaign to promote himself politically and build a groundswell of support.

What **political party** did Harrison **join**?

Harrison was a member of the Whig Party and opposed many tenets of Andrew Jackson's Democratic Party. Harrison was one of several Whig candidates who vied for the presidency following Jackson's two terms. He lost to Jackson's hand-picked successor, Martin Van Buren, in the election of 1836.

PRESIDENCY

Whom did **Harrison defeat** for the presidency in the election of **1840**?

Harrison got revenge against Martin Van Buren for his loss in the Election of 1836. Van Buren's chances dimmed after the Panic of 1837 and the economic depression that befell the country. Harrison managed to win the support of the Whig Party and carried the election handily, particularly the electoral vote count. He won the electoral vote 234 to 60.

What **aspersions** did the **Democrats call Harrison** during the campaign?

Democratic supporters called Harrison "Granny Harrison" in reference to his advanced age. They also accused him of being noncommittal on issues, calling him "General Mum." They also focused on spelling his last name backwards: "Nosirrah."

What was **unusual** about Harrison's **inauguration**?

Harrison gave the longest inauguration speech in presidential history. He delivered a speech of more than 8,400 words that took nearly two hours to deliver. He delivered the speech in wet, cold weather in March.

What was unique about **Harrison's age** at his inauguration?

At age sixty-eight, Harrison was the oldest president ever at the time of his inauguration, a record unbroken until Ronald Reagan was sworn in at the age of nearly seventy in 1989. Harrison also was the first president from the state of Ohio, though he wouldn't be the last. Ohio has been called the "mother of presidents" because eight presidents were from the state, including: Harrison, Ulysses S. Grant, Rutherford B. Hayes, James Garfield, Benjamin Harrison, William McKinley, William Howard Taft, and Warren G. Harding.

Who was Harrison's **secretary of state**?

Daniel Webster was Harrison's secretary of state. Webster actually served as secretary of state for three different presidents: Harrison, his successor John Tyler, and later Franklin Pierce. He was a leading senator during his day and also considered one of the country's finest lawyers. He argued more than two hundred cases before the U.S. Supreme Court. Considered a great orator, he also was a great oral advocate in Court. He argued some of the most famous cases in American history, including *Dartmouth College v. Woodford* (1819), *Gibbons v. Ogden* (1824), and *McCullough v. Maryland* (1819).

How did Harrison **die**?

Harrison died from pneumonia on April 4, 1841, after serving just over thirty days in office as president. He became the first president to die in office. Harrison may have contracted pneumonia after being caught in a harsh downpour of rain a few weeks after his inauguration. Others have speculated that his two-hour inaugural speech in wet, cold weather may have contributed to his rapid decline in health.

What were Harrison's **last words**?

His last words allegedly were: "Sir, I wish you to understand the principles of government. I wish them carried out. I ask nothing more."

JOHN TYLER

(1790–1862)
10th President, 1841–1845
Party Affiliation: Whig
Chief Opponent: None

EARLY LIFE AND FAMILY

Where and when was John Tyler **born**?

John Tyler Jr. was born at Greenway Plantation in Charles City County, Virginia, to John Tyler Sr. and Mary Armistead Tyler on March 29, 1790.

What was his **father's occupation**?

John Tyler Sr. was a planter, lawyer, judge, and politician. He served in the Virginia House of Delegates and as governor of Virginia. He also served on the Virginia Court of Appeals and later as a federal district court judge appointed by President James Madison.

What **tragedy** befell young John and his family?

His mother died when he was only seven years old. A housekeeper and his four older sisters cared for young John in his early years.

President John Tyler.

> ## What other president was born in Charles City County, Virginia?
>
> Coincidentally, William Henry Harrison—under whom Tyler served as vice president and whom he succeeded—was also born in Charles City County, Virginia.

Did John Tyler have any **siblings**?

Yes, John Tyler had seven siblings. He was the second oldest son. He had four older sisters.

What was his **education**?

He attended local schools under a Scottish schoolmaster named William McMurdo. He then attended preparatory school at his father's alma mater, William & Mary, when he was twelve years old. He then went to college at William & Mary, where he graduated in 1807.

At William & Mary, who was his **favorite professor**?

His favorite educator was Reverend James Madison, the president of the college, and a second cousin to the fourth president of the United States. Tyler was attracted to the dynamism of Madison's lectures.

How **old** was Tyler when he **graduated college**?

He graduated college at age seventeen. He was one of four commencement speakers at his graduation.

Who was his **wife**?

At age twenty-three, he married Letitia Christian, the daughter of a wealthy merchant, on March 29, 1813. She died in 1842 during his presidency and, while still president, he married again, this time to actress Julia Gardiner Tyler in 1844. The second marriage caused controversy, as Tyler was thirty years older than Julia.

Did he have any **children**?

He had eight children with his first wife, Letitia. Their names were Mary, Robert, John, Letitia, Elizabeth, Anne Contesse, Alice, and Tazewell. He then had seven more

149

children with his second wife, Julia. Their names were David Gardiner, John Alexander, Julia Gardener, Lachlan, Lyon Gardiner, Robert Fitzwater, and Pearl. Tyler had fifteen children—the most of any president in history.

Which of Tyler's children became president of his alma mater, The College of William & Mary?

Lyon Gardiner Tyler became president of The College of William & Mary in 1888 and served for more than thirty years until 1919.

EARLY CAREER

What occupation did Tyler choose after graduation from college?

Tyler chose the field of law, following in his father's footsteps. He learned law under his father and his cousin Samuel Tyler, and then worked in the Richmond-based law office of Edmund Randolph, the nation's first U.S. attorney general.

When did he become licensed as an attorney?

He was accepted into the bar at age nineteen, younger than the normal age of admission into the legal field at that time. However, Tyler excelled at law, specializing in criminal law.

When did Tyler join the military?

Tyler joined the Charles City Rifles, a local militia group organized to defend the state against the British during the War of 1812. He was appointed captain of the local group, which never saw any combat action.

POLITICAL OFFICES

What was Tyler's first political position?

Tyler won a seat in the Virginia House of Delegates in 1811 when he was only twenty-one years old. He won reelection four more times to the political body, which held annual elections. He left in 1821 after winning a seat in the U.S. House of Representatives. He also served in the Virginia House of Delegates from 1823 to 1825 and from 1838 to 1840.

Whom did he **defeat** to **win** a place in the **U.S. House of Representatives**?

He defeated Virginia Speaker of the House Andrew Stevenson in a special election that was held after the death of Representative John Clopton.

What **political vision** did Tyler show as a **U.S. representative**?

Tyler followed a vision of states' rights that followed in the tradition of Thomas Jefferson. He disagreed with some of the proposals brought forth by Henry Clay that gave more power to the federal government. For example, he opposed a bill that called for the creation of the Second National Bank.

What were Tyler's **views on slavery**?

Tyler believed that slavery was evil, but that it was a necessary evil. He believed that the Southern economy needed slavery and could not support itself without it.

Why did Tyler **decide to not seek reelection** in December 1820?

Tyler became frustrated because he often was in the minority, as Congress passed limitations on slavery in the Compromise of 1820 and supported the national bank. He also suffered an unknown stomach illness in 1819 that persisted well beyond the election.

After leaving the House, what did Tyler do?

Tyler returned to the practice of law, though he did not enjoy it as much as he did when he was younger. He even got into a fight with someone that he had vigorously cross-examined at an earlier time.

What were his **next political positions**?

Tyler returned to the Virginia House of Delegates in 1823 and then became the governor of Virginia in 1825. After this, he successfully challenged incumbent John Randolph for a position in the U.S. Senate. Randolph was a controversial figure in part because he engaged in some unusual behavior, such as dressing and undressing in the Senate chamber. He also fought a duel with Henry Clay. Tyler narrowly defeated Randolph by five votes in the state legislature.

What **political party** did Tyler belong to while a **senator**?

Tyler served in the U.S. Senate from 1827 until 1836. Originally, he had supported President Andrew Jackson in the election of 1828, attracted by Jackson's hostility to the national bank. However, Tyler grew wary of Jackson's expansion of federal power. Tyler voted to censure Jackson for removing monies from federal banks. Tyler started to shift his allegiance from Jackson's Democratic Party to the newly formed Whig Party led by Henry Clay. He resigned his Senate seat in 1836 in part because he would not vote to remove Jackson's censure. After resigning, Tyler later officially joined the Whig Party.

After resigning his Senate seat, what did Tyler do?

Tyler returned to Virginia and won another seat in the Virginia House of Delegates in 1838 and became the body's Speaker. He also took time to care for his wife Letitia, who had suffered a stroke. He lost an attempt to return to the U.S. Senate in 1839.

What was Tyler's next political position after failing to return to the Senate?

The Whig Party chose Tyler, who was popular politically in some segments of the South, as a running mate for William Henry Harrison. The two ran under the immortalized campaign slogan "Tippecanoe and Tyler Too." When Harrison defeated incumbent Martin Van Buren for the presidency, John Tyler became vice president.

PRESIDENCY

What does the U.S. Constitution say about what happens if a president dies or is removed from office?

Article II, Section 1 provides:

> In case of the removal of the President from Office, or of his Death, Resignation, or Inability to discharge the Powers and Duties of said office, the Same shall devolve to the Vice President, and the Congress may by law provide for the case of removal, death, resignation or inability, both of the President and Vice President, declaring what officer shall then act as President, and such officer shall act accordingly, until the disability be removed, or a President shall be elected.

The Twelfth Amendment, added to the Constitution in 1804, says that should the president die, "the Vice President shall act as President."

The question became whether Tyler should simply act as president until a new president was elected or chosen by Congress, or whether he would become the new president. Tyler acted swiftly and definitively, declaring that he should assume the presidency.

What negative nicknames were ascribed to Tyler at this time?

Some referred to him as "His Accidency" or the "Accidental President." His critics charged that he was not worthy of the office of the presidency.

> ## Who informed Vice President Tyler that President Harrison had died?
>
> Francis Webster, the son of Secretary of State Daniel Webster, and Robert Beale, the doorkeeper of the U.S. Senate, traveled to Tyler's home near Williamsburg, Virginia, to deliver the untimely news about Harrison.

What was **Tyler's age** at the time he **became president**?

Tyler was fifty-one years of age when he became the president, making him the youngest person up to that point to hold the office of chief executive.

Who were Tyler's **original Cabinet members**?

Tyler inherited all of Harrison's original Cabinet members: Daniel Webster as secretary of state, Thomas Ewing as secretary of the treasury, and John Bell as secretary of war.

What **significant treaty** was signed **in 1842** during the first full year of Tyler's presidency?

The Webster-Ashburton Treaty was a significant diplomatic achievement that significantly reduced conflict between Great Britain and the United States. The nub of the treaty was the working out of an agreed-upon border between the state of Maine and the Canadian province of New Brunswick. The treaty was named after Secretary of State Daniel Webster and British diplomat Alexander Baring known as Lord Ashburton. Fortunately for the United States, Ashburton had a personal interest in bringing peace to the northeast region, as he owned a significant chunk of land in Maine and did not want to see full-blown conflict in the area.

How did Tyler **run afoul** of his **own political party**?

Tyler was never really a good fit for the Whig Party. He joined the party to oppose President Andrew Jackson, a Democrat whom he viewed as dangerous. But, Tyler advocated states' rights positions, while the Whig Party generally advocated an expansion of federal power. Tyler angered Henry Clay and other leading Whigs by opposing the creation of a national bank. Twice, Tyler vetoed bills supporting its creation. After the second veto, Tyler's entire Cabinet—except for Secretary of State Daniel Webster—resigned in protest.

When his **Cabinet resigned**, what did Tyler do?

Upon learning of the actions of his Cabinet members, Tyler simply appointed new Cabinet members within a matter of days. Tyler actually has the record for the most Cabinet members of any one-term president.

Why did **Daniel Webster** eventually **resign** from Tyler's Cabinet too?

Webster resigned from Tyler's Cabinet because the president continued to support the annexation of Texas. Webster opposed the idea of annexation in part because it would be a large slave state. Tyler replaced Webster with Abel P. Upshur, and later John C. Calhoun.

What did the **Whig Party do** to Tyler?

The Whig Party essentially disowned Tyler. President Tyler became a president without a political party.

What **issue most concerned** Tyler?

Tyler wholeheartedly supported the annexation of Texas, something that Whig candidate Henry Clay opposed. Tyler was able to obtain a promise from the eventual Democratic party candidate (and ultimately his successor) James K. Polk that if Tyler dropped out of the race, Polk would support the annexation of Texas.

What was a bit **different** about Tyler's new **wife, Julia**?

At age twenty-three, she was the youngest first lady in history. She was given to extravagant displays and preoccupation with titles. Her press agent came up with her title of "The Lovely Lady Presidentress." She also ordered that the song "Hail to the Chief" be played whenever her husband appeared at official and public events.

She also interjected herself in political discussions. For example, she actively supported the annexation of Texas.

Who was Tyler's **only U.S. Supreme Court appointee**?

Samuel Nelson, a New York jurist, was Tyler's only appointment to the U.S. Supreme Court. Nelson had served as a New York state circuit judge and on the New York Supreme Court. He served twenty-seven years on the U.S. Supreme Court. Nelson was not Tyler's first choice, as the Senate rejected several of his earlier nominations, including his secretary of the treasury John C. Spencer, Edward King, Reuben Walworth, and John Read. Tyler actually had two vacancies to fill, but the Senate would not accept his nominations, or would refuse to vote on them.

Which **future president** did Tyler **offer** the job of U.S. **Supreme Court Justice**?

Tyler offered the position to James Buchanan, a U.S. senator from Pennsylvania and a lawyer. Buchanan declined the offer and many years later became the fifteenth president of the United States.

POST PRESIDENCY

What did Tyler do **after leaving the White House**?

Tyler retired to his Virginia plantation, Sherwood Forest, in Charles City County. He planted crops and even purchased more slaves. His wife Julia had seven children starting in 1846.

What **peace commission** did Tyler propose?

Tyler proposed a peace conference to be held in Washington, D.C., that could work out a way to avoid a civil war. The Virginia legislature approved his idea and Tyler went to Washington to meet with President Buchanan. In February 1861, the peace commission met and elected Tyler as their president. However, the commission could not stem the tide, as several Southern states seceded from the Union. Tyler grew dissatisfied with the commission's progress and later voted against the proposal from the peace commission. Tyler eventually supported Virginia's move to secede from the Union.

Did **Tyler participate** in the **Confederacy**?

Yes, Tyler helped Virginia join the Confederate States of America and later won a seat in the Confederate House of Representatives.

When did Tyler **die**?

Tyler died on January 18, 1862, in Richmond, Virginia. He was buried in Richmond next to the grave of James Monroe. However, there was no official mention of his passing and no flags flew at half-mast in Washington, D.C., as is customary when a president dies.

JAMES K. POLK

(1795–1849)
11th President, 1845–1849
Party Affiliation: Democrat
Chief 1844 Opponent: Henry Clay (Whig)

EARLY LIFE AND FAMILY

Where and when was James K. Polk **born**?

James K. Polk was born in Mecklenburg County, North Carolina, to Samuel and Jane Knox Polk on November 2, 1795.

What was his **father's occupation**?

Samuel Knox was a land surveyor and landowner who prospered after moving his family to Columbia, Tennessee, in 1806. He later opened a general store that was quite successful and led to other business opportunities. Samuel had an interest in a steamboat operation and was a director in a local bank. His wealth enabled him to fund his son James's education.

Did he have any **siblings**?

Yes, James K. Polk was the oldest of ten children. His nine siblings were named Jane, Lydia, Franklin, Marshall, John, Naomi, Ophelia, William, and Samuel.

What caused Polk to **start** his **education relatively late** in life?

As a child, James suffered from poor health. Because he was chronically ill, he did not attend regular school until a relatively advanced age. When he was seventeen, his parents took him to a doctor who performed surgery on James to remove urinary stones. Some speculate that it was this operation that later prevented James Polk and his wife from having children.

What was his **early education**?

After recovering from surgery, James was well enough to attend school regularly. He attended a Presbyterian school in Mount Zion, Tennessee, and then Bradley Academy in Murfreesboro, Tennessee. At both schools, Polk distinguished himself academically.

A Currier & Ives reproduction of the official portrait of President James K. Polk.

Did he **marry**?

Polk married Sarah Childress in January 1824, in Murfreesboro, Tennessee. James was twenty-eight years old at the time, while Sarah was only twenty.

Did he have any **children**?

James and Sarah never had any children. The two were devoted to each other until James's death. It has been said that upon Polk's death, Sarah dressed in mourning for the rest of her life.

EARLY CAREER

Where did James **attend college**?

He attended the University of North Carolina in Chapel Hill. He entered as a sophomore in 1816 and graduated in 1818 at the top of his class, giving the commencement address.

What college **classmates of Polk** also became **prominent in politics**?

William Henry Haywood Jr., John Y. Mason, George Dromgoole, and William Dunn Moseley all went to college with Polk and had political careers. Haywood served as a U.S. senator for North Carolina. Mason served as the U.S. secretary of the navy for both President John Tyler and Polk and also served as Polk's attorney general. Dromgoole served in the U.S. House of Representatives for Virginia. Moseley became the first governor of Florida in 1845.

What did Polk do **after graduating college**?

Polk studied law under well-known lawyer Felix Grundy, who previously had served in the Kentucky legislature and on the Kentucky Supreme Court. Grundy was a friend of Andrew Jackson and later became a U.S. senator from Tennessee and U.S. attorney general under President Martin Van Buren.

Polk studied under Grundy for two years and was admitted to the Tennessee Bar in June 1820.

What job did **Felix Grundy help Polk** land?

Grundy's connections helped Polk land a job as a clerk in the state Senate in Murfreesboro, Tennessee. Polk learned and loved the legislative process from this up-close vantage point. Polk later returned the favor when he was governor, appointing Grundy as a U.S. senator to replace the Whig Hugh Lawson White.

What **type of law** did Polk practice?

Polk practiced law in Columbia after finishing his studies under Grundy. He handled property law and debt collection cases. He even argued a case before the U.S. Supreme Court, *Williams v. Norris* (1827).

Did Polk have any **military service**?

Polk never served in actual combat but he did join a local militia in 1821 and rose to the rank of colonel.

POLITICAL OFFICES

What was Polk's **first political position**?

Polk won a seat to the Tennessee House of Representatives in 1823 by defeating two-term incumbent William Yancey. He served in the Tennessee legislature until 1825, when he ran for a seat in the U.S. House of Representatives.

How **long** did Polk serve in the **U.S. House of Representatives**?

He served seven terms in the U.S. House of Representatives from 1825 until 1839. He was never defeated in running for his seat in the House of Representatives. He left to run for governor in 1839.

How did **Polk support President Jackson** in the House of Representatives?

Andrew Jackson was Polk's primary political mentor. Polk later was even known as "Young Hickory" in reference to Jackson's famous moniker. Polk consistently supported Jackson's positions in the House. As a member and later chairman of the Ways and Means Committee, Polk opposed the Second National Bank and its president Nicholas Biddle. He supported President Jackson's position against John C. Calhoun's threatened secession by supporting the Force Bill, which would enable the president to ensure state compliance with federal law. Polk had even more power to support Jackson when he became Speaker of the House.

How did Polk fare as **speaker of the House**?

Polk consistently supported President Jackson and furthered the interests of the Democratic Party over the other major party—the Whigs. Polk presided over a deeply divided House—one that featured 108 Democrats, 107 Whigs, and 24 member of other parties. He tried to support President Van Buren's mission of an independent Treasury Department that would place federal governmental money in governmental, rather than private, institutions. Unfortunately for Van Buren and Polk, Whig opposition was too much. He left the position as speaker in part because the Whig party was growing in popularity, to some extent due to the Panic of 1837, which harmed the Van Buren administration and, consequently, the Democratic Party.

Whom did Polk **defeat** for **governor of Tennessee**?

Polk defeated two-time incumbent Newton Cannon for governor by a very narrow margin in 1839. Polk won by just more than two thousand votes in an election in which there were more than one hundred thousand votes cast. He lost in his reelection bid in 1841 to Tennessee legislator James C. "Lean Jimmy" Jones, who was an effective stump speaker on the campaign trail. In 1843, Polk once again tried to regain the governor's seat, but lost to Jones again—this time by approximately 3,200 votes.

PRESIDENCY

Why was Polk called the **"dark horse" candidate**?

In 1844, James K. Polk did not appear on the radar screen as the next president of the United States. He had just lost two consecutive bids for the governorship of Tennessee.

No one thought a candidate who could not win his own state could win the presidency. Additionally, the front-runner for the Democratic Party at the 1844 convention was former President Martin Van Buren.

However, Van Buren made a serious blunder by publicly coming out against the annexation of Texas—adding the state to the Union—as did Whig candidate Henry Clay. Perhaps Van Buren and Clay wanted to avoid the thorny slavery question that was so divisive in the country. President Andrew Jackson saw an opportunity for his protégé, and with the help of other key politicians, managed to move Polk onto a later ballot at the Democratic convention.

As Van Buren could not obtain the necessary majority votes, it became clear that someone else would have to emerge. It turned out to be James K. Polk who became the Democratic Party nominee.

Whom did Polk defeat in the general election to win the presidency?

Polk defeated the legendary U.S. senator from Kentucky, Henry Clay—John Quincy Adams's former secretary of state and also a former speaker of the House of Representatives. Clay had also run for the presidency in 1832, losing to incumbent President Andrew Jackson and in 1840 when he lost the Whig nomination to William Henry Harrison, who would later become president. The Whigs thought that Clay could defeat the lesser known Polk. One of their campaign slogans was "Who is James K. Polk?"

Polk defeated Clay by an electoral vote margin of 170 to 105. However, he carried the popular vote by a mere 1.4 percent margin. Ironically, Polk won the presidency even though he did not carry his home state of Tennessee. He remains the only president to win the White House race while losing his own state.

What member of Polk's cabinet was a holdover from the Tyler administration?

James K. Polk did keep one member of President Tyler's cabinet on his own cabinet: John Y. Mason. Polk probably kept Mason because the two knew each other at the University of North Carolina. Mason served as President Tyler's secretary of the navy. In the Polk administration, Mason served as U.S. attorney general and then secretary of the navy again.

What member of Polk's cabinet later became president in his own right?

Polk's secretary of state, James Buchanan, later became the fifteenth president of the United States. Polk and Buchanan frequently clashed during their time together. Polk often acted as his own secretary of state to achieve his objectives.

161

The Polk residents in Columbia, Tennessee.

Why is **Polk considered** a **great president**?

Polk is considered by many historians to be a great president because he had several major accomplishments in his one term in office. In fact, Polk's secretary of the navy, George Bancroft, an esteemed historian, said that Polk articulated four major goals upon assuming office: (1) lower the tariffs; (2) create an independent treasury; (3) annex Oregon to the United States; and (4) obtain California from Mexico.

Polk accomplished all four of these major objectives. Twentieth-century president Harry Truman said of Polk: "He said exactly what he was going to do and he did it."

What **measure** led to Polk's success in **lowering the tariff**?

The Walker Tariff Act of 1846, named after Polk's secretary of the treasury, Robert J. Walker, achieved the president's objective in lowering the tariffs that had been passed by the Whigs in 1842. Polk faced significant opposition in Congress. Vice President George M. Dallas cast the tie-breaking vote in the Senate that led to the law's successful passage.

What was Polk's **financial plan** with regard to the **Treasury**?

Polk wanted to avoid creating a national bank and have the government's money placed in private banks. Polk followed the example of Martin Van Buren, who had called for an independent treasury during his presidency. Unlike Van Buren, Polk managed to have his measure—which he called the Constitutional Treasury Act—passed into law. It lasted until 1913, when Congress created the Federal Reserve System.

How did Polk **obtain Oregon**?

Polk refused to back down from the British and remained steadfast in his demands that the British drop claims to the Oregon territory. Polk allegedly told at least one member of Congress: "The only way to treat John Bull [a name for Great Britain] is to look him in the eye." He acquired what is present-day Oregon, Washington, and part of Idaho. He obtained land up to the forty-ninth parallel, though not all the way to the "54-40" parallel that was desired by some in the "All Oregon" campaign.

> ## What member of Polk's cabinet later lived to the age of ninety?
>
> George Bancroft, a politician, was born in 1800 and did not pass away until 1891. He served as Polk's secretary of navy, during which time he helped create the United States Naval Academy at Annapolis. He is considered a great historian, particularly for his multivolume set entitled *A History of the United States*.

What **war did Polk wage** that led to greater territory for the United States?

Fulfilling the Democrat phrase "manifest destiny," Polk engaged the United States in the Mexican-American War that led to the eventual annexation of California. Tensions were already hot between the two countries after the annexation of Texas, which had begun in earnest at the end of the Tyler administration, but was completed officially in Polk's term.

But Polk wanted more for the country—the provinces of New Mexico and California. Mexican troops had crossed the Rio Grande and killed American soldiers in the dispute. Polk sent Zachary Taylor—his presidential successor—into the region. Taylor achieved several victories over the Mexican army at Palo Alto and Resaca de la Palma. Taylor later defeated Mexican forces at Buena Vista in 1847. American armies led by either Taylor or General Winfield Scott actually took Mexico City during the conflict.

After the United States conquered Mexico City, Mexico realized that it had better sell its land in New Mexico and California and end the war. Some speculated that the United States should simply take control of all of Mexico. This was known as the "All Mexico" campaign. Polk faced resistance to the war from many in the country, and decided to obtain peace and enlarge the country with more than a half a million square miles.

What was Polk's **relationship** with his **generals Zachary Taylor and Winfield Scott**?

Polk did not get along with either Zachary Taylor or Winfield Scott. The source of the animus appears to be political. Taylor and Scott were Whigs, while Polk was a die-hard Democrat. Polk suspected that the two men—who were considered heroes for their military successes—held presidential ambitions. On this point, Polk proved correct, as Taylor became the twelfth president of the United States and Scott became the Whig candidate for the presidency in 1852.

Who were Polk's **Supreme Court appointees**?

Polk's first successful nominee was Levi Woodbury, a loyal Democratic supporter of President Andrew Jackson and Polk. Woodbury, a U.S senator and former governor from New Hampshire, had served in Jackson's administration as secretary of the treasury and secretary of the navy. He served on the U.S. Supreme Court for only six years.

Polk's second successful nomination was Robert C. Grier, a Pennsylvania state judge who had been a loyal Jacksonian Democrat and political organizer for years. Grier served on the Court for approximately twenty-four years.

What Polk **nominee did not receive confirmation** by the Senate?

Polk nominated George Washington Woodward, a Pennsylvania state judge as associate justice in 1845. However, the Senate refused to confirm Woodward. Polk speculated in his diary that James Buchanan, his secretary of state who also was from Pennsylvania, had worked against the nomination. Buchanan had requested that Polk nominate John M. Read, another Pennsylvanian, to the Supreme Court.

What was Polk's **position on slavery**?

Polk said that slavery was an evil institution, but he was a slaveholder during his adult life. His political position was that it was up to individual states to determine whether slavery should exist within their borders. In his will, he called for all his slaves to go to Sarah and upon her death, to be freed. Sarah lived more than forty years after his death, so his will was trumped by the Emancipation Proclamation and the Thirteenth Amendment of the U.S. Constitution.

POST PRESIDENCY

Why did Polk **not accomplish much** after his term in office?

Unfortunately, Polk only lived a mere three months after leaving the White House. He did not get much time to enjoy the home that he and his wife, Sarah, had purchased from Felix Grundy in Nashville. He passed away at the age of fifty-three. He frequently suffered from diarrhea and stomach ailments.

What significant **personal event** occurred near his death?

Polk agreed to be baptized, insisting that it be done by a Methodist minister. Throughout his adult life, he often attended a Presbyterian church with his wife, Sarah, who was a devout religious advocate.

ZACHARY TAYLOR

(1784–1850)
12th President, 1849–1850
Party Affiliation: Whig
Chief 1848 Opponents: Lewis Cass (Democratic) and Martin Van Buren (Free Soil)

EARLY LIFE AND FAMILY

Where and when was Taylor **born**?

Zachary Taylor was born in Orange County, Virginia, to Richard and Sarah Taylor on November 24, 1784.

What was his **father's occupation**?

Richard Taylor was a distinguished military veteran, planter, and politician. He served in the Revolutionary War, reaching the level of lieutenant colonel. Just after his son Zachary was born, Richard moved his family from Virginia to Kentucky, where he eventually acquired more than ten thousand acres. He served as a justice of the peace and held office in the Kentucky legislature.

Did he have any **siblings**?

Yes, Taylor had seven siblings—four brothers and three sisters. His brothers were named Hancock, William, George, and Joseph. His sisters were named Elizabeth, Sarah, and Emily.

Major General Zachary Taylor by engraver John Sartain.

Which of Taylor's daughters married Jefferson Davis, future president of the Confederacy?

Sarah Knox Taylor married Jefferson Davis, who had served as an officer under the command of Zachary Taylor. Taylor opposed the wedding, as he did not want his daughter to marry someone in the military. Taylor and his wife, Margaret, did not attend the wedding. Tragically, Sarah contracted malaria and died only three months after marriage.

What was his **early education**?

Taylor's education was relatively limited. He had private tutoring intermittently, but he did not attend a place of higher learning. Taylor never enjoyed academics much; he preferred helping with the management of the family plantation and engaging in athletics. He must have been very fit, since his biographers report that he once swam across the Ohio River to Indiana and back.

Did he **marry**?

He married Margaret Mackail Smith on June 21, 1810, in Louisville, Kentucky.

Did he have any **children**?

Yes, Taylor and his wife had seven children. They were named Ann, Sarah, Octavia, Margaret, Mary Elizabeth, and Robert. Two of his children, Octavia and Margaret, died as children.

Which of his sons **entered politics** and became a **general**?

Richard Taylor, who lived in Louisiana, served in the Confederate army during the Civil War, rising to the level of major general. In 1855, he won a seat in the Louisiana Senate. He began his political career, like his father, as a Whig. But he later switched to the Know Nothing Party, and then the Democratic Party. He achieved several military victories with smaller forces than his Union counterparts, winning the Battle of Mansfield and the Battle of Pleasant Hill during the Red River campaign. He was the last Confederate general to surrender.

Which of Taylor's daughters later served as the **official White House hostess**?

Taylor's daughter Mary Elizabeth "Betty" Taylor served as the White House's official hostess because her mother, First Lady Margaret Taylor, was chronically ill.

MILITARY CAREER

How did he **begin his military career**?

Taylor first served in the Kentucky militia in 1806, finding it more to his liking than running a plantation. He managed to obtain a commission as a lieutenant with the local infantry from his famous second cousin—then U.S. Secretary of State James Madison, the future fourth president of the United States.

What **future president** did **Taylor serve under** beginning in 1810?

Taylor served under William Henry Harrison, the future ninth president of the United States, at Fort Knox in Vincennes, Indiana. His command of Fort Knox impressed Harrison.

What **wars** did **Taylor participate in** during his long military career?

Taylor served in the War of 1812; the Black Hawk War of 1832; the Second Seminole War, which began in 1837; and the Mexican-American War, which began in 1846.

Where did Taylor successfully **fight against** the great **chief Tecumseh**?

Taylor—then a captain—successfully defended Fort Harrison with a group of fifty men from a Tecumseh-led force of more than four hundred men in the War of 1812. The event is sometimes called the "Siege of Fort Harrison." His success earned him the rank of brevet major, the first time this honor was ever awarded. A designation of "brevet" signified that an officer displayed particular courage during military service.

Why did Taylor **temporarily leave the military**?

When the War of 1812 ended, Taylor was demoted back to captain. He resigned his commission and moved back to his Springfield plantation. But he preferred military over civilian life, and rejoined the army. His second cousin—now President James Madison—restored his rank and he was assigned to Fort Howard near Green Bay, Wisconsin.

What did Taylor do in the **Black Hawk War**?

Taylor, then a colonel, commanded troops into action during the Black Hawk War in 1832. He served under General Henry Atchinson, who faced later criticism for not being decisive enough in his military judgments. Taylor performed well in command, leading his troops to victory at the decisive Battle of Bad Axe near present-day Victory, Wisconsin. The Native American leader Black Hawk, war chief of the Sauk Indians, surrendered at this battle.

A lithograph portraying future President Taylor hunting down Seminole Indians in Florida.

What **famous battle** did Taylor win during the **Second Seminole War**?

Taylor led troops into battle during the Second Seminole War at the Battle of Okee-chobee on Christmas day 1837 against a group of Seminole Indians. Taylor had superior numbers than Indian chief Billy Bowlegs. Both sides declared victory, though the U.S. forces suffered more casualties. Taylor received another promotion to brigadier general for bravery during this conflict. He was given command of all U.S. troops in Florida.

How did Taylor become a **bona fide military hero**?

Taylor became a military hero due to several victories during the Mexican-American War, which began in 1846. Now a general, Taylor defeated Mexican forces at Palo Alto and then at Resaca de la Palma. Taylor and the Americans had superior artillery fire and were able to inflict many more casualties. He was awarded two gold medals for these victories.

Taylor further entrenched himself into the country's consciousness as a hero after he led his troops to victory at Monterey. President Polk, a diehard Democrat, became displeased with Taylor, whom he saw as a possible Whig candidate. Polk also believed that Taylor had granted too generous terms to the Mexicans following the taking of Monterrey. Polk then replaced Taylor with General Winfield Scott on a mission to march to Mexico City.

169

Taylor vowed not to resign and instead did something unexpected against presidential orders. With a much smaller force he engaged the Mexicans at the Battle of Buena Vista in February 1847. The Mexican leader Santa Anna could not defeat Taylor's much smaller military force. This battle ensured that Taylor had presidential possibilities.

PRESIDENCY

Whom did **Taylor defeat** to win the **election of 1848**?

Taylor, the candidate for the Whig party, defeated Democrat Lewis Cass by an electoral vote count of 163 to 127. Cass had lost the Democratic nomination to James K. Polk in 1844. A senator from Michigan, Cass later served as secretary of state for the fifteenth president, James Buchanan.

What **third-party candidate helped Taylor** win the election?

Martin Van Buren, the eighth president, ran as a third-party candidate for the Free Soil Party. Historians contend that Van Buren, who was from New York, drew enough voters away from Cass to turn the thirty-six electors to Taylor. Historians believe that if Van Buren was not in the race that Cass would have carried New York and perhaps the election.

Who was his **vice president**?

Millard Fillmore from New York was Taylor's vice president. The Whigs believed that they needed a Northerner as vice president to balance the ticket, as Taylor was a Southerner. The Whigs also wanted someone who had outstanding political credentials because Taylor had no political experience. Fillmore fit the bill.

What **new position was created** in Taylor's **cabinet**?

The secretary of the interior was a position that began with Taylor's administration. Held by Thomas Ewing of Ohio, the secretary of the interior was responsible for Indian issues, pensions, and other matters.

> ## What was unusual about the date of Taylor's inauguration?
>
> Taylor refused to take the oath of office on Sunday March 4, 1849, because of his religious faith. Because Taylor refused, the Senate's president pro tempore, David Rice Acheson, technically served as the unofficial president for that one day.

What **scandal** befell the Taylor administration?

The Galphin Affair involved the Galphin family in Georgia who had a claim against the United States dating back to the 1770s. The government paid the family's claim but the family asserted that it was entitled to interest in the amount of six-figures. The government paid the fee, but soon it was revealed that Taylor's secretary of war, George M. Crawford, had previously represented the Galphin family and stood to gain from the payment. Taylor was upset by the matter and thought of replacing several members of his cabinet. But he was never able to carry out his plan, since he died soon afterwards.

What **significant treaty** did the government sign during Taylor's presidency?

The Clayton-Bulwer Treaty of 1850 established that any new canal constructed in Central America was to be neutral, not under the control of either the United States or Great Britain. Neither side was supposed to colonize or exercise dominion over any part of Central America. The treaty was named after U.S. Secretary of State John M. Clayton and British minister to the United States Henry Lytton Bulwer.

What was Taylor's position on the **Compromise of 1850**?

The Compromise of 1850 was a federal law created largely by influential congressman Henry Clay to address the increasingly divisive issue of slavery. Under the Compromise of 1850, California would be admitted as a free state (a state where slavery was not allowed), while other territories, such as New Mexico and Utah, could decide for themselves whether to allow slavery. The bill also contained other measures favorable to slave owners. Taylor opposed the measure and said that he would veto it if it came to his desk. He died before Congress passed the law. His vice president, Millard Fillmore, signed the measure into law.

Why was Taylor's **position on slavery** surprising to some?

Taylor opposed the spread of slavery. This surprised some because Taylor was from Louisiana and, previously, Kentucky. He also owned slavers on his large plantation. But Taylor was a strong nationalist, and feared that the slavery question would tear

171

An 1848 Currier & Ives portrait of President Zachary Taylor.

apart the union. He strongly disagreed with those Southerners who advocated for secession.

When did Taylor **die**?

Taylor died on July 9, 1850, of gastroenteritis at the White House in Washington, D.C.

What were his **last words**?

Taylor's last words were: "I am about to die. I expect the summons very soon. I have tried to discharge my duties faithfully. I regret nothing, but I am very sorry that I am about to leave my friends."

MILLARD FILLMORE

(1800–1874)
13th President, 1850–1853
Party Affiliation: Whig
Chief Opponent: None

EARLY LIFE AND FAMILY

Where and when was he **born**?

Millard Fillmore was born in Morovia, New York, to Nathaniel and Phoebe Fillmore on January 7, 1800.

What did his **father do** for a living?

Nathaniel was a farmer in Vermont and New York.

Did Fillmore have any **siblings**?

Yes, he was the second oldest of nine children. His siblings were Olive, Cyrus, Almon, Calvin, Julia, Darius, Charles, and Phoebe.

What was his **early education**?

Fillmore's early education was very limited. At the age of fourteen, he served as an apprentice to learn the clothing trade. He learned to make clothing as a wool carder.

Where did he **attend school**?

At age nineteen, he attended New Hope Academy in New Hope, New York, to further his education. He later fell in love with his teacher Abigail Powers, who was only a few years older than he was.

Who was his **wife**?

Fillmore married Abigail Powers on February 5, 1826.

Did he have any **children**?

Yes, Fillmore and his wife had two children: a son named Millard Powers Fillmore and a daughter named Mary Abigail Fillmore. The son, called Powers, later became a lawyer and a federal court clerk. The daughter died at the age of twenty-two from cholera, though she charmed many as the acting White House hostess during Fillmore's presidency.

EARLY CAREER

What **profession** did Fillmore **initially pursue**?

He pursued the study of law, first under Judge Walter Wood of Montville, New York, and then under Buffalo attorneys Asa Rice and Joseph Clary. He entered the bar in 1823 and began practicing law in East Aurora, Illinois.

Which **two future politicians** did Fillmore **practice law** with in the 1830s?

Fillmore practiced law in Buffalo with Nathan K. Hall, creating a law firm called Fillmore and Hall in 1834. Hall served as a member of the U.S. House of Representatives for two years in the late 1840s. Fillmore would later name Hall as postmaster general of the United States. Hall left that position in 1852, after Fillmore nominated him to serve as a federal district court judge in New York. He held that position for twenty-four years until his death in 1874.

In 1836, Fillmore and Hall added attorney Solomon G. Haven to the firm, which became known as Fillmore, Hall, and Haven. Solomon G. Haven also became a prominent politician, becoming the mayor of Buffalo in 1846, and later serving three terms in the U.S. House of Representatives.

What **other job** did Fillmore do in the **private sector** while serving as a congressman?

Fillmore worked as an insurance agent for New York Life Insurance Co. and Buffalo Mutual Fire Insurance Company.

POLITICAL OFFICES

What was Fillmore's **first political position**?

Fillmore ran for the New York State Assembly as a member of the Anti-Masonic party. He won his seat and was reelected twice, serving a total of three one-year terms from 1829-31. Fillmore was helped immensely by his friendship with Thurlow Weed, a newspaper publisher influential in New York politics. Weed met Fillmore at an Anti-Masonic party meeting and backed him publicly.

What **law** did **Fillmore help** move through the **New York legislature**?

Fillmore was instrumental in obtaining the passage of a law in New York that forbade the imprisonment of individuals for debts.

When did Fillmore get **elected** to the **U.S. Congress**?

Fillmore became a member of the U.S. House of Representatives in 1833 as a member of the Whig Party and served in the Twentieth-third Congress from 1833 to 1835. He returned to Congress for three more successive terms from 1836 to 1842. By this time, he had moved from the Anti-Mason to the Whig Party.

What **powerful position** did Fillmore hold in **Congress**?

Fillmore served as chairman of the House Ways and Means Committee from 1841 to 1843. The head of this committee has a great deal of power with respect to tax and tariff measures that are introduced in Congress. From this position, Fillmore helped lead the Tariff of 1842 to passage.

Vice President Millard Fillmore (right) shown with 1848 running mate President Zachary Taylor.

What **two political defeats** did Fillmore suffer after not running for reelection to Congress?

Fillmore lost in bids for the vice presidency in 1844 and for New York governor later that year. Fillmore sought the vice presidency for the Whig Party alongside candidate Henry Clay. However, the nomination for vice president went to Theodore Frelinghuysen of New Jersey. Fillmore then ran as the Whig Party candidate for governor, but narrowly lost to Democratic nominee Silas Wright, a former U.S. Senator. After these defeats, Fillmore went back to practicing law.

What was Fillmore's **next political position**?

Fillmore became New York's state comptroller by defeating incumbent Azariah Cutting Flagg. While not sounding very prestigious, it was a powerful position in the state, as the office of comptroller controlled banks, canals, and other key aspects of the state.

Why did the **Whigs select Fillmore** as **vice presidential candidate** in 1848?

Although the Whig Party did not choose Fillmore as its vice presidential candidate in 1844, things changed four years later and Fillmore won the nomination in 1848. Some have speculated that this occurred because Fillmore was from the North, which

A depiction of the U.S. Senate in session during debates that resulted in the Compromise of 1850. Daniel Webster (standing at right) addresses the Senate, presided over by Vice President Millard Fillmore.

provided a good contrast to presidential candidate Zachary Taylor, who was a Southerner from Louisiana.

PRESIDENCY

How did Fillmore **become president**?

Fillmore became president after President Zachary Taylor died in office on July 9, 1850. He took the oath of office on Monday July 10, 1850, from Judge William Cranch, the chief justice of the U.S. Court of Appeals for the District of Columbia.

Who was **his vice president**?

Fillmore did not have a vice president. Fillmore was only the second person—the first being the tenth president, John Tyler—to assume the presidency from the position of the vice presidency.

Who served as his **secretary of state**?

Daniel Webster served as Fillmore's secretary of state, just as he had for former Whig presidents William Henry Harrison and John Tyler. The influential Webster was a lead-

177

ing United States senator earlier in his career and one of the finest lawyers ever to argue before the U.S. Supreme Court.

Who was Fillmore's **attorney general**?

John J. Crittenden, the former governor of Kentucky, served as Fillmore's United States attorney general. Crittenden previously had served in that capacity for Whig president William Henry Harrison. Crittenden later served in Congress in both the House and Senate.

What **famous bill** did Fillmore sign into law?

Fillmore signed into law the Compromise of 1850, a measure designed to reduce tensions between the slave and free states. Introduced and guided by Senator Henry Clay, the measure had many different provisions. Several of them dealt with the increasingly divisive issue of slavery. Under this law, California was admitted as a free state, the territories of New Mexico and Utah would decide for themselves, and the Fugitive Slave Law was enforced. Under this provision, slave owners had the ability to enter nonslave states to retrieve their slaves and claim them as their property.

What **foreign country** did Fillmore try to **open trade** with?

Fillmore sent Commodore Matthew Perry to Japan to open up trade with this closed empire. Japan traded only with the Netherlands among Western countries and Fillmore felt that it would help the United States to have access to this Eastern power. Japan officially opened up trade with the United States under Fillmore's successor, Franklin Pierce.

Who served as the **White House hostess** instead of his wife?

Fillmore's daughter Mary Abigail Fillmore often served as the White House hostess instead of his wife, Abigail, who was more reserved.

Who was his lone **Supreme Court appointee**?

Fillmore nominated Benjamin R. Curtiss to the U.S. Supreme Court in 1851. Curtiss had graduated from Harvard Law School in 1831, having studied under the legendary Justice Joseph Story. He also was a member of the Massachusetts House of Representatives. Curtiss was one of only two dissenters on the Court in the infamous *Dred Scott v. Sandford* (1857) decision in which the majority of the Court sanctioned the practice of slavery. Curtiss resigned his position on the Court later that year, it is thought partly because of dispute over the Dred Scott decision and possibly for pecuniary reasons.

During the Fillmore administration, attempts were made to establish relations with the isolationist country of Japan. Commodore M.C. Perry's crew is shown here coming ashore to meet the Japanese in 1853.

After he resigned from the Court, he resumed his law practice and flourished. He argued several cases before the U.S. Supreme Court and later served as chief counsel for President Andrew Johnson during his impeachment proceedings.

POST PRESIDENCY

Did Fillmore **seek reelection**?

Fillmore could not win reelection even among his own party—the Whigs. The party instead nominated war hero General Winfield Scott, who would lose to Democratic nominee Franklin Pierce. Fillmore suffered the same fate as John Tyler, a Whig vice president who could not gain his party's nomination.

What **personal tragedies** befell Fillmore shortly after leaving office?

Fillmore's wife, Abigail, developed pneumonia after attending the inauguration of her husband's successor, Franklin Pierce. She died less than a month after leaving the White House in March 1953. Then, Fillmore's only daughter, Mary, died at the age of twenty-two in 1854 from cholera. Historians believe that these deaths may have inspired Fillmore to make a return to the national political stage.

179

Fillmore was the first president to create a library in the White House. His wife, Abigail, a lifelong teacher, took the lead in creating a library in the second floor in the Oval Room.

Under what **third party** did Fillmore **attempt** to regain the **presidency**?

In the election of 1856, Fillmore ran as a third-party candidate for the Know-Nothing Party (also known as the American Party). The Know-Nothing Party was known for its anti-immigrant stance and for its positions against what it saw as increasing Catholic influence in American life. Fillmore accepted the nomination, but finished a distant third in the election behind Democrat James Buchanan, the winner, and Republican candidate John C. Frémont. Fillmore did manage to carry one state, Maryland, and its eight electoral votes.

Whom did Fillmore **marry after he left** the White House?

In 1858, Fillmore married wealthy widow Catherine McIntosh, whose first husband was a merchant from Troy, New York. The two remained married until Fillmore's death in 1874.

What were Fillmore's **contributions** to the city of **Buffalo**?

Fillmore made lasting contributions to the city of Buffalo in his post-presidential years. He had become the first chancellor of the University of Buffalo in 1846, and he officially held that position until his death in 1874. He also founded the Buffalo Historical Society in 1862 and served as the group's first president. He founded a hospital in the city and an animal rights group.

When did he **die**?

Fillmore died on March 8, 1874, in Buffalo, New York, from a stroke.

FRANKLIN PIERCE

(1804–1869)
14th President, 1853–1857)
Party Affiliation: Democrat
Chief 1852 Opponent: Winfield Scott (Whig)

EARLY LIFE AND FAMILY

Where and when was Pierce **born**?

Franklin Pierce was born in Hillsborough, New Hampshire, to Benjamin and Anna Kendrick Pierce on November 23, 1804. He remains the only president in history born in New Hampshire.

What did Pierce's **father do** for a living?

Benjamin Pierce was a farmer, military veteran, and a politician. He served in the Revolutionary War, seeing action at the Battle of Bunker Hill, Saratoga, and other conflicts. He won election to the New Hampshire legislature and served as governor of the state.

Did Pierce have any **siblings**?

Yes, Pierce had seven siblings, including four brothers and three sisters. His brothers were Benjamin Kendrick, John Sullivan, Charles Grandison, and Henry Dearborn. His three sisters were Nancy, Harriett, and Charlotte (who died as an infant.)

Portrait of President Franklin Pierce.

Pierce's father had one daughter from a previous marriage, but she died before Franklin Pierce was born.

What was his **early education**?

He attended school at a schoolhouse in Hillsborough. He later enrolled at Hancock Academy in nearby Hancock, New Hampshire, and then at Francestown Academy in Francestown, New Hampshire. He received a fine education that enabled him to gain admission to Bowdoin College.

What **famous college classmates** of Pierce's became literary giants?

At Bowdoin College, Pierce befriended Nathaniel Hawthorne and Henry Wadsworth Longfellow. Pierce and Hawthorne were classmates and Longfellow graduated in the next class. Hawthorne produced novels and short stories, the best known being *The Scarlet Letter*. He also wrote a biography of his friend Pierce entitled *The Life of Franklin Pierce* (1852). Longfellow was a great poet known for such works as "Paul Revere's Ride" and the "Song of Hiawatha."

Who was his **wife**?

Pierce married Jane Means Appleton on November 19, 1834, in Amherst, New Hampshire. Her father, Jesse, was a former president of Bowdoin University, her husband's alma mater.

Did he have any **children**?

Yes, Franklin and Jane Pierce had three boys, all of whom died young. Their first son, Franklin Jr., died a few days after his birth. Their second son, Frank Robert, died at age four. Their third son, Benjamin or "Bennie," died from a freak railway accident before his parent's eyes at age eleven.

EARLY CAREER

What **career**—other than politics—did Pierce **pursue**?

He studied law under various attorneys, including John Burnham in Hillsborough and future U.S. Supreme Court Justice Levi Woodbury in Portsmouth, New Hampshire. Part of his legal education took place at the law school in Northampton, Massachusetts. He was admitted to the bar in September 1827, and opened a law practice.

What **other job** did Pierce have as he studied law?

Pierce worked as the postmaster of Hillsborough beginning in 1824. His father Benjamin had held the position before him.

POLITICAL OFFICES

When did he become a **state legislator**?

He won election to the New Hampshire legislature in 1829 when he was only twenty-four years old. He served four terms in the state legislature, including a stint as speaker from 1831 to 1832. He left the state legislature to become a member of the U.S. House of Representatives in 1833.

How **long** did he serve in the **U.S. House of Representatives**?

Pierce served from 1833 to 1837 in the U.S. House of Representatives, supporting the policies of President Andrew Jackson and the Democratic-Republican party. During this time, he befriended two fellow representatives: James K. Polk, the Speaker of the House and future president, and Jefferson Davis, his future secretary of war and later the president of the Confederacy.

Why did Pierce **leave the House**?

Pierce left the House after he moved up the ranks again and was elected to the U.S. Senate. He was only thirty-two years old when he became a U.S. senator, the youngest in the body at that time. He continued to support of the policies of his party and the administration of President Martin Van Buren. He served in the Senate until 1842.

Why did he **leave the Senate**?

Pierce left the Senate in 1842 for several reasons, including the fact that the Whig party began to take control of Congress. He also wanted to make more money and to please his wife, who was unhappy with the political life.

Between leaving the Senate and his eventual presidency, **what did Pierce do**?

He practiced law and continued to participate in party activities. He worked as chairman of the Democratic Party in New Hampshire and campaigned actively for James K. Polk. As a result, when Polk became president he appointed Pierce as U.S. district attorney in New Hampshire. Polk served in that position from 1845 to 1847.

> ### What events during his military career were later seized by his opponents during the campaign?
>
> Pierce fell off his horse twice and fainted while leading his forces at the Battle of Contreras and later at Churubusco. Allegedly, comments by a fellow officer led to accusations that Pierce was a coward. Actually, Pierce showed bravery by wishing to fight alongside his men and even pleading with General Scott to let him lead his brigade rather than rest behind the lines.

What prestigious **political position** offered by President Polk did Pierce **decline**?

Polk offered Pierce the position of U.S. attorney general when his previous attorney general, Nathan Clifford (a future U.S. Supreme Court Justice) became U.S. envoy to Mexico. Pierce declined the position and instead offered himself for service in the Mexican–American War.

What was Pierce's **military experience**?

Pierce volunteered in Concord, New Hampshire. His political connections led to his commission as a colonel and later a promotion to brigadier general. He followed in his father's footsteps by leading men into battle. Ironically, he served under General Winfield Scott—his future presidential opponent.

PRESIDENCY

Why was Pierce a **dark horse candidate** for president in 1852?

At the Democratic Convention in 1852, Pierce was not considered a contender for the party's nomination. The four leading candidates were: Lewis Cass of Michigan, who had lost to Zachary Taylor in 1848; James Buchanan of Pennsylvania, who had been Polk's secretary of state (and who would succeed Pierce as president); Stephen Douglas of Illinois (later best known for running against Abraham Lincoln); and William L. Marcy (who would become Pierce's secretary of state).

Cass led on the early ballots and later Buchanan led, but no candidate could acquire the necessary majority. Pierce was first proposed on the thirty-fifth ballot as a compromise candidate. He gradually gained support and became the nominee on the forty-ninth ballot.

Who was Pierce's **opponent** in the presidential **election**?

Pierce's opponent was Mexican–American War hero Winfield Scott, who had served in a leading capacity in the United States Army for many years. Known as "Old Fuss and Feathers," Scott presented a formidable challenge and contrast to Pierce, particularly given the charges made against Pierce about his fainting spells while in battle. However, the Whig Party was divided on the slavery question and that appeared to hurt Scott's chances. Scott's antislavery position cost him votes with many Southern Whigs. Pierce ended up winning in an electoral vote landslide 254 to 42.

Who was Pierce's **vice president**?

Pierce's running mate was William Rufus King of Alabama, a former U.S. senator. King died after only forty-five days in office and no replacement was named.

What was most **unusual about Pierce's cabinet** aside from the vice presidency?

Pierce is the only president who had the rest of his cabinet serve the entire term. There were no resignations, dismissals, retirements or deaths among the members: Secretary of State William L. Marcy, Secretary of the Treasury James Guthrie, Secretary of War Jefferson Davis, Attorney General Caleb Cushing, Secretary of the Navy James C. Dobbin, Postmaster General James Campbell, and Secretary of the Interior Robert McClelland.

What **land purchase** did Pierce's administration oversee that increased U.S. land in the southwest?

The Gadsden Purchase, named after U.S. minister to Mexico, James Gadsden, added the southern edge of Arizona and parts of New Mexico to the United States. The U.S. purchased the land from Mexico pursuant to a treaty signed by President Pierce on June 24, 1853.

What **major piece of legislation** dealing with the **slavery** question was signed into law by President Pierce?

Pierce signed into law the Kansas-Nebraska Act of 1854, which allowed settlers in those two territories to decide for themselves whether to outlaw slavery. Many in the

Considerable violence broke out after President Pierce signed the Kansas-Nebraska Act of 1854. In this political cartoon, the Democrats are blamed for the chaos that ensued.

North opposed this law because it led to the spread of slavery. Sponsored by Senator Stephen Douglas, the bill was designed to further progress on an intercontinental railroad, but devolved into a bitter dispute about the intractable slavery question. Opposition to the bill led to the creation of what became known as the Republican Party.

President Pierce believed that the states and territories had the right to decide for themselves whether or not to allow slavery. Because he was a Northerner who did not oppose slavery, he was sometimes pejoratively referred to as a "doughface."

What **manifesto** revealed the administration's possible **plans to annex Cuba**?

The Ostend Manifesto was a document drafted by former U.S. Senator Pierre Soule which outlined the United States' plans to acquire Cuba from Spain. It also revealed that the United States might use military force against Spain if more diplomatic efforts failed. Someone leaked the contents of the manifesto to the press, which published the document. This caused President Pierce and his secretary of state William Marcy to back away from the Ostend Manifesto.

Who was President Pierce's lone **Supreme Court appointee**?

Pierce appointed Alabama lawyer and politician John A. Campbell, considered one of the finest advocates of his day. Originally from Georgia, Campbell graduated college at age fourteen and became a lawyer at the age of eighteen. Pierce nominated Campbell for a seat on the Supreme Court on the advice of several sitting justices.

Though he personally disfavored secession, Campbell resigned from the Court in 1861 after his home state of Alabama seceded from the Union. He joined the Confederate government as assistant secretary of war. He was in charge of enlisting men to fight in the war. After the war, Campbell was imprisoned for four months in Fort Pulaski, Georgia. President Andrew Johnson ordered his release, but Campbell was destitute upon his release. Campbell traveled to New Orleans and rebounded by establishing a very successful law practice. He argued a number of times before the U.S. Supreme Court, in such well known cases as the *Slaughterhouse Cases* (1873) and *Ketchum v. Duncan* (1877).

POST PRESIDENCY

Did Pierce **seek reelection**?

Yes, Pierce sought to run again for president but he could not win the nomination for the election of 1856. The three main contenders were Pierce, James Buchanan, and Stephen Douglas. Buchanan and Douglas were leading contenders for the nomination in 1852, when Pierce emerged as the dark horse candidate who won the nomination. This time, Buchanan emerged as the front-runner and eventually captured the nomination—and later the presidency. Pierce never again ran for the presidency, though supporters urged him to run in 1860 and 1864.

Did Pierce hold any **political office after leaving** the presidency?

No, Pierce returned to Concord, New Hampshire, with his wife, Jane. They traveled overseas but Jane could not shake her bouts with depression, which increased after the tragic death of their third son, "Bennie." She died in 1863. Pierce died several years later in October 1869.

Why was Pierce **unpopular** in his post-presidency days?

Many perceived that Pierce sympathized with the South, as he spoke out against northern attempts to curb slavery in the South. While he supported the North during the war, he maintained a friendly correspondence with his former secretary of war, Jefferson Davis.

What **law school** is **named after** the former president?

Franklin Pierce Law Center in Concord, New Hampshire, is named after the former president. Founded in 1973, this private school is slated to merge with the University of New Hampshire. An undergraduate institution, Franklin Pierce University was founded in 1962 in Rindge, New Hampshire.

When did Pierce **die**?

Pierce died on October 8, 1869, in Concord, New Hampshire, from dropsy (edema) at the age of 64.

JAMES BUCHANAN

(1791–1868)
15th President, 1857–1861
Party Affiliation: Democrat
Chief 1856 Opponents: John C. Frémont (Republican), Millard Fillmore (Know-Nothing)

EARLY LIFE AND FAMILY

Where and when was Buchanan **born**?

James Buchanan Jr. was born in Cove Gap, Pennsylvania, to James Buchanan Sr. and Elizabeth Speer Buchanan on April 23, 1791.

What was his **father's occupation**?

Buchanan's father, James Buchanan Sr., emigrated from Ireland. He worked as a store owner and a justice of the peace. He also dabbled in real estate and became a wealthy merchant.

Did James Buchanan have any **siblings**?

Yes, Buchanan had ten siblings—four brothers and six sisters. Their names were John, William Speer, George Washington, Edward, Mary, Elizabeth Jane, Maria, Sarah, Elizabeth, and Harriet.

Official portrait of President James Buchanan.

Was Buchanan homosexual?

He may have been. Some historians have pointed out that Buchanan lived for more than twenty years with William Rufus King, who later served a short time as Franklin Pierce's vice president. Some referred to Buchanan and King as "Siamese twins" and Andrew Jackson referred to King as "Miss Nancy." Another politician once referred to King as "Mrs. B." However, there is no conclusive proof as to Buchanan's sexual orientation.

What was his **early education**?

Buchanan studied at Old Stone Academy in Mercersburg, Pennsylvania. He then attended Dickinson College Carlisle, Pennsylvania. He graduated college in only two years, though he was briefly expelled from college for allegedly participating in drunken, disorderly behavior.

Did he ever **marry**?

No, Buchanan is the only president in U.S. history to never marry. He was engaged to Anne Coleman, who was the daughter of a millionaire who owned a prosperous iron mine. The engagement broke off in 1819 and a short time later Coleman died. Some have speculated that she killed herself.

What **other tragedy** befell Buchanan shortly after Coleman's death?

Buchanan's father, James Buchanan Sr., died in a carriage accident in 1821, only two years after Coleman's death.

EARLY CAREER

What did Buchanan do when the U.S. became embroiled in the **War of 1812**?

Though he opposed the war, Buchanan volunteered to serve his country under Judge Henry Shippen. He marched with his unit to Baltimore to serve under Major Charles S. Ridgely of the Third Cavalry.

What did Buchanan do **after graduating** from college?

After graduation, Buchanan studied law under attorney James Hopkins in Lancaster, Pennsylvania. Hopkins was considered the best lawyer in Lancaster. Buchanan studied under Hopkins for two year and a half years. In 1813, Buchanan received admission to the Pennsylvania bar.

How was Buchanan as a **lawyer**?

Buchanan was a highly respected lawyer who built an impressive practice in Lancaster. He handled estates, family law cases, and property claims. He also defended several prominent politicians in legal matters. For example, he successfully defended Judge Walter Franklin in an impeachment proceeding before the Pennsylvania state Senate. Jean H. Baker in her biography *James Buchanan* in the American Presidents Series writes that he became "one of the best known lawyers in southern Pennsylvania."

Given his impressive career as a lawyer with political connections, did Buchanan ever **aspire** to be a **U.S. Supreme Court justice**?

Yes, when Buchanan was serving as President James K. Polk's secretary of state, he asked Polk if he could be nominated to the U.S. Supreme Court. Earlier, President John Tyler had offered Buchanan a seat on the high court, but Buchanan declined. From 1843 to 1845, there were several openings on the Supreme Court, as Justices Smith Thompson and Gabriel Duvall had died and esteemed Justice Joseph Story had retired. Buchanan asked Polk for a seat on the Court but then withdrew the request, fearing that he might not be confirmed. Then, he changed his mind once again, and decided to ask Polk for the appointment. Polk declined his request and Buchanan remained as secretary of state.

What **other legal-political position** did Buchanan decline?

President Martin Van Buren offered Buchanan the position of U.S. attorney general in 1838, but Buchanan declined.

POLITICAL OFFICES

What was Buchanan's **first elected office**?

Buchanan won election in October 1814 to the Pennsylvania House of Representatives as a member of the Federalist Party. He served two terms in the state House before losing in an attempt for a seat in the U.S. House of Representatives.

When did Buchanan become a **member** of the **U.S. House of Representatives**?

Buchanan won a seat in the U.S. House of Representatives in October 1820. His term began in 1821 and he stayed in that position for several terms until deciding not to seek reelection in 1830. During his tenure in the House, he chaired the House Judiciary Committee beginning in 1829. It was also during his tenure in the House that Buchanan's Federalist Party dissolved and he became a Democratic-Republican.

Who appointed him as **minister to Russia**?

President Andrew Jackson, whom Buchanan supported during his days in the House, appointed Buchanan as minister to Russia in 1831.

What was Buchanan's **next political position**?

After serving as minister to Russia, Buchanan was elected to the United States Senate in 1834 as a member of the Democratic Party, winning over Joel B. Sutherland, James Clarke, and Amos Ellmaker. He served three terms in the Senate, winning reelection in 1837 and 1843. In 1837, he served as chairman of the Senate's Foreign Relations Committee.

For whom did Buchanan serve as **secretary of state**?

Buchanan made his first run for president in the election of 1844 but he did not obtain the nomination of the Democratic Party; it fell instead to dark horse candidate James K. Polk. Buchanan did become Polk's secretary of state. But it was a tough position for Buchanan, as Polk would carry out the responsibilities of the job when he and Buchanan disagreed openly on political matters, something that happened quite often.

When did Buchanan **originally retire** from politics?

Buchanan retired from politics after serving as secretary of state. He had sought the Democratic Presidential nomination again in 1848, when the nod went to Lewis Cass of Michigan. After Cass lost the presidential election to Whig candidate Zachary Taylor, Buchanan left Washington, D.C. and returned to his home in Lancaster. He purchased a large estate called Wheatland and reared his niece Harriet Lane, the orphaned daughter of his sister.

When did Buchanan **return to politics**?

Buchanan returned to politics and once again sought the Democratic nomination in the election of 1852. He lost out once again, this time to Franklin Pierce, who went on to win the presidency. Pierce appointed Buchanan as minister to Great Britain. As minister to Great Britain, Buchanan had a role with U.S. minister to Spain, Pierre Soule, in drafting the Ostend Manifesto, which justified the U.S. annexation of Cuba.

195

PRESIDENCY

Whom did **Buchanan defeat** to win the **Democratic Party nomination** in 1856?

Buchanan entered the Democratic convention as a leading contender for the nomination, but he faced serious contenders in U.S. Senator Stephen Douglas, the Democratic Party candidate in 1848 Lewis Cass, and presidential incumbent Franklin Pierce. Buchanan captured the nomination.

Whom did he **defeat** in the **general election?**

Buchanan defeated John C. Frémont of the newly formed Republican Party and the third-party candidate former President Millard Fillmore, who ran under the banner of the Know Nothing Party. Frémont was known as the "Pathfinder of the West" for his explorations in the western United States and for his exceptional military career. A former U.S. senator from California, Frémont had the support of many abolitionists but the abolitionist stance of the Republican Party was not well received in the South and other parts of the country. Buchanan captured 174 electoral votes, Frémont 114, and Fillmore 8.

Who was Buchanan's **vice president?**

John C. Breckenridge of Kentucky served as Buchanan's vice president. He was a member of the U.S. House of Representatives and became the vice president at the age of thirty-six. He remains the youngest person in American history to serve as vice president. He later served in the administration of the Confederate government. He ran for the presidency in the election of 1860 as a southern Democrat, but lost to Republican Abraham Lincoln.

What other **former presidential candidate** served in Buchanan's **cabinet?**

Lewis Cass, the Democratic candidate for president in the election of 1848, served as Buchanan's first secretary of state from 1857 until 1860. Cass resigned from the office after Buchanan refused to heed his advice on protecting federal interests in the South. Cass realized that Southern forces were close to moving on federal property and close to secession. Buchanan probably realized it too but chose to be more conciliatory toward Southern states. Jeremiah S. Black replaced Cass as Buchanan's secretary of state.

What **family members lived with Buchanan** during his **White House** years?

Buchanan's niece Harriet Lane—the daughter of Buchanan's sister Jane—served as the White House hostess during President Buchanan's tenure in office. Harriet's mother and father had died by the time she was eleven years old. James Buchanan became her guardian and took care of her.

Buchanan also took care of his nephew James Buchanan Henry, the son of Harriet Buchanan and James Henry. When his parents died, James Buchanan also became young James's guardian. Buchanan educated his nephew, including paying his way to Princeton University. James Buchanan Henry served as secretary to the president for his uncle and later became an assistant U.S. attorney in New York.

The U.S. Supreme Court ruled against Dred Scott's claim to freedom in the 1857 case *Dred Scott v. Sanford,* a ruling President Buchanan supported.

What **controversial Supreme Court decision** occurred during Buchanan's presidency?

In 1857, the U.S. Supreme Court issued its decision in *Dred Scott v. Sanford,* which ruled that slaves were not citizens and that Dred Scott could not be considered a free man, even though he had left slavery and moved to a free state. Buchanan allegedly corresponded with Supreme Court justices before the decision was rendered early in his tenure as president. Buchanan contacted Supreme Court Justice John Catron, asking whether the decision would be decided before his inauguration. He allegedly pressured Justice Robert Grier—a fellow Pennsylvanian—to vote with the majority against Dred Scott.

What **economic problem** surfaced during the Buchanan administration?

The Panic of 1857 that began before Buchanan assumed office plagued him and the American economy throughout his tenure. The panic began in part after the collapse of the New York branch of the Ohio Life Insurance Company, a major force in the American economy. Thousands of American businesses and numerous banks collapsed during this economic depression. The country did not recover until after the U.S. Civil War.

Which **states seceded** from the Union **before Buchanan left office**?

A few weeks after Abraham Lincoln was elected—but while Buchanan was still in office—South Carolina seceded from the Union on December 20, 1860. Mississippi, Florida, Alabama, Georgia, and Louisiana seceded from the Union in January 1861. Texas seceded on February 1, 1861. The four other states that seceded—Virginia, Arkansas, North Carolina, and Tennessee—did so after Lincoln was sworn into office.

197

Buchanan was blamed for failing to act effectively in preventing war. Upon his death in 1868, an obituary in the *New York Times* read: "he met the crisis of secession in a timid and vacillating spirit, temporizing with both parties, and studiously avoiding the adoption of a decided policy."

Who was Buchanan's lone U.S. **Supreme Court appointee**?

In 1858, Buchanan nominated Nathan Clifford, a politician from Maine who had served in the U.S. House of Representatives and had served as President James K. Polk's attorney general. Clifford, who supported the right of states to decide for themselves the slavery question, was narrowly confirmed in the Senate by a 26 to 23 vote. Clifford served on the Court until his death in 1881.

POST PRESIDENCY

Did Buchanan **seek reelection**?

No, Buchanan did not seek reelection. He allegedly told his successor, Abraham Lincoln: "My dear sir, if you are as happy on entering the White House as I on leaving, you are a very happy man indeed."

What **book** did **Buchanan write** during his retirement?

Buchanan wrote *Mr. Buchanan's Administration on the Eve of the Rebellion* in 1866. The three-hundred-page book outlined the growing dispute between Northern and Southern states over the intractable problem of slavery. He explained that few too many leaders were willing to find a compromise to slavery and economic issues between the different regions of the country. He blamed the Republican party and anti-abolitionist agitation for the secession and subsequent Civil War.

When did he **die**?

Buchanan died at Wheatland (his estate) at the age of seventy-seven from pneumonia on June 1, 1868.

ABRAHAM LINCOLN

(1809–1865)
16th President, 1861–1865
Party Affiliation: Republican
Chief 1860 Opponents: John C. Breckenridge (National Democrat),
Stephen A. Douglas (Democrat), and John C. Bell (Constitutional Union)
Chief 1864 Opponent: George B. McClellan (Democrat)

EARLY LIFE AND FAMILY

Where and when was Lincoln **born**?

Lincoln was born near Hodgeville, Kentucky, in Hardin County to Thomas and Nancy Hanks Lincoln on February 12, 1809.

What **tragedy** befell Lincoln when he was young?

Lincoln's mother, Nancy, died when young Abe was only nine years old. Nancy Hanks Lincoln was only thirty-four years of age at her death. Thomas Lincoln then married Sarah Bush Johnston, who was a good stepmother to the youngster.

Did he have any **siblings**?

Yes, Lincoln had an older sister named Sarah Grigsby, who died giving birth at age twenty-one. He had a younger brother named Thomas, who died in infancy. When his father married Sarah Bush Johnston, they had three children named John, Matilda, and Sarah.

Photographic portrait of President Abraham Lincoln by Anthony Berger.

> ## After whom was Lincoln named?
>
> Lincoln was named after his paternal grandfather, Abraham Lincoln, who fought in the Virginia militia during the Revolutionary War.

What did Lincoln's **father do** for a living?

Lincoln's father, Thomas, worked as a carpenter and a farmer. The Lincoln family was not wealthy and lived in a log cabin home.

Where did the family **live during Lincoln's youth**?

They lived in the log cabin near Hodgeville, where Abraham was born. They later moved to another farm near Knob Creek in the same county. In 1816, the family moved across the Ohio River to Spencer County, Indiana. In 1830, the family moved to Macon County, Illinois.

Did Lincoln have a **good relationship** with his **parents**?

Lincoln had a good relationship with his mother before she died. He also adored his stepmother, referring to her as his best friend. She understood his love of reading and helped him acquire materials to read. However, Lincoln had a poor relationship with his father, Thomas. His father believed that Abraham was lazy with his chores and could not understand why his son preferred to read rather than work splitting logs or other farm work. Some have said that his father even physically abused him. It is telling that when his father died, Abraham Lincoln did not attend the funeral.

Who was Lincoln's **first love**?

As a young man in New Salem, Lincoln was attracted to Ann Rutledge, the daughter of local leader James Rutledge. She died of typhoid fever in 1835, a death that severely depressed Lincoln.

Who was Lincoln's **wife**?

At age thirty-three, Lincoln married twenty-three-year-old Mary Todd on November 4, 1842. She would battle depression for much of her adult life, but Lincoln remained a devoted husband to her.

Did he have any **children**?

Yes, Lincoln and Mary had four sons: Robert Todd, Edward, William, and Thomas. Edward died at age three, William at age eleven, and Thomas at age eighteen. Only

203

> ## What sport did Lincoln excel at as a young man?
>
> **A**pparently, Lincoln was very strong and was adept at wrestling. He engaged in a celebrated wrestling match with Jack Armstrong in New Salem that further endeared him to the town.

Robert Todd, the oldest son, lived a full life. He later served as secretary of war to James Garfield and Chester A. Arthur. He also worked as U.S. ambassador to Great Britain under President Benjamin Harrison.

What was Abraham Lincoln's **early education**?

Growing up on the frontier, Lincoln had very little formal education. He later said that he had one year of formal schooling. He did, however, learn from some good teachers—Zacariah Riley and Caleb Hazel.

EARLY CAREER

What were Lincoln's **first jobs**?

Lincoln worked as a ferryboat pilot and a rail-splitter in his youth. He would take passengers along the Ohio River for his boss James Taylor. He also earned the nickname "Rail-splitter" for his effectiveness in splitting logs. Later, Lincoln worked as a store clerk in New Salem, Illinois, for owner Dennis Offutt. He enjoyed the work at the store and was very popular among the customers. He also worked for a time as a blacksmith.

When he moved to New Salem, Illinois, as a young adult, Lincoln worked several jobs. He opened a general store with William Berry, but the store failed. He also landed a job as the postmaster of New Salem—a job he enjoyed. He was also the deputy county surveyor. These two jobs earned him enough money to start his political career.

What was Lincoln's **military service**?

Lincoln volunteered to fight in the Black Hawk War. Though elected captain of his local regiment, Lincoln and his troops never saw any combat action.

What **other career**—other than politics—would Lincoln engage in through much of young adult life?

Lincoln read law books supplied by Bowling Green, the justice of the peace in New Salem, Illinois. He traveled to hear celebrated defense attorney John A. Brackenridge defend a person convicted of murder. Lincoln studied law diligently and eventually was admitted to the Illinois bar in 1836.

In 1837, he moved to Springfield and practiced law for several years with John Stuart. He then practiced law with Stephen T. Logan, a former judge. Lincoln left practicing with Logan in 1844 to enter a law partnership with William Herndon, who once had clerked for Lincoln.

POLITICAL OFFICES

Did Lincoln win his **first political race**?

No, Lincoln lost in his first attempt at political office, losing a race for a seat in the Illinois House of Representatives in 1832. He finished eighth in the race.

When did he **first win a race**?

Lincoln won his first political race in 1834 as a Whig candidate running for the Illinois legislature. He served three more terms. He roomed with Springfield lawyer John T. Stuart, who further encouraged Lincoln's study of the law. In 1836, he became chairman of the finance committee and advocated for a series of measures that improved the state's railroad and canal systems.

When did Lincoln **become** a **U.S. congressman**?

Lincoln lost his first race for U.S. Congress to John J. Hardin—who was also an attorney—in 1842. Hardin was a cousin to Lincoln's wife, Mary. In 1846, however, Lincoln won a seat in the U.S. House of Representatives by defeating Peter Cartwright. In the House, he attracted attention for voicing his opposition to President Polk and the Mexican–American War. He introduced the "Spot Resolutions," which demanded that President Polk document the exact location (or spot) where blood was spilled on American soil. Polk had argued that such violence on American soil justified the Mexican–American War.

What **positions** did Lincoln **decline**?

Lincoln actively supported the Whig presidential campaign of Zachary Taylor, who became the country's twelfth president. Taylor offered Lincoln the position of governor of the Oregon territory, but Lincoln declined that appointment. Instead, Lincoln had wanted the job of commissioner of the General Land Office, but Taylor declined to appoint him. Lincoln therefore retired from politics and resumed his legal career.

After resuming a law career, how did his **legal career fare**?

Lincoln's legal career boomed. He handled admiralty, criminal, and patent law cases, while also representing several railroad companies in the Midwest. He sometimes sat as a special judge or prosecutor for local courts. He even handled cases that went before the U.S. Supreme Court. For example, he and Herndon successfully represented a railroad company in a damages action brought by a displaced property owner in *The Alton and Sangamon Railroad Company v. Carpenter* (1852).

Did Lincoln ever become a **U.S. senator**?

No, Lincoln lost in his bids for a seat to the U.S. Senate. In 1855, he lost to Lyman Trumbull. In the midst of running for the Senate, Lincoln switched from the Whig Party to the Republican Party, which opposed slavery. Lincoln blasted the Kansas-Nebraska Act, introduced by Democratic Senator Stephen Douglas—legislation that repealed the Missouri Compromise and eventually propelled the country into civil war.

As a Republican, Lincoln again challenged popular incumbent Stephen Douglas for a seat in the Senate. Lincoln and Douglas carried on a series of memorable debates during the campaign, appropriately called the Lincoln–Douglas debates. Quoting from a verse in the Bible (Mark 3:25), Lincoln said at one debate: "A house divided against itself cannot stand," referring to the increasing sectional conflicts in the country. The two politicians engaged in seven debates. One of the key issues concerned the question of slavery and its extension into territories and new states. Douglas defeated Lincoln in a close election. While Lincoln had strong popular support, the Democratic-controlled state legislature gave the nod to Douglas by a fifty-four to forty-six vote.

PRESIDENCY

Who was the **original front-runner** for the **Republican ticket** in the **1860 presidential election**?

William H. Seward—who would later serve as Lincoln's secretary of state—was the front-runner. Seward edged Lincoln by more than seventy votes on the first ballot. But Lincoln gradually gained support and captured the nomination.

Who were **Lincoln's opponents** in the 1860 election?

His opponents were his familiar nemesis Stephen A. Douglas of the Democratic Party, John C. Breckenridge from the Southern Democratic Party or the National Democratic Party, and John C. Bell of the Constitutional Union Party. Lincoln captured 180 electoral votes, Breckenridge obtained 72, Bell garnered 39, and Douglas (who was second in the popular vote) managed only 12 electoral votes.

Why did Lincoln change vice presidents for his second term?

Lincoln approved of Andrew Johnson as his vice president for his second term. It was an unusual choice given that Johnson was a Democrat from Tennessee and, therefore, belonged to a different political party from his president. However, Johnson was a so-called "War Democrat" who showed loyalty to the Union. Lincoln and others realized that rather than running with his current vice president, Hannibal Hamlin, who was from Maine, Lincoln would gain more political support by choosing a Southerner like Johnson.

Who was Lincoln's **vice president** for his first term?

Hannibal Hamlin, a Maine lawyer and politician, was Lincoln's vice president during his first term. Hamlin entered politics as a Democrat, but switched his allegiance to the Republican Party because of the slavery issue. He was a staunch abolitionist. Some opponents even suggested that Hamlin was part black. Lincoln dropped Hamlin in favor of Andrew Johnson as his vice president running mate for the election of 1864.

What **member** of Lincoln's **cabinet** later became a **Supreme Court Justice**?

Lincoln's secretary of the treasury was Salmon P. Chase, a man who had challenged Lincoln for the 1860 Republican nomination for the presidency. Chase served several years as Lincoln's secretary of the treasury before resigning in June 1864. Lincoln later nominated him to serve on the U.S. Supreme Court, where he served until his death in 1873. Chase, a former member of the Free Soil Party, was an ardent abolitionist.

Who was Lincoln's **secretary of state**?

William Seward served as Lincoln's secretary of state. Originally a political rival in the Republican nomination in 1860, Steward later became a loyal and staunch ally of Lincoln's. He later served as secretary of state for President Andrew Johnson and engineered the purchase of Alaska, a move originally criticized as "Seward's Folly."

What **measures** did Lincoln take that **arguably violated constitutional liberties**?

Lincoln believed that the Union must be preserved above all else. To that end, he justified certain measures as necessary during a time of war. For example, he suspended the writ of habeas corpus—a guarantee in the Constitution that essentially ensures that the government will not detain a person without legal justification.

Lincoln suspended the writ and had federal officers arrest numerous political leaders in the state of Maryland whom he suspected of leading the state into secession. He had thousands of Southerners arrested and tried in military courts without the normal panoply of constitutional protections. He even ordered the censorship of certain newspapers critical of the Union war effort.

When did the **Civil War begin**?

The Civil War began just more than a month after Lincoln's inaugural address in March 1861. On April 12, 1861, Confederate forces fired upon Fort Sumter in South Carolina. Lincoln called for an army to reclaim federal property and tensions escalated, with additional states seceding. The Civil War lasted until April 9, 1865, when leading Confederate general Robert E. Lee surrendered to Union general Ulysses S. Grant. Less than a week later, President Lincoln was assassinated.

Whom did Lincoln defeat for **reelection in 1864**?

Lincoln's opponent in the 1864 election was Democrat George B. McClellan, Lincoln's former head general in the Civil War. Lincoln had fired McClellan as the head general of the Union army and replaced him with General Ambrose Burnside. Lincoln's 1864 campaign slogan was "don't swap horses in the middle of the stream." He trounced McClellan, winning 212 electoral votes to McClellan's 21.

President Lincoln meets with General George B. McClellan at the Antietam battlefield during the Civil War. McClellan later ran against Lincoln in the 1864 presidential election.

Who were Lincoln's **chief generals** during the Civil War?

Initially, Lincoln's chief Union general was George B. McClellan. However, in 1862 Lincoln replaced McClellan with Ambrose Burnside. Later, Lincoln replaced Burnside with Joseph Hooker, who lasted less than six months as head commander. Lincoln then turned to George Meade, but Lincoln felt he was not aggressive enough in the war effort. Finally, Lincoln named future eighteenth president Ulysses S. Grant as his supreme commander. Lincoln rejected a proposal to replace Grant, saying: "I can't spare this man. He fights."

What was the **Emancipation Proclamation**?

The Emancipation Proclamation refers to an executive order issued by President Lincoln in September 1862, announcing his intention to free the slaves from states that had seceded from the Union. It also refers to the official January 1863 order that listed several states in which the proclamation applied. Lincoln waited to issue the Proclamation until the Union army made a strong showing in battle. After the Union army performed well at the bloody Battle of Antietam, Lincoln made the pronouncement. One effect of the ruling was that it allowed African Americans to join the Union army. In the words of George McGovern in his biography of Lincoln, it also represented "the beginning of the end of slavery in the United States" and "changed the whole nature of the war." This act earned Lincoln the nickname "The Great Emancipator."

An 1888 reproduction of the text of Lincoln's "Emancipation Proclamation."

What was the **Gettysburg Address**?

The Gettysburg Address was a speech given by President Lincoln on November 19, 1863, at the dedication at the Soldiers' National Cemetery in Gettysburg, Pennsylvania, the site of an important Union Civil War victory several months earlier. Lincoln talked about the meaning of the war as a human struggle for equality. The address begins with familiar words to Americans: "Four score and seven years ago our fathers brought forth on this continent a new nation, conceived in liberty, and dedicated to the proposition that all men are created equal." It is considered one of the greatest speeches in world history.

What **acts** were passed during Lincoln's tenure that provided a **boon for railways**?

Congress passed and Lincoln signed the Pacific Railway Acts of 1862 and 1864. These acts provided federal assistance to the Union Pacific and Central Pacific Railroads to build a transcontinental railroad from Missouri to the Pacific Ocean.

The box at Ford's Theater where Lincoln was assassinated by John Wilkes Booth.

What law signed by Lincoln **helped small farmers** obtain more land?

Lincoln signed into law the Homestead Act of 1862, which provided a mechanism by which farmers could apply for federal land grants in the Midwest. Under this law, a farmer could gain title to up to 160 acres in the western United States if he and his family lived and worked on the land for a period of five years. The law greatly encouraged westward movement in the United States.

Who was President **Lincoln's assassin**?

John Wilkes Booth assassinated President Lincoln at Ford's Theatre in Washington, D.C., on April 14, 1865. Booth was a popular actor who toured the country. He also was a Confederate sympathizer who had a deep hatred of President Lincoln. He and his associates plotted to kill President Lincoln, Secretary of State William Seward, and Vice President Andrew Johnson. They hoped to throw the federal government into disarray. Only Booth succeeded in killing his target. As an actor who knew John Ford, the owner of the theatre, Booth got access to various parts of the building. Booth shot Lincoln in the back of the head while he sat in the presidential box at the theatre. Then Booth leaped from the box onto the stage. Federal authorities later shot and killed Booth on April 26 in a barn outside of Washington.

One of Booth's co-conspirators, Lewis Powell, was assigned to kill Secretary of State William Seward. Powell went to Seward's home, knocked the secretary's son Frederick to the floor, and attacked Seward while he was sleeping. He managed to stab Seward several times, but the secretary of state recovered. Later, Powell was apprehended, and he was executed in July 1865.

Who were Lincoln's **Supreme Court appointees**?

Lincoln nominated five justices to the U.S. Supreme Court: Noah Swayne, Samuel Miller, David Davis, Stephen Field, and Salmon P. Chase. Swayne was a former United States attorney in Ohio and a distinguished lawyer. Miller served on the Court for more than twenty-seven years and wrote more opinions than any other justice of his era. Davis had served as Lincoln's campaign manager for his 1860 presidential campaign. Field ended up serving more than thirty-four years on the U.S. Supreme Court and remains the second longest serving Justice in Supreme Court history. Lincoln nominated Chase for the position of Chief Justice, replacing Chief Justice Roger B. Taney.

POST PRESIDENCY

On what **currency** is President **Lincoln's image**?

President Lincoln's visage appears on the $5 bill and the penny. It wasn't until the early twentieth century that Lincoln appeared on the $5 bill, but he has appeared on the penny since 1909.

When was the **Lincoln Memorial** built?

The Lincoln memorial, still a popular tourist attraction in Washington, D.C., was dedicated in 1922. Located on the National Mall, it remains one of the country's favorite pieces of architecture.

What **rooms** in the **White House** are **named after Lincoln**?

The Lincoln Sitting Room and the Lincoln Bedroom are both named after President Lincoln. Located on the second floor, the sitting room is relatively small room, while the bedroom is a guest suite used by distinguished visitors of the president to the White House.

What **universities and colleges** are **named after President Lincoln**?

Lincoln College (originally Lincoln University), located in Lincoln, Illinois, was formed in 1865 and named after the president while he was still alive. Other schools named after the former president include: Lincoln Center Institute, Lincoln Land Community College, Lincoln Law School of Sacramento, Lincoln Law School of San Jose, Lincoln Memorial University, Lincoln School, Lincoln University in California, Lincoln University in Missouri, and Lincoln University in Pennsylvania.

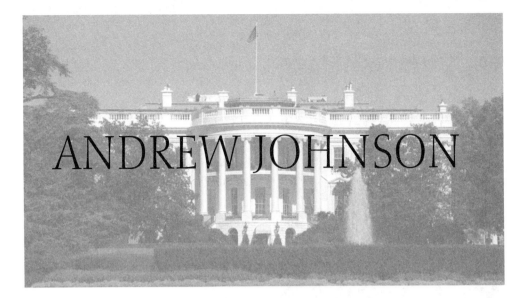

ANDREW JOHNSON

(1808–1875)
17th President, 1865–1869
Party Affiliation: Democrat/National Union
Chief Opponents: None.

EARLY LIFE AND FAMILY

Where and when was Johnson **born**?

Johnson was born in Raleigh, North Carolina, to Jacob Johnson and Mary McDonough Johnson on December 12, 1809.

What did his **parents do** for a living?

Jacob Johnson worked as a host at a local inn named Casso's, but died when Andrew was only three years old. He passed away a month after carrying out a heroic rescue. He fell ill from complications after diving into an ice cold pond to save two men, including the editor of the *Raleigh Star*. Andrew Johnson's mother, Mary, worked as a spinner and a weaver to support her family.

What **work** did Johnson have to do **as a boy**?

Johnson worked as an apprentice to a tailor when he was a young boy. Because he had to work to help his family survive, Johnson had no formal education. He worked for

Portrait of President Andrew Johnson.

many years for James J. Selby of Raleigh, who taught Johnson and his brother the tailoring trade.

Did he have any **siblings**?

Yes, Andrew Johnson had one brother named William.

Did he **marry**?

At age nineteen, Johnson married seventeen-year-old Eliza McCardle. Tragically, McCardle—like Johnson—lost her father at an early age.

Did he have any **children**?

Yes, Andrew Johnson and Eliza McCardle had five children: Martha, Charles, Mary, Robert, and Andrew Jr. Martha served as White House hostess for her mother, who was often ill. She later married David T. Patterson, who became a U.S. senator. Charles became a doctor and a veteran of the Union army. He died after being thrown from his horse during the war. Mary lived in Calver County, Tennessee, and was married twice. Robert became a lawyer and served as his father's private secretary during the White House years. Andrew became a journalist, founding the *Greeneville Intelligencer*.

EARLY CAREER

What did **Johnson do** for a living?

He continued plying his trade as a tailor, capitalizing on the skills he learned as a young boy. He worked in this trade in Raleigh, North Carolina; Carthage, North Carolina; and later at Laurens, South Carolina. In 1826, he moved his family to Greeneville, Tennessee, where he opened a tailor shop.

How did he transition from a **tailor to a politician**?

Johnson's tailor shop was very popular, as he was skilled at his craft. He liked to listen to political debates and was well read even though he had no formal education. He met

> ## How did Johnson differ from his Southern colleagues in the Senate?
>
> Johnson was the only sitting Southern senator who did not resign his seat in the U.S. Senate when the Southern states seceded and formed the Confederacy. Johnson was a Unionist and he worked to support and preserve and defend the Union.

his wife in Greeneville, and she helped him to increase his knowledge. Gradually, Johnson became more interested in politics and began to engage in political discussions.

POLITICAL OFFICES

What were Johnson's **first political positions**?

Johnson became involved in local politics in Greeneville, Tennessee. He served as an alderman beginning in 1829, and later as mayor of the city in 1833.

When did he become a **state congressman**?

In 1835, Johnson won election to the Tennessee House of Representatives, where he served a single term. He won election again in 1839. Johnson frequently defended the interests of smaller farmers and mountaineers against the wealthy elite. In 1841, he served as a member in the Tennessee Senate.

When did he become a **U.S. congressman**?

Johnson won election to the U.S. House of Representatives in 1843. Like in the state congress, Johnson advocated on behalf of the poor and dispossessed. He argued for a measure that would provide for free land for farmers who had lost their land. After serving a term as governor of Tennessee, Johnson won election to the United States Senate in 1857. He pushed for the adoption of the Homestead Act, which gave up to 160 acres of undeveloped land to settlers willing to move and settle out in the Midwest and West.

To what position did **Lincoln appoint Johnson** in **1862**?

Lincoln appointed Johnson as military governor of Tennessee in 1862. Johnson steadfastly defended the Union, sought to quell rebellion, and worked to further the causes of preserving the Union.

What was Johnson's next position **after military governor**?

In 1864, Lincoln and party leaders selected Johnson to run as Lincoln's vice president. Lincoln was a Republican and Johnson was a Democrat. While it was (and is) extremely unusual for running mates to come from different parties, Lincoln believed that Johnson as a Southern, pro-war Democrat would help ensure his reelection.

PRESIDENCY

How did Johnson **become president**?

Assassin John Wilkes Booth killed President Abraham Lincoln by shooting him at Ford's Theatre in Washington, D.C. Lincoln died on April 14, 1865. The next morning, Vice President Andrew Johnson became the next president of the United States. Johnson became the first person to assume the presidency after the murder of a president. He followed in the footsteps of John Tyler and Millard Fillmore, as the third vice president to assume the presidency after his successor died in office. The key difference was that William Henry Harrison and Zachary Taylor died of natural causes, while Lincoln was assassinated.

Who **swore Johnson in** as president?

Salmon P. Chase, the Chief Justice of the U.S. Supreme Court, swore in Johnson to the office of the presidency. Most presidents are now sworn in by the sitting Chief Justice of the U.S. Supreme Court.

Who served as Johnson's **vice president**?

Johnson did not have a vice president, as he had been Lincoln's vice president. In those days, a new vice president was not selected.

How did **Johnson spar with Congress** during his presidency?

Johnson and the thirty-ninth Congress—composed of the so-called "Radical Republicans"—sparred mightily over the period of Reconstruction—the period of time given to the rebuilding of the Union after the Civil War. Johnson favored a quick process by which the former Confederate states would be re-admitted to the Union. Johnson also did not support some of the civil rights measures passed by Congress that were designed to ensure a measure of equality to the recently freed slaves.

Johnson vetoed the renewing of the Freedmen's Bureau, an agency that provided federal assistance to recently freed individuals. Johnson felt that this measure—like other federal civil rights legislation—invaded the sovereignty, or power, of the state governments.

Johnson also sought to block passage of the Civil Rights Act of 1866 and later the Fourteenth Amendment to the U.S. Constitution. Once again, Johnson believed that the federal Congress had exceeded its powers and invaded the states' sphere.

Why was **Johnson impeached**?

The U.S. House of Representatives vehemently felt that President Johnson was not doing his job properly. They initially attempted to impeach him in November 1867 for a variety of reasons, but the vote failed 57 to 108. However, the House found a new reason to impeach President Johnson after he removed Secretary of War Edwin Stanton from office in violation of a newly enacted federal law known as the Tenure of Office Act.

The Tenure of Office Act prohibited the president from discharging members of his cabinet until a successor had gone through official Senate approval. Congress had passed the law in large measure to protect Stanton, whom Johnson wanted out of office. Johnson ignored the Tenure of Office of Act and had Stanton—who had barricaded himself in his office—removed.

A few days later the House impeached President Johnson. Under the Constitution, the House can impeach a president (and other federal officials), but the Senate has the power to try and convict the person. The Senate has to vote by a two-thirds margin to actually remove the person from office via impeachment. The Senate voted thirty-five to nineteen that Johnson was guilty and should be impeached. This was one vote shy of the necessary two-thirds majority. Thus, Johnson survived the impeachment process and remained in office.

Which **senators' courageous votes saved Johnson** from being found guilty in the Senate vote?

Seven Republican senators refused to join their colleagues and voted not guilty on the charges. They were Lyman Trumbull of Illinois, James W. Grimes of Iowa, Edmund G. Ross of Kansas, William P. Fessenden of Maine, John B. Henderson of Nevada, Joseph F. Fowler of Tennessee, and Peter Van Winkle of West Virginia. The seven paid a steep price for their vote. None of them were reelected to the Sen-

President Johnson is served impeachment papers. He was later found innocent of the charges against him.

A political cartoon satirizing President Johnson and Secretary of State William Seward for purchasing Alaska from Russia. The move was criticized at the time but history proved it to be a smart move.

ate. The deciding vote was cast by Ross. He rebounded to later serve as governor of the New Mexico territory in the 1880s.

How did history **vindicate Johnson** with respect to the **Tenure of Office Act**?

In 1926, the U.S. Supreme Court ruled in *Myers v. United States* that President Woodrow Wilson could remove Postmaster Frank Myers from office without congressional approval. The Court ruled that the Tenure of Office Act was unconstitutional—as Johnson argued years earlier—because the executive branch has sole power to remove executive branch officials without legislative interference.

What **significant land purchase** occurred under Johnson's presidency?

The United States acquired the territory of Alaska from Russia on April 9, 1867, for a little more than $7 million. Critics ridiculed the purchase as excessive and labeled it "Seward's Folly" after Secretary of State William Seward. However, history showed that it was a very wise move by the government. President Johnson approved of the measure.

What was **one of** Johnson's **last official acts** as president?

Johnson granted unconditional amnesty to all former members of the Confederacy. He did this on Christmas Day in 1868.

Did Johnson **appoint** anyone to the **U.S. Supreme Court**?

No, Johnson is one of only a few sitting presidents to never have an opportunity to add someone to the U.S. Supreme Court. Johnson nominated former U.S. Attorney General Henry Stanbery to the Court in 1868 to replace John Catron, but the Senate did not confirm him. Stanbery had resigned his position as attorney general in 1868 to defend Johnson during the impeaching proceeding. Johnson then sought to reappoint Stanton as attorney general, but the Senate would not confirm him. Congress simply would not accept President Johnson's appointments. Congress reduced the number of seats on the U.S. Supreme Court to avoid having to accept anyone nominated by Johnson.

Did Johnson **seek reelection**?

Yes, Johnson ran for reelection at the Democratic National Convention in New York City in July 1868. Johnson never led on any of the ballots, finishing second to George Pendleton on the first ballot with sixty-five votes. Horatio Seymour became the party's candidate as the support for Johnson diminished.

POST PRESIDENCY

What **political office** did Johnson gain in his **post-presidency years**?

Johnson lost a bid for the U.S. Senate in 1868, but he won election in 1874 to serve as a U.S. senator representing his home state of Tennessee. He served in the Senate until his death in 1871. He remains the only president to serve in the United States Senate after being president.

When did he **die**?

He died on July 31, 1875, in Carter County, Tennessee, after suffering a second stroke.

Where is **Johnson buried**?

Johnson is buried in Greenville, Tennessee. His body was buried in the American flag, with his head placed on a copy of the United States Constitution.

ULYSSES S. GRANT

(1822–1885)
18th President, 1869–1877
Party Affiliation: Republican
Chief 1868 Opponent: Horatio Seymour (Democrat)
Chief 1872 Opponent: Horace Greeley (Liberal Republican)

EARLY LIFE AND FAMILY

Where and when was Grant **born**?

Grant was born in Point Pleasant, Ohio, to Jesse Root Grant and Hannah Simpson Grant on April 27, 1822.

What was his **father's occupation**?

Jesse Root Grant worked as a tanner. His father's business grew prosperous, and eventually he owned stores in Ohio, Kentucky, Illinois, and Wisconsin. Ulysses S. Grant named his youngest son after his father.

What was his **early education**?

Grant learned at local schools in Georgetown, Ohio. At age fourteen, he entered the Maysville Seminary in Kentucky, and then the Presbyterian Academy in Ripley, Ohio.

He graduated from this academy at age seventeen and then gained admittance to the U.S. Military Academy.

Did he have any **siblings**?

Yes, Grant had five younger siblings: Clara, Virginia, Abel, Orvil, and Mary.

Did he **marry**?

Grant married Julia Boggs Dent on August 22, 1848, in St. Louis, Missouri. Grant was twenty-six years old and Julia was twenty-two. The couple's parents did not approve of the marriage. Julia's parents did not want their daughter to marry a military man, while Grant's parents disapproved of the Dent family because they owned slaves.

A painting by Christian Schussele depicts the Civil War hero General Grant.

Did he have any **children**?

Yes, they had four children: Frederick, Ulysses, Ellen, and Jesse. The oldest child, Frederick Dent Grant, later served as U.S. minister to Austria-Hungary and became commissioner of police in New York City. Ulysses S. Grant Jr. became an assistant U.S. attorney and successful lawyer in private practice. Ellen "Nellie" Grant was originally named Julia after her mother. However, at eighteen months, she was renamed Ellen after Grant's mother, who had recently died. Jesse Root Grant, the youngest child, sought the Democratic Party presidential nomination in 1908, but lost to William Jennings Bryan.

MILITARY CAREER

How did Grant fare at **West Point**?

Grant was an average student at West Point, though he did show some proclivity for mathematics. He also showed excellent aptitude as a horseman. He graduated twenty-first out of a class of thirty-nine cadets in 1843. His last-year roommate was Frederick T. Dent, the brother of his future wife, Julia.

What was Grant's birth name?

Grant's name at birth was Hiram Ulysses Grant, honoring his maternal grandfather and the Greek mythological hero. Years later, Congressman Thomas Lyon Hamer recommended Grant for admission to the United States Military Academy. However, Hamer mistakenly referred to the seventeen-year-old Hiram Ulysses Grant as "Ulysses Simpson Grant." Grant used the name for the rest of his life.

Where did Grant **first serve**?

Grant became commissioned as an officer and served near St. Louis, Missouri, at Jefferson Barracks beginning in September 1843. Grant served in the Fourth U.S. Infantry.

In **which war** did Grant see his **first combat action**?

Grant served in the Mexican–American War beginning in 1846. He served under two eminent generals—Zachary Taylor and Winfield Scott. Grant followed in the footsteps of these two leaders in becoming a presidential candidate. Taylor served as the nation's twelfth president, while Scott lost the presidential election of 1852 to Franklin Pierce. Grant earned a promotion to second lieutenant during the Mexican–American War.

Grant served as quartermaster of the Fourth Infantry while a twenty-four-year-old lieutenant. He proved himself well, earning the respect of his fellow officers and soldiers.

Where did Grant serve next **after the Mexican–American War**?

He served at various posts through the next decade, including Madison Barracks in Sacketts Harbor, New York, Detroit, San Francisco, and Fort Vancouver in the Oregon Territory. Though promoted to captain in 1853, he did not enjoy his service at Fort Vancouver and resigned from the military in 1854.

What did Grant do **after leaving the army**?

Grant tried his hand at farming and real estate to little success. He worked farmland in White Haven, Missouri, that had been given to Ulysses and Julia by her parents as a wedding present. He built a house on his land that he named "Hardscrabble." He also sold lumber and worked on land owned by his father-in-law, Colonel Dent.

After farming did not work out economically, Grant worked at one of his father's leather-good stores in Galena, Illinois, in May 1860. The store was managed by his brothers Simpson and Orvil.

223

How did Grant **return to the military**?

Grant joined the army with a group of volunteers in Galena, Illinois. As a West Point graduate and Mexican War veteran, he became the natural leader of the volunteers. He became colonel of a local regiment and faced off against Confederate troops at Belmont, Missouri. He later became commander of the southeast Missouri district.

What were Grant's **initial victories** that brought him acclaim?

Grant secured victories in Tennessee, capturing Fort Henry on the Cumberland River and then Fort Donelson near the Tennessee River. His win at Fort Donelson in 1862 constituted the first major Union victory of the war. He earned the nickname "Unconditional Surrender" Grant for telling one of his subordinates: "No terms except an unconditional and immediate surrender can be accepted."

What **other major victories** did Grant achieve?

Grant captured Jackson, Mississippi, in April 1863, and then Vicksburg, Mississippi, in July 1863. He later won several battles in Chattanooga, Tennessee, in November 1863. This series of victories earned him the trust of President Abraham Lincoln, who named him supreme commander of the Union army.

In April 1865, Grant defeated Confederate forces led by General Robert E. Lee at the Battle of Five Forks near Petersburg, Virginia. He took Richmond, Virginia, shortly thereafter, which culminated in Lee surrendering to Grant at Appomattox Court House on April ninth. This surrender effectively ended the Civil War.

What **position** did Grant ultimately **refuse from President Andrew Johnson**?

Johnson removed Secretary of War Edwin Stanton. He temporarily appointed Grant, who served on an interim basis for a short time before officially declining the position.

PRESIDENCY

How did Grant **become president**?

Grant was a war hero of the highest order. The Republicans heralded him as their next nominee. In Chicago at the 1868 Republican convention, the party nominated him as its candidate on the first ballot. He ran against Democrat Horatio Seymour from New York. Grant handily defeated Seymour by a 214 to 80 electoral vote margin.

Who was Grant's **first vice president**?

Grant's vice president for his first term was Schuyler Colfax of Indiana, who was Speaker of the House. Colfax believed that Grant would not run for reelection and that he could then rise to the presidency. But Grant took a liking to the presidency and decided to run for reelection in 1872. Colfax tried to regain the vice presidency, but Grant knew Colfax's ambition and favored Henry Wilson, who became Grant's vice president for his second term.

Whom did Grant **defeat** in his **reelection** bid in the election of 1872?

Grant defeated newspaper editor and Liberal Republican Horace Greeley, who also had the support of the Democratic Party. Greeley ran on a platform of cleaning up the government, noting several scandals during Grant's first term. However, Grant still had enough good will from his Civil War record and the financial panic of 1873 had not happened yet. Greeley died on November 29, 1872, after the popular vote but before the electoral vote. Grant garnered 286 electoral votes to Greeley's 66 pledged votes. Because Greeley had died, his 66 votes were spread among other candidates.

What **financial crisis** occurred during Grant's first term?

Black Friday happened on September 24, 1869, in Grant's first term as president. It occurred when two Wall Street speculators, Jay Gould and Jim Fisk, attempted to buy up all the gold at the financial markets. Their attempts to corner the market led to a financial panic that forced the closing of the stock market. Unfortunately, Gould and Fisk were friends with Grant's brother-in-law Abel Rathbone Corbin, husband to Grant's sister Virginia.

What **other financial crisis** occurred during Grant's time as president?

The Panic of 1873, a worldwide economic depression, occurred during President Grant's tenure. Eighteen thousand businesses failed, including a quarter of the nation's railroads. The panic began in the United States with the failure of Jay Cooke & Company, a major bank. Unemployment reached a high of nearly fifteen percent. This panic lasted until 1879.

What were some of the **other scandals** rocked the Grant administration?

In 1875, Secretary of the Treasury Benjamin Bristow exposed the Whiskey Ring Scandal, which involved officials and businessmen supposedly pocketing millions of dollars in liquor taxes. Many officials allegedly bribed Internal Revenue Service (IRS) agents and others, including IRS supervisor John McDonald and Grant's private secretary Orville E. Babcock.

The Indian Trading Scandal also rocked the Grant administration, and impeachment charges were brought against Secretary of War William W. Belknap for allegedly accepting a bribe over an Indian trading post position. He became the first member of a presidential cabinet to be impeached. Although he resigned immediately, the House impeached him. The Senate acquitted him because he had already resigned.

The Delano Affair also rocked the Grant administration. Secretary of the Interior Columbus Delano allegedly took bribes for fraudulent land grants. He resigned from office in October 1875.

Photographic portrait of President Grant by Matthew B. Brady.

What **significant treaty** did Grant's administration bring about that improved relations with **Great Britain**?

Grant's able secretary of state, Hamilton Fish, oversaw the negotiation of the Treaty of Washington in 1871. This treaty normalized relations with Great Britain and solved several thorny problems, ranging from the northwestern border of the United States to the sinking of Union ships by British-built Confederate ships. These damages were known as the "Alabama Claims." Under the treaty, Great Britain agreed to pay more than $15 million in damages for the sinking of American ships.

What efforts at **helping African Americans** occurred during Grant's first term?

Grant issued a proclamation that celebrated the Fifteenth Amendment, which had ensured recently freed slaves the right to vote. He also approved of the passage by Congress of a civil rights law known as the Ku Klux Klan Act of 1871, which sought to reduce violence against blacks.

What significant **part of the federal government** did Congress **create** during the Grant administration?

On June 22, 1870, Grant signed into law a bill passed by Congress that created the U.S. Department of Justice. The new bill went into effect on July 1, 1870, and provided great support for the U.S. attorney general. The law created the prestigious position of U.S. solicitor general, who to this day handles much litigation on behalf of the federal government before the U.S. Supreme Court. Benjamin Bristow served as the first solicitor general.

POST PRESIDENCY

What did Grant do for the **first few years after leaving** the presidency?

Grant and his wife, Julia, traveled the world for more than two years. They went to Europe, the Middle East, China, Japan, India, and Russia. He also traveled to Mexico and Cuba. He was hailed as a great war hero and enjoyed enormous prestige abroad.

Did Grant **seek the presidency again**?

Yes, Grant was promoted as a possible candidate during the 1880 Republican party nomination. Senator Roscoe Conkling and other so-called members of the Stalwart wing of the Republican Party advanced Grant as their candidate. The Stalwarts were named for their ardent opposition to many of the policies of President Rutherford B. Hayes (Grant's successor as president) regarding Reconstruction. However, Grant lost the nomination to James A. Garfield on the thirtieth-sixth ballot by a vote of 399 to 306. Garfield later won the presidential election and became the country's twentieth president.

How did Grant **earn a living** after he left the presidency?

He served as the president of the Mexican Southern Railway for a short time and then became a silent partner in his son's New York City investment firm, Grant and Ward. Ulysses Grant Jr. ran the firm along with Ferdinand Ward, who later embezzled money and caused the project to fail. Ward served a jail sentence for his crime, but the former president was left destitute.

What did Grant **do for money** after he became broke?

Grant's friend William H. Vanderbilt assumed title to Grant's house, which enabled Grant to maintain residence in his home. He became a writer and wrote accounts of several of his Civil War battles, including Shiloh and Vicksburg. He then wrote his memoirs, which focused largely on his involvement and observations made during the Mexican War and the Civil War. He finished the memoirs—working eight hours a day—just a few days before his death.

When did Grant **die**?

Grant died on July 23, 1885, at the age of sixty-three of throat cancer.

227

RUTHERFORD B. HAYES

(1822–1893)
19th President, 1877–1881
Party Affiliation: Republican
Chief 1876 Opponent: Samuel J. Tilden (Democrat)

EARLY LIFE AND FAMILY

Where and when was Rutheford B. Hayes **born**?

Rutherford Birchard Hayes was born in Delaware, Ohio, to Rutherford and Sophia Birchard Hayes on October 4, 1822.

What did his **father do** for a living?

Rutherford B. Hayes's father, Rutherford Hayes, worked as a farmer and merchant. The father also invested in a local distillery. Hayes's father had moved his family to Ohio from Wilmington, Vermont, in 1817. Sadly, he died of malaria in 1822 two months before Rutherford B. Hayes was born. The widowed Sophia Birchard Hayes rented out the farmland and another house in the city for income.

Did Hayes have any **siblings**?

Yes, he had an older sister named Fanny. She would marry and move to Columbus, Ohio, as Fanny A. Platt. She died in 1856, while giving birth to stillborn twins. He also

President Rutherford B. Hayes.

had an older brother named Lorenzo, who drowned at age four, when Rutherford was only two.

What **other family members lived with** Hayes, his sister, and mother?

Arcena Smith, a cousin to his mother, lived with the family, as did Rutherford's uncle Sardis Birchard. Sardis, a lifelong bachelor, was a successful businessman and banker. He helped rear Rutherford and served as his mentor. Sardis paid for Rutherford's education and became his guardian.

What was Rutherford Hayes's **early education**?

He attended a local school in Delaware, Ohio, and at age fourteen, he attended the Norwalk Seminary, a Methodist school in Norwalk run by Reverend Jonah Chaplin. When Hayes was fifteen, he attended a private academy in Middletown, Connecticut, run by Isaac Webb. At age sixteen, Hayes entered Kenyon College in Gambier, Ohio.

Was Hayes a **good college student**?

Hayes was an exceptional student, graduating first in his class in 1842. He made many important contacts in college, including future U.S. Supreme Court Justice Stanley Matthews and future Michigan congressman Rowland E. Trowbridge. While in college, he delved into literature and theater, and engaged in political discussions. He also began reading law at the law firm Sparrow & Matthews in Columbus.

Did he **marry**?

In December 1852, the thirty-year-old Hayes married twenty-one-year-old Lucy Ware Webb in Cincinnati. She strongly opposed both slavery and alcohol.

Did he have any **children**?

Yes, Rutherford and Lucy Hayes had eight children: Sardis Birchard, James Webb, Rutherford Platt, Frances, Scott Russell, Joseph, George Crook, and Manning Force. Sardis followed in his father's footsteps by attending Harvard law school and became a successful real estate lawyer. James served as his father's secretary during the White House years and later founded a successful business. He also distinguished himself in military action, winning a Congressional Medal of Honor for bravery during the Spanish–American War. Rutherford Platt graduated from Cornell, and then worked as a successful banker in Asheville, North Carolina. Frances settled in Fremont, Ohio, and married. Scott Russell became a successful railroad executive. The other three children—Joseph, George Crook, and Manning—all died as infants.

EARLY CAREER

What did Hayes do **after earning his undergraduate degree**?

Though he was learning law at the law firm in Columbus, his uncle Sardis wanted young Rutherford to have a formal legal education at an institution of higher learning. Hayes entered Harvard Law School and remained there until 1845. During his time at Harvard, he met former President John Quincy Adams, Henry Wadsworth Longfellow, and famed lawyer and politician Daniel Webster.

After law school at Harvard, what did Hayes do?

He became admitted to the bar in Marietta, Ohio, but then set up a law practice in Lower Sandusky (later called Fremont), Ohio, with Ralph P. Buckland. His uncle Sardis and his cousin John R. Pease lived in Lower Sandusky. He handled cases in this region, but also had time to travel to Texas and other parts of the country.

When did he **move to Cincinnati**?

Hayes moved to Cincinnati in 1849, and established a law practice in that growing city. He handled many different types of cases, including criminal defense. He pleaded an insanity defense on behalf of a disabled girl named Nancy Farrer. Though she was convicted and sentenced to death, the prosecutors and others praised Hayes for his able defense and deftness in courtroom argument. Hayes pursued an appeal on behalf of Farrer, and she eventually was placed in an insane asylum. In December 1853, he formed another law firm called Corwine, Hayes & Rogers.

How did Hayes's **legal practice** deal with the **slavery issue**?

Hayes became more active in politics and supported abolition. He began to represent fugitive slaves, who sought their freedom once they set foot in a free state like Ohio. With future U.S. Supreme Court Justice Salmon P. Chase, he helped secure the freedom of Rosetta Armstrong.

The future President Hayes married Lucy Ware Webb, who was active in campaigning against slavery and alcohol.

What **position did Hayes turn down** in 1856?

Hayes became active in politics as a member of the Whig Party and later the Republican Party. He was offered a judgeship, but turned it down.

What public **legal position** did he **accept** in **1858**?

Hayes became Cincinnati's city solicitor in 1858, after the city council narrowly appointed him following the death of the incumbent. He won reelection in 1859 and 1860, before losing in 1861.

Whom did he **support** in the **presidential election** of **1860**?

Hayes supported the candidacy of Abraham Lincoln in 1860. He served as vice chairman of the Republican Executive Committee of Hamilton County.

POLITICAL OFFICES

When was Hayes **first elected to Congress**?

While still fighting for the Union, supporters nominated him as a Republican candidate for the U.S. House of Representatives in Hamilton County, Ohio. He refused to leave the war effort to campaign but still won the election, as news of heroism in war served him well. He served two terms in the House and played a key role in the passage of a measure that expanded the Library of Congress.

What was his **next political position**?

Hayes ran for governor of Ohio and won in 1867, defeating Democrat Allen G. Thurman. He ran on a platform of universal suffrage for men, including blacks. Hayes said during the campaign: "Honest colored men are preferable to white traitors." As governor, he promoted education, prison reform, passage of the Fifteenth Amendment

What was distinctive about Hayes's military service?

Hayes fought for the Union during the Civil War. He organized a group of volunteers and then joined the Twenty-third Ohio Infantry. He served as a major, but rose up to the rank of major general. He was injured multiple times during the war, including at the Battle of South Mountain in Maryland in September 1862. Several times he suffered injuries because his horse was shot; for example, this occurred at the Battle of Cedar Creek in October 1864. He played a key role in the Union victory at the Battle of Cloyd's Mountain in Pulaski County, Virginia, that led to the Union destroying a key Confederate railroad. He resigned from the army in June 1865. He distinguished himself with bravery and courage during his military service during the Civil War, fighting in fifty engagements.

(guaranteeing the right to vote), and better treatment for the insane. He won reelection in 1869 over Democrat George Pendleton, but left office in 1872. He did not want to run for a third consecutive term, believing that a two-term limit was appropriate.

What **election** did Hayes **lose**?

Hayes ran for Congress somewhat reluctantly in 1872. He lost the election to General Henry B. Banning, who had the support of Democrats and the Liberal Republicans.

After leaving the Ohio **governorship**, what did he do?

Hayes returned to the practice of law, opening an office at Sixth and Walnut Streets in Cincinnati. In 1873, his uncle Sidas deeded his estate Spiegel Grove in Fremont to Hayes and his family. Hayes moved to Fremont in part to be near his ailing uncle, who died in 1874.

What **position** offered by President Ulysses S. **Grant** did Hayes **decline**?

President Grant offered Hayes the position of assistant treasurer for the U.S. government in Cincinnati. He declined the position.

Whom did **Hayes defeat** for an unprecedented **third term** as **governor**?

Hayes could not stay retired from public service for long. He defeated Judge Alphonso Taft (father of future President William Howard Taft) for the Republican nomination, and then ousted Democratic incumbent William Allen to become the first man to serve three terms as governor of Ohio.

PRESIDENCY

Who was the **front-runner** for the **Republican nomination** for president in **1876**?

James G. Blaine of Maine, who had served several years as Speaker of the House of Representatives, was the clear front-runner for the Republican nomination in 1876. A gifted orator, Blaine nearly captured the nomination, landing only twenty-seven votes short. Hayes was in fifth place for the first four ballots behind Blaine as well as Oliver P. Morton of Indiana, Benjamin H. Bristow of Kentucky, and Roscoe Conkling of New York. Hayes, however, won the nomination on the seventh ballot.

Who was Hayes's **opponent** in the **general election**?

Democrat Samuel J. Tilden of New York was Hayes's opponent in the general election. Tilden had served as city counselor for New York City, New York State legislator, and governor. In his public life, he was instrumental in taking down the corrupt William "Boss" Tweed and Tammany Hall, an organization that controlled New York City politics. As governor, he had dismantled the corrupt Canal Ring, a group of politicians and others who had gotten rich over fraudulent canal repair contracts.

What was **unusual and controversial** about the **election of 1876**?

The election of 1876 was unusual because Tilden won the popular vote by nearly three hundred thousand votes, but ended up one electoral vote shy of winning the election. On the night of the election, Tilden had clearly captured the popular vote and was only one electoral vote short of winning the election. However, the states of Florida, South Carolina, Oregon, and Louisiana could go to Hayes, which would give him 185 electoral votes.

Democrats charged that fraud in the vote counting occurred in several of the Southern states. They pointed out that in several Southern states, there were Republican-controlled election boards that engineered the outcome. But, apparently, each party engaged in fraud. Some Democratic party members threatened and intimidated blacks from voting. Some Republicans intervened and had some blacks vote multiple times. The result was hotly contested, as Democrats and Republicans each set forth conflicting electoral vote results for Tilden and Hayes respectively.

In January 1877, Congress established a fifteen-member electoral commission to resolve the issue and decide which set of electoral ballots to accept. It was made up of seven Democrats, seven Republicans, and one independent. There were five U.S. Senators, five members of the U.S. House of Representatives, and five U.S. Supreme Court Justices. However, the independent—Justice David Davis of Illinois—was elected to

> ## Because of the disputed election, what unfavorable nicknames did Hayes acquire?
>
> Some called him "Rutherfraud." Others called him "Ole 8-7." Still others referred to him as "His Fraudulency." Hayes's presidency was tainted in many people's eyes by the unusual nature of the election.

the Illinois legislature. Davis's slot on the election commission was filled by another sitting U.S. Supreme Court Justice Joseph Bradley, a Republican from New Jersey. The commission ended up voting eight to seven, along party lines, in favor of Hayes. Some referred to this as the "Compromise of 1877," as some key Republican leaders (though not Hayes personally) bargained for the victory on the promise of removing federal troops from Southern states.

Who was Hayes's **vice president**?

His vice president was William Wheeler from New York. He had been a district attorney and a member of the New York state legislature for many years before serving in the U.S. House of Representatives. He was known for his probity in a state that had been rocked by scandal. However, he was not very well known on the national political scene at all.

Who was his **secretary of state**?

Hayes's secretary of state was William M. Evarts of New York, who had served as attorney general under President Andrew Johnson before resigning to defend the president on impeachment charges.

What happened with **Reconstruction**?

Hayes wanted to move the country to a position of national unity. He wanted to remove federal troops from the South and attract more Southerners into the Republican Party. He also had to deal with outraged Democrats, who were enraged over the disputed election results. Whatever the precise motivations, Hayes did remove federal troops out of the Southern states. This had disastrous consequences for blacks in those states, who suffered under Jim Crow segregation laws and other tools of intimidation.

What appointment did Hayes give to **Frederick Douglass**?

Hayes appointed the great black abolitionist advocate Frederick Douglass to the position of marshal of the District of Columbia. This appointment was opposed by many Democrats.

What did Hayes do with respect to **Chinese immigration**?

More and more Chinese immigrated to the United States in the 1860s and 1870s. Much of the workforce in California consisted of Chinese laborers. When the Chinese began competing for jobs with others, pressure built to curb the level of immigration. Congress passed a law that abrogated a treaty the U.S. signed with China that specifically allowed Chinese immigration. Hayes vetoed this measure and authorized Secretary of State Evarts and a commission headed by James B. Angell to negotiate a new treaty with China. The Treaty of 1880 allowed the government to limit immigration from China, but also provided for the protection of rights for Chinese already in the United States.

In a very progressive move, President Hayes appointed prominent African American abolitionist Frederick Douglass to be marshal of Washington, D.C.

What executive order targeted **civil service reform**?

In June 1877, Hayes issued an executive order that sought to limit federal government officials from engaging in partisan political activity. He wanted to end the practice of patronage and increase the efficiency of federal governmental agencies. The order prohibited federal government officials from participating in "the management of political organizations, caucuses, conventions, or election campaigns."

Who were his **U.S. Supreme Court appointees**?

Hayes's two successful Supreme Court nominees were John Marshall Harlan of Kentucky and William B. Woods of Georgia. Harlan became known as "the Great Dissenter" for his lone dissents in the *Civil Rights Cases* (1883) and *Plessy v. Ferguson* (1896). Though from a slave owning family in Kentucky, Harlan had farsighted views and ruled that segregation was unconstitutional. Woods, formerly a judge on the 5th Circuit, served only six years on the Court.

POST PRESIDENCY

Did Hayes seek **reelection**?

No, Hayes did not seek reelection. He had promised to be a one-term president and he kept that promise. After having to deal with a recalcitrant Democratic-controlled Congress, he welcomed retirement.

What did Hayes do in **retirement**?

He retired to Spiegel Grove in Fremont, Ohio, and pursued many charitable and humanitarian causes. He served as president of the National Prison Association and advocated for greater emphasis on rehabilitation. He presided over the Slater Education Fund for Freemen, which awarded many scholarships to African Americans, including W. E. B. DuBois. He served on the board of trustees of the Ohio State University, Ohio Wesleyan University, and Western Reserve University. He also worked with the Peabody Education Fund.

When did Hayes **die**?

He died on January 17, 1893, in Fremont, Ohio.

JAMES A. GARFIELD

(1831–1881)
20th President, 1881
Party Affiliation: Republican
Chief 1880 Opponent: Winfield Scott Hancock (Democrat)

EARLY LIFE AND FAMILY

Where and when was Garfield **born**?

James Abram Garfield was born in a log cabin in Orange, Ohio, to Adam and Eliza Garfield on November 19, 1831.

What did his **parents do** for a living?

His father, Adam, worked as a farmer and for a time worked as a supervisor in the construction of canals. He died of complications from a severe cold when James Garfield was eighteen months old. Eliza also worked at farming to support her family after her husband's death. When Garfield was a boy, his mother remarried to a man named Alfred Belden whom Garfield did not like.

Did he have any **siblings**?

Yes, Garfield had four older siblings: James who died as an infant; Mehitabel, Thomas, and Mary.

President James Garfield.

What was Garfield's **early education**?

He attended a local school in Orange, Ohio, before attending Geauga Academy in Chester, Ohio. In 1851, he entered the Western Reserve Eclectic Institute in Hiram, Ohio, which was run by the Disciples of Christ, the church his family followed. While attending school, he worked as a janitor and teacher at local district schools in nearby cities.

Did Garfield **marry**?

The twenty-six-year-old Garfield married Lucretia "Crete" Rudolph, also twenty-six, on November 11, 1858, in Hiram, Ohio. She was a schoolteacher who taught in Cleveland and Bayou, Ohio.

Did he have any **children**?

Yes, James and Lucretia had seven children, five of whom survived to adulthood: Harry Augustus, James Rudolph, Mary, Irvin, and Abram. Harry Augustus Garfield became a lawyer and a law professor at Western Reserve University. He then taught at Princeton University and became the president of Williams College. James Rudolph also became a lawyer, graduating with his older brother at Columbia Law School. James served in the Ohio state Senate and later served as secretary of the interior under President Theodore Roosevelt. Mary married Joseph Stanley-Brown, who became an investment banker. Irvin McDowell Garfield also graduated from Columbia Law School and started a successful law firm in Boston. Abram Garfield went to the Massachusetts Institute of Technology and became a respected architect.

EARLY CAREER

What **occupation** was **Garfield attracted to** as a youth?

Garfield wanted to become a sailor when he was a boy. He read stories about adventures at sea and thought that would be better than his poverty-stricken life. At age sixteen, he left home for the Cleveland docks. Rejected for a job because of his age, he worked on a canal boat called the *Evening Star* that was owned by his cousin Amos

Letcher. He fell overboard numerous times. After one fall, he caught a fever and went home. His mother convinced him to resume his studies and further his education.

Where did he **graduate college**?

He first attended Western Reserve Eclectic Institute, which was later renamed Hiram College. He then transferred to Williams College in 1854, where he excelled. He learned Latin and Greek. He was the school's debating champion and also excelled in athletics. He edited the *Williams Quarterly,* the school's newspaper, and was president of a student literary society. At Williams, he heard a speech by Ralph Waldo Emerson, a leading intellectual of the time. Emerson's speech moved Garfield to pursue excellence in education and beyond. He graduated with honors in 1856, and delivered a speech at graduation.

What did Garfield do **after graduating** from Williams?

He worked as a traveling preacher for the Disciples of Christ and then went back to Western Reserve Eclectic, which was now called Hiram College. He inspired countless students with his lectures on the classical languages. At the age of twenty-six, he became the president of the college.

What was Garfield's **next career**?

Garfield left teaching to pursue a career in law. He studied law for two years and then became certified as an attorney in 1861.

What did Garfield do when the **Civil War broke out**?

Garfield volunteered for service and began as a lieutenant colonel. He later became a colonel of the 42nd Ohio Volunteer Infantry. Many of his soldiers were young men he had taught, and they displayed great loyalty to their former teacher. He fought at the Battles of Middle Creek, Shiloh, and Chickamauga. At the Battle of Chickamauga in January 1863, he distinguished himself with bravery through enemy fire. Major General William Rosecrans, for whom Garfield served as chief of staff, praised him as having the skills of a great commander.

POLITICAL OFFICES

What was his **first political position**?

His first political position was as a member of the Ohio state Senate in 1859. He served in that capacity until the outbreak of the Civil War in 1861.

When did he **first** get **elected** to the **U.S. House of Representatives?**

President Garfield's five children: (left to right) Mary, James Rudolph, Harry Augustus, Irvin, and Abram.

Garfield won election as a member of the U.S. House of Representatives while still a soldier in the Union army. He defeated his Democratic candidate D. B. Woods by a large margin even though he didn't campaign for the position. President Abraham Lincoln, whom Garfield had supported in Ohio, encouraged Garfield to take the position.

He served as a U.S. congressman for seventeen years until he ran for president in 1880. He served as chairman of the Banking and Currency Committee and the Military Affairs Committee. In 1874, he became the House minority leader for the Republicans, as the Democrats were in the majority.

In what **scandal** was he **implicated?**

Garfield was implicated in the Credit Mobilier scandal that came to light during the Grant administration. He was accused of accepting ten shares of Credit Mobilier stock and a three hundred dollar loan from a company that had engaged in an illegal business venture with Union Pacific Railroad. He also allegedly accepted legal fees from a company that bid on a government contract for street repairs in Washington, D.C. Garfield had to testify before a legislative committee as to the Credit Mobilier scandal. He avoided any serious problems to his reputation and career.

PRESIDENCY

Was Garfield the **front-runner** for the **1880 Republican nomination?**

No, he was not even on the radar screen. Former President Ulysses S. Grant emerged as a front-runner, along with James G. Blaine of Maine, who had nearly captured the nomination four years earlier in 1876. Another leading candidate was John Sherman of Ohio, whom Garfield voted for and served as campaign manager. Garfield attracted attention with his speechmaking abilities when he nominated Sherman. The convention went through thirty-five ballots, but none of the three leading contenders—Grant, Blaine, or Sherman—could garner enough votes. Garfield began to emerge as a com-

> ## How close was the election of 1880?
>
> It was a very close race, as the popular vote was nearly a dead heat. Each candidate garnered more than 4.45 million votes and each carried nineteen states during the election. But, Garfield won the electoral vote count 214 to 155.

promise candidate and supporters of Blaine and Sherman voted for Garfield as someone who could defeat Grant. On the final tally, Garfield received 399 votes to Grant's 306.

Who was his **opponent** in the **general election**?

The Democratic candidate Winfield Scott Hancock of Pennsylvania challenged Garfield in the 1880 general election. Hancock had graduated from West Point and distinguished himself with his service in the Mexican, Seminole, and U.S. Civil War. He later served as military governor of Louisiana and Texas. Originally, it was thought that Samuel J. Tilden would be the Democratic Party's nominee, given that many thought he had been cheated out of the previous presidential election. However, Tilden withdrew his name from consideration and Hancock emerged as the leading contender.

Who was Garfield's **vice president**?

Chester A. Arthur of New York was his vice president. Arthur was a supporter of powerful New York politician Roscoe Conklin. To appease Conklin and the Stalwart wing of the Republican Party, Arthur was offered the job of vice president. Little did he know that he would become president less than a year later.

Who was Garfield's **secretary of state**?

James G. Blaine, one of the front-runners for the Republican nomination in 1876 and 1880, ended up serving as Garfield's secretary of state. Blaine resigned his position after Garfield was assassinated. He finally obtained the Republican Party nomination in 1884, but lost to Democrat Grover Cleveland. He later served as secretary of state to President Benjamin Harrison.

Who was his lone U.S. **Supreme Court appointee**?

Garfield nominated Stanley Matthews of Ohio to the U.S. Supreme Court. President Rutherford B. Hayes originally had sent Matthews's name to the Senate, but the Senate refused to act. Garfield resubmitted Matthews's name and the Senate confirmed him by one vote. Matthews served on the Court until his death in 1889.

The assassination of President Garfield at the hands of Charles Julius Guiteau.

To which **issue** did **Garfield devote** much of his **attention** as president in 1881?

Garfield pushed for civil service reform in Congress. Ironically, Garfield's death inspired others to support civil service reform and Congress passed a major initiative in that regard when Vice President Chester A. Arthur became the next president.

What **ended Garfield's presidency** so early?

A strange man named Charles Julius Guiteau ended Garfield's presidency by shooting him in Elberton, New Jersey, on July 2, 1881. Guiteau, a member of the Stalwart wing of the Republican Party, had supported Garfield during the presidential election. He somehow thought that his support merited him an appointment of an ambassador position. The administration politely rejected Guiteau, which sent him into a rage. He began stalking the president for a couple months and finally got the nerve to follow through with his murderous intentions. Guiteau claimed that he had killed Garfield to "unite the Republican Party and save the Republic."

When did Garfield **die**?

Garfield did not die immediately, but he never recovered. Although surgeons removed the bullets from his body, he was bedridden until his death on September 19, 1881.

CHESTER A. ARTHUR

(1829–1886)
21st President, 1881–1885
Party Affiliation: Republican
Chief 1880 Opponent: None

EARLY LIFE AND FAMILY

Where and when was Arthur **born**?

Chester Alan Arthur was born in Fairfield, Vermont, to the Reverend William Arthur and Malvina Stone Arthur on October 5, 1829.

Who was the future **president named after**?

He took his first name from Dr. Chester Abell, the physician who delivered him. He took his middle name, Alan, from his paternal grandfather Alan Arthur.

What did his **father** do for a living?

The Reverend William Arthur taught school in Dunham, Quebec, before eloping with his future wife, Malvina Stone, to Vermont. In 1828, he became a Baptist preacher. He preached in a number of churches in Vermont and New York. A strong abolitionist, William Arthur passed down these feelings to his son Chester.

245

President Chester A. Arthur.

Did he have any **siblings**?

Yes, he had seven siblings who lived to adulthood: Regina, Jane, Almeda, Ann, Malvina, William, and Mary.

Did he **marry**?

Yes, the thirty-year-old Arthur married twenty-two-year-old Ellen "Nell" Lewis Herndon on October 25, 1859, in New York City. She died in 1880 at age forty-two, before Arthur became president. He never recovered from her death.

Did he have any **children**?

Yes, he and his wife had three children, including two that lived to adulthood. William Lewis Herndon was born first in 1860, but died before age three of an apparent brain hemorrhage. Chester Alan Arthur Jr., born in 1864, graduated from Princeton University and then Columbia Law School. However, he did not go into politics or even practice law. Rather, he seemed to enjoy the good life and traveled extensively. Ellen "Nell" Herndon Arthur, named after her mother, was born in 1871. She married Charles Pinkerton and lived in New York City.

What was his **early education** like?

Arthur learned from his father during his early years. He then attended a school in Union Village, New York. At age fifteen, he attended the Lyceum in Schenectady, New York. He edited the school newspaper.

EARLY CAREER

Where did he **attend college**?

Arthur attended Union College in 1845, where by all accounts he had a good time. He managed to graduate in the top third of his class in 1848 and taught school in a nearby town during breaks.

After graduation what career did Arthur pursue?

Arthur taught school after graduating college. He taught in North Pownall, Vermont, before becoming principal at a private academy in Cohoes, New York.

> ## What political charge did some opponents allege regarding Arthur's birth?
>
> Some opponents alleged that Arthur was born in Canada, instead of Vermont. This would have disqualified him from serving as either vice president or president. No proof was ever established that he was born anywhere other than Vermont.

When did Arthur **turn to law**?

To support himself, Arthur pursued a career in law, studying in Ballston Spa, New York, while still teaching. He later studied under attorney Erastus D. Culver in New York City. Culver, an ardent abolitionist, handled many cases and fought against the Fugitive Slave Act. Arthur enjoyed this work and later became admitted to the New York bar in 1854.

What was his **first legal job** after admission to the bar?

Arthur worked as a junior partner at the law firm where he had learned his trade; the firm became known as Culver, Parker, and Arthur.

What **famous case** did he handle that led to **desegregation**?

Arthur successfully represented Lizzie Jennings, a black woman ejected from a streetcar because of her race. Arthur's legal representation led to the desegregation of New York City's public transportation.

With whom did Arthur form his **next legal partnership**?

Arthur formed a law partnership with Henry D. Gardiner in 1856. The two traveled to Kansas for a time, interested and horrified over reports they read about "Bleeding Kansas" and the abolition battle there. The venture was not successful and the attorneys came back to New York.

What was Arthur's **military career** like?

Arthur served in the New York militia during the Civil War. He began his service in 1858 as a brigade judge advocate, and rose to quartermaster general by the time he left near the end of 1862. As assistant quartermaster general, he supplied soldiers with food, proper uniforms, and equipment. Arthur saved the government money by contracting out services to the private sector. Governor Edwin Morgan, who had given

Arthur his job and rank, praised him for his abilities: "He displayed not only great executive ability and unbending integrity, but great knowledge of Army regulations."

POLITICAL OFFICES

How did Arthur **become involved in politics**?

Arthur supported Abraham Lincoln in the 1864 election and Ulysses S. Grant in the 1868 election. He had become very active in the Republican Party in his home state. He served as state chairman of the party's executive committee. His political party work, however, detracted from his law practice. He managed to land a job for a short period of time as counsel to the New York tax commission.

What **lucrative political position** did President Grant and Roscoe Conkling help Arthur land?

Arthur had ingratiated himself to powerful New York politician and U.S. Senator Roscoe Conkling and to President Grant. This association paid off. Grant appointed him to the position of collector of the port of New York. In this job, he supervised the busiest port in the United States. He not only acquired a very nice salary, but he could obtain a piece of collected fees from those who did not pay the proper tariffs. Arthur served in this position from 1871 until 1878.

Who **removed Arthur** from this position as collector of the port of New York?

President Rutherford B. Hayes, who despised patronage and the spoils system, campaigned on the promise to clean up government. After hearing complaints, Hayes appointed John Jay—grandson of the first U.S. Supreme Court Chief Justice and *Federalist Paper* co-author John Jay—to investigate the New York port. The Jay Commission investigated and found problems. The Commission did not find Arthur personally guilty of anything, but criticized him for looking the other way while employees received appointments after making political contributions. The report also noted that Arthur often arrived to work late. Hayes ordered Secretary of the Treasury John Sherman to remove Arthur from his lucrative position. Roscoe Conkling vigorously defended Arthur and, for a time, President Hayes backed off his original demands. When Congress went into recess in 1878, Hayes again ordered Sherman to remove Arthur and replaced him with Alonzo Cornell, a city naval officer.

The controversy endeared Arthur to the Stalwart wing of the Republican Party, led by Conkling. It also gave Arthur some national political exposure.

What did **Arthur do after** his **removal**?

Arthur resumed law practice and then Roscoe Conkling rewarded him with the chairmanship of the New York Republican Party. Arthur managed the party's get-out-the-vote and fundraising efforts.

How did Chester A. Arthur **become vice president**?

Arthur entered the 1880 Republican National Convention as a loyal member of the Stalwart faction of the Republican Party, led by the influential Conklin. At the 1880 Republican convention, the Stalwarts backed former President Ulysses S. Grant for an unprecedented third term in office. Another faction of the Republican Party backed James G. Blaine. These Republicans were called "Half-Breeds" because they had divided loyalties to Grant when he was president and to civil service reform.

The Stalwarts and Half-Breeds supported Grant and Blaine as their respective candidates. Soon, more party members began questing for a compromise candidate. That candidate proved to be James A. Garfield, who eventually defeated Grant and emerged the victor during the contentious nomination process. The Garfield camp thought that Arthur would make an excellent choice as vice president, as a way to appease the Stalwart, pro-Grant wing of the Republican Party. Because Garfield was only forty-eight years old, no one expected that Arthur would have a big role in the government, including Arthur himself.

Did **Roscoe Conkling support Arthur** taking the vice presidency?

No, Senator Conkling did not like the idea, in part because it was the Garfield camp who had approached Arthur, not him. When Arthur informed Conkling that he had been offered the vice presidency, Conkling allegedly said: "Well, sir, you should drop it as you would a red hot shoe from the forge." But, Arthur disagreed, responding: "The office of the vice president is a greater honor than I ever dreamed of attaining."

PRESIDENCY

Why was **Arthur embroiled** in **controversy** when President **Garfield was shot**?

Charles Guiteau, the assassin that shot President Garfield in July 1881, committed his heinous act in part because he was a strident supporter of the Stalwart wing of the Republican Party. President Garfield was not a Stalwart and Arthur was. Guiteau allegedly said after the shooting: "I did it and will go to jail for it. I am a Stalwart and Arthur will be president."

249

Whom did Arthur hire to redecorate the White House?

Arthur thought that the White House needed serious upgrading. For this project, he enlisted the services of Louis Comfort Tiffany, the son of Tiffany and Company founder Charles Lewis Tiffany. Louis Comfort Tiffany later became world renowned for his glassmaking.

When did Arthur **officially become president**?

Garfield died on the evening of September 19, 1881. Early the morning of September 20, 1881, a state judge swore in Chester A. Arthur as the country's new president. He later took another oath of office, this time administered by Chief Justice of the U.S. Supreme Court Morrison Waite.

Which **relative** of a famous **former president** did Arthur keep on his **cabinet**?

Arthur replaced most of the cabinet named by President James Garfield when he succeeded as president. A notable exception was Arthur's choice as secretary of war, Robert T. Lincoln. The oldest son of President Lincoln, Robert Lincoln continued to serve as Arthur's secretary of war.

What major **civil service reform bill** did Arthur sign into law?

President Arthur—the former beneficiary of party politics—signed into law the Pendleton Act in 1883. Named after Democratic senator George Pendleton of Ohio, this measure sought to ensure that civil servants would be hired based on merit, not political party connections. Arthur biographer Zachary Karabell writes in *Chester Alan Arthur: The American Presidents Series:* "The Pendleton Civil Service Act is the most memorable piece of legislation to emerge from Chester Arthur's Presidency."

What measure did Arthur sign with regard to **Chinese immigration**?

Arthur reluctantly signed the Chinese Exclusion Act of 1882, which suspended or banned further Chinese immigration to the United States for ten years. Arthur opposed the measure, but signed it for pragmatic reasons.

What did Arthur do about the **tariff issue**?

The tariff issue divided the country and the political parties. Democrats wanted lower tariffs, while Republicans desired higher tariffs. President Arthur appointed a tariff commission to investigate and report on the matter. This work eventually led to the congressional passage of a broad-based tariff law pejoratively dubbed the "Mongrel Tariff" because it had inconsistent provisions that did not change the overall tariff rate much at all. Arthur took heat in the press for not being active enough in the process.

Who were his **U.S. Supreme Court appointees**?

Arthur nominated Horace Gray and Samuel Blatchford to the U.S. Supreme Court. Gray, former a jurist on the high court in Massachusetts, served nearly eleven years on the Court. Blatchford, a former federal district court judge and a federal appeals court judge, also served eleven years on the Court. Blatchford is the first person in American history to serve at all three levels of the federal judiciary: federal district court, federal appeals court, and the U.S. Supreme Court.

Did Arthur try for **another term**?

Yes, Arthur did believe that he deserved another term in office. His name was on the ballot at the 1884 Republican Party nomination convention. However, he did not fare well and the nomination went to Republican rival James Blaine.

During President Arthur's administration, Chinese immigration to the United States was becoming a political issue. The president signed the Chinese Exclusion Act of 1882, which suspended or banned further Chinese immigration to the United States for ten years. Arthur opposed the measure, but signed it for pragmatic reasons.

POST PRESIDENCY

What happened to Arthur **after leaving the White House**?

Arthur suffered from Bright's Disease, an ailment that attacks the kidneys. Consequently, Arthur spent his short post-presidency period suffering from this malady. He passed away on November 18, 1886, and was buried in New York City next to his wife, Ellen.

GROVER CLEVELAND

(1837—1908)
22nd President, 1885–1889
24th President, 1893–1897
Party Affiliation: Democrat
Chief 1884 Opponent: James G. Blaine (Republican)
Chief 1892 Opponent: Benjamin Harrison (Republican)

EARLY LIFE AND FAMILY

Where and when was Grover Cleveland **born**?

Stephen Grover Cleveland was born in Caldwell, New Jersey, to Richard Falley and Ann Neal Cleveland on March 18, 1837. When he was nearly twenty, he began signing his name S. Grover Cleveland and a few years later dropped the "S" altogether.

What was his **father's job**?

The Yale-educated Richard Falley was a Presbyterian minister, who moved his family to Fayetteville, New York, when young Grover—as he came to be called—was four years old. The family then moved to Clinton, New York, when Grover was fourteen years old.

Who was Grover **named after**?

His father, Richard, named his son after Stephen Grover, the first minister at the First Presbyterian Church of Caldwell, New Jersey, where his father was minister at the time.

President Grover Cleveland.

Did Grover Cleveland have any **siblings**?

Yes, he had eight siblings: Anna, William, Mary, Richard Cecil, Margaret, Lewis, Susan, and Rose.

What was his **early education**?

Cleveland first attended school at age eleven in Fayetteville, New York. He attended the Clinton Liberal Institute and the Fayetteville Institute. He loved debate and had planned on attending college at nearby Hamilton College, where his brother William was a student. However, his father's untimely death in 1853 stymied those plans.

Did he **marry**?

Yes, forty-nine-year-old Grover Cleveland married twenty-one-year-old Frances Folsom at the White House on June 2, 1886. He remains the only president to marry in the White House.

Did he have any **children**?

Yes, Grover and Frances had five children: Ruth, Esther, Marion, Richard Folsom, and Francis Glover. Ruth—known as "Baby Ruth" in the press—died at age twelve. Esther, the only child in American history to be born in the White House, married a British military officer. Marion married twice and worked with the Girl Scouts organization on a national level. Richard Folsom graduated from Harvard Law School and later served as general counsel to the Public Service Commission in Baltimore, Maryland. Francis Grover graduated from Harvard, earning his degree in drama.

EARLY CAREER

What were Grover's **first jobs** as a youth?

Grover worked on the Erie Canal as a youth and then as a store clerk at age fifteen. He went on to teach at the New York Institute for the Blind, where his older brother William taught and then served as principal. Grover wanted to attend college but did not have the funds.

Did Cleveland father a child out of wedlock?

Cleveland allegedly fathered a child out of wedlock with a Maria Halpin, when Cleveland was sheriff of Erie County. Maria named the child Oscar Folsom Cleveland—after Cleveland and his law partner and future father-in-law. Cleveland allegedly had the unstable Halpin placed in a mental institute and paid for the child's expenses at an orphanage. The issue nearly doomed Cleveland's presidential chances in 1884. Some ardent Republicans would chant at rallies: "Ma! Ma! Where's my pa? Gone to the White House, ha, ha, ha."

What **career** did Grover first choose?

He initially thought about following in his father's footsteps to the ministry. However, he really wanted to practice law. He borrowed money from a neighbor, Ingham Townsend, who always admired young Grover, to go out west. Many years later he repaid the loan with interest and thanked Townsend for her generosity.

In what city did Grover choose to **lay down his roots**?

Grover decided to move west. First, he stopped off in Buffalo to visit his favorite uncle Lewis F. Allen, a wealthy farmer. His uncle hired Grover as a clerk and an editor. Allen enlisted his nephew to help him finish a short book he was writing entitled *Short-Horn Herd Book*. His uncle introduced him to several prominent lawyers. Grover then began studying law at Rogers, Bowen, and Rogers.

Where did Grover **practice law**?

He clerked at Rogers, Bowen, and Rogers, and after he gained admission to the New York bar in 1859, he officially joined the firm as a lawyer. Former president Millard Fillmore practiced with this firm as well.

How did Cleveland **avoid war service**?

Cleveland avoided the draft and service in the Civil War by paying Polish immigrant George Brinske one hundred and fifty dollars to be his substitute. Cleveland claimed, rightfully according to his biographers, that he was the chief supporter of his mother and sisters.

What was his **next job** in the **legal field**?

In January 1863, Cleveland accepted an appointment to be an assistant district attorney for Erie County, New York. His boss—district attorney C.C. Torrance—relied heavily on

President Cleveland married Frances Folsom while he was in the White House. He was the only president to marry while in office.

Cleveland and his superior work ethic. When Torrance ended his term, Democratic leaders nominated Cleveland as the district attorney. He narrowly lost to future U.S. House of Representatives member and Republican Lyman K. Bass. Ironically, Cleveland later practiced law with Bass.

After losing the race for D.A., what did Cleveland do?

He briefly formed a law partnership with Isaac K. Vanderpoel. However, Vanderpoel left to become a high-ranking police official. Cleveland then joined forces with attorneys Albert P. Laning and Oscar Folsom (the father of his future wife) to form the law firm Laning, Cleveland, and Folsom. By all accounts Cleveland prepared well and excelled as an attorney.

POLITICAL OFFICES

Cleveland left the law firm for what political position?

In 1870, Cleveland accepted the Democratic nomination for sheriff of Erie County and won the position. He had to perform a variety of duties, including serving as executioner. Twice, he pulled the lever that killed convicted murderers. Detractors would later deride him as "The Buffalo Hangman."

What was his next political position?

His next political position was serving as the mayor of Buffalo. He promised to clean up city government and he did, exposing a plan to overcharge the city for road construction. He quickly made a reputation as an incorruptible politician—something considered rather uncommon.

Why was Cleveland the mayor of Buffalo for such a short time?

Cleveland served as mayor briefly because he ran for governor of New York and won. He defeated Charles J. Folger, a federal appeals court judge, to win the position handily by more than 190,000 votes.

What **marked Cleveland's term** as governor?

Cleveland made his mark by refusing patronage requests from the notorious Tammany Hall, a New York political machine known for backroom dealings and underhanded ways. He also vetoed numerous measures—a trait that would also characterize his tenure as president. He approved of a state civil service reform measure and also set aside for preservation more than a million acres near Niagara Falls.

PRESIDENCY

Whom **did he defeat** in the **1884** presidential election?

Cleveland defeated Republican James G. Blaine of Maine to win the presidency for his first term. Blaine had vied for the Republican nomination in 1876 and 1880, but lost to eventual presidents Rutherford B. Hayes and James A. Garfield, respectively. Blaine had served many years in Congress, including as Speaker of the House for six years. Democrats seized upon Blaine's close connection to the railroad industry to sully his name. One common chant was: "Blaine! Blaine! James G. Blaine! Continental liar from the state of Maine!" The vote was extremely close, as Cleveland captured the electoral vote 219 to182 and barely had an edge in the popular vote. Cleveland captured the electoral votes in twenty states, while Blaine won in eighteen.

Whom **did Cleveland defeat** in the **1892** presidential election?

Cleveland defeated incumbent President Benjamin Harrison to recapture the White House in the 1892 election. Cleveland captured 277 electoral votes to 145 for Harrison and 22 for third-party candidate James Weaver, who ran under the Populist banner. Cleveland captured the electoral votes in twenty-three states, compared to sixteen for Harrison and four for Weaver.

Who were Cleveland's **vice presidents**?

In Cleveland's first term, Thomas Hendricks of Indiana served as vice president until his death only nine months into his term in 1885. Hendricks had served in the U.S. House of Representatives, served as Indiana's governor, and ran as Samuel Tilden's vice presidential candidate in 1876. He tried for the presidency in 1880 and 1884. After Hendricks's death, Cleveland did not choose a replacement.

In Cleveland's second term, Adlai Ewing Stevenson of Illinois served as his vice president. A former member of the U.S. House of Representatives, Stevenson had served as assistant postmaster general during Cleveland's first term as president. He later ran as William Jennings Bryan's vice presidential candidate in 1900. His grand-

> ## What is unique about Grover Cleveland's tenure as president?
>
> **G**rover Cleveland is the only person in American history to serve two noncon-secutive terms as president of the United States. He is both the twenty-second and twenty-fourth president in American history, as he lost after his first term to Republican Benjamin Harrison. However, Cleveland defeated Harrison in a rematch four years later to return to the White House for a second term.

son and namesake, Adlai Ewing Stevenson, ran as the Democratic nominee for president in 1952 and 1956, losing to Republican Dwight D. Eisenhower.

What **law** passed in Cleveland's first term as president sought to **assimilate the Native Americans**?

Congress passed and Cleveland signed into law the Dawes Act, which sought to assimilate Native Americans into American life. Under the measure, many reservation lands were divided into separate plots. Native Americans who renounced their tribal allegiances were then granted these parcels of land.

What law did Cleveland sign that **regulated railway rates**?

Cleveland signed into law the Interstate Commerce Act of 1887, which created the Interstate Commerce Commission, a federal agency that monitored the railway rates. The law was designed to ensure that such rates would be "reasonable and just."

What **presidential power** did **Cleveland use more** than all previous presidents combined?

President Grover Cleveland believed strongly in the veto power. Just as he was called the "Veto Governor," he became the "Veto President." He vetoed more than four hundred bills during his first term in office—more than all other previous presidents combined. In his two terms, Cleveland vetoed 586 bills. The only president who vetoed more bills than Cleveland was Franklin Delano Roosevelt, who served three full terms and part of a fourth term. Many of Cleveland's vetoes were against bills that would provide pensions and private relief to many veterans. Cleveland believed in limited government and fiscal conservatism, which caused him to veto many bills that called for great government spending.

What **member** of his **second-term cabinet** served in **two different positions**?

Richard Olney served as U.S. attorney general the first two years of Cleveland's second term and then as secretary of state the last two years, after Walter Q. Gresham died in office. A Harvard-educated lawyer, Olney performed well in both positions. As secretary of state, he forcefully advanced the country's positions on foreign-policy issues. In the twentieth century, he would turn down two federal government positions from President Woodrow Wilson.

What **financial problem befell the country** during Cleveland's second term?

The failure of the Philadelphia and Reading Railroad brought about the Panic of 1893. After the major railroad collapsed, numerous banks followed suit. It was considered the country's worst economic depression until the Great Depression in 1929.

The Panic of 1893 resulted when a large railroad company and several banks financially collapsed. It was the worst financial crisis America had experienced up to that time.

What **strike** caused Cleveland to intervene and employ **federal troops**?

President Cleveland sent in federal troops to resolve the Pullman Strike of 1894. The Pullman Palace Car Company had reduced employee wages in the declining economic market, which outraged many workers. Cleveland sought a court order against the strikers. He said: "If it takes the army and navy of the United States to deliver a postcard in Chicago, that card will be delivered."

What **financial law** passed during Harrison's term in office did Cleveland oppose and **push to repeal**?

Cleveland opposed the Sherman Silver Purchase Act of 1890, which required the federal government to buy a fixed amount of silver each month. The law allowed the federal government to release more paper money backed by silver. The farming community had supported the law as a way to increase the economy and ease the amount of debt. Cleveland believed that the law had harmed the economy, in part by draining the federal government of its gold supply.

Who were Cleveland's U.S. **Supreme Court appointees**?

During his first term as president, Cleveland appointed Lucius Q. C. Lamar, his former secretary of the interior, to the U.S. Supreme Court. The Senate barely confirmed Lamar by a vote of thirty-two to twenty-eight, in part because he has served for the Confederacy in the Civil War. He served only five years on the Court. Cleveland also appointed Melville W. Fuller as chief justice as a replacement Morrison Waite. Fuller served on the Court for twenty-two years and proved an able administrator of the Court.

During his second term as president, Cleveland appointed Edward D. White, who served twenty-seven years on the Court, as an associate justice until 1910, when President William Howard Taft elevated him to Chief Justice. He became the first justice to serve as both associate justice and chief justice. Cleveland's second appointment during his second term was Rufus Peckham, a conservative justice who served thirteen years on the Court. He is best known for writing the Court's majority opinion in *Lochner v. New York* (1905), where the Court struck down a law limiting the number of hours bakery employees could work under a freedom-of-contract theory.

POST PRESIDENCY

At what **college** did Cleveland **devote much** of **his energies** in retirement?

Cleveland devoted much of his energies to Princeton University, where he was named a lecturer in public affairs in 1899. He moved to the Princeton, New Jersey area on the suggestion of his friend and professor Andrew West. He bought a nice estate there and named it "Westlake" after his friend. A few years later, he served on the university's board of trustees. The press sometimes dubbed him "The Sage of Princeton." He quarreled with Princeton president and future Democratic president Woodrow Wilson over the location of a graduate school.

What **else did Cleveland do** in retirement?

He worked at a leading New York law firm. He also wrote articles for numerous magazines and authored several books, including *Presidential Problems* (1904), *Fishing and Shooting Sketches* (1906) and *Good Citizenship* (1908).

When did he **die**?

He died in June 24, 1908, of heart failure. Allegedly, his last words were: "I have tried so hard to do right."

BENJAMIN HARRISON

(1833—1901)
23rd President, 1889–1893
Party Affiliation: Republican
Chief 1888 Opponent: Grover Cleveland (Democrat)

EARLY LIFE AND FAMILY

Where and when was Benjamin Harrison **born**?

Benjamin Harrison was born in North Bend, Ohio, to John Scott Harrison and Elizabeth Irwin Harrison on August 20, 1883. Elizabeth was John's second wife.

After whom was **Benjamin named**?

He was named after his paternal uncle, Dr. Benjamin Harrison, and his great-grandfather, Benjamin Harrison V, who signed the Declaration of Independence.

What **relative** of his was a **former U.S. president**?

Benjamin Harrison's grandfather was none other than William Henry Harrison, the former war hero turned president. William Henry Harrison was the ninth president of the United States, though his tenure was cut tragically short by his untimely death just forty-one days into his presidency. When William Henry Harrison was president, his grandson Benjamin was only seven years old.

President Benjamin Harrison.

What did his **father do** for a living?

John Scott Harrison worked as a farmer most of his life. He also served in the U.S. House of Representatives from 1853 to 1857.

Did he have any **siblings**?

Yes, Benjamin Harrison had five full siblings and two half-siblings (from his father's first marriage). His full-blooded siblings were: Irwin, Mary Jane, Carter, Anna, and John Scott. His two-half siblings were Elizabeth and Sarah.

What was his **early education**?

Harrison first learned from several tutors at a log cabin on his father's property. At age fourteen, his father sent him to Farmers' College, a school in Cincinnati that offered preparatory and college-level classes. His older brother Irwin also attended this school. At Farmers' College, Benjamin learned from Professor Robert Hamilton Bishop. He also met his future wife at this school.

Did he **marry**?

Yes, Benjamin Harrison married twice in his life. In 1853, the twenty-year-old Harrison married twenty-one-year-old Carolina Lavinia Scott. She died in October 1892, right before Harrison's reelection campaign. The sixty-two-year-old Harrison remarried on April 6, 1896, to thirty-seven-year-old Mary Scott Lord Dimmick—the niece of his first wife.

Did he have any **children**?

Yes, Benjamin Harrison had three children—two from his first marriage and one from his second marriage. The two children from his first marriage were Russell Benjamin Harrison and Mary Scott Harrison. Russell served in both houses of the Indiana legislature, practiced law and published a newspaper. Mary married J. Robert McKee, one of the founders of General Electric.

The child from his second marriage was Elizabeth Harrison, who graduated from New York University law school and later published an investment newsletter.

EARLY CAREER

Where did he go to **college**?

In 1850, Harrison attended Miami University in Oxford, Ohio. He excelled academically and became president of the Union Literary Society. He graduated third in his class in 1852.

The home of President Harrison in Indianapolis, Indiana.

After graduating college, what did Harrison do?

He moved to Cincinnati to learn the law under prominent attorney Bellamy Storer. He gained admission to the bar in 1854, a year after marrying Caroline.

What **city** did Harrison **move to** after gaining admission to the bar?

Harrison and his wife decided to move to Indianapolis. His cousin William Sheets, who had achieved success in business, had encouraged the young couple to move to that city. After a year practicing on his own, Harrison joined a practice with William Wallace, a flourishing attorney and the son of a former governor. The law firm of Wallace and Harrison prospered.

What were his **next jobs** in the **legal field**?

In 1857, Harrison won election as the city attorney for Indianapolis. The next year he became an official in the local Republican Party. In 1860, Harrison ran for the position of reporter of the Indiana Supreme Court. The reporter would compile the court's judicial opinions and oversee their publication into legal books. He defeated older Democratic attorney Michael Kerr to win the position.

What did Harrison do in the **military**?

After meeting with Indiana governor Oliver Morton about helping with the war recruitment effort, Harrison decided to join the war effort more directly. Morton commissioned him a second lieutenant in the 70th Indiana Regiment. He rose to become brigadier general and distinguished himself well in battle. He served under Major General Joseph Hooker and saw significant combat action, including the Battle of Resaca and the Battle of Peachtree Creek, both in Georgia.

After the war, what did Harrison do?

He continued work as the state supreme court reporter and continued his private legal practice. He made a good living and attracted the attention of powerful politicians. President Ulysses S. Grant appointed him to defend the government in a suit by Lambdin Milligan, a lawyer who was a vocal opponent of the war. Federal officials arrested Milligan, who responded with a lawsuit that eventually reached the U.S. Supreme Court, which sided with Milligan in the famous case *Ex parte Milligan* (1866). The Supreme Court ruled that federal officials exceeded their lawful authority in arresting Milligan and hauling him before a military tribunal.

Because of the Court's decision, Milligan's case went back to a trial court for a jury hearing. Grant appointed Harrison to argue for the government before the jury. Harrison was an excellent attorney and he persuaded the jury to award Milligan only nominal damages—a total of five dollars.

POLITICAL OFFICES

What political **election** did Harrison **lose in 1876**?

Harrison lost the race for Indiana governor, narrowly dropping the contest to Democratic candidate James D. Williams.

When did Harrison earn a spot in the **U.S. Congress**?

After campaigning in Indiana for himself and for Presidents Ulysses S. Grant and Rutherford B. Hayes, Harrison attracted national party attention. President James Garfield offered Harrison a spot in his cabinet, but Harrison declined. The Indiana legislature elected him to the U.S. Senate. He served in the Senate from 1881 until 1887.

What did Harrison do as a **U.S. senator**?

He supported the Pendleton Act, which provided much needed civil service reform. He supported measures to give Union veterans healthy pensions. He supported measures to improve the navigation of the Mississippi River. He also promoted federal aid for educational efforts, particularly in the South. He also opposed the Chinese Exclusion Act of 1882. He later served as chairman of the Territories Committee in the Senate.

PRESIDENCY

Who was **Harrison's opponent** in the **1888** presidential election?

Harrison had secured the Republican Party nomination in 1888 and squared off against the incumbent president Grover Cleveland. Harrison favored a protective tariff, while Cleveland did not. Harrison won the electoral vote and the presidency by a vote of 233 to168. However, he did lose the popular vote to Cleveland, albeit very narrowly.

Who was his **vice president**?

His vice president was New Yorker Levi P. Morton, founder of the banking firm L.P. Morton and Company. Morton had served as minister to France under President James Garfield and later was elected as governor of New York. He lived to be ninety-six years old.

Who were Harrison's **secretaries of state**?

Harrison tabbed James G. Blaine as his secretary of state. Blaine had served as secretary of state for both James Garfield and Chester A. Arthur and had been the Republican presidential nominee in 1884. Blaine resigned in 1893, in part because he was considering another run at the Republican nomination. Harrison's second secretary of state was John W. Foster of Indiana, who had been a skilled diplomat, serving as minister to Mexico, Russia, and Spain.

What law did Harrison sign that **helped veterans**?

Harrison signed into law the Dependent and Disability Pensions Act of 1890, which gave benefits to military veterans and their dependents when the veterans were disabled for reasons unrelated to military service.

What famous **anti-trust law** did he sign in 1890?

Harrison signed into law the Sherman Antitrust Act of 1890. This important law sought to curb the excesses of big business monopolies. Named after prominent U.S. senator John Sherman, the law is still the most important piece of antitrust legislation in the United States.

What **tariff** bearing a future president's name did Harrison sign?

Harrison signed into law the so-called McKinley Tariff Act of 1890, named after U.S. senator William McKinley of Ohio, who would later go on to become president. This tariff established a very high tariff rate (48 percent) in order to protect U.S. industry. However, the tariff was unpopular and contributed to displeasure with the Republican Party and Harrison.

Which **future president** did Harrison appoint to the position of **civil service commissioner**?

In 1889, Harrison appointed a young Theodore Roosevelt to the position of civil service commissioner. Roosevelt traveled the country and fought hard to enforce the Pendleton Act and further civil service reform.

Who were Harrison's U.S. **Supreme Court appointees**?

Harrison had four Supreme Court appointments: David J. Brewer, Henry B. Brown, George Shiras, and Howell E. Jackson. Brewer was the nephew of former U.S. Supreme Court Justice Stephen Field and a strong conservative. He served for more than twenty years on the Court. Brown served for fifteen years. He dissented in the Supreme Court's decision in *Pollock v. Farmers' Loan and Trust Co.* (1895), where the majority of the Court invalidated a federal income tax. Shiras served for eleven years and often voted for big business interests during his tenure. Jackson, from Tennessee, only served two years. His appointment was a bit unusual in that Harrison, a Republican, nominated Jackson, a Democrat, to the bench. Jackson had distinguished himself as a federal appeals court judge.

Did Harrison **seek reelection**?

Yes, Harrison sought a second term, but lost in the election of 1892 to the man he defeated in 1888—former president Grover Cleveland. Cleveland captured 277 electoral votes to Harrison's 145. His campaign was also harmed by the Populist Party candidacy of James Weaver, who took 22 votes himself.

POST PRESIDENCY

What did Harrison do **after leaving the White House**?

Perhaps the most surprising thing he did—especially to his children—was that he married a woman twenty-five years younger than him, Mary Scott Lord Dimmick, his first wife's niece. His children adamantly opposed the union. He also resumed the practice of law and wrote a great deal. He served as counsel for the country of Venezuela in a border dispute with British Guiana. President William McKinley appointed him to the Permanent Court of Arbitration.

What **books did he author** during his retirement?

He wrote two books in his retirement period—*This Country of Ours* (1897) and *Views of an Ex-President* (1901).

When did he **die**?

Harrison died of the flu in March 13, 1901, in Indianapolis, Indiana, at the age of sixty-seven.

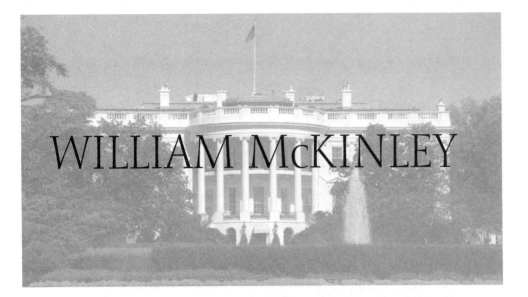

WILLIAM McKINLEY

(1843–1901)
25th President, 1897–1901
Political Party: Republican
Chief 1896 and 1900 Opponent: William Jennings Bryan (Democrat)

EARLY LIFE AND FAMILY

Where and when was he **born**?

William McKinley Jr. was born in Niles, Ohio, to William McKinley and Nancy Allison McKinley on January 29, 1843. He dropped the Jr. suffix after the death of his father in 1892.

What did his **father do** for a living?

William McKinley Sr. worked as an iron manufacturer just as his father before him had done.

What was his **early education**?

McKinley attended a public school in Niles, Ohio. At age eleven, he attended the Poland Seminary, a Methodist school in Poland, Ohio. He matriculated to Allegheny College at age seventeen, but dropped out for health reasons after a year.

President William McKinley.

Did William McKinley Jr. have any **siblings**?

Yes, he had seven siblings: David, Anna, James, Mary, Helen, Sarah, and Abner.

Did he **marry**?

A twenty-seven-year-old William McKinley married twenty-three-year-old Ida Saxton on January 25, 1871. She was the daughter of a successful banker in Canton, Ohio.

Did he have any **children**?

Yes, William and Ida had two children—Katherine and Ida. Sadly, both children died in childhood. Katherine lived to age four and Ida died before reaching her first birthday.

EARLY CAREER

After leaving **college**, what did McKinley do?

He taught school at the Kerr School District in Poland, Ohio, and then worked at the city's post office.

When did he **join the military**?

An eighteen-year-old McKinley volunteered for the Union forces in his native Ohio. He joined the 23rd Ohio Volunteer infantry in June 1861. He served more than four years during his service. He rose from the rank of private to brevet major. He saw action in numerous Civil War battles, including the Battles of Opequon, Cedar Creek, Antietam, Kernstown, Berryville, and Clay's Mountain. His commander for part of his service was none other than Rutherford B. Hayes—the future nineteenth president of the United States and a fellow Ohioan.

How did McKinley distinguish himself with **heroism** during the **Civil War**?

At the Battle of Antietam in September 1862 some of the Union soldiers were trapped and not able to cross the river with their fellow soldiers. The nineteen-year-old McKin-

273

ley, serving as commissary to the unit, loaded a wagon and rode back to give food and drink to the trapped soldiers. He drove the wagon through hostile Confederate gunfire and completed his mission successfully. McKinley narrowly missed meeting his end, as his wagon was hit by Confederate cannon fire.

What did McKinley do **after the war**?

McKinley decided to pursue a career in law. He attended Albany Law School for a year, but did not graduate. Instead—as was often done at that time—he learned, or "read" the law under a practicing attorney. McKinley read law under Judge Charles Glidden.

What legal **job** did he **win** in an **election**?

McKinley won election as the prosecutor for Stark County, Ohio, even though the county was largely Democratic. He served one term before losing a reelection bid in 1871. After losing, McKinley returned to the private practice of law.

POLITICAL OFFICES

When did he become a **U.S. congressman**?

McKinley won election to the U.S. House of Representatives in 1876, defeating Democrat Leslie L. Sanborn. He won reelection twice more before losing a razor-thin race to Democrat Jonathan H. Wallace, who successfully challenged an original eight vote lead for McKinley.

He returned to the House after defeating D. R. Paige in an 1884 election. Once again, he earned reelection twice before losing to John G. Warwick in an 1890 election.

Why did McKinley **lose the 1890 election**?

He lost largely because of an unpopular tariff bill that he championed as chairman of the House Ways and Means Committee. The so-called McKinley Tariff imposed incredibly high taxes on foreign-produced goods, but the impact of the law drove up consumer prices. As a result, the measure was not very popular. Many Republicans in Congress—including McKinley—lost their seats as a result of the economic issues.

What was McKinley's **next political position**?

McKinley became governor of Ohio in 1892, a position he held for two terms until his presidential run four years later in 1896. He had to exert his authority to monitor labor unrest, even sending out the National Guard to help quell public disturbances.

President McKinley's cabinet.

However, McKinley also tried to reign in the excesses of employers in their harsh treatment of unions and union members. On balance—like his mentor Rutherford B. Hayes (who was also a former governor of Ohio), McKinley was a popular governor.

PRESIDENCY

Whom did **McKinley defeat** to win the **1896 Republican nomination**?

McKinley overwhelmingly captured the 1896 Republican nomination for the presidency, defeating Thomas B. Reed of Maine, Levi P. Morton of New York, Matthew Quay of Pennsylvania, and William B. Allison from Iowa. Reed was the Speaker of the House, Morton was the governor of New York as well as President Benjamin Harrison's former vice president, Quay and Allison were United States senators. McKinley captured more than 660 votes, while Reed—the next closest—garnered just more than eighty votes.

Whom did **McKinley defeat twice** to win the presidency?

McKinley defeated a thirty-six-year-old lawyer who had practiced in Illinois and Nebraska named William Jennings Bryan, a talented attorney who argued many times before the U.S. Supreme Court. Known as the "Great Commoner," Bryan advocated

275

the free-silver cause, which would call for the federal government to allow farmers and debtors to deposit bullions and receive silver coins in return. Essentially, it was a policy that favored those in debt (which included many farmers) over the investors (the banks). Bryan captured the Democratic Party nomination three times—in 1896, 1900, and 1908.

McKinley defeated Bryan in both the election of 1896 and 1900. In 1896, McKinley won the electoral vote count 271 to 176 in 1896, and 292 to 155 in the election of 1900.

Who were McKinley's **vice presidents**?

McKinley's first vice president was Garret Augustus Hobart, a New Jersey politician who had served in both branches of the state congress but had failed in his bid for the United States Senate. Hobart died in office and the position was not filled for the remainder of McKinley's first term.

His second vice president was a promising politician from New York named Theodore Roosevelt. A striking figure in personality and performance, Roosevelt assumed the presidency after McKinley's assassination.

Which members of McKinley's **cabinet** later won a **Nobel Peace Prize**?

Theodore Roosevelt—McKinley's second vice president—won the Nobel Peace Prize in 1906 when, as president, he negotiated an end to the Russo-Japanese War. Elihu Root—McKinley's second secretary of war—also won the Nobel Peace Prize in 1912 for his efforts in attempting to bring different countries together for arbitration purposes. Root replaced Russell A. Alger as secretary of war after McKinley asked for Alger's resignation. Root later served as secretary of state under Theodore Roosevelt. Root lived to be more than ninety years of age.

Which member of McKinley's **cabinet** set a **record** for the longest **continuous service** as a **cabinet member**?

James Wilson served as secretary of agriculture for McKinley's entire presidency. He continued in that same role under presidents Theodore Roosevelt and William Howard Taft. He had previously been a member of the U.S. House of Representatives and a professor of agriculture at Iowa State University.

What **major war** did the U.S. successfully **wage** during McKinley's presidency?

The United States prevailed over Spain in the Spanish–American War of 1898. For a time McKinley resisted growing public sentiment for the U.S. to stop Spain from perpetrating alleged atrocities in nearby Cuba, including hauling civilians into concentration camps. Some leading journalists led the call for McKinley to initiate military action. A cataclysmic turning point occurred with the explosion and subsequent sinking of the U.S.S. *Maine,* a U.S. warship sent to Havana, Cuba. The circumstances surrounding the destruction of the ship remain cloudy. Whatever the cause, the effect was that McKinley asked Congress for a declaration of war in April 1898.

Congress agreed by a wide margin in the House and a narrow margin in the Senate. U.S. armed forces dominated, notably Theodore Roosevelt and his band of so-called "Rough Riders" who won the Battle of San Juan. The battle earned Roosevelt national hero status and ultimately the vice presidency.

The sinking of the U.S.S. *Maine* in Cuba's Havana Harbor set off the Spanish–American War of 1898.

By a peace agreement, the United States gained control of Spanish interests in Guam, Puerto Rico, and the Philippines. Guam and Puerto Rico remain U.S. territories to this day. U.S. occupation in the Philippines led to the Philippine–American War, which lasted several years beginning in 1899. It lasted until the administration of President Theodore Roosevelt.

What **future state** did **McKinley annex** during his tenure?

During his presidency, the United States annexed the Republic of Hawaii by the Newland Resolution—named after U.S. congressman Francis G. Newland. Hawaii became a United States territory in 1898. It remained a territory until it was admitted as the fiftieth state in 1959.

What **law passed** during McKinley's tenure seemed to help the **economy**?

McKinley signed into the law the Gold Standard Act of 1900, which made just gold—not gold and silver—the standard for redeeming paper currency. This provision—along with the ending of the economic depression known as the Panic of 1893—ensured that McKinley would be reelected to a second term.

Who was his lone **U.S. Supreme Court appointee**?

McKinley appointed Joseph McKenna, his attorney general, to the U.S. Supreme Court in 1898. He served nearly twenty-seven years on the Court before his death. Previously, he had been a member of the U.S. House of Representatives. Thus, McKenna is one of the few leaders to have served in all three branches of the federal government.

277

T. Dart Walker painted this depiction of the assassination of President McKinley at the hands of anarchist Leon F. Csolgosz.

Who **killed William McKinley**?

Leon F. Csolgosz shot President McKinley on September 6, 1901, in Buffalo, New York, at a concert hall named The Temple of Music. McKinley was attending the Pan-American Conference there. Csolgosz was a self-avowed anarchist who believed that McKinley represented an oppressive government that exploited the working class. McKinley died eight days later on September 14, 1901.

Csolgosz was not a formal member of the Anarchist party but he attended several lectures and speeches by the group. He particularly enjoyed a speech by noted anarchist Emma Goldman. Historians believe that Csolgosz was inspired by the assassination of the King Umberto I of Italy by Gaetano Bresci.

Csolgosz stood trial later that month. A jury convicted him and recommended a sentence of death. He was executed on October 29, 1901. His last words reportedly were: "I killed the president because he was the enemy of the good people—the good working people. I am not sorry for my crime."

THEODORE ROOSEVELT

(1858–1919)
26th President, 1901–1909
Party Affiliation: Republican
Chief 1904 Opponent: Alton B. Parker (Democrat)

EARLY LIFE AND FAMILY

Where and when was he **born**?

Theodore Roosevelt Jr. was born in New York City to Theodore Roosevelt Sr. and Martha Bulloch Roosevelt on October 27, 1858. His nickname as a child was "Teedie."

What did his **father do** for a living?

Theodore Roosevelt Sr. worked some in the family business of manufacturing plate glass. Theodore Sr.'s father, Cornelius, had made a fortune in real estate in Manhattan as well. This gave Theodore Sr. the opportunity to devote his energies to different charities. He did much philanthropic work with hospitals and museums.

What was Theodore Jr.'s **early education**?

He did not have much formal schooling in the traditional sense. This was due, in part, to the fact that he was beset with asthma when he was three years old. However, his family's affluence enabled him to travel around the world. He saw much of Europe

The future President Roosevelt poses in 1905 with members of the Rough Riders.

when he was ten years old. Private tutors helped young Teddy learn French, German, and other subjects.

Who were his **siblings**?

He had three siblings: an older sister named Anna, a younger brother named Elliott, and a younger sister named Corinne.

How did he acquire his **interests in athletics**?

His father built a gym in the family home and strongly encouraged his son to maintain his health through vigorous exercise. It was advice that Theodore Jr. took to heart for most of his life.

Did he **marry**?

Roosevelt married twice in his life. He married Alice Hathaway Lee on October 27, 1880, in Brookline, Massachusetts. She died February 14, 1884, of kidney failure shortly after giving birth to the couple's daughter, Alice Lee. In a horrible coincidence, that same day (Valentine's Day) Theodore also lost his mother, Martha. He wrote in his diary: "And when my heart's dearest died, the light went out from my life forever."

In December 2, 1886, he married Edith Carow Roosevelt in London. She lived until 1948—nearly thirty years longer than her husband.

Which of his siblings was the father of a future first lady?

Theodore's younger brother Elliott was the father of Anna Eleanor Roosevelt, who later became the wife of future President Franklin Delano Roosevelt. Eleanor Roosevelt is one of the most famous First Ladies in American history.

Who were his **children**?

Roosevelt had one child by his first marriage named Alice. She lived till the age of ninety-six, passing away in 1980. He had five children by his second marriage: Theodore, Kermit, Ethel, Archibald, and Quentin. Theodore Jr., a Harvard graduate, served with distinction during World War I, earning a Purple Heart. He later served as assistant secretary of the navy under President Warren G. Harding, governor of Puerto Rico under President Calvin Coolidge, and governor-general of the Philippines by President Herbert Hoover. He later served in World War II and participated in the Battle at Normandy. Kermit graduated from Harvard, served in World War I, and became a successful businessman. During World War I, he flew as a pilot for the army and died in the service of his country. Ethel married a doctor and served as a nurse at an American hospital in Paris during World War I. Archibald graduated from Harvard, served in both World Wars, and became a successful investment banker. Quentin flew as an Army pilot during World War I and died in the service of his country.

EARLY CAREER

Where did Roosevelt **attend college**?

He attended Harvard University in Cambridge, Massachusetts, in 1876. In his second year of college, his father passed away at the age of forty-six from stomach cancer. Though devastated with grief, Roosevelt stayed at Harvard and graduated in June 1880. He joined the Art Club, the Rifle Club, and edited a school newspaper. He also boxed for his college team.

After graduating college, what did Roosevelt do?

He married Alice Hathaway Lee a few months after his graduation. He then enrolled in Columbia Law School. While a law student, he wrote a book entitled *The Naval War of 1812*. He did not graduate from law school. Instead, he left school to run for political office at the age of twenty-three.

281

What did he do **after** the **death of his first wife** and his **mother** in 1884?

Theodore Jr. left his child Alice with his older sister Anna and traveled out west. He moved to the Badlands in the Dakota Territory, where he became a rancher at Elk Horn. During his two years out west, he learned the ways of the cowboys, but still found time for reading and writing. He wrote a book on Thomas Hart Benton, a famous U.S senator from Missouri, and another book entitled *Hunting Trips of a Ranchman*.

Roosevelt and his second wife, Edith, pose with grandson Richard Derby, son of the Roosevelts' daughter Ethel.

What **other books** did he **write** before resuming his political career?

He wrote a book on Founding Father Gouverneur Morris and another work entitled *New York*. He also worked on a four-volume series, *The Winning of the West*.

POLITICAL OFFICES

What was his **first political office**?

He won a place in the New York state assembly in 1882, representing Albany. He won reelection twice in 1883 and 1884. While an assemblyman, he attracted public attention by targeting a corrupt judge named T.R. Westbrook, who aided financier Jay Gould. Although Westbrook was eventually cleared of the investigation, his image suffered, and he may have committed suicide.

What political **race** did Roosevelt **lose in 1886**?

Theodore Roosevelt ran for mayor of New York City in 1886 as a Republican with the moniker "Cowboy of the Dakotas." He finished third behind Democrat Abram Hewitt and Socialist Henry George.

What was his **next political position**?

President Benjamin Harrison appointed Roosevelt to the position on the Civil Service Commission in 1889. He worked tirelessly against the spoils system and for civil ser-

Why didn't Roosevelt win the Medal of Honor?

His heroism at San Juan Hill merited Roosevelt the Medal of Honor. However, Roosevelt penned an open letter in which he criticized the army and the politicians for their slow withdrawal of American troops from Puerto Rico, even though there was a spread of malaria. The secretary of war and President McKinley were not pleased and some even thought that Roosevelt might face a court martial. However, nothing came of this, due to Roosevelt's immense popularity. President Bill Clinton later posthumously awarded Roosevelt his Medal of Honor in January 2001.

vice reform. He believed that President Harrison—whom he supported in the 1888 and 1892 presidential elections—did not pursue civil service reform goals with enough zest. Roosevelt performed well in this position, so much so that President Grover Cleveland, a Democrat, reappointed Roosevelt for another term.

What did he do **after leaving** the **Civil Service Commission**?

Roosevelt left the Civil Service Commission in 1895 to serve as president of the Board of Police Commissioners of New York City. He took to this job with his characteristic zeal, sometimes even checking up on individual patrolmen to see if they were doing their jobs properly.

What political position did President **William McKinley appoint** him to?

McKinley appointed Roosevelt to the position of assistant secretary to the navy. He worked under the easygoing John Long, who gladly let Roosevelt do the heavy lifting. Roosevelt worked to increase the number of naval ships and even gave orders to Commodore George Dewey about moving his ships from Japan to Hong Kong to monitor Spanish ships, when it seemed as if America might enter war with Spain over the conflict in Cuba.

Why did Roosevelt **resign** as **assistant secretary of the navy**?

Roosevelt resigned his post in 1898 to volunteer to serve in the Spanish–American War of 1898. He entered as a lieutenant colonel under the leadership of Colonel Leonard Wood, his friend who had earned the Medal of Honor for his combat record. Roosevelt trained with Wood's men at San Antonio. His so-called "Rough Riders" were a tough military unit that later achieved great success during the war, particularly at the Battle of San Juan Hill near Santiago, Cuba, when Roosevelt was a full colonel and personally led his troops into combat. He left the conflict as a genuine military hero.

283

Teddy Roosevelt campaigned from the caboose of a train, a strategy his cousin Franklin D. Roosevelt would make famous in his "whistle stop" campaign.

He later wrote a book about his experiences in Cuba, aptly titled *Rough Riders*.

After the war, what election did Roosevelt win?

Roosevelt campaigned and won election as governor of New York. During his tenure as governor, he continued his reform-minded ways, rid the city of racial segregation in the public schools, and pushed for stronger regulations for workplace safety. He also dealt easily and effectively with the media—something not all presidents have been able to do through the years.

Why didn't Roosevelt run for reelection as governor?

Roosevelt would have run for another term as governor, but through the cagey machinations of New York political figure Tom Platt, he became the country's vice-president. President William McKinley needed a vice presidential candidate for his run at a second term. Platt—who wanted Roosevelt out as New York governor because of his independent streak and zeal for reform—saw an opportunity to press for Roosevelt as the vice presidential nominee at the 1900 Republican nominating convention.

PRESIDENCY

How did Roosevelt become president?

Vice President Roosevelt became president after Leon Csolgosz assassinated President William McKinley. He followed in the footsteps of John Tyler, Millard Fillmore, Andrew Johnson, and Chester A. Arthur as vice presidents who became president following the untimely death of the sitting president. At age forty-two, Theodore Roosevelt became the youngest person up to that time to become president.

Whom did Roosevelt defeat in the 1904 election to win his first full term?

Roosevelt defeated Alton B. Parker, the former chief justice of the New York Court of Appeals (the state's highest court), to win the presidency. He captured 336 electoral votes to only 140 for Parker. The former jurist, who had resigned his position from the bench after receiving the Democratic nomination, returned to the private practice of law after losing the election.

Who was Roosevelt's **vice president**?

Roosevelt did not have a vice president for the years after McKinley's assassination. However, his vice president for his full term was Charles W. Fairbanks, a U.S. senator from Indiana. Fairbanks later sought the Republican nomination for president in 1916, but did not succeed. However, he was chosen to be the running mate of Charles Evans Hughes, the Republican presidential candidate that year. Hughes and Fairbanks lost that election to Woodrow Wilson and Thomas Marshall.

What **member** of Roosevelt's **cabinet** later became **president of the United States**?

William Howard Taft served as Roosevelt's secretary of war from 1904 to 1908. Taft later succeeded Roosevelt as the country's twenty-seventh president.

What **major trust** did Roosevelt **break up** during his first couple years in office?

Roosevelt instructed his attorney general Philander C. Knox to investigate the Northern Securities Trust, a conglomeration of James J. Hill's Great Northern Railroad, E. H. Harriman's Union Pacific Railroad, and J. P. Morgan's Northern Pacific Railroad. Northern Securities Trust served as a holding company for their collective earnings. Roosevelt earned his reputation as a trust-buster extraordinaire, as the U.S. Supreme Court ruled in 1904 that the company did violate the Sherman Anti-Trust Act.

What other **labor crisis** did Roosevelt **resolve** in his first term?

Roosevelt intervened in the United Mine Workers' strike in eastern Pennsylvania. The United Mine Workers union found it difficult to bargain with the mine operators. After coal prices skyrocketed, Roosevelt threatened to take over the mines as a federal receivership unless the two sides could reach a bargain. The operators agreed to binding arbitration with the net result that the workers received a ten percent wage raise and the operators received a ten percent price increase for coal.

What famous **canal was started** during Roosevelt's presidency?

The United States wanted a canal built through Central America. Roosevelt wanted the canal to go through Panama, then under the control of Columbia. In January

1903, the United States signed a treaty which allowed the construction of the canal across Panama. When Columbia balked at the treaty, Roosevelt encouraged the Panamanians to rise up and declare their independence. The U.S. recognized Panama as an independent country. Construction began on the canal in 1904 and it was completed in 1914.

Why was Roosevelt called "The Great Conservationist"?

Roosevelt actively promoted the goal of conserving the country's natural resources. He supported a federal law providing for the construction of dams and aqueducts in the west. He supported the first Federal Bird Reservation at Pelican Island. He expanded the National Forestry Service and set aside 230 million acres for preserves, parks, and refuges.

In what war did Roosevelt serve as mediator?

Roosevelt mediated between the Russians and the Japanese, who had been embroiled in the Russo-Japanese War of 1904 to 1905. The two countries sent representatives to Portsmouth, New Hampshire, which culminated in the Treaty of Portsmouth. For his efforts, Roosevelt received the Nobel Peace Prize in 1906.

Who were Roosevelt's U.S. Supreme Court appointees?

Roosevelt made three Supreme Court appointments: Oliver Wendell Holmes, William R. Day, and William H. Moody. Holmes, formerly a justice on the Massachusetts Supreme Judicial Court, became one of the most famous justices in Supreme Court history. He served thirty years on the Court from 1902 until 1932, leaving at the age of ninety. Holmes became known for his judicial restraint and for his powerful First Amendment opinions. William R. Day, the former U.S. secretary of state under President William McKinley, served on the Court from 1903 until 1922. William R. Moody, who had served as Roosevelt's navy secretary and U.S. attorney general, served on the Court from 1906 until 1910.

> ## Who tried to assassinate Theodore Roosevelt when he ran for president again in 1912?
>
> John Flammang Schrank, a thirty-six-year-old man, shot Roosevelt outside a hotel in Milwaukee, Wisconsin. Fortunately, the bullet hit his breast pocket, which contained his metal eyeglass case. While bleeding, Roosevelt still managed to deliver his speech of nearly an hour. He reportedly said: "It takes more than one bullet to kill a Bull Moose."
>
> Schrank believed that a ghost of William McKinley had appeared to him in his dream and instructed him to kill Roosevelt. He spent the rest of his life in mental hospitals.

POST PRESIDENCY

Did Roosevelt **try** to gain the **presidency** again?

Yes, Roosevelt ran for president in 1912. He did not run in 1908, content to support his former cabinet member and friend William Howard Taft for president. However, Roosevelt became alarmed at the conservative direction of Taft's administration. Roosevelt, the leader of the progressive wing of the Republican Party, sought the party's nomination in 1912. This election marked the beginning of state primaries in which voters in respective states selected the candidate and party delegates would then cast the state's votes for that candidate.

After Taft won the nomination, Roosevelt left the Republican Party and formed the Progressive Party, which later became known as the Bull Moose Party. Roosevelt came in second in the election, capturing eighty-eight electoral votes and more than four million popular votes. He even won the states of New York and California. However, the split between Taft and Roosevelt enabled Democrat Woodrow Wilson to win the nomination.

Did Roosevelt **support World War I**?

Yes, and he even offered his services to create a volunteer unit, as he did during the Spanish–American War of 1898. However, President Woodrow Wilson declined his offer. All of his sons—Theodore, Kermit, Archibald, and Quentin—served in World War I. Quentin lost his life in the war, after his plane was shot down by the Germans.

What were some of the **books Roosevelt wrote** in his post-presidential period?

Roosevelt wrote more books than any president in American history. Some of the books he wrote in his post-presidential period were *African Game Trails, The New*

287

Nationalism, Theodore Roosevelt: An Autobiography, America and the World War, Fear God and Take Your Own Part, The Foes of Our Own Household, and *International Duty.*

When did Roosevelt **die**?

Roosevelt died on January 6, 1919, of a coronary embolism. He was buried in Oyster Bay, New York.

WILLIAM HOWARD TAFT

(1857–1930)
27th President, 1909–1913
Party Affiliation: Republican
Chief 1908 Opponent: William Jennings Bryan (Democrat)

EARLY LIFE AND FAMILY

Where and when was he **born**?

William Howard Taft was born in Cincinnati, Ohio, to Alphonso Taft and Louisa Maria Torrey Taft, on September 15, 1857 in Cincinnati, Ohio.

Did William Howard Taft have any **siblings**?

He had two half-brothers, Charles and Peter, who were products of his father's first marriage to Fanny Phelps. Fanny Phelps Taft died at age twenty-nine. Alphonse Taft then married Taft's mother, Louisa. Taft had three full siblings: Henry, Horace, and Frances.

Which of his **siblings** became a member of the **U.S. Congress**?

Charles Phelps Taft, William Howard Taft's half-brother, served in the U.S. House of Representatives from 1895 to 1897. A graduate of Yale University and Columbia Law School, Charles Phelps Taft practiced law and then became owner of the newspaper *The Cincinnati Times-Star.*

President William Howard Taft.

What did his **father do** for a living?

Alphonso Taft had a distinguished legal and political career. A Yale graduate, Taft studied law and became a successful lawyer and jurist. He served several terms as a Superior Court judge in Cincinnati. He accepted an appointment from President Ulysses S. Grant to be his secretary of war in 1876 for a few months, and then his U.S. attorney general for two years, 1876 to 1878. President Chester A. Arthur appointed him minister to Austria-Hungary in 1882 and minister to Russia in 1884.

What was Taft's **early education**?

He attended Sixteenth District public school in his early years. He then went to Woodward High School, earning his high school diploma in 1874 and graduating second in his class. He went on to attend Yale University, graduating second in a class of 132 in 1878.

Did he **marry**?

William Howard Taft married Helen "Nellie" Herron on June 19, 1886, in Cincinnati. She outlived Taft by thirteen years and died in 1943.

Did he have any **children**?

Yes, William and Helen had three children: Robert, Helen, and Charles. Robert Alphonso Taft graduated from Yale University and Harvard Law School. He later served in the United States Senate from 1939 to 1953. His leadership in the Republican Party earned him the moniker "Mr. Republican."

Helen Herron Taft earned her undergraduate degree from Bryn Mawr College. She married Yale history professor Frederick Johnson Manning. Helen became dean of her alma mater in 1917. She left to pursue a doctorate degree from Yale University. Afterwards, she returned to Bryn Mawr, where she served as dean for many years. After leaving the deanship, she taught history at the college until her retirement in 1957.

Charles Phelps Taft, named after William's half-brother, earned both his undergraduate and law degrees from Yale University. He served from many years on the Cincinnati city council and also served as mayor of the city from 1955 to 1957. His moniker was "Mr. Cincinnati."

EARLY CAREER

After graduating college, what did Taft do?

Taft entered the University of Cincinnati law school, graduating in 1880. During his law school days, he worked as a courthouse reporter for the *Cincinnati Commercial* and received admission to the Ohio bar.

Taft—seen here traveling with his wife and friends on a ship bound for the Philippines—was named commissioner of the Philippines by President McKinley.

What was his **first job** in the **law?**

Taft's first legal position was as assistant prosecuting attorney in Hamilton County, Ohio. He chose this job even though it paid less than a full-time job as a reporter with the *Cincinnati Commercial.*

What did he do after **leaving this legal post?**

Taft then entered private practice with attorney Harlan Page Lloyd, but he yearned for a place on the bench. His career ambition was to serve on the U.S. Supreme Court.

POLITICAL POSITIONS

To what position did the **Ohio governor appoint him** in 1887?

Governor Joseph B. Foraker appointed Taft to fill a vacancy on the Ohio Superior Court in Cincinnati. Taft was only thirty years old at the time, but the governor was impressed with his keen legal mind. Taft filled out the remainder of the term and then won reelection. It was the only election in which he would participate until capturing the presidency in 1908.

President Benjamin **Harrison** then **appointed him** to what position?

President Benjamin Harrison appointed Taft to the prestigious position of U.S. solicitor general. The solicitor general has the opportunity to represent the government before the U.S. Supreme Court. Therefore, Taft went on to argue numerous cases before the Court.

What was his **next position**?

President Harrison appointed Taft as a judge on the U.S. Court of Appeals for the 6th Circuit. This court hears federal cases on appeal from federal district courts in Tennessee, Kentucky, Ohio, and Michigan. Taft served on the 6th Circuit for eight years from 1982 until 1900.

Why did he **leave the 6th Circuit judgeship**?

Taft left the 6th Circuit because President William McKinley appointed him to become commissioner of the Philippines. Taft had hoped that McKinley had called him to Washington, D.C., to offer him a position on the U.S. Supreme Court. Instead, Taft accepted the position with the understanding that if an opening arose on the Supreme Court, he would be strongly considered.

What did Taft **accomplish** in the **Philippines**?

Taft performed well in his role as commissioner and then governor-general of the Philippines. He took the job with zeal and it showed. He upgraded the health standards in the country, created a civil service system, established a governing legal document, and limited corruption. At times he clashed with Major General Arthur

MacArthur—father of future general Douglas MacArthur—over the treatment of Filipinos. During his tenure in the Philippines from 1901 to 1904, Taft even turned down two offers from President Theodore Roosevelt to serve on the U.S. Supreme Court.

What was Taft's **next political position**?

President Roosevelt named Taft as his secretary of war. As head of the War Department, Taft supervised work on the Panama Canal and met with Japanese leaders about the Russo-Japanese War. He quelled a potential crisis in Cuba, even serving as provisional governor for a time in 1906. In these positions, Taft showed his characteristic excellent work ethic and good diplomacy skills.

PRESIDENCY

Whom did **Taft defeat** to win the **Republican nomination**?

President Roosevelt had announced that he would not seek a third term. Taft for his part was more interested in one day becoming Chief Justice of the U.S. Supreme Court, but his wife, Nellie, pushed him to run for president. Roosevelt called him to the White House and told Taft that he was his handpicked successor. Roosevelt helped ensure that Taft had smooth sailing at the 1908 Republican nominating convention.

Whom did **Taft defeat** to win the presidency?

Taft defeated familiar Democratic presidential aspirant William Jennings Bryan. Taft had the advantage of being the successor to the popular Theodore Roosevelt. Bryan said that Roosevelt had actually taken many Democratic positions during his administration, but that argument did not work with the majority of the voting public. Taft won the electoral vote by 321 to 162.

Who was his **vice president**?

James S. Sherman, a longtime member of the U.S. House of Representatives from New York, served as Taft's vice president for most of his term. Sherman died in office in 1912 before Taft completed his term.

Who was his **secretary of state**?

Philander C. Knox served as Taft's secretary of state. Previously, he had served as U.S. attorney general under both presidents William McKinley and Theodore Roosevelt. He sought the Republican nomination for president in 1908, but lost to his future boss Taft.

Knox is credited with implementing the "Dollar Diplomacy" policy. He served as a U.S. senator from Pennsylvania and sought the Republican presidential nomination in 1920.

What was **"Dollar Diplomacy"**?

Dollar Diplomacy referred to the U.S. policy toward gaining economic footholds in countries in Central and South America. Taft and Knox formulated a plan that would use U.S. strength to set up favorable economic positions for U.S. business interests. The term is used pejoratively by some who criticized the United States for overreaching and exploiting foreign countries for economic gain.

What did Taft do with respect to **trusts**?

Taft pursued the goal of breaking up large trusts as much as Roosevelt did. The difference was that Taft pursued the goal just as much—if not more than—Roosevelt, but did not make big pronouncements like his predecessor. The federal government filed ninety antitrust suits during Taft's tenure—more than those filed during the Roosevelt administration. His administration won victories over the Standard Oil Company and the American Tobacco Company.

What **major law** signed by Taft gave the federal government greater **control over railroad rates**?

Taft signed into law the Mann-Elkins Act of 1910, which gave the Interstate Commerce Commission (ICC) more authority over railroad rates. It also gave the ICC control over the telephone and telegraph industries. Congress abolished this agency in 1995.

What **two states** were **admitted to the Union** during Taft's administration?

New Mexico and Arizona became the forty-seventh and forty-eighth states respectively during the time that Taft was president. Thus, the Taft presidency oversaw the completion of the full continental United States. Only Alaska and Hawaii would be added to the current total of fifty.

What **amendment** was added to the **Constitution** during Taft's administration?

The necessary number of thirty-six states ratified the 16th Amendment and it became a part of the Constitution in February 1913 before Taft left office. The amendment provides: "The Congress shall have the power to lay and collect taxes on incomes, from whatever source derived, without apportionment among the several States, and without regard to any census or enumeration."

After serving as president, Taft happily took the job of Chief Justice of the U.S. Supreme Court, the only U.S. president to ever hold a post as Supreme Court justice.

Who were Taft's U.S. **Supreme Court appointees?**

It was fitting that Taft—a lover of the judicial branch and a future Chief Justice of the U.S. Supreme Court—had more appointments to the U.S. Supreme Court than any other single-term president in history. He appointed five men as associate justices: Horace H. Lurton, Charles Evan Hughes, Willis Van Devanter, Joseph R. Lamar, and Mahlon Pitney. He also elevated sitting associate justice Edward D. White from associate justice to chief justice.

Lurton served on the Court from 1910 until 1914. Taft had served with him on the 6th U.S. Circuit Court of Appeals. Hughes, the governor of New York, served on the Court as an associate justice from 1910 to 1916. He left the bench to run for president. He captured the Republican nomination, but lost a close election to incumbent Woodrow Wilson. Devanter served on the court more than twenty-five years from 1911 to 1937. He served with Chief Justice Taft, the man who had appointed him. Lamar served five years on the Court from 1911 to 1916. Pitney served ten years on the Court from 1912 to 1922. Taft elevated Edward D. White from associate justice to chief justice in 1910. White served as chief justice until his death in 1921. Taft succeeded White as chief justice.

POST PRESIDENCY

Did Taft **seek reelection?**

Yes, but he faced considerable opposition in his own party. His former mentor and friend Theodore Roosevelt believed that Taft had not followed his progressive policies and questioned Taft's leadership skills. Taft managed to capture the Republican Party nomination through some deft political maneuvering, but Roosevelt simply created a third party—the Progressive or Bull Moose Party. This doomed the Republicans and enabled Democrat Woodrow Wilson to win the election.

What did Taft do **after losing** his reelection bid?

Taft became a professor at Yale University, teaching law. He served in that capacity from 1913 until 1921. During this time, he wrote a book entitled *Our Chief Magistrate and His Powers,* published in 1916. He also managed to reconcile with Roosevelt in 1918.

When and where did he **die**?

Taft, who was the largest president in U.S. history, suffered from several health problems after he left the presidency, including high blood pressure and heart disease. He died on March 8, 1930, in Washington, D.C. He remains the only person in United States history to serve as a president of the United States and Chief Justice of the U.S. Supreme Court. In fact, no other president has ever served in any capacity on the Supreme Court.

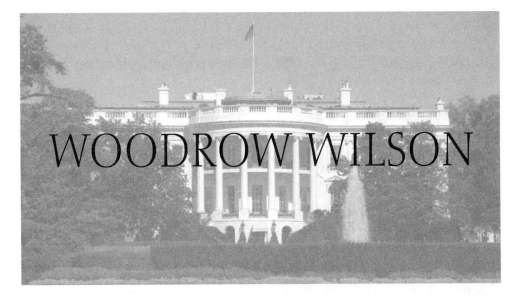
WOODROW WILSON

(1856–1924)
28th President, 1913–1921
Party Affiliation: Democrat
Chief 1912 Opponents: Theodore Roosevelt (Bull Moose) and William Howard Taft (Republican)
Chief 1916 Opponent: Charles Evans Hughes (Republican)

EARLY LIFE AND FAMILY

Where and when was he **born**?

Thomas Woodrow Wilson was born in Staunton, Virginia, to Joseph Wilson and Janet Woodrow Wilson on December 28, 1856. Known as "Tommy" as a youngster, he later dropped his first name to the initial T. and then dropped it altogether. He claimed this was based on a request from his mother (whose maiden name was Woodrow).

What did his **father do** for a living?

Joseph Wilson served as a Presbyterian minister and a teacher of theology. He moved around to various churches, which explains why the family left Virginia. When young Woodrow was one year old, the family moved from Virginia to Augusta, Georgia, and later to Columbia, South Carolina.

Did he have any **siblings**?

Yes, Wilson had three siblings: Marion, Annie, and Joseph.

What was his early **education**?

Wilson could not read until he was nearly ten years old because he suffered from dyslexia. However, he attended school at age twelve in Columbia, South Carolina. He received tutoring from a minister at the Presbyterian seminary at which his father worked. His studies improved enough that he entered Davidson College at age sixteen in 1873. Failing health required him to drop out after one year. He reentered college in 1875 at the College of New Jersey (now called Princeton). There, he excelled in public speaking, edited *The Princetonian,* and graduated in 1879.

President Woodrow Wilson.

Did he **marry**?

Yes, Wilson had two marriages. In 1885, he married Ellen Louise Axson in Savannah, Georgia. She passed away while he was president in August 1914. Then, on December 18, 1915, Wilson—while president—married widower Edith Bolling Galt. He was fifty-eight and she was forty-three. Some in the press had a field day with this second marriage. She outlived Wilson by nearly forty years, passing away in 1961.

Did he have any **children**?

Yes, Wilson had three daughters by his first marriage. They were Margaret, Jessie, and Eleanor. Margaret Woodrow Wilson was a talented singer who later worked in the advertising business. Jessie Woodrow Wilson married Francis B. Sayre, who later became a Harvard law professor. She was active in the League of Women Voters. His youngest daughter, Eleanor Randolph Wilson, married her father's secretary of the treasury, William G. McAdoo Jr., in 1914 in a wedding held at the White House. She later wrote a book entitled *The Woodrow Wilsons* (1937).

EARLY CAREER

What did Wilson do **after graduating college**?

He entered law school at the University of Virginia. Wilson found that the law was in his words a "hard taskmaster." He persevered in law school for a year and a half, before leaving to return to his parent's home in Wilmington, North Carolina.

Did he **graduate** from **law school**?

No, Wilson left law school midway through his second year and never returned. He continued to study and read the law, however. He gained admittance to the bar in 1882.

What did he do **after becoming a lawyer**?

Wilson moved to Atlanta, Georgia, and opened up a law practice with his friend Edward I. Renick. He found the practice of law dreary and distasteful, realizing that he preferred to study writing, literature, and politics. "I throw away law books for histories," he acknowledged.

After law practice, what **education** did Wilson pursue?

Wilson dissolved his business with attorney Renick and entered John Hopkins University to obtain his doctorate degree in political science. He received his Ph.D. from John Hopkins in 1886. While a doctoral student, he published his first book, *Congressional Government: A Study in American Politics* (1885). Wilson remains the only president in history to obtain a doctorate degree.

Wilson then **taught** at which colleges and universities?

Wilson taught at Bryn Mawr College in Pennsylvania; Wesleyan University in Middleton, Connecticut; and then at his alma mater, Princeton, beginning in 1890. While at Princeton, he taught short courses at John Hopkins and New York Law School. His prominence as a leader in academics grew. The Universities of Illinois and Virginia offered him the position of university president. Princeton—wanting to keep him—also offered him the position of president in 1902. He accepted and remained president of Princeton until 1910.

What was Wilson's **first political office**?

Wilson defeated Republican Vivian M. Lewis to become governor of New Jersey. As governor, Wilson sought the passage of the state's first workers' compensation law and a public utilities commission that would regulate rates. He also sought to reform election law in the state by supporting a law that called for direct party primaries and sought to reduce the power wielded by party bosses.

PRESIDENCY

Whom did **Wilson defeat** to win the **Democratic** presidential **nomination** in **1912**?

Wilson defeated Joseph Beauchamp "Champ" Clark, the Speaker of the House of Representatives from Missouri; Oscar Wilder Underwood, a U.S. congressman from Alabama; and Governor Judson Harmon from Ohio. On the first ballot, Clark received more votes than Wilson and the other candidates. Later in the process, William Jennings Bryan endorsed Wilson, which caused a seismic shift in the delegate voting. Wilson ended up prevailing on the forty-sixth ballot.

Whom did he **defeat** for the **1912 general presidential election**?

Wilson defeated two former presidents: incumbent Republican President William Howard Taft and the third-party candidacy of former President Theodore Roosevelt, who broke from the Republican ranks to form the Progressive, or Bull Moose, Party. In simplest terms, Roosevelt and Taft split much of the Republican vote, enabling Wilson as the lone Democrat to capture the election. He garnered 435 electoral votes to 88 for Roosevelt and only 8 for Taft.

Whom did he defeat in the **1916** to **win a second term** as president?

Wilson defeated Republican Charles Evans Hughes, a former associate justice of the U.S. Supreme Court and governor of New York. Hughes left the Court to run for president. This was a very close race with Wilson winning 277 electoral votes to 254 for Hughes. The popular vote was close as well.

"I Summon you to Comradeship in the Red Cross"
Woodrow Wilson

Who was Woodrow Wilson's only **vice president** for his two terms in office?

Thomas R. Marshall of Indiana served as Wilson's only vice president. Marshall had served as the governor of Indiana. He opposed U.S. involvement in World War I, but loyally supported the administration and the war effort in Wilson's second term. He sometimes ran cabinet meetings when Wilson was overseas.

Who were Wilson's **secretaries of state**?

Wilson had three secretaries of state during his two terms in office: William Jennings Bryan, Robert Lansing, and Bainbridge Colby. Bryan, the former three-time Democratic presidential nominee, served as Wilson's first secretary of state.

A Red Cross poster from World War I featuring a quote from President Wilson.

Suffragists campaigning in New York City for women's voting rights in 1915. The Nineteenth Amendment to the Constitution finally granted these rights in 1920.

Wilson respected Bryan, who had helped him get the nomination back in 1912. However, Bryan opposed Wilson's strong position concerning German aggression and the sinking of the RMS *Lusitania*. Bryan believed in complete neutrality by the United States. He resigned because of this issue. Lansing, an expert in international law, fell out of favor with President Wilson because he disfavored the League of Nations and suggested that Vice President Marshall should take over for Wilson during a period when the president was debilitated. Colby, another lawyer-politician, supported Wilson's policies, including the League of Nations. He later practiced law with Wilson.

What **federal agency** did Wilson **petition Congress to create** during the first term of his presidency?

Wilson pushed for the creation of the Federal Trade Commission as a way to ensure that the government could maintain a degree of regulatory control over the practices of large businesses. It was designed to stop the spread of monopolies.

What **important antitrust law** did Wilson sign during his first term?

Wilson signed into law the Clayton Antitrust Act of 1914, named after its chief congressional sponsor, U.S. Representative Henry De Lamar Clayton Jr. This law extended federal authority that began with the Sherman Antitrust Law of 1890. Under the Clayton Anti-Trust Act, Congress could regulate price discrimination and mergers and

303

What was "The Fourteen Points" speech and what were the points in that speech?

The Fourteen Points refers to a speech President Wilson delivered before the U.S. Congress on January 8, 1918, that outlined his fourteen provisions that a peace treaty to end World War I must contain. Those fourteen points were: (1) an open peace process free of secret diplomacy; (2) free navigation on the seas; (3) equality of trade between nations free from economic conditions; (4) reduction of national armaments; (5) review of colonial claims with consideration given to the concerned population; (6) evacuation of Russian territory by other countries; (7) the removal of troops from Belgium and recognition of it again as an independent sovereign state; (8) freeing of all French territory and French acquisition of the Alsace-Lorraine territory; (9) realignment of borders of Italy; (10) a chance for autonomy for the people of Austria-Hungary; (11) evacuation and restoration of Rumania, Serbia, and Montenegro; (12) sovereignty for the Turkish part of the Ottoman Empire, but recognition of other nationalities under Turkish rule; (13) a free Poland; and (14) a general association of all member nations.

acquisitions that led to monopolistic tendencies. The law also provided a safe harbor for union activities, such as strikes and pickets.

What caused Wilson to **believe** that the United States must **enter World War I**?

At the outbreak of World War I, Wilson emphasized that the United States would maintain a position of neutrality. Hostilities continued to escalate, particularly submarine battles between Germany and Great Britain. On May 7, 1915, a German submarine sank the British ship *Lusitania*. Nearly 1,200 people died in the attack, including 128 Americans. The sinking of this ship, which was carrying some munitions, changed public perception about the war in the United States. The next year, German submarines torpedoed English and French ships that contained a few Americans. The United States and Wilson strongly demanded that the Germans desist from such activity. In early 1917, Wilson called for "peace without victory" between the fighting nations. That did not work, and the German submarine warfare continued. In April 1917, Wilson asked Congress for a declaration of war.

How was Wilson involved in the **peace process**?

Wilson led the American delegation to the Paris Peace Conference in late January 1919. At this conference, the Allied countries outlined the terms of the ultimate peace agreement, including the Treaty of Versailles. This treaty signaled the end of World

IRS agents destroy a large still in 1922. Prohibition was passed during Wilson's administration with the Eighteenth Amendment. It was incredibly unpopular and was eventually repealed in 1933 with the Twenty-first Amendment.

War I and placed blamed for the war on the Germans. The Paris Peace Conference also called for a League of Nations, a precursor to the modern-day United Nations. Wilson actively promoted the idea of a League of Nations, even touring around the United States to get support. For his efforts, he received the Nobel Peace Prize in 1919.

What **laws** did President Wilson sign during the time of World War I that **limited First Amendment freedoms**?

President Wilson signed into law the Espionage Act of 1917 and the Sedition Act of 1918. Though parts of the Espionage Act of 1917 are still law today, some of the provisions were applied to punish antiwar, dissident political speech. Individuals faced lengthy prison terms for circulating leaflets critical of the U.S. war effort and the draft. The U.S. Supreme Court began to develop a body of law explaining the meaning of the First Amendment free-speech clause ("Congress shall make no law … abridging the freedom of speech….") in response to cases that involved convictions of Socialists, anarchists, and other political dissidents.

Where did President Wilson stand on **race relations**?

President Wilson did not do very well on race relations. Allegedly, his favorite movie was D. W. Griffith's *The Birth of a Nation Woods, formerly a judge on the 5th Circuit, served*   305 *only six years on the Court* (1915), which glorified the Ku Klux Klan. He did not overrule members of his cabinet who adopted segregationist policies. He did not send in federal troops when race riots occurred in East St. Louis, Missouri, and Chicago, Illinois.

What **three constitutional amendments** were passed while Wilson was president?

The Seventeenth Amendment, Eighteenth Amendment, and Nineteenth Amendments were passed during Wilson's presidency. The Seventeenth Amendment provided for direct popular elections of U.S. senators. Previously, state legislatures had elected senators. The controversial Eighteenth Amendment created Prohibition, the outlawing of alcoholic beverages. It was later repealed by the Twenty-First Amendment. The Nineteenth Amendment gave women the right to vote.

Who were Wilson's U.S. **Supreme Court appointees**?

Wilson appointed three men to the U.S. Supreme Court: James C. McReynolds, Louis D. Brandeis, and John H. Clarke. McReynolds, who was from Tennessee, previously had served as Wilson's U.S. attorney general. He served nearly twenty-seven years on the Court. Brandeis, the Court's first Jewish justice, served twenty-three years on the Court. He is considered one of the finest thinkers and writers of opinion to ever serve on the Court. Clark, a former federal district court judge from Ohio, served on the Court nearly six years.

POST PRESIDENCY

With whom did Wilson **briefly practice law** with **after leaving** the White House?

Wilson set up a law firm with his former secretary of state Bainbridge Colby in 1921. However, Wilson's health prevented him from practicing to any real extent.

What **book was published** during his post-presidency period?

Wilson's book on the League of Nations, *President Wilson's Case for the League of Nations* (1923), was published during his post-presidential period.

When and where did he **die**?

Woodrow Wilson died on February 3, 1924, in Washington, D.C., of complications from the flu.

WARREN G. HARDING

(1865–1923)
29th President, 1921–1923
Party Affiliation: Republican
Chief 1920 Opponent: James Cox (Democrat)

EARLY LIFE AND FAMILY

Where and when was Harding **born**?

Warren Gamaliel Harding was born in Corsica, Ohio, to George Tryon Harding and Phoebe Elizabeth Dickerson Harding on November 2, 1865. His father wanted to name his son Winfield, but Phoebe preferred the idea of naming him after his great-uncle

Who was his **great-uncle**?

Warren Gamaliel Harding was a Methodist chaplain at a Wisconsin prison.

What did his **parents do** for a living?

George Tryon Harding owned a farm and taught. He later studied medicine at Western College of Homeopathy in Cleveland, Ohio. Dr. Harding built his medical practice in Caledonia, Ohio. Harding's mother was a midwife who later gained her license to practice medicine from the Ohio State Medical Board.

Did Harding have any **siblings**?

Yes, Harding was the oldest of eight children, six of whom lived past childhood. His siblings that lived past childhood were Charity, Mary, Abigail, George, and Phoebe.

What was his **early education**?

Harding studied at a one-room schoolhouse near his home in Caledonia. He entered Ohio Central College in 1880, in Iberia, Ohio, and graduated two years later in 1882. While at college, he helped form a college newspaper called the *Iberia Spectator*. The experience endeared him to newspapers and journalism.

Did he **marry**?

Yes, Harding married Florence Mabel Kling DeWolfe on July 8, 1891. "Flossie" —as she was called—had been married once before to banker Henry DeWolfe.

President Warren G. Harding.

Harding met his future wife through his sister Charity, as Florence taught Charity to play the piano.

Why did her **father oppose the marriage**?

Florence's father, Amos Kling, did not like Harding for at least two reasons. First, Harding had written critical editorials of Kling's real estate and money lending practices. But Kling also heard rumors that Harding, who was from a pro-abolitionist family, had African-American blood. By this time, Harding was in the newspaper business and a rival publisher spread the rumor about his heredity. Kling yelled a racial slur at Harding on a public street and threatened to harm him if Harding married his daughter. Many years later, in 1907, Kling apologized for his treatment of his son-in-law and paid for a lengthy European tour for the couple.

Did he have any **children**?

Harding and his wife, Florence, did not have any children. However, Harding allegedly had a daughter through an extramarital affair with Nan Britton, a woman thirty years younger than him. Britton claimed in the book *The President's Daughter* (1927) that

> ## What was unusual about Harding in relation to his father in terms of life span?
>
> **H**arding was the first president whose father outlived him. Harding died in office in 1923, while his father lived until 1928. John F. Kennedy Jr. is the only other president in American history who died before his father.

Harding fathered her child. It has never been conclusively proven that Harding was the biological father of the child. The daughter—Elizabeth Ann Blaesing—was born in 1919 and passed away in 2005.

EARLY CAREER

What was Harding's **first job after graduating college**?

Harding worked as a teacher at the White Schoolhouse near Marion, Ohio. Harding later said it was the most difficult job of his career.

What were his **next vocations**?

Harding briefly studied law, but did not like it. He read famous English legal scholar William Blackstone's *Commentaries* on the law, but was impatient to start a career and earn some money. First, he tried his hand at the insurance business. He did not like that job, either. He then found an area he liked—the newspaper business.

What **newspapers** did Harding **work for**?

Harding first worked as a reporter for the *Marion Mirror*. With his father's financial assistance, Harding bought the *Marion Star* with two friends. He later bought out his two associates, and ran the newspaper with his wife. The daily newspaper became a success. Harding also started a weekly newspaper devoted to political issues. *The Weekly Star* became a platform for Harding to support causes of the Republican Party.

What **health issue** did Harding face in the **early 1890s**?

Harding had to place himself in a sanitarium in Battle Creek, Ohio, because of a nervous breakdown in 1890. He went back to the sanitarium at least five times, because he had frayed nerves and a nervous stomach.

POLITICAL OFFICES

What was his **first election**?

Harding ran for county auditor in Marion County, an area that generally voted Democratic. As a result, the Republican Harding lost his very first election.

What was the **first election** that he **won**?

Harding won his first election when he ran for the Ohio State Senate in 1899. He served two terms in the Senate until 1903. He later became majority leader. He gave the eulogy in the state Senate for President William McKinley after the assassination.

What was his **next political position**?

Harding then became lieutenant governor of Ohio in 1903, serving under Governor Myron T. Herrick. During this tenure, he traveled the state and acquired a good reputation for his speech-making abilities. He briefly retired from politics in 1905 and returned to the newspaper business.

Did Harding ever **run for governor**?

Yes, Harding ran for governor of Ohio in 1910, but lost to Democrat incumbent Judson Harmon, who had served as U.S. attorney general under President Grover Cleveland. Harding lost by more than one hundred thousand votes.

When did Harding become a **U.S. senator**?

Harding defeated Democrat Timothy Hogan, state attorney general of Ohio, and Progressive candidate Arthur L. Garford to win a seat in the U.S. Senate in 1914. He served in the Senate until he became president of the United States. Harding was the first sitting U.S. senator to be elected president, followed many years later by John F. Kennedy and Barack Obama.

President Harding speaks at a session of the House of Representatives, with Calvin Coolidge sitting behind him at left.

PRESIDENCY

Whom did he **defeat to win** the **Republican nomination** in **1920?**

Harding is considered by some historians as a dark horse candidate. He was not expected to win the nomination. The favorites were Leonard Wood; Frank Lowden, the governor of Illinois; and Hiram Johnson, a U.S. senator from California. Harding emerged as a compromise candidate and captured the nomination.

Whom did he **defeat** to win the presidential **election of 1920?**

Harding defeated Democrat James M. Cox. Ironically Cox—like Harding—was from Ohio and worked in the newspaper business. Cox also had served in the U.S. House of Representatives and as governor of Ohio. However, Harding was able to capitalize on growing discontent with the Democratic administration of Woodrow Wilson. Harding captured the election in a landslide, 404 to 127 on electoral votes. Harding also won more than 60 percent of the popular vote.

Who was his **vice president?**

Calvin Coolidge of Massachusetts served as Harding's vice president. Coolidge had served as lieutenant governor and then governor of Massachusetts. He later became president after Harding died in office.

313

Who was his **secretary of state**?

Charles Evans Hughes, the former governor of New York and associate justice on the U.S. Supreme Court, served as Harding's secretary of state. Hughes had been the Republican Party's presidential nominee in 1916, but lost a close election to Democratic incumbent Woodrow Wilson. Hughes maintained his position as secretary of state even when Coolidge took over as president. He later became Chief Justice of the U.S. Supreme Court.

What **future president** (other than Vice President Coolidge) served on Harding's **cabinet**?

Herbert Hoover, the future thirty-first president of the United States, served as Harding's secretary of commerce. Harding gave Hoover the choice of serving as either secretary of the interior or secretary of commerce. Hoover wanted the position of secretary of commerce. Harding chose Albert B. Fall for his secretary of the interior.

What famous **scandal** did **Albert B. Fall** create?

Fall, whom Harding befriended in the U.S. Senate, was responsible for the infamous Teapot Dome scandal. Teapot Dome was an oil field in public land in Salt Creek, Wyoming, Fall's home state. As secretary of the interior, Fall leased the petroleum lands to Sinclair Oil without any competitive bidding. Fall also had leased the Elk Hills Naval Petroleum Reserve in central California to wealthy oilman Edward Doheny. During Harding's administration, it was revealed that Doheny had given a personal loan of $100,000 to Fall. For his conduct, a jury found Fall guilty of bribery in 1929 and sentenced him to one year in prison. He became the first person from a presidential administration to serve time in prison for official political actions.

What **other scandals** beset the Harding administration?

Harding had named Charles R. Forbes as director of the War Insurance Risk Board, which became the Veterans Bureau. Forbes had a distinguished war record and was a friend of both President Harding and his wife, Florence. However, Forbes engaged in corruption by embezzling money from contractors, giving them low-priced bids for building veteran hospitals. He was convicted in 1925 and served more than a year in prison. Charles F. Cramer, legal advisor for the Veterans Bureau, committed suicide.

Another scandal involved Harry M. Daugherty, Harding's attorney general. Daugherty allegedly accepted bribes from bootleggers. He resigned from his position in 1924 (when Coolidge was president). He was never charged with a crime for this allegation. However, he did face other criminal charges for bribes. Two juries deadlocked and he never was convicted of anything. It is interesting that Daugherty's assistant, Jess

> ## What famous political figure did Harding grant clemency to while president?
>
> Harding freed Eugene Debs, the prominent labor organizer and Socialist candidate for president, who had vigorously dissented and protested U.S. involvement in World War I. Harding ordered that Debs be freed for time served, but did not grant him an official pardon. Harding also freed many others who had been convicted under the Sedition Act of 1918.

Smith, destroyed his personal papers and committed suicide shortly after Harding asked for his resignation.

It was perhaps because of these so-called "friends"—sometimes loosely referred to as the "Ohio Gang"—that Harding lamented: "My God, this is a hell of a job. I have no trouble with my enemies.... But my damn friends, they're the ones that keep me walking the floor at night."

What **federal bureau** did **Harding establish** to regulate federal spending?

Harding supported and signed into law the Budget and Accounting Act of 1921, which created the Bureau of the Budget. This law created the General Accounting Office, which regulates spending by the federal government to this day.

What **speech** on **civil rights** by Harding was considered **controversial** at that time?

Harding delivered a speech on October 26, 1921, at Capitol Park in Birmingham, Alabama. He told the Southern audience that the time had come for political equality for blacks. He told the audience, which the *New York Times* called a conservative estimate of one hundred thousand people, that he would speak frankly to the audience "whether you like it or not." He did say that social equality was not attainable, but called for political equality for blacks. "I would say let the black man vote when he is fit to vote; prohibit the white man voting when he is unfit to vote."

Who were his U.S. **Supreme Court appointees**?

Harding appointed four men to the U.S. Supreme Court: William Howard Taft, George Sutherland, Pierce Butler, and Edward Sanford. Harding named Taft—the former president of the United States—as Chief Justice of the U.S. Supreme Court after the death of Edward D. White. Taft served on the Court until his death in 1930. Sutherland served

The funeral train transporting the body of President Harding to Chicago in 1923.

on the Court for sixteen years. He is one of the few Supreme Court justices born in another country (England). He had served in the U.S. Senate representing the state of Utah. Butler, who was the first justice from Minnesota, served on the Court for seventeen years. Sanford, who had served as an assistant U.S. attorney general under President Theodore Roosevelt, served on the court for seven years. Before his nomination, he served as a federal district court judge in Tennessee.

When did he **die**?

Harding died in office on August 2, 1923 at the Palace Hotel in San Francisco, California.

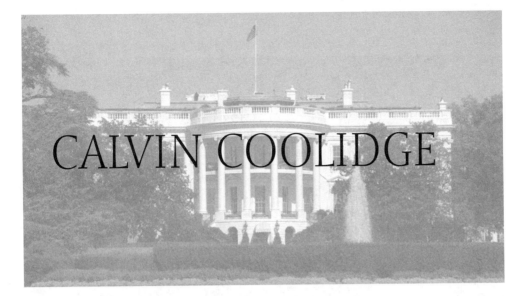

CALVIN COOLIDGE

(1872–1933)
30th President, 1923–1929
Party Affiliation: Republican
Chief 1924 Opponents: John W. Davis (Democrat), Robert M. LaFollette (Progressive)

EARLY LIFE AND FAMILY

Where and when was he **born**?

John Calvin Coolidge was born in Plymouth, Vermont, to John and Victoria Moor Coolidge on July 4, 1872. He is the only president in history to be born on the Fourth of July. He dropped the name John after graduating college.

What did his **father do** for a living?

John Calvin Coolidge worked as a farmer and successful storekeeper but also held political offices. He served in both the Vermont House of Representatives and Senate, and was a constable and selectman.

Did Calvin have any **siblings**?

Yes, Calvin had a younger sister named Abbie. She died at age fifteen from acute appendicitis when Calvin was eighteen.

317

President Calvin Coolidge.

What **other tragedy** befell the Coolidge family?

Calvin's mother, Victoria, died when he was only twelve years old. The loss affected Coolidge greatly, and he always kept a picture of her with him.

What was his **early education**?

Calvin Coolidge attended an elementary school in Plymouth, Vermont. After elementary school, he entered Black River Academy in Ludlow, Vermont, the same school his mother had attended. Initially, he failed the entrance exam to Amherst College, so he enrolled at St. Johnsbury Academy in Ludlow, as preparation for college. He then entered Amherst and graduated in 1895.

Did he **marry**?

Yes, Calvin Coolidge married Grace Anna Goodhue on October 4, 1905, in Burlington, Vermont. Grace outlived the president by twenty-four years.

Did he have any **children**?

Yes, Calvin and Grace Coolidge had two sons: John and Calvin Coolidge Jr. John, who lived into his nineties, graduated from his father's alma mater, Amherst College, and became a successful businessman. He worked as a railway executive and later owned a printing company. The other son, Calvin Jr., died from a toe infection after playing tennis with his older brother. Calvin Jr. died at age sixteen in 1924, when his father was president.

EARLY CAREER

What did Coolidge do **after graduating** from Amherst College?

Coolidge studied law at Hammond and Field, a law firm in Northampton, Massachusetts. He learned the tools of the legal trade from seasoned attorneys John C. Hammond and Henry P. Field. These fellow Amherst graduates took the young Coolidge under their wings.

When did he **become a lawyer**?

Coolidge became a licensed attorney admitted to the Massachusetts bar in 1897 at the age of twenty-five. He opened his own law practice and worked effectively as an advocate for various business clients.

In what **other activity besides law** did Coolidge engage?

Like his father, Coolidge became interested in politics. A staunch Republican, Coolidge followed in the footsteps of his legal mentors Hammond and Field. He served as local party chairman in 1904.

POLITICAL OFFICES

What were his **first local political positions**?

Coolidge became active in Republican Party politics, following in the footsteps of his legal mentors Hammond and Field. He won a seat on the Northampton City Council where he served from 1899 to 1900. He then served for a few years as city solicitor.

When did he become a **state legislator**?

Coolidge served in the Massachusetts General Court—the name for the Massachusetts legislature. He served in both the State House and Senate. He served first in the House and then in the Senate from 1912 to 1915. In his last year in the Senate, he served as the body's president.

After his terms in the **Senate**, what did Coolidge do?

Coolidge then ran successfully for the position of lieutenant governor under the ticket with gubernatorial candidate Samuel McCall. Coolidge served two terms under McCall and then ran for governor when McCall decided not to seek a third term.

Whom did he **defeat** to become **governor of Massachusetts**?

Coolidge defeated Democrat Robert W. Long in 1919 and again in 1920 to win the governorship. During his time as governor, Coolidge earned national recognition for his handling of a police strike. Coolidge relied on the state militia and stood firm against the strike, stating: "There is no right to strike against the public safety by anybody, anywhere, any time."

What was his **next political position**?

Coolidge captured the vice presidential nomination for the Republican Party on the first ballot. Warren G. Harding emerged as the presidential candidate. After Harding won the election, Coolidge served as vice president. At this election, the Democrats nominated James Cox as their presidential candidate and New York politician Franklin D. Roosevelt as their vice president. Roosevelt would go on to become the longest serving president in U.S. history. As vice president, Coolidge rarely intervened in Senate affairs, though he enjoyed presiding over them and listening to the debates. It was because of his hands-off approach that he earned the nickname "Silent Cal."

PRESIDENCY

How did Coolidge **become president**?

Coolidge became president because Warren G. Harding died in office in August 1923. His father, a notary public, swore in his son to the office of the presidency at nearly 3:00 A.M. on August 3, 1923.

Who was his **vice president**?

Coolidge did not have a vice president for his first couple years, as he filled out Harding's first term. After he won the election of 1924, his vice president was Charles G. Dawes, who had served capably as the first director of the Budget Bureau under President Harding. He later earned fame for his role in determining the reparations that Germany must pay after World War I. Dawes won the Nobel Peace Prize for his efforts in 1925. He was a great-great grandson of William Dawes, who rode with Paul Revere on the famous "Midnight Ride," warning colonists about the impending British forces near Lexington and Concord.

Who was Coolidge's **secretary of the treasury**?

Andrew W. Mellon served as his secretary of the treasury, just as he did for President Warren G. Harding. He served in the same capacity for Coolidge's successor, Herbert Hoover.

Whom did Coolidge **defeat** in the election of **1924**?

Coolidge defeated Democrat John W. Davis and Progressive Robert M. LaFollette Sr. to win the election in 1924. Coolidge garnered 382 electoral votes to 136 for Davis and 13 for LaFollette. His campaign used the slogan: "Keep Cool with Coolidge."

Davis, a former congressman from West Virginia, is known for his outstanding legal career. He argued approximately 140 cases before the U.S. Supreme Court. He argued many cases before the High Court as solicitor general under President Woodrow Wilson. LaFollette was the former governor of Wisconsin, who had a lengthy career in the U.S. Senate.

The inauguration of Calvin Coolidge. Chief Justice Taft swore in the nation's thirtieth president.

What **policy of peace** did Coolidge's administration successfully pursue?

Coolidge's administration—most notably his secretary of state Frank B. Kellogg—helped pull off the Kellogg-Briand Pact. This pact—named after Kellogg and French diplomat Aristide Brand—called for countries to avoid war and try to resolve disputes through the peace process. More than sixty countries agreed to the terms. For his efforts, Kellogg received the Nobel Peace Prize in 1929.

What **tax policies** did Coolidge pursue?

Coolidge signed into law two bills that reduced income taxes and eliminated the gift tax. The most significant of these laws, the Revenue Act of 1926, lowered taxes significantly across the board. He kept corporate taxes at a lower level than his predecessors. Coolidge's policies seemingly helped the economy, as unemployment dropped and businesses profited. The stock market rose during Coolidge's time in the White House.

What measure did Coolidge sign that was significant for the **aviation industry**?

Coolidge signed into law the Air Commerce Act of 1926, which gave the federal government power over the commercial aviation industry. The measure also created the first two commercial air routes.

Many years after Coolidge's death, which president honored Coolidge by putting his portrait in the White House?

President Ronald Reagan removed a portrait of President Harry Truman and replaced it with one of Calvin Coolidge. Reagan admired Coolidge's stance on reducing the size and involvement of the federal government in American's day-to-day lives and his policies favoring business and reducing taxes.

Who was his lone U.S. **Supreme Court appointee**?

Coolidge appointed his U.S. attorney general Harlan Fiske Stone, his former classmate at Amherst, to the Supreme Court as an associate justice. Stone served sixteen years as an associate justice before President Franklin D. Roosevelt elevated him to Chief Justice in 1941. Stone wrote many opinions protective of civil liberties.

POST PRESIDENCY

Did Coolidge **seek reelection** in 1928?

No, Coolidge announced that he would not run for president in 1928. Instead, he supported his eventual successor, Herbert Hoover.

What **writing did Coolidge do** in his retirement?

He wrote *The Autobiography of Calvin Coolidge* (1929). He also wrote articles for several newspapers, such as *The Saturday Evening Post*. And he wrote a popular column titled "Calvin Coolidge Says" or "Thinking Things Over with Calvin Coolidge."

When did he **die**?

Coolidge died of a heart attack on January 5, 1933, in Northampton, Massachusetts.

HERBERT HOOVER

(1874–1933)
31st President, 1929–1933
Party Affiliation: Republican
Chief 1928 Opponent: Alfred Smith (Democrat)

EARLY LIFE AND FAMILY

Where and when was he **born**?

Herbert Clark Hoover was born in West Branch, Iowa, to Quakers Jesse Clark Hoover and Huldah Randall Minthorn Hoover on August 10, 1874.

What did his **father do** for a living?

Jesse worked as a blacksmith and a salesman of farm equipment in addition to serving on the local town council. He died at age thirty-four when young Herbert was only six years old. Hoover's mother died when he was only nine years old.

After his parents died, where did Hoover go?

At age ten or eleven, after living with other relatives, Hoover went to live with his uncle, Henry Minthorn, who was a doctor and a school official. Dr. Minthorn later became successful in real estate.

Hoover relaxing with his wife, Lou Henry.

Did Hoover have any **siblings**?

Yes, Herbert Hoover had two siblings: an older brother named Theodore and a younger sister named Mary.

What was his **education**?

Hoover attended school beginning at age five at the West Branch Free School in West Branch, Iowa. When he moved to Oregon, he attended the Friends Pacific Academy. In 1891, he entered Stanford University; at age seventeen, he was the youngest person in his class.

What **activities and jobs** did Hoover try at **Stanford University**?

Hoover met John Caspar Branner, the head of the university's geology department. Hoover worked for Branner and helped him create a project that won a prize at the Chicago World Fair. He also landed summer jobs with the U.S. Geological Survey. He became treasurer of his class and drafted a student constitution that lasted for decades. He served as a manager for the baseball and football teams.

What other **key person** did Hoover **meet at Stanford**?

Hoover met his future wife, Lou Henry, at Stanford. The two eventually married on February 10, 1889, in Monterey, California.

Did he have any **children**?

Yes, the Hoovers had two children: Herbert Jr. and Allan. Herbert Jr. graduated from Stanford and later Harvard Business School. He worked as an engineer, and later as a diplomat under President Eisenhower. Allan also graduated from Stanford and Harvard Business School. He worked as a mining engineer, and later as a rancher in California.

EARLY CAREER

When did he **graduate college**?

Hoover graduated from Stanford in 1895 with a degree in geology. He had trouble locating employment after graduation, and ended up working at a gold mine pushing carts of ore. But by 1896 he managed to land a job with Louis Janin, a mining engineer in San Francisco. While officially he had an office job, his knowledge of mines made him valuable to Janin, who recommended young Hoover for employment with the London firm of Bewick, Moreing, and Company. The company hired the twenty-two-year-old Hoover and sent him to Australia to evaluate prospective mines.

Where did his **work** for the **mining company** take Hoover?

In 1898, Bewick, Moreing, and Company transferred Hoover to China, offering him an even more lucrative position to supervise a new mining operation. Hoover survived the Boxer Rebellion, an uprising by those who advocated against foreign presence, wanting to drive the "foreign devils" out of the country. While in China, Hoover made a heavy profit for his company—and himself—with coal deposits. By 1901, he left China a much wealthier man and relocated to London as a full partner in the firm. For several years, he traveled the globe for the company, including return trips to Australia.

What did Hoover do **after leaving Bewick, Moreing, and Company**?

Hoover ventured out on his own in 1908, starting a consulting company. His company had offices in New York, San Francisco, Paris, among other locations. He owned shares in several different companies and made a veritable fortune, amassing a net worth of more than $4 million.

When did Hoover become **involved in politics**?

Hoover became involved in politics in 1912, supporting former President Theodore Roosevelt in his run as the Progressive, or Bull Moose, candidate. He contributed $1,000 to Roosevelt's campaign.

What **post** with his **alma mater** did Hoover accept at this time?

In 1912, Hoover became a trustee of Stanford University, a position he held for decades. He worked to initiate plans to build a hospital, a gymnasium, and other improvements at Stanford.

What **humanitarian role** did Hoover play that thrust him into the spotlight?

Hoover played a large role in London at the outbreak of World War I. He headed up the "Committee of American Residents in London for Assistance of American Travellers." This organization helped more than 120,000 Americans who were stranded in Europe at the outbreak of World War I. Then, Hoover received a summons from the U.S. embassy in Belgium, asking for his assistance. He became a key leader with the Commission of Relief in Belgium. He worked tirelessly to ensure that food and other provisions were given to Belgians, who faced the prospect of starvation. During this time, he even negotiated with the German government on occasion to ensure the delivery of relief supplies.

POLITICAL OFFICES

What position did President Woodrow **Wilson give to Hoover**?

President Woodrow Wilson tabbed Hoover the head of the U.S. Food Administration. Hoover worked endlessly to put out messages of food conservation. He even became eponymous; a new word was coined—"hooverize"—meaning to save in the interests of the larger economy and the country. While considered an effective administrator, sometimes he faced criticism for his blunt and heavy-handed manner.

He later served on the Supreme Economic Council and became economic advisor to President Woodrow Wilson at the Versaille Peace Conference. He was considered so effective in these roles that President Wilson pegged Hoover as a worthy successor. Among those who supported him for president in 1920 was future opponent Franklin Delano Roosevelt, then assistant secretary of the navy.

What **political party** did **Hoover choose**?

Hoover announced in March 1920 that he was a Republican, though he went on to elaborate that he wanted the party to adopt certain positions. But the conservative Republicans feared his dalliances with Progressivism, and he was not seriously considered for the 1920 nomination.

What **cabinet position** did President **Harding offer** to Hoover?

Harding named Hoover his secretary of commerce. Hoover served in that role from 1921 until 1928, under both Harding and his successor Calvin Coolidge. Hoover expanded the Commerce Department significantly, so much so that some dubbed him the "the secretary of commerce … and under-secretary of everything else." Others called him "the grand marshal of economic policy at home as abroad." His department regulated radio, air travel, the census, and housing. And he attempted to wrest control of various activities and aspects from other departments.

When coal miners went on strike, President Harding tabbed Hoover, not the secretary of labor, to handle the situation.

What **position** did **Coolidge offer Hoover**?

President Coolidge offered Hoover the position of secretary of agriculture when the existing secretary, Henry C. Wallace, died. Hoover declined the position, choosing to remain as secretary of commerce.

What **natural disaster** once again catapulted Hoover to prominence?

The Mississippi River flood of 1927 caused great damage, breaking the dams and levees of the Mississippi River. This caused millions of dollars worth of flood damage with more than half a million people displaced from their homes. President Coolidge appointed Hoover to handle the fallout and help administer relief efforts. Several governors communicated directly with Hoover, not President Coolidge, for aid and government help. This turn of events placed Hoover as the front-runner to succeed Coolidge as president.

PRESIDENCY

Whom did **Hoover defeat** to win the **Republican nomination**?

Hoover dominated the Republican convention in Kansas City, garnering 837 votes on the first ballot. Governor Frank Lowden of Illinois and Senator Charles Curtis of Kansas were the next closest with 72 and 64 votes respectively. Hoover had the backing of former president Theodore Roosevelt and Secretary of the Treasury Andrew Mellon.

Whom did he **defeat** in the **general election**?

Hoover defeated Democrat Alfred Smith of New York handily to win the election. A four-time governor of New York, Smith was the first person of the Catholic faith to be nominated for president. Hoover trounced Smith in the election, winning 444 electoral votes to Smith's mere 87.

Who was Hoover's **vice president**?

Charles Curtis of Kansas served as Hoover's vice president. Born on Indian land in North Topeka, Curtis was one-fourth Kaw Indian. He served in both the U.S. House of

What is a "Hooverville"?

During the Great Depression, the throngs of unemployed began constructing ramshackle homes in destitute communities that became known as "Hoovervilles." This unflattering name stemmed from hatred for a president who people felt was failing to help them. "Hooverville" was first coined in a 1930 newspaper article and it was first used for a town outside the Chicago area.

Representatives and the U.S. Senate. He ran as Hoover's running mate for a second term, but when Hoover lost the election to Franklin Delano Roosevelt, Curtis left politics and returned to the practice of law.

What **relative** of a **former president** was on Hoover's **cabinet**?

Charles Francis Adams III, a great-grandson of the sixth president, John Quincy Adams, served as Hoover's secretary of the navy. He also was a famous yachtsman, who was inducted into the America's Cup Hall of Fame.

What horrible **economic depression** plagued Hoover's administration?

The defining moment of Herbert Hoover's presidency was the Great Depression, marked by the horrific stock market crash on October 24, 1929—so-called "Black Tuesday." Unemployment ravaged the country and poverty struck many who were previously in the middle class. Hoover, who had successfully relied on the private sector in part for his humanitarian relief efforts, faced criticism for not providing enough assistance from the federal government for emergency relief.

What significant **federal entity** did **Hoover create** for prisons?

Hoover oversaw the creation of the Federal Bureau of Prisons in 1930. This organization oversees the administration of the federal prison system. Under its first director, Sanford Bates, the bureau instituted training for prison guards, built new prisons such as Alcatraz, and improved health care for inmates. Hoover's interest in penal reform had escalated after a notorious riot at the Leavenworth penitentiary in Kansas in 1929.

What significant **labor legislation** was signed by President Hoover?

President Hoover signed into law without comment the Norris-LaGuardia Act of 1932, named after Senator George Norris of Nebraska and Representative Fiorello LaGuardia of New York. This law prohibited judges from issuing injunctions, or court orders, limiting peaceful labor striking.

This 1938 photo by Ben Shawn depicts a destitute family in Centerville, Ohio, one of the many "Hoovervilles" that sprang up across the country during the Great Depression.

Who were Hoover's U.S. **Supreme Court appointees**?

Hoover appointed three men to the U.S. Supreme Court: Charles Evans Hughes, Owen J. Roberts, and Benjamin N. Cardozo. Hughes, a former Republican nominee for president and secretary of state, had previously served as an associate justice from 1910 to 1916, then resigned to run for president. In 1930, Hoover appointed him Chief Justice of the U.S. Supreme Court, where he served until his death in 1941. Owen J. Roberts was nominated to the Supreme Court by Hoover after his first nominee, John J. Parker, was denied confirmation by the Senate. Roberts, who was involved in the prosecution of the Teapot Dome scandals by President Calvin Coolidge, served on the Court for fifteen years. Cardozo, formerly a well-respected jurist in New York, served on the Court for six years.

POST PRESIDENCY

Did Hoover seek **reelection**?

Yes, Hoover ran for reelection. He garnered his party's nomination, but lost the election badly to Democratic nominee Franklin Delano Roosevelt. Hoover could manage only 59 electoral votes to 472 for Roosevelt.

To what position did President Harry **Truman appoint Hoover**?

President Truman appointed Hoover to a leading position in the Food Supply for World Famine. Truman allegedly told him: "You know more about feeding nations and people than anybody in the world." He later appointed Hoover to head the Commission on Organization of the Executive Branch of the Government. The organization became known as the Hoover Commission during Hoover's chairmanship. There were two different commissions, the first in 1947 to 1949 and the second in 1953 to 1955. President Dwight D. Eisenhower appointed Hoover to the second Hoover Commission in 1953.

What **books** did Hoover **write** in his post-presidency period?

Hoover wrote several books, including a collection of essays that criticized the Roosevelt administration titled *The Challenge to Liberty* (1934). He also wrote *The Basis of Lasting Peace* with Hugh Gibson and *The Memoirs of Herbert Hoover* (1958). One of his books, *The Ordeal of Woodrow Wilson* (1958), became a national bestseller.

When did he **die**?

Hoover died at the age of ninety on October 20, 1964, in New York City.

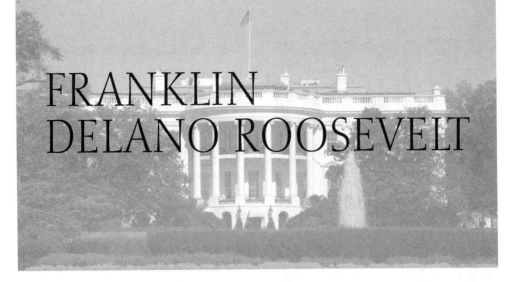

FRANKLIN DELANO ROOSEVELT

(1882–1945)
32nd President, 1933–1945
Party Affiliation: Democrat
Chief 1932 Opponent: Herbert Hoover (Republican)
Chief 1936 Opponent: Alf Landon (Republican)
Chief 1940 Opponent: Wendell Willkie (Republican)
Chief 1944 Opponent: Thomas E. Dewey (Republican)

EARLY LIFE AND FAMILY

Where and when was Roosevelt **born**?

Franklin Delano Roosevelt (FDR) was born in Hyde Park, New York, to James Roosevelt and Sara Delano Roosevelt on January 30, 1882. He was named after his great-uncle Franklin Hughes Delano.

What was his **father's occupation**?

Born into a wealthy and prominent family, James Roosevelt graduated from Harvard Law School, but did not practice law. Instead, he became a successful businessman, venturing into various financial projects. He was a founder of Consolidated Coal Company and president of the Southern Railway Security Company.

Did Franklin Roosevelt have any **siblings**?

Yes, he had one half-brother. Roosevelt's father, James, had previously been married to Rebecca Howland, who died in 1876. James and Rebecca had one son, James "Rosy" Roosevelt.

President Franklin D Roosevelt.

What was Roosevelt's **early education**?

He learned from private tutors in his early years. In 1896, he attended a private boarding school in Massachusetts called Groton School, led by headmaster Endicott Peabody. He received an excellent education at this academy, as did all four of his sons. He then attended Harvard, where he majored in political science and government. He did not excel academically, but graduated in 1904. While in college, he was the editor-in-chief of the *Harvard Crimson*.

Did he **marry**?

Franklin Roosevelt married his distant cousin Eleanor Roosevelt on March 17, 1905, when FDR was twenty-three and Eleanor was twenty. Eleanor Roosevelt became one of the most significant First Ladies in the history of the United States. She contributed mightily to the president's policies. After FDR's death, President Harry Truman appointed her to the U.S. delegation to the United Nations.

Did he have any **children**?

Yes, Franklin and Eleanor Roosevelt had six children, five of whom lived to adulthood. The five were Anna, James, Elliott, Franklin Jr., and John. Anna achieved prominent success in journalism and public relations. James served in the U.S. House of Representatives. Elliott was a successful businessman and served as mayor of Miami Beach. Franklin Jr. graduated from Harvard and the University of Virginia Law School. Like his older brother James, he served in the U.S. House of Representatives. Later, he was named chairman of the Equal Employment Opportunity Commission. John graduated from Harvard and became a successful business owner and stockbroker.

The Roosevelts had another boy, born between James and Elliott, whom they named Franklin Jr. He died as an infant, and five years later the Roosevelts gave their next baby the same name.

Which **former presidents** was FDR most closely **related** to?

FDR was a fifth cousin of former president Theodore Roosevelt, a man he admired greatly. FDR also was related quite distantly to presidents Ulysses S. Grant and Zachary Taylor.

> ## After a failed turn in politics, what disease crippled Roosevelt?
>
> In 1921, Roosevelt contracted polio, a disease that crippled his lower body. It took at least three years of rehabilitation before his body recovered some feeling and movement. But he never regained full strength and mobility in his lower body.

EARLY CAREER

After graduating from Harvard, what did Roosevelt do?

Roosevelt attended Columbia Law School from 1904 to 1907. He did not graduate from Columbia, dropping out after he passed the bar exam in 1907.

After leaving Columbia University, what did FDR do?

FDR joined the Wall Street law firm of Carter, Ledyard & Milburn. He practiced corporate law, though contemporaries recalled that he had his eye on politics more than advancing in the career of law.

When did FDR return to law practice?

He first returned to the practice of law in 1920 after losing the election as vice president along with presidential candidate James M. Cox. He joined the firm of Emmett, Martin, and Roosevelt in New York City.

He also practiced law with Basil O'Connor in New York City from 1924 until 1933. Roosevelt met O'Connor, a Harvard law graduate and promising attorney, in New York City in 1920. O'Connor served as a legal adviser to Roosevelt. The two formed their own law partnership in 1924 and practiced until Roosevelt became president of the United States.

POLITICAL OFFICES

What was his first political office?

FDR first served as a New York state senator from 1911 to 1913. He established himself as a leading progressive against the political machine at Tammany Hall. He advocated for farmers and union workers, and supported voting for women and other progressive positions.

What **position** did President **Wilson offer Roosevelt**?

President Woodrow Wilson appointed Roosevelt to the position of assistant secretary of the navy. Ironically, this was the same position that his famous cousin and former president Theodore Roosevelt had held back in 1897. Franklin Roosevelt pushed for the expansion of the navy and supported U.S. entry into World War I sooner than many of his contemporaries.

Why did he **leave his job** as **assistant secretary of the navy**?

Roosevelt left this position in 1920 because he was the Democratic vice presidential candidate alongside presidential candidate James M. Cox. Roosevelt campaigned hard for Cox and himself, but they lost the election to the Republican ticket of Warren G. Harding and Calvin Coolidge.

Roosevelt as a young man in 1913, when he was still an attorney.

What speech marked **Roosevelt's political comeback**?

In 1924, FDR gave a speech at the Democratic National Convention in New York City in support of the Democratic contender Alfred E. Smith, the governor of New York. Roosevelt gave a terrific speech—sometimes called the "Happy Warrior" speech—that earned significant applause. However, the Democrats ended up choosing John W. Davis as their presidential nominee. Smith did receive the Democratic nomination in 1928. That same year, President Roosevelt wrote a book on Smith entitled *The Happy Warrior*.

What **political position** did Roosevelt have **before running for president**?

Roosevelt served as governor of New York from 1929 until 1933. He defeated Albert Ottinger for his first term and Charles H. Tuttle for his second term. He created a governmental agency to assist the rising number of unemployed persons in the state. He also furthered his progressive agenda by reducing work hours and expanding the coverage of the state workers' compensation law.

PRESIDENCY

Whom did **Roosevelt defeat** to win the **1932 Democratic nomination** for president?

Roosevelt defeated Alfred E. Smith of New York, the Democrat's presidential candidate in 1928, and Texas-based John Nance Garner, the Speaker of the House.

Who were his **opponents** in his **four presidential elections**?

In the 1932 election, Roosevelt defeated incumbent Republican president Herbert Hoover, whose campaign was doomed because the Great Depression began during his administration. Roosevelt won the electoral vote by a margin of 472 to 59.

In the 1936 election, Roosevelt defeated Alf Landon, the governor of Kansas, by another overwhelming margin—523 to 8. In the 1940 election, Roosevelt won over Wendell Wilkie, a Republican from Indiana. Wilkie was an unusual candidate for president, as he had never held elective office. Roosevelt defeated him by a margin of 449 to 82. In the 1944 election, Roosevelt faced Republican Thomas E. Dewey, the governor of New York. Roosevelt beat Dewey by an electoral vote count of 432 to 99.

Who **tried to kill** President **Roosevelt before** he was officially **sworn in** as president?

Guiseppe Zangara, a thirty-two-year-old Italian-born bricklayer, tried to assassinate President-Elect Roosevelt in Miami, Florida. Apparently, he had also thought about killing President Hoover. Zangara was motivated in his violent actions by the belief that the president was responsible for massive unemployment and for his own physical ailments. Zangara missed Roosevelt, but did kill Chicago mayor Anton Cermak and wounded several others. Cermak allegedly told FDR on the way to the hospital: "I'm glad it was me and not you, Mr. President."

Who were Roosevelt's **vice presidents**?

Roosevelt had three vice presidents during his tenure as president: John Nance Garner, Henry Agard Wallace, and Harry S. Truman. Garner, the Speaker of the House, had been

President Roosevelt signs the declaration of war against Germany.

considered a leading candidate for the 1932 Democratic nomination, but he urged his supporters to throw their support behind Roosevelt. He served as Roosevelt's vice president for his first two terms. He disagreed with Roosevelt over the president seeking a third term, believing in the tradition of a two-term maximum. Garner challenged Roosevelt for the Democratic nomination, but did not win.

Wallace served as Roosevelt's vice president from 1941 to 1945. He had served as secretary of agriculture for the president's first two terms. Roosevelt, on the advice from many in the Democratic Party leadership concerned about Wallace's unpopular views on closer ties with the Soviet Union, decided to remove Wallace from the vice president position and later installed him as secretary of commerce.

Roosevelt's last vice president was Harry S. Truman. Truman, who served only eighty-two days in that capacity (his tenure was cut short by Roosevelt's death) had previously served a decade as a U.S. senator from Missouri.

Who was the **first female member** of a presidential **cabinet**?

Roosevelt chose Frances Perkins as his secretary of labor, and she served in that position for his entire tenure as president. Roosevelt had appointed her to the position of New York industrial commissioner when he was governor. Perkins and Secretary of the Interior Harold L. Ickes were the only members of Roosevelt's cabinet to stay on the entire tenure of his presidency.

What **constitutional amendment** was **passed** during Roosevelt's tenure?

The Twenty-first Amendment was ratified in 1933, the first year of Roosevelt's presidency. The Twenty-first Amendment repealed the Eighteenth Amendment, which had established Prohibition. Upon signing the measure, Roosevelt said in part: "I trust in the good sense of the American people that they will not bring upon themselves the curse of the excessive use of intoxicating liquors, to the detriment of health, morals, and social integrity."

What was the **New Deal**?

The New Deal is the name given to a series of economic programs initiated by FDR and his administration to improve the American economy that continued to be mired in the Great Depression. In his inaugural address, Roosevelt promised a "new deal" for the "forgotten people."

The New Deal focused on relief, recovery, and reform. It consisted of the creation of the Social Security system, the Federal Deposit Insurance Corporation, and the Civilian Conservation Corps, which gave jobs to many unemployed young men. Another law passed as part of the New Deal was the Fair Labor Standards Act of 1938, which provide better working conditions for laborers.

Roosevelt garnered popular support for many of his New Deal programs through a series of speeches to the American public known as the "Fireside Chats." Roosevelt gave thirty "Fireside Chats" during 1933 and 1934. They contributed greatly to the popularity of the president and showcased his leadership skills.

What was Roosevelt's **position on World War II**?

Roosevelt saw the threat that Hitler's Germany presented to the Western world. While maintaining a position of official neutrality, he reached an understanding with British Prime Minister Winston Churchill that Germany must be stopped. They issued the Atlantic Charter, which sought to ensure that democracy would flourish and triumph over totalitarian regimes. His leadership—along with that of Churchill and, to a lesser extent, Joseph Stalin of Russia—contributed greatly to the victory of the Allied forces over Germany, Japan, and the other Axis powers.

When Japan attacked the United States at Pearl Harbor on December 7, 1941, Roosevelt showed forceful leadership and resolve in the face of a direct threat to national security and existence. He wrote a memorably evocative appeal to Congress, asking for a declaration of war: "Yesterday, December 7, 1941—a date which will live in infamy—the United States of America was suddenly and viciously attacked by naval and air forces of the Empire of Japan."

What **controversial executive order** did Roosevelt sign that **interned Japanese Americans**?

On February 19, 1942, President Roosevelt signed Executive Order 9066, which stated, in part:

> I hereby authorize and direct the Secretary of War, and the Military Commanders whom he may from time to time designate, whenever he or any designated Commander deems such action necessary or desirable, to prescribe military areas in such places and of such extent as he or the appropriate Military

339

Commander may determine, from which any or all persons may be excluded, and with respect to which, the right of any person to enter, remain in, or leave shall be subject to whatever restrictions the Secretary of War or the appropriate Military Commander may impose in his discretion

While the law did not specifically mention the Japanese, military commanders used this executive order to intern more than 110,000 Japanese Americans for the duration of the war. First Lady Eleanor Roosevelt opposed the measure. Even FBI director J. Edgar Hoover opposed the measure, believing that the Japanese spies had been caught shortly after the attack on Pearl Harbor on December 7, 1941.

What was the **Court Packing Plan**?

Roosevelt was angered by the actions of the Supreme Court in striking down many of his New Deal laws. He supported a measure that would allow the president to appoint a new justice every time an existing justice reached seventy years of age, with a maximum of six additional justices. This plan did not get very far, because it was met with widespread opposition. However, some speculate that pressure from Roosevelt caused at least some members of the Court to look with a bit more favor on some New Deal measures. Whatever the case, the Court continued to consist of nine members and this has stayed constant.

Who were Roosevelt's U.S. **Supreme Court appointees**?

FDR appointed nine men to the U.S. Supreme Court, elevating Harlan Fiske Stone from the position of associate justice to chief justice, and then appointing eight associate justices. They were Hugo Black, Stanley Reed, Felix Frankfurter, William O. Douglas, Frank Murphy, James Byrnes, Robert Jackson, and Wiley Rutledge.

Stone had served as an associate justice from 1925 to 1941. Roosevelt elevated him to chief justice in 1941, where he served for five years. He was an effective chief justice who contributed greatly to the development of constitutional law in his tenure on the Court. The appointment was different than most because FDR, a Democrat, appointed Stone, who was a Republican. Usually, a president will appoint a justice from his political party.

Black, a former U.S. senator from Alabama, served on the Court for nearly thirty-four years, from 1937 until 1971. Though he had been a member of the Ku Klux Klan early in his career, he developed into a strong defender of individual freedoms on the Court. He was known for his strident defense of First Amendment freedoms until the waning years of his tenure.

Reed served on the Court for nineteen years from 1938 to 1957. A former solicitor general, Reed left the Court at age seventy-three. He lived until he was ninety-five, making him the longest living Supreme Court justice in American history. Felix Frankfurter, a noted Harvard law professor, served on the Court

A World War II poster inspired by President Roosevelt's idea of the Four Freedoms.

from 1939 until his death in 1962. Formerly with the American Civil Liberties Union, Frankfurter surprised some by turning into the defender of the doctrine of judicial restraint.

Douglas, the former chairman of the Securities and Exchange Commission, served on the Court for more than thirty-six years from 1939 until 1975. He served more years on the Court than any other justice in history. He was the Court's ultimate defender of individual liberties. Murphy, the former mayor of Detroit and U.S. solicitor general, served on the Court nearly ten years from 1940 to 1949. He, too, consistently voted with Black and Douglas on civil liberties questions.

Byrnes served on the Court for little more than a year between 1941 and 1942. He left the Court to become the director of Economic Stabilization. He later served as secretary of state for President Harry Truman and governor of South Carolina.

Robert H. Jackson, formerly Roosevelt's U.S. attorney general, served on the Court from 1941 to 1954. He is known for serving as the chief prosecutor at the Nuremberg Trials of Nazi war criminals in the mid-1940s. He is considered one of the Court's best writers. Wiley Rutledge, a former law school dean, served on the Court from 1943 to 1949. He was a consistent liberal vote on the Court and a defender of religious freedom principles.

President Roosevelt meets with Soviet Union leader Joseph Stalin (left) and British Prime Minister Winston Churchill.

How did Roosevelt's **presidency end**?

Roosevelt died in office on April 12, 1945, just as his fourth term was beginning.

What **constitutional amendment** was passed in **response** to FDR's **long tenure** as president?

The Twenty-second Amendment—sometimes dubbed the "FDR Amendment"—prohibits anyone from serving as president for more than two full terms. Ratified in 1951, the measure provides:

> No person shall be elected to the office of the President more than twice, and no person who has held the office of President, or acted as President, for more than two years of a term to which some other person was elected President shall be elected to the office of the President more than once. But this Article shall not apply to any person holding the office of President, when this Article was proposed by the Congress, and shall not prevent any person who may be holding the office of President, or acting as President, during the term within which this Article becomes operative from holding the office of President or acting as President during the remainder of such term.

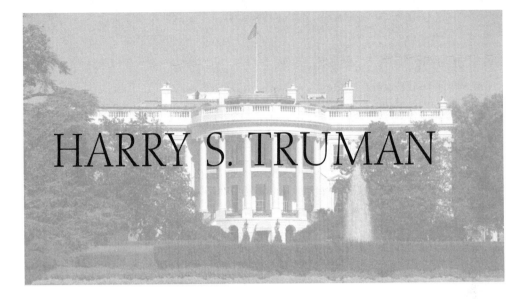

HARRY S. TRUMAN

(1882–1974)
33rd President, 1945–1953
Party Affiliation: Democrat
Chief 1948 Opponents: Thomas E. Dewey (Republican),
Strom Thurmond (Dixiecrat), Henry Wallace (Progressive)

EARLY LIFE AND FAMILY

Where and when was he **born**?

Harry S. Truman was born in Lamar, Missouri, to John and Martha Truman on May 8, 1884. He is the only president in U.S. history to have been born in Missouri.

What did his **father do** for a living?

John Truman worked as a farmer and cattle salesman.

Did Harry Truman have any **siblings**?

Truman had two younger siblings: a brother named John Vivian and a sister named Mary Jane.

What was Truman's **early education**?

He attended public grade school in Noland, Missouri. His family moved to Independence, Missouri, when he was still a youngster. He then went to Independence High School in Independence, Missouri. He graduated from high school in 1901.

343

Did he **marry**?

Truman married Elizabeth "Bess" Wallace on June 28, 1919, in Independence, Missouri. Bess outlived her husband by nearly ten years, living until age ninety-seven.

Did he have any **children**?

Yes, Harry and Bess had one daughter, Margaret Truman. She became a singer and later an author of both fiction and nonfiction books.

EARLY CAREER

What did Truman do **after graduating** from **high school**?

He initially planned to go to college, but his father suffered financial loss and Truman went to work at a variety of jobs to help the family. He worked as a timekeeper for a railroad, a mailroom clerk, a bank clerk, and a bookkeeper. He then returned to his family's home near Grandview, Missouri, to help run the farm.

What was his **military service**?

Truman joined the Missouri National Guard in 1905, leaving after six years. When the country entered World War I, Truman reenlisted in the National Guard. His unit became a regular army force. He served in the One Hundred and Twenty-Ninth Field Artillery and saw combat action in Europe at the Vognes Mountains near the France-Germany border. He left the war as a major.

What did Truman do **after the war**?

He opened a clothing store in Kansas City, Missouri, with Eddie Jacobsen, a comrade from World War I. The store did well for a couple years but went under in 1922. For more than a decade, Truman made installment payments to pay off his creditors. Because he had once owned a clothing store, he earned the nickname "The Haberdasher."

POLITICAL OFFICES

What was his **first political position**?

Truman won election as judge of Jackson County, Missouri, in 1922, an administrative rather than judicial position. He won with the backing of local political leader Thomas

What was unusual about the 1948 election?

The election was unusual because the newspapers and pollsters wrongly predicted that Dewey would defeat Truman. The *Chicago Tribune* published an article in its early edition on election day with the headline "Dewey Defeats Truman." Many political pundits also wrongly predicted that Dewey would prevail.

"Boss Tom" Pendergast. Truman had served in World War I with Pendergast's nephew James. Truman lost reelection in 1924, but won the position of presiding judge of Jackson County in 1926. He held this position until 1934.

When did he serve in the **U.S. Senate**?

Truman served in the U.S. Senate from 1935 until 1945, when he became vice president under Franklin D. Roosevelt. With assistance from Pendergast, he defeated Republican incumbent Roscoe Conkling Patterson to win the seat. As a senator, Truman vigorously supported FDR's New Deal programs. He later served as chairman of the Special Committee to Investigate the National Defense Program.

What was his **next political position**?

Truman left the U.S. Senate after President Roosevelt asked him to be his vice presidential running mate. Roosevelt had initially considered James F. Byrnes, William O. Douglas, and Truman. Truman served only eighty-two days as vice president before Roosevelt passed away.

PRESIDENCY

Whom did Truman defeat to **win** his **first full term** as president?

In 1948, Truman defeated Republican Thomas E. Dewey, Dixiecrat Strom Thurmond, and Progressive Henry Wallace to win the election. Dewey, the governor of New York, had been the Republican presidential candidate in 1944. Thurmond, a U.S. senator from South Carolina, led the Dixiecrats. This splinter group of Southern Democrats split with other members of the party because the Dixiecrats opposed the granting of more civil rights to blacks. Wallace, whom Truman had replaced as FDR's vice president, led the Progressive Party. He was too liberal to garner much public support. Truman captured the election with 303 electoral votes to 189 for Dewey, 39 for Thurmond, and 0 for Wallace.

Truman assumed the presidency after FDR's death in early 1945. Here he is in October 1945 greeting constituents.

Who was Truman's **vice president**?

Truman did not have a vice president for the remainder of FDR's fourth term. The Twenty-fifth Amendment would later require that a vice president be replaced when a turn of events caused the office to be vacated. For Truman's first full term, his vice president was Alben W. Barkley of Kentucky. He had served in both the U.S. House and Senate.

Which **member** of Truman's **cabinet** served in **two different positions**?

George C. Marshall served as Truman's secretary of state from 1947 to 1949 and as his secretary of defense from 1950 to 1951. Marshall had been Franklin D. Roosevelt's chief military advisor and was a key figure in Allied strategy during World War II. He won the Nobel Peace Prize in 1953 because of the famous program named after him—the Marshall Plan—which outlined the economic rebuilding of Europe following the devastating war.

Which **member** of Truman's **cabinet** later won a **Pulitzer Prize**?

Dean Acheson served as Truman's fourth secretary of state after Edward R. Stettinius Jr., James F. Byrnes, and George C. Marshall. Acheson won the Pulitzer Prize for his 1969 memoir, *Present at the Creation*. He later served as an unofficial advisor to John F. Kennedy and Lyndon B. Johnson.

What was the **Fair Deal**?

Truman's "Fair Deal" was the name given to his policies for improving the lives of average Americans. His domestic "Fair Deal" program included federal funding for housing, increases in the minimum wage, improved civil rights, and increased Social Security benefits.

What was the **Truman Doctrine**?

The Truman Doctrine was a foreign policy perspective that stressed that the United States must help other countries to contain and prevent the spread of Communism. Truman said in a 1947 speech: "I believe it must be the policy of the United States to support free peoples who are resisting attempted subjugation by armed minorities or

When did Truman learn there was an atom bomb?

Truman did not learn of the existence of the atom bomb until he assumed office as president in April 1945. As vice president, he had no clue about its development. At the end of a cabinet meeting, Secretary of War Henry L. Stimson informed him about the bomb.

by outside pressures." His comments referred to U.S. aid to Greece and Turkey to counter the threat of Soviet influence.

The Truman Doctrine helped lead to active U.S. involvement in the North Atlantic Treaty Organization—a military agreement between various European countries known by its acronym NATO.

Did **Truman** exercise the **veto power often**?

Yes, Truman exercised his presidential veto powers approximately 250 times, which placed him third, behind Franklin Delano Roosevelt and Grover Cleveland.

What **ultimate weapon** did Truman sanction in order to **end World War II**?

Truman ordered the use of the atomic bomb on Japan, when they would not surrender. He reasoned that the dropping of the bomb would save American lives, as more soldiers would be killed invading Japan. It was estimated that half a million American troops or Allied forces would have died if an invasion had taken place in Japan. The first bomb was dropped on Hiroshima on August 6, 1945. When Japan refused to surrender, Truman ordered the dropping of another atomic bomb on Nagasaki, Japan, on August 9, 1945. Japan asked for peace the very next day and surrendered soon after that.

What **other war** was the U.S. involved in **while Truman was president**?

The Korean War took place between 1950 and 1953. At the end of World War II, Korea, which had been conquered by Japan, was divided into North and South Korea. North Korea was a communist country, while South Korea was a democratic country. When North Korea invaded South Korea, Truman believed military action was necessary to stop the spread of Communism.

Which famous **general clashed with Truman** and was relieved of duty because of this?

Truman clashed with General Douglas MacArthur over combat maneuvers during the Korean War. MacArthur's soldiers and UN troops had pushed North Korean forces past

President Harry S. Truman.

the 38th Parallel (the dividing line between North and South Korea). However, when MacArthur pushed into North Korea, China sent thousands of troops there, forcing a retreat by the UN forces.

MacArthur urged the president to approve of military action against China. Truman, fearing the development of World War III, declined. This led to the Korean War ending in a stalemate rather than a clear victory. MacArthur publicly challenged Truman's authority, declaring that "there is no substitute for victory." Truman fired MacArthur for challenging his authority as commander in chief.

What **executive order** did Truman issue that **changed the composition** of the **military**?

Truman issued Executive Order 9981 in July 26, 1948, which called for "equality of treatment and opportunity for all persons in the armed forces without regard to race, color, religion, or national origin." This led to the desegregation of the American military and is considered a milestone in the quest for civil rights in the United States.

What **action by Truman** led to a **ruling against him** by the U.S. Supreme Court?

Facing a strike by steelworkers during the Korean War, Truman invoked his powers as commander in chief and seized the steel mills. He claimed that such seizure for the government was necessary as an emergency measure during the war. The owners of the steel mills sued in court for an injunction and ultimately prevailed. The U.S. Supreme Court ruled 6 to 3 in *Youngstown Sheet and Tube Co. v. Sawyer* (1952) that the actions of the executive branch infringed upon the fundamental principle of separation of powers. The Court reasoned that Truman's actions invaded the province of the legislative branch, as the seizure of the steel mills could only be done (if at all) by an act of Congress.

Interestingly, the attorney for the steel mills was attorney John W. Davis, the 1924 Republican Party presidential nominee who lost to Calvin Coolidge.

What **famous saying** was on President **Truman's desk**?

Truman had a sign on his desk that read "The Buck Stops Here." It became a mantra associated with Truman, who recognized that he had to make tough decisions as the country's commander in chief.

Who tried to **assassinate President Truman**?

On November 1, 1950, Griselio Torresola and Oscar Collazo, Puerto Rican nationalists, shot at guards outside the Blair House—the house in Washington, D.C. where President Truman lived while the White House was being renovated. The two men wanted to draw worldwide attention to the cause of independence for Puerto Rico.

One guard and Torresola were killed during the gunfire. Collazo and two guards were injured. Collazo was convicted and sentenced to death. Truman, who did not believe in capital punishment, commuted his sentence to life in prison. He became eligible for parole in 1966, but remained in prison until President Jimmy Carter granted him clemency and he was released for time served.

Who were Truman's U.S. **Supreme Court appointees**?

Truman appointed one chief justice and three associate justices. He appointed Frederick M. Vinson, his secretary of the treasury, to the Court in 1946 where he served seven years. He was not regarded as a great leader of the Court; some members of the Court viewed him as a politician, not a judge.

Truman appointed Harold Burton, Tom Clark, and Sherman Minton as associate justices. Burton, a U.S. senator from Ohio, served thirteen years on the Court. Clark, Truman's U.S. attorney general, served on the Court for eighteen years. He resigned from the Court when his son Ramsey was named U.S. attorney general. Minton, a former U.S. senator from Indiana, had been a judge on the U.S. Court of Appeals for the Seventh Circuit before his nomination. He served seven years on the Court.

POST PRESIDENCY

What **books did Truman write** in his post-presidential period?

Truman authored three books: *Year of Decisions* (1955), *Years of Trial and Hope* (1956) and *Mr. Citizen* (1960).

When did he **die**?

Truman died on December 26, 1972, in Kansas City, Missouri, at the age of eighty-eight.

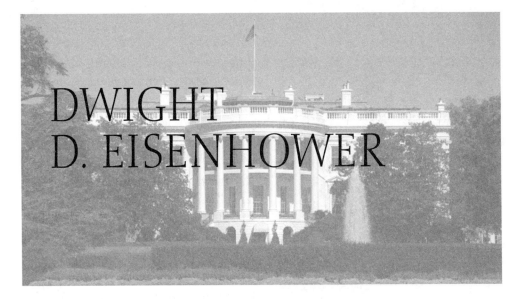

DWIGHT D. EISENHOWER

(1890–1969)
34th President, 1953–1961
Party Affiliation: Republican
Chief 1952 and 1956 Opponent: Adlai Stevenson (Democrat)

EARLY LIFE AND FAMILY

Where and when was Eisenhower **born**?

David Dwight Eisenhower was born in Denison, Texas, to David and Ida Eisenhower on October 14, 1890. Because his father was named David, family members called the son Dwight. He later changed his name to Dwight David Eisenhower when he enrolled at West Point.

What did his **father do** for a living?

David Jacob Eisenhower worked as a store owner, mechanic, and manager of a gas company.

Did he have any **siblings**?

Eisenhower had five brothers who lived to adulthood: Arthur, Edgar, Roy, Earl, and Milton. Arthur had a successful banking career in Kansas City. Edgar worked as an attorney. Earl worked as an engineer and later served in the Illinois House of Representatives. Roy had a career as a pharmacist. Milton served as the president of three

Eisenhower married the future first lady, Marie "Mamie" Geneva Doud, on July 1, 1916.

different universities during his career: Kansas State, Pennsylvania State, and John Hopkins University.

What was Eisenhower's **early education**?

He attended local public schools in Abilene, Kansas. He graduated from Abilene High School in 1909. During high school, he played basketball and football.

Who was his **wife**?

Eisenhower married Marie "Mamie" Geneva Doud on July 1, 1916, in Denver, Colorado. Eisenhower was twenty-five and Marie was nineteen at the time of their marriage.

Did he have any **children**?

Yes, Dwight and Marie had two sons: Doud, who was born in 1919, and John, who was born in 1922. Doud Dwight Eisenhower died at age three in 1921. Still living at the time of this writing, John Sheldon Doud Eisenhower had a military career and then wrote several books on military history. For example, he authored *Allies: Pearl Harbor to D-Day* (1982). He also served as U.S. ambassador to Belgium from 1969 to 1971.

MILITARY CAREER

What did Eisenhower do **after graduating high school**?

Eisenhower entered the U.S. Military Academy at West Point in 1911 and graduated in 1915. He excelled at football for the army before suffering a knee injury. His knowledge of the game impressed the coaches, who asked him to coach the junior varsity team.

Did he see **combat** in **World War I**?

Eisenhower requested an overseas deployment, but did not receive it. Instead, he served as a training instructor at Fort Oglethorpe, Georgia, and a commander at Camp Colt, Pennsylvania, where he studied tank warfare.

In what field of study did Eisenhower excel?

Eisenhower attended the Command and General Staff Training School in Leavenworth, Kansas, from 1925 to 1926, where he excelled. He finished first in a class of more than 270.

Under which famous generals did he work or serve?

He worked, served under, or learned from many famous generals, including George Patton, Fox Conner, John J. Pershing, and Douglas A. MacArthur. Patton taught him much about tank warfare. Conner served as a key mentor to Eisenhower, teaching him military history and strategy. Some dubbed him "the man who made Eisenhower." Eisenhower referred to Conner as "the ablest man I ever knew."

Pershing sent Eisenhower to the Army War College, and then to France. MacArthur taught the junior officer administration and attention to detail when Eisenhower served under the famous general's staff in the Philippines and elsewhere.

When did Eisenhower become a general?

He was promoted to brigadier general in September 1941, to major general in March 1942, and to full general in February 1943. He led the successful Allied excursion into North Africa and defeated enemy forces, leading to an invasion of Italy. In December 1943, President Franklin D. Roosevelt named him supreme allied commander. He planned the attack at D-Day on Normandy, and directed the final attack on Germany that effectively ended the war. He was promoted to a five-star general in December 1944.

When he returned home after World War II, what military position did he take?

After his successful management of the invasion in northern Africa and the Allied invasion at D-Day in Normandy, France, leading to the eventual subjugation of Germany, Eisenhower was a genuine war hero. When he returned to the United States, he was named army chief of staff.

What was his next non-military position?

Eisenhower was named president of Columbia University in 1948. He was largely a figurehead.

What well-received memoir did he write that was published in 1948?

Eisenhower's military memoir, *Crusade in Europe,* was published in 1948. It was a critical and commercial success.

General Eisenhower meeting with paratroopers in England just before the D-Day invasion in June 1944.

To what position did President **Truman appoint Eisenhower** in 1950?

Truman appointed Eisenhower to the position of supreme commander of the North Atlantic Treaty Organization (NATO) in late 1950. He served in this position until accepting the Republican presidential nomination.

PRESIDENCY

Whom did he **defeat** to win the **Republican nomination** in **1952**?

Eisenhower defeated Ohio Senator Robert Taft, the son of former President William Howard Taft, to win the Republican nomination. He also defeated Earl Warren, the governor of California, whom Eisenhower would later appoint as Chief Justice of the U.S. Supreme Court.

Whom did he **defeat** to win the **presidency** in both 1952 and 1956?

Eisenhower defeated Democrat Adlai E. Stevenson, the grandson of Grover Cleveland's vice president. Stevenson served as governor of Illinois. President John F. Kennedy later appointed Stevenson as U.S. ambassador to the United Nations. Eisenhower

> ## What was unusual about Eisenhower as president?
>
> **E**isenhower was one of only four presidents in history (the others being Zachary Taylor, Ulysses S. Grant, and Herbert Hoover) who never held public office before the presidency. Prior to 1952, it was uncertain which political party Eisenhower would support. Both major political parties courted him as a candidate. Eisenhower described himself as a "liberal Republican."

handily defeated Stevenson by an electoral vote count of 442 to 89 in 1952, and an electoral vote count of 457 to 73 in 1956.

Who was his **vice president**?

His vice president was Richard M. Nixon from California, who had served as a member of the U.S. House and Senate. Nixon served as vice president for all of Eisenhower's two terms. He later lost the presidency in a close race with Democratic candidate John F. Kennedy. Nixon retired from politics for a time, but returned with a vengeance, winning the presidency in 1968 and again in 1972.

Who were Eisenhower's **secretaries of state**?

Eisenhower had two secretaries of state during his two-term presidency: John Foster Dulles and Christian A. Herter. Dulles served from 1953 to 1958 and Herter served from 1959 to 1961. Dulles, who died in office, crafted an aggressive foreign policy against Communism. Herter, who had served as governor of Massachusetts, had been undersecretary of state for Dulles.

What **significant internal improvement** occurred during Eisenhower's early years?

Eisenhower signed into law the Highway Revenue Act, which provided federal funds to states for constructing interstate highways.

What **famous clash** did Eisenhower have **with a governor over civil rights**?

Eisenhower sent in federal troops to ensure that Arkansas governor Orval Faubus would not attempt to block nine African American students from attending the previously all-white Central High School in Little Rock, Arkansas. In the wake of the Supreme Court's desegregation decision in *Brown v. Board of Education* (1954), the city school board recognized its obligation to desegregate. However, Governor Faubus

355

President Dwight Eisenhower.

> ## What were Eisenhower's catchy campaign slogans?
>
> His 1952 campaign slogan was "We Like Ike." His 1956 campaign slogan was "Peace and Prosperity."

used the Arkansas National Guard to block the school to prevent the integration. He did this in defiance of a federal court order mandating integration.

Eisenhower met with Faubus personally and came away from the meeting thinking that Faubus understood he must not defy a federal court order. However, days later Faubus defiantly refused to agree and said he would support segregation. Eisenhower then sent in federal troops to ensure that the "Little Rock Nine" could attend Central High. Federal troops from the 101st Airborne Division surrounded the school, controlled the crowd, and ensured integration. Eisenhower told his U.S. attorney general Herbert Brownell to use force if necessary to save lives and ensure integration.

What was the **"Domino Principle"**?

The "Domino Principle" was a term used by President Eisenhower to explain the threat of Communist expansion. He explained that the spread of Communism would have severe ramifications: "You have a row of dominoes set up, you knock over the first one, and what will happen to the last one is the certainty that it will go over very quickly."

What was the **U-2 incident**?

The U-2 incident was a diplomatic crisis that occurred in May 1960, when the Soviet Union shot down an American U-2 spy plane piloted by CIA agent Gary Powers. A few weeks before an international summit, Powers flew the U-2 plane over the Soviet Union in attempts to gather photographic evidence of Soviet military and missile capabilities. The Soviets shot down the plane.

The United States and President Eisenhower claimed that the plane was not a spy plane but a weather forecasting plane that had unintentionally flown off course. Soviet premier Nikita Khrushchev announced that Powers was captured as a prisoner. The incident proved a great embarrassment to the United States and Eisenhower, as the administration was caught in a lie.

Whatever **happened** to CIA agent **Gary Powers**?

Powers was sentenced to three years in prison followed by seven years of hard labor by Soviet authorities. In February 1962, the United States and the Soviet Union exchanged

The Eisenhower home, located in Gettysburg, Pennsylvania.

prisoners. The United States turned over Soviet spy Rudolf Abel, who was really KGB Colonel Vilyam Fisher, for Powers and American student Frederic Pryor.

Powers later worked for Lockheed Martin as a test pilot from 1963 to 1970. He had to leave Lockheed Martin after the publication of his memoir, *Operation Overflight: A Memoir of the U-2 Incident* (1970).

Who were Eisenhower's U.S. **Supreme Court appointees**?

He appointed five men to the U.S. Supreme Court—one as chief justice and four as associate justices. In 1953, Eisenhower appointed Earl Warren, the governor of California and a political rival, as chief justice of the U.S. Supreme Court. Warren led the Court until 1969. He showed great leadership on the Court, including marshalling together a unanimous opinion in the famous school desegregation decision in *Brown v. Board of Education* (1954). Warren established his place in history as the head of the so-called Warren Court, which desegregated public schools, enhanced constitutional protections for those charged with crimes, and breathed life into many other provisions of the Bill of Rights.

Eisenhower appointed four men as associate justices: John Marshall Harlan II, William J. Brennan, Charles Whittaker, and Potter Stewart. Harlan, the grandson of John Marshall Harlan I, had a distinguished career as a lawyer and had been on the U.S. Court of Appeals for the Second Circuit for a year. He believed in the principles of judicial restraint and precedent and often dissented from some of the broader rulings of his colleagues.

Brennan, a jurist on the New Jersey Supreme Court, served on the Court for thirty-four years from 1956 to 1990. He authored many important First Amendment decisions during his tenure, including the famous libel law case *New York Times Co. v. Sullivan* (1964), which made it much more difficult for public officials to sue their critics for libel.

Whittaker, who had attended law school with Harry Truman in Kansas City, served on the Court from 1957 to 1962. Previously, he had worked as both a federal district court judge and a federal appeals court judge before his rapid ascent to the U.S. Supreme Court. Stewart, who had served on the U.S. Court of Appeals for the 6th Circuit, held his place on the Court from 1959 until 1981. He was known for his defense of free-press rights, as well as his famous statement on obscenity: "I know it when I see it."

Did **Eisenhower agree** with **Warren Court** rulings?

He disagreed with some of them, certainly. He did not agree with the Court's historic decision in *Brown v. Board of Education* (1954). To his credit, however, he did use federal forces to enforce outright defiance of Court decisions. He wrote in his memoirs: "Like many political moderate conservatives, I felt that some Supreme Court justices were too often using their own interpretations of the law to remake American society according to their own social, political, and ideological precepts."

POST PRESIDENCY

What **books did Eisenhower write** in his post-presidential period?

Eisenhower wrote his two volume memoir, *The White House Years*. The first volume was *Mandate for Change, 1953–1956* (1965) and the second volume was *Waging Peace, 1956–1961* (1966). He also wrote another book entitled *At Ease: Stories I Tell to Friends* (1967).

What **athletic accomplishment** did he achieve in retirement?

Eisenhower, a golf aficionado, scored a hole-in-one on February 2, 1968, at the Seven Lakes Country Club in Palm Springs, California.

When did he **die**?

Eisenhower died on March 28, 1969, at Walter Reed Army Hospital in Washington, D.C.

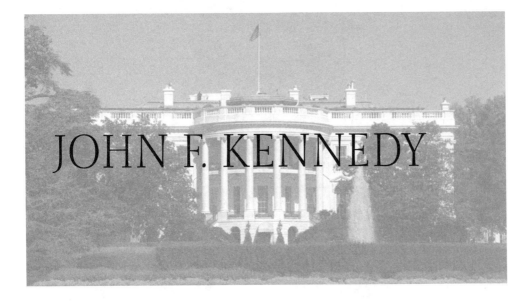

JOHN F. KENNEDY

(1917–1963)
35th President, 1961–1963
Party Affiliation: Democrat
Chief 1960 Opponent: Richard M. Nixon (Republican)

EARLY LIFE AND FAMILY

Where and when was he **born**?

John F. Kennedy was born in Brookline, Massachusetts, to Joseph and Rose Kennedy on May 29, 1917.

What did his **father do** for a living?

Joseph Patrick Kennedy was a successful businessman and public official. He worked as a bank president, made large amounts of money in the stock market, and formed a liquor distributorship that profited him handsomely. President Franklin D. Roosevelt appointed him as chairman of the Securities and Exchange Commission. He later served as U.S. ambassador to Great Britain.

Did John F. Kennedy have any **siblings**?

Yes, John F. Kennedy had eight siblings: five sisters and three brothers. They were Joseph Jr., Rosemary, Kathleen, Eunice, Patricia, Robert, Jean, and Edward.

President John F. Kennedy.

Which of his **siblings** also **ran for president**?

Robert F. Kennedy and Edward M. Kennedy both ran for president. Robert served as John's U.S. attorney general and later became a U.S. senator from New York. He likely would have captured the 1968 Democratic nomination for president, but was assassinated. Edward served as a U.S. senator from Massachusetts from 1962 until his death in 2009. He was the fourth-longest serving U.S. senator in American history—behind Robert Byrd, Daniel Inouye, and Strom Thurmond.

First Lady Jackie Kennedy was as young and glamorous as her husband. Together, they were the beloved rulers of "Camelot." Five years after the assassination, she married shipping magnate Aristotle Onassis.

What was Kennedy's **early education**?

He attended Dexter School in Brookline, Massachusetts, and Riverdale Country Day School in New York for elementary school. He then studied at the Canterbury School in New Milford, Connecticut. After that, he attended Choate Rosemary Hall, a prep school in Willington, Connecticut, from 1931 to 1935.

Did he **marry**?

Yes, John F. Kennedy married Jacqueline L. Bouvier on September 12, 1953. Widowed in 1963, she was remarried in 1968 to Greek tycoon Aristotle Onassis.

Did he have any **children**?

Yes, John and Jackie Kennedy had two sons and a daughter. Caroline Kennedy, born in 1957, graduated from Radcliffe and then Columbia Law School. She has co-authored two well-received legal books with Ellen Alderman entitled *In Our Defense: The Bill of Rights in Action* (1991) and *The Right to Privacy* (1995). She expressed interest in the U.S. Senate vacancy created after Hillary Clinton made her run for the 2008 Democratic presidential nomination. She later withdrew for undisclosed personal reasons.

John F. Kennedy Jr., born in 1960, graduated from Brown University and New York University Law School. He worked as a prosecutor in the office of the Manhattan district attorney and later started his own magazine, *George.* He died in a plane crash in 1999.

The third child was Patrick, who died only two days after his birth in 1963.

EARLY CAREER

Where did Kennedy go to **college**?

He initially enrolled at Princeton University in the fall of 1935, but had to withdraw for health reasons in December. He then attended Harvard University from 1936 to 1940, graduating cum laude.

What did he do **after graduating college**?

He attended Stanford Business School in 1940 to 1941 before leaving to travel to South America.

What was his **military service**?

Kennedy served in the U.S. Navy from 1941 to 1945, rising to the rank of lieutenant. His PT boat was attacked by a Japanese destroyer in August 1943. He managed to swim to safety, saving the life of a fellow soldier in the process. He won a Purple Heart and the Navy and Marine Corps Medal.

What did he do **after leaving the military**?

Kennedy worked as a journalist for the *Chicago Herald-American* and for the International News Service.

POLITICAL OFFICES

What was his **first political office**?

Kennedy's first political office was as a U.S. representative for Massachusetts in 1947. He served in the House from 1947 to 1953, defeating Republican Lester Bowen to win his seat. He served on the House Education and Labor Committee.

When did he become a **U.S. senator**?

He won a seat in the U.S. Senate in 1953 with a victory over incumbent Senator Henry Cabot Lodge Jr. Kennedy served in the Senate until 1961, working on various committees. He did not come out strongly against controversial Republican Senator Joseph McCarthy, who went overboard in his condemnation of Communists. It is speculated that Kennedy did not denounce McCarthy because he was a friend of the Kennedy family and Robert Kennedy had worked on his staff.

What **book** did Kennedy write while he was a senator that earned him a *Pulitzer Prize*?

Kennedy authored the book *Profiles in Courage* (1956), which won a Pulitzer Prize in 1957. The book examined eight U.S. senators who showed courage in taking unpopular stands. The senators profiled in the book included: John Quincy Adams, Daniel Webster, Thomas Hart Benson, Sam Houston, Edmund G. Ross, Lucius Lamar, George Norris, and Robert Taft.

What **position** did **Kennedy seek** in **1956**?

Kennedy sought the Democratic vice-presidential nomination in 1956. He nearly captured the nomination, but lost to U.S. senator from Tennessee Estes Kefauver.

PRESIDENCY

Whom did **Kennedy defeat** to win the **1960 Democratic presidential nomination**?

Kennedy defeated Lyndon B. Johnson, a U.S. senator from Texas, Hubert Humphrey, a U.S. senator from Minnesota, and Adlai Stevenson of Illinois, the failed nominee from 1952 and 1956. Kennedy won the nomination on the first ballot with a lead of 806 to 409 for Johnson.

Whom did he **defeat** to win the **presidency**?

Kennedy defeated Eisenhower's vice president Richard M. Nixon to win the presidency. Nixon's running mate was none other than Kennedy's former senatorial opponent Henry Cabot Lodge Jr. Kennedy won the nomination with an electoral vote margin of 303 to 219. The popular vote was razor-thin, with Kennedy carrying 49.7 percent of the vote to 49.5 percent for Nixon. Kennedy had been helped in the election by a series of television debates between the two candidates. Nixon had hammered on Kennedy's youth and lack of experience, but Kennedy came off quite well on television.

Who was his **vice president**?

To the chagrin of some of his supporters, Kennedy chose Lyndon B. Johnson of Texas as his running mate. The two did not see eye-to-eye on some issues, but Johnson helped Kennedy carry the key state of Texas in the election. On Kennedy's assassination, Johnson assumed the presidency and later won reelection in 1964.

Who was his **attorney general**?

John F. Kennedy named his brother Robert as U.S. attorney general. Critics charged nepotism, but Robert Kennedy proved an effective and capable attorney general. He showed great leadership during the civil rights movement and fought against labor corruption.

What was the **Bay of Pigs** invasion?

This was a failed plan begun in the Eisenhower administration but approved by President Kennedy. After Communist leader Fidel Castro came to power in Cuba in 1959, the U.S. government looked at him as a threat. The Central Intelligence Agency (CIA) trained thousands of Cuban nationals, who were to be brought back to Cuba to lead an uprising. The nationals were to land on a beach in the Bay of Pigs. The U.S. government would provide air support once the Cuban nationals initiated an uprising.

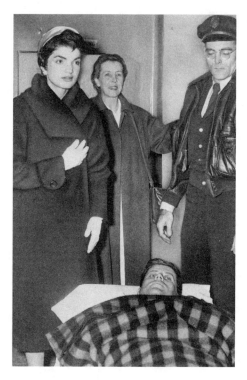

Kennedy leaves the hospital after back surgery. Many Americans did not realize that their president suffered from excruciating back pain for much of his adult life.

The plan failed miserably, as the CIA-trained nationals were overwhelmed by Castro's forces. The U.S. did not provide air support. Kennedy accepted responsibility for the failure.

What was the **Cuban Missile Crisis**?

The Cuban Missile Crisis referred to a tense situation that some feared would lead to a nuclear war between the United States and the Soviet Union. President Kennedy learned that there was a missile base being constructed in Cuba using Soviet materials. The world tensed, as Soviet ships headed toward Cuba. Kennedy forcefully declared that the United States would search all Soviet ships heading towards Cuba. The Soviet ships turned away and sailed back home. Kennedy's Secretary of State Dean Rusk said: "We're eyeball to eyeball and I think the other fellow just blinked."

What did **Kennedy do** in the area of **civil rights**?

Kennedy called for Congress to pass major civil rights legislation. Tragically, he died before seeing that objective accomplished. Under President Johnson, Congress passed

> ## What famous phrase did Kennedy utter at his inaugural address?
>
> **K**ennedy famously told the public during his inaugural address on January 20, 1961: "And so, my fellow Americans: Ask not what your country can do for you—ask what you can do for your country."

the historic Civil Rights Act of 1964, which prohibited racial discrimination in public employment, public accommodations, and other aspects of society. Kennedy sent in federal troops to protect civil rights protestors, including the Freedom Riders in the South. He established the President's Committee on Equal Employment Opportunity and issued an executive order that prohibited government contractors from discriminating "on the basis of race, creed, color, or national origin." He also used the public platform of the presidency to condemn segregation and racial discrimination.

What well-known **volunteer program** did **Kennedy establish**?

Kennedy established the Peace Corps by executive order in March 1961. Its stated purpose was "to promote world peace and friendship through a Peace Corps, which shall make available to interested countries and areas men and women of the United States qualified for service abroad and willing to serve, under conditions of hardship if necessary, to help the peoples of such countries and areas in meeting their needs for trained manpower." Kennedy named his brother-in-law, Robert Sargent Shriver Jr., as the Peace Corps first director.

What did Kennedy do with respect to the **space program**?

Kennedy played a vital role in the development of the U.S. space program. He claimed that a major goal of the country was to place a man on the moon before the end of the decade (an objective that was accomplished in 1969). Under Kennedy's watch, the National Aeronautics and Space Administration (NASA) launched Project Mercury with a goal of putting American astronauts in space. Kennedy did not want to lag behind the Soviet Union, which was aggressively pursuing its own space program.

Who were Kennedy's U.S. **Supreme Court appointees**?

Kennedy appointed two men to the U.S. Supreme Court: Byron White and Arthur J. Goldberg. White, a former college and pro football star, was a deputy attorney general under Robert Kennedy. He served on the Court for more than thirty years from 1962 to 1993. Goldberg, Kennedy's secretary of labor, served on the Court from 1962 to 1965. He resigned from the Court to become U.S. ambassador to the United Nations.

367

The president and first lady on November 22, 1963, in Dallas, Texas, just before Kennedy was shot to death by Lee Harvey Oswald.

When was **Kennedy assassinated**?

Kennedy was killed on November 22, 1963, in Dallas, Texas, while he rode in an open motorcade. A number of shots rang out from near the Texas School Book Depository building. Two bullets struck the president, hitting him in the neck and head. Rushed to a local hospital, he was pronounced dead almost immediately.

The accused assassin was Lee Harvey Oswald, a communist sympathizer who worked at the book depository. Two days later, Jack Ruby, a Dallas nightclub owner, shot Oswald, as police were transporting him to a local jail. Ruby was convicted and sentenced to death. He gained a new trial, but died in prison of lung cancer awaiting the new trial date.

Who was **behind** the **Kennedy assassination**?

That is a question that may never be answered. President Johnson, who assumed the position after Kennedy's death, appointed a commission to examine the circumstances of the assassination. Chaired by U.S. Supreme Court Justice Earl Warren, the Warren Commission concluded: "The shots which killed President Kennedy and wounded Governor Connally were fired by Lee Harvey Oswald." A House Committee in 1979 concluded that there probably was a conspiracy behind the Kennedy assassination, but was "unable to identify the other gunman or the extent of the conspiracy."

Numerous theories have abounded over the years, including some that maintain that the mafia, the CIA, Fidel Castro, or anti-Vietnamese groups were involved in the plot to kill President Kennedy. Many still don't believe that Lee Harvey Oswald acted alone.

LYNDON B. JOHNSON

(1908–1973)
36th President, 1963–1969
Party Affiliation: Democrat
Chief 1964 Opponent: Barry Goldwater (Republican)

EARLY LIFE AND FAMILY

Where and when was he **born**?

Lyndon Baines Johnson was born near Stonewall, Texas, to Sam Ealy Johnson Jr. and Rebekah Baines Johnson on August 27, 1908.

Who was he **named after**?

Lyndon Johnson was named after W. C. Linden, a family friend and popular attorney. His parents agreed to name their son after the lawyer, but his mother changed the spelling to Lyndon.

What was his **father's occupation**?

Sam Ealy Johnson Jr. worked as a teacher, farmer, and legislator. He was serving in the Texas House of Representatives when his son Lyndon was born. He later worked as a state railroad inspector.

371

President Lyndon Johnson.

Did he have any **siblings**?

Yes, Lyndon Johnson had four siblings: three sisters and a brother. They were named Rebekah, Josefa, Sam Houston, and Lucia.

What was his **early education**?

He attended public elementary school near Stonewell and in Johnson City. He later attended Johnson City High School from 1921 to 1924. He loved debating in high school, and even then had a goal of being a successful politician.

Did he **marry**?

He married Claudia "Lady Bird" Taylor on November 17, 1934, in San Antonio, Texas. Her childhood nurse said that she was as pretty as a "ladybird," which is how she acquired her nickname. She outlived her husband by more than thirty years, passing away in her nineties in 2007. In 1977, President Gerald Ford awarded her the Presidential Medal of Freedom and in 1988 President Ronald Reagan presented her with the Congressional Medal of Honor. She was actively involved in the implementation of the Head Start Program, vocal in her support of civil rights, and passionate about the conservation and beautification of America.

Did he have any **children**?

Yes, Lyndon and Lady Bird had two daughters: Lynda Bird Johnson and Luci Baines Johnson.

EARLY CAREER

What did Johnson do **after graduating high school**?

Johnson took a variety of odd jobs in Texas and California after he finished high school. He worked as a dishwasher, elevator operator, and member of a road construction crew before deciding that he should heed his mother's advice and go to college.

Where did he go to **college**?

Johnson attended Southwest Texas State Teachers College from 1927 to 1930. It later became known as Southwest Texas State and then Texas State University—San Marcos. He participated on the college debating team while working a variety of jobs to earn extra money. He also edited the school newspaper. While in college, he taught at a largely Mexican school in Cotulla, Texas. He also became involved in politics, even directing the campaign of a state senatorial candidate.

What did he do **after graduating college**?

Johnson taught public speaking at a high school in Pearsall, Texas, and then taught public speaking at Sam Houston High School in Houston, Texas.

Why did he **leave teaching**?

He left teaching because of a political opportunity. He became secretary to Democrat Richard M. Kleberg Sr., who served seven terms in the U.S. House of Representatives. Johnson worked as Kleberg's secretary from 1931 to 1934. While in this position, he was elected speaker of the "Little Congress," a name given to a group of congressional aides. He made many political connections in this group.

What **position** did he have next that was in the **education field**?

Johnson received an appointment as the head of the National Youth Association in Texas. From this position, Johnson was able to create jobs and educational opportunities for young people. He served in this position until running for Congress.

POLITICAL OFFICES

When did Johnson serve in the **U.S. House of Representatives**?

Johnson won election to the U.S. House of Representatives in 1937, where he served until 1949, when he made a successful move to the U.S. Senate. As a member of the House, he strongly supported the policies of Franklin D. Roosevelt. He served on the Naval Affairs Committee.

While a member of the House, what **military service** did Johnson perform for his country?

He joined the Naval Reserves in 1940, and then served in the Navy from December 1941 to July 1942. Roosevelt placed him on an observation mission under General Douglas MacArthur in Australia and New Guinea. Johnson went as an observer on an air bombing strike on a Japanese airbase in New Guinea. The Japanese shot down several planes, but Johnson's plane and its occupants survived. He was awarded a Silver Star. He left the military because President Roosevelt ordered all congressmen to return to their legislative duties.

When did he serve in the **U.S. Senate**?

Johnson first ran for a seat in the Senate in 1941, but lost to Texas governor and popular radio personality Wilbert Lee "Pappy" Daniel. However, he won a controversial

Then still vice president, Lyndon Johnson visits a Saigon textile factory in 1961 that was being supplied with American cotton.

election in 1948 over Governor Coke Stevenson. He won by such a scant margin that he was dubbed "Landslide Lyndon." Allegations have been made through the years that Johnson and his team used unsavory means to win the election.

Whatever the circumstances of his narrow victory, Johnson became a fixture in the U.S. Senate, serving from 1949 until 1961. He was the first chairman of the Senate's Aeronautics and Space Science Committee. He also worked as the chair of the Armed Services Defense Preparedness Subcommittee. He initially voted against civil rights legislative, but in 1957 switched course and became a supporter of such legislation.

What **office** did he **seek in 1960**?

Johnson's name was mentioned as a presidential candidate in 1956, but he was named as a serious contender in 1960. He finished second to President John F. Kennedy. Some historians believe that Kennedy offered the vice-presidential slot to Johnson, realizing that he needed Johnson to help him carry several Southern states—particularly Texas. The Kennedy–Johnson ticket won a close election over Republicans Richard M. Nixon and Henry Cabot Lodge Sr.

PRESIDENCY

How did Johnson **become president**?

Lyndon Baines Johnson became the thirty-sixth president of the United States when President John F. Kennedy was assassinated on November 22, 1963, in Dallas, Texas, as

375

part of a motorcade rally. Johnson was riding two cars behind President Kennedy. Later that day, Johnson took the oath of office and became president.

Whom did **he defeat** in the presidential **election of 1964**?

Johnson defeated Republican candidate Barry Goldwater, a U.S. senator from Arizona, to win the election. Goldwater became a hero of the conservative movement after the publication of his book *The Conscience of a Conservative* (1960). Johnson trounced him in the election by an electoral vote count of 486 to 52.

Who was his **vice president**?

Hubert Humphrey of Minnesota served as Johnson's vice president from 1965 to 1969. A former pharmacist, Humphrey served in the U.S. Senate from 1949 until becoming Johnson's vice president. He later became the Democratic presidential nominee in 1968, but lost to Republican candidate Richard M. Nixon.

A protestor urges President Johnson to take more action to defend African American civil rights activists in Selma, Alabama, where protest marches led to violence by state police.

Who were his **attorneys general**?

Johnson had three U.S. attorneys general: Robert Kennedy, Nicholas Katzenbach, and Ramsey Clark. Kennedy had served as his brother's attorney general, but he and Johnson did not get along. Kennedy left the position to run for a Senate seat in New York. Nicholas Katzenbach had served as a deputy attorney general under Robert Kennedy, and then succeeded his former boss. He left the position in 1966 to become undersec-

> ## How was Johnson able to see so many of his programs passed into law?
>
> Johnson won the presidency in a landslide election in 1964 over Barry Goldwater. Furthermore, the Democrats had large control over both Houses of Congress—295 to 140 in the House of Representatives and 67 to 33 in the Senate. This dominance over the Republican Party enabled Johnson and the Democratic-controlled Congress to initiate, pass, and implement nearly all of Johnson's social programs.

retary of state. William Ramsey Clark, the son of U.S. Supreme Court Justice Tom Clark, served as Johnson's third U.S. attorney general. He was known for his staunch defense of civil liberties.

What **measures signed** by Johnson provided more **protection to the environment**?

Johnson signed into law the Air Quality Act of 1967, the Clean Water Restoration Act of 1966, and the Water Quality Act of 1965. These bills required states to take measures to ensure cleaner water and better air quality standards.

What major pieces of **civil rights legislation** did Johnson sign into law?

Johnson signed into law the Civil Rights Act of 1964, the Voting Rights Act of 1965, and the Fair Housing Act of 1968. The Civil Rights Act of 1964 banned discrimination in places of public accommodation, employment, and by government agencies. It is considered the lynchpin of the Civil Rights Movement during the 1950s and 1960s. The Voting Rights Act of 1965 prohibited discriminatory practices that various states and locales had erected to reduce African American voting. The Fair Housing Act of 1968 outlawed racial discrimination in the purchase and renting of homes.

What was **"The Great Society"**?

"The Great Society" was Lyndon Johnson's term—similar to Franklin D. Roosevelt's "New Deal"—for a fairer, inclusive society free of racism and poverty. Johnson told a crowd in 1964: "In your time we have the opportunity to move not only toward the rich society and the powerful society, but upward to the Great Society. The Great Society rests on an abundance and liberty for all. It demands an end to poverty, and racial injustice, to which we are totally committed in our time."

Lyndon Johnson signing the 1968 Civil Rights Act.

What **programs** were key components of the **Great Society**?

The Great Society covered various areas of life, including education, health, civil rights, internal improvements, labor, and culture. Johnson's plan included the Medicare and Medicaid programs, which provided health care for the elderly and poor. It also included the creation of the Job Corps, which provided educational and occupational opportunities for troubled youth. One famous recipient of the Job Corps program was a young man from Texas named George Foreman, who later became a two-time world heavyweight boxing champion. With respect to culture, the National Foundation for the Arts and Humanities was created and the Corporation for Public Broadcasting was formed.

What was Johnson's **position toward Vietnam**?

Johnson's presidency was defined by two things: increasing federal government funding of social programs ("The Great Society") and increased military engagement in Vietnam. Johnson's administration was popular for its social programs, but there was growing protest over U.S. involvement in Vietnam. Most historians assess Johnson as a great social reformer who became overwhelmed by the Vietnam War.

The United States entered the conflict in a major way after the U.S. destroyer *Maddox* was attacked by North Vietnamese torpedo boats in the Gulf of Tonkin. Johnson asked for the authority from Congress to defend American lives in Vietnam in the so-called Tonkin Gulf Resolution. After this resolution, Johnson authorized air strikes on North Vietnam. More than 460,000 American troops were in Vietnam by May 1967.

Who were his **U.S. Supreme Court appointees**?

Johnson nominated two men as associate justices to the U.S. Supreme Court: Abe Fortas and Thurgood Marshall. Fortas, a leading Washington, D.C., lawyer who had argued successfully before the Court in the famous case *Gideon v. Wainwright* (1963)—among others—served on the Court from 1965 to 1969. Johnson viewed Fortas as a possible successor to Chief Justice Earl Warren. He nominated Fortas for chief justice, but opposition arose and there were reports that Fortas received money from financier Louis Wolfson, who was under investigation for wrongdoing by the Securities and Exchange Commission. Fortas denied wrongdoing, but resigned from the Court.

Marshall had won great recognition as an attorney in several civil rights cases. In 1961 John F. Kennedy appointed him to the U.S. Court of Appeals for the Second Circuit. Johnson made history when he chose Marshall to be the first African American solicitor general in 1965, and then appointed him to the U.S. Supreme Court in 1967, where he served until 1991. Marshall was known for his opposition to the death penalty and opinions protective of freedom of speech.

POST PRESIDENCY

What **book** did **Johnson write** in his **post-presidential period**?

He wrote his memoirs *The Vantage Point: Perspectives of the Presidency, 1963–1969* (1971).

When did he **die**?

Johnson died on January 22, 1973, as he was transported from his ranch to San Antonio, Texas. He had suffered his third heart attack earlier in the day.

RICHARD M. NIXON

(1913–1994)
37th President, 1969–1974
Chief 1968 Opponents: Hubert Humphrey (Democrat) and
George Wallace (American Independent)
Chief 1972 Opponent: George McGovern (Democrat)

EARLY LIFE AND FAMILY

Where and when was he **born**?

Richard Milhous Nixon was born in Yorba Linda, California, to Frank and Hannah Nixon on January 9, 1913.

What did his **father do** for a living?

Frank Anthony Nixon worked as a farmer in Yorba Linda. He then moved his family to Whittier, where he worked in the oil fields before building a gas station and opening a convenience store.

Did he have any **siblings**?

Yes, Nixon had four brothers: Harold, Francis Donald, Arthur, and Edward. Arthur and Harold died of tuberculosis at ages seven and twenty-three respectively. Francis Donald became a restaurant owner, while Edward is an entrepreneur and author.

President Richard Nixon.

What was his **early education**?

He attended elementary school in his birthplace of Yorba Linda, and then in Whittier when his family moved there. He went to Fullerton High School for a couple years before transferring to Whittier High School on his junior year. He graduated first in his class in 1930, excelling in debate.

Did he **marry**?

Yes, Nixon married Thelma Catherine "Pat" Ryan on June 21, 1940, in Riverside, California. She died in 1993—one year before the former president.

Did he have any **children**?

Yes, Richard and Pat Nixon had two daughters: Patricia and Julie. Patricia married Edward Cox, who became a corporate attorney in New York City. Julie married David Dwight Eisenhower, grandson of former president Dwight D. Eisenhower. She has authored several books, including a biography of her mother entitled *Pat Nixon: The Untold Story*.

EARLY CAREER

Where did Nixon **go to college**?

Nixon earned a scholarship to Harvard University, but his family had no money to send him across country. Instead, he enrolled at Whittier College, where he graduated in 1934—second out of a class of eighty-five. Once again, he excelled at debate and he played on his college football team.

What did he do **after college**?

Nixon earned a scholarship to Duke University Law School in Durham, North Carolina. He graduated third out of twenty-five students in 1937. He was president of his graduating class.

After finishing law school, where did he go to **practice law**?

Nixon returned home to Whittier, where he gained admission to the California bar in 1937. He first practiced commercial law with the Whittier-based firm of Wingert and Bewley. He later helped open up a different branch of the firm and later became a partner in Bewley, Knoop, and Nixon.

What was his **first job** in Washington, D.C.?

Nixon took a job with the Office of Price Administration in December 1941 in Washington, D.C. While he took a cut in pay, he felt that D.C. was the place to be to further his political ambitions. He did not enjoy life as a bureaucrat with the OPA.

What was his **military career**?

Nixon joined the navy in August 1942. Even though he was a Quaker, Nixon decided to support his country in the war effort. He was sent to Iowa, California, and then to the South Pacific Combat Air Transport Command in New Caledonia. He later served in Alameda, California, and then Philadelphia. While he never saw any combat action, he performed his administrative duties quite well, rising to the level of lieutenant commander.

POLITICAL OFFICES

When did Nixon serve in the **U.S. House of Representatives**?

Nixon served in the U.S. House of Representatives from 1947 to 1950. He won his position by upsetting incumbent Democrat Jerry Voorhis. He served on the House Education and Labor Committee. He also served as a member of the House Un-American Activities Committee. In that capacity, Nixon questioned Alger Hiss, a former government attorney accused of espionage.

When did Nixon move to the **U.S. Senate**?

Nixon served as a U.S. senator from 1951 to 1953. He won his seat by defeating Democrat Helen Gahagan Douglas, an actress turned politician. His campaign materials linked her to the Communist Party, causing a local newspaper to refer to him as "Tricky Dick"—a nickname that would stick for the rest of his career. He served on the Government Operations Committee, and an investigation subcommittee led by Senator Joe McCarthy.

What was his **next political position**?

Nixon served as vice president to President Dwight D. Eisenhower for both of Eisenhower's presidential terms. Nixon traveled to various foreign countries during his time as vice president, even debating Soviet premier Nikita Khrushchev in the "Kitchen Debate" in Moscow in 1959.

Whom did **Nixon defeat** to win the **1960 Republican nomination** for president?

Nixon was the favorite to win the Republican nomination given that he had served as vice president for eight years. Some speculated that New York governor Nelson Rocke-

> ## Why did Nixon lose the 1960 presidential election?
>
> **N**ixon had an advantage as the vice president to a popular president. However, Democratic candidate John F. Kennedy possessed charisma, good looks, and a good debating presence. Nixon and Kennedy sparred in front of national audiences in four televised debates on September 26, October 7, October 14, and October 21. Television favored Kennedy; his air of confidence dispelled the notion that he was too inexperienced. Political commentators often cite Kennedy's good looks and honed oratory skills as key to his winning favor with the voting public. Kennedy narrowly won the election.

feller could pose a formidable challenge, but he endorsed Nixon instead of running against him. Nixon won on the first ballot with 1,321 votes to only 10 for Senator Barry Goldwater of Arizona.

How did Nixon do in the **1962 California gubernatorial election**?

In the 1962 California gubernatorial election, Nixon lost to incumbent Democrat Edmund G. "Pat" Brown, the father of Jerry Brown. Nixon bitterly told the press after the loss: "You won't have Nixon to kick around anymore, because, gentleman, this is my last press conference."

After the **two failed elections**, what did Nixon do?

Nixon practiced law in New York at the law firm of Nixon, Mudge, Rose, Guthrie, and Alexander from 1963 to 1968. The firm dissolved in 1995. During his time with the firm, he argued *Time v. Hill* (1967), an invasion of privacy case against the press, before the U.S. Supreme Court.

PRESIDENCY

Whom did **Nixon defeat** to win the **Republican nomination** in **1968**?

Nixon entered the 1968 Republican nomination as the front-runner, but there were some serious contenders. They included Nelson Rockefeller, the governor of New York who would later be President Gerald Ford's vice president, and Ronald Reagan, the governor of California who would win the presidency in 1980. Nixon was nominated on the first ballot with more than 690 votes.

Nixon meets Soviet leader Nikita Khrushchev.

Whom did **he defeat** to win the **1968 general election**?

Nixon defeated Democrat Hubert Humphrey of Minnesota and American Independent candidate George Wallace of Alabama. Humphrey was a longtime member of the U.S. Senate and had served as President Lyndon B. Johnson's vice president. Wallace, a governor of Alabama, had some popularity among some whites in the South for his position against desegregation. Nixon won in a close election with an electoral vote count of 301 to 191 votes for Humphrey and 46 for Wallace.

Whom did **he defeat** to win the **1972 general election**?

Nixon defeated Democrat George McGovern to win reelection in 1972. McGovern served as a U.S. senator from South Dakota. He was an outspoken critic of the Vietnam War and favored busing to fully integrate the public schools—an issue that Nixon spoke out heavily against. Nixon trounced McGovern in one of the most lopsided elections in history. He garnered 520 electoral votes to only 17 for McGovern.

Who were Nixon's **vice presidents**?

Nixon's two vice presidents were Spiro Agnew and Gerald R. Ford. Agnew, the former governor of Maryland, was a colorful character known for his ability to turn a phrase. He once referred to the press as "nattering nabobs of negativism." Federal prosecutors accused him of accepting bribes while governor of Maryland and as vice president. He worked out a deal with prosecutors where he pled no contest to income tax evasion charges. He was fined and placed on a three-month probation.

Nixon filled his vice presidency vacancy under Section 2 of the Twenty-fifth Amendment, which provides: "Whenever there is a vacancy in the office of the Vice President, the President shall nominate a Vice President who shall take office upon confirmation by a majority vote of both Houses of Congress." Nixon chose U.S. Representative Gerald Ford.

What **did Nixon do** with respect to **Vietnam**?

President Nixon did reduce American troops in Vietnam, but he broadened U.S. involvement in the region by approving of secret bombing of Cambodia and Laos. He

> ## What significant event happened with the American space program?
>
> On July 20, 1969, astronaut Neil Armstrong walked on the moon with the historic words: "I'm going to step off the LM now. That's one small step for man; one giant leap for mankind." Nixon spoke to Armstrong and his colleague Buzz Aldrich, saying: "For every American, this has to be the proudest day of our lives."

also sent in ground troops to Cambodia in 1970, and then began bombing in Laos in 1971. Critics charged that Nixon was "widening down" the war. In 1972, Nixon even authorized bombing in North Vietnam.

What **foreign policy successes** did Nixon have in his administration?

Nixon had many accomplishments in the foreign policy arena. He opened a new era of relationship between the United States and China. Nixon was the first president to visit China, a country with which the U.S. had no diplomatic relations. Nixon and Chinese leader Mao Tse-tung appeared together in public, a sight many would never have predicted given the hostilities between the two nations. The breakthrough in U.S.–China relations arguably forced the Soviet Union to come to the table with the United States because it feared a better relationship between the two powers that were its greatest rivals. This culminated in President Nixon and Soviet leader Leonid Brezhnev signing the Strategic Arms Limitations Talks, called SALT. Under this agreement, the superpowers agreed to curtail missile development and slow the arms race that seemingly threatened world peace.

Who was **Henry Kissinger**?

Henry Kissinger played a key role in the administration's foreign policy from Vietnam to China to the Soviet Union and elsewhere around the world. He served first as Nixon's national security advisor, and then in 1973 became Nixon's secretary of state. He helped negotiated the Paris Peace Accords, which effectively ended U.S. involvement in Vietnam. For this, he won the 1973 Nobel Peace Prize, along with North Vietnamese leader Le Duc Tho, who refused the award. Kissinger also crafted the policy of détente (the easing of strained relations) with the Soviet Union and prepared the way for Nixon's historic visit and agreement with China. Kissinger stayed on as President Gerald Ford's secretary of state.

What was the **Watergate scandal**?

The Watergate scandal refers to a series of events in President Nixon's administration that culminated in his ignominious resignation. It began when five members of the

Committee to Reelect the President (CREEP) broke into the Democratic national committee headquarters at the Watergate Hotel in Washington, D.C.

Washington Post reporters Carl Bernstein and Bob Woodward uncovered a massive plan by the Nixon administration that included spying and sabotage to support the president's reelection campaign. Twenty-five of Nixon's aides served prison sentences as a result of their participation in the subsequent Watergate cover-up. Eventually, the House Judiciary Committee began impeachment hearings against Nixon and he resigned from office.

What was the **Saturday Night Massacre?**

The Saturday Night Massacre was the October 20, 1973, controversy involving President Nixon, the Justice Department, and the Special Prosecutor. Nixon had hired Archibald Cox to serve as the special prosecutor to look into Watergate. Cox asked Nixon for audio tapes recorded in the Oval Office and other key rooms in the White House. Nixon refused, but said he would turn over edited transcripts. When Cox balked, Nixon wanted him fired.

Nixon ordered U.S. Attorney General Elliot Richardson to fire Cox, but Richardson refused and resigned. Nixon then ordered Assistant U.S. Attorney General William Ruckelshaus to fire Cox, but he also refused and had resigned earlier. Ultimately, Solicitor General Robert Bork fired Cox. Richardson and Ruckelshaus held a press conference, decrying the actions. Richardson declared: "At stake, in the final analysis, is the very integrity of the government processes I came to the Department of Justice to help restore."

What **case did Nixon lose** before the U.S. Supreme Court on **executive privilege?**

In *United States v. Nixon* (1974), the U.S. Supreme Court unanimously ruled eight to zero that President Nixon did not have an executive privilege to ignore a subpoena from the Watergate special prosecutor to turn over the tapes. Nixon had installed an extensive audio taping system in the White House. The special prosecutor Leon Jaworksi proceeded to indict several individuals. Nixon refused to turn over the tapes, but would provide edited transcripts of numerous tapes. Nixon claimed that as president he did not have to turn over the tapes. The Supreme Court disagreed:

> The President's need for complete candor and objectivity from advisers calls for great deference from the courts. However, when the privilege depends solely on the broad, undifferentiated claim of public interest in the confidentiality of such conversations, a confrontation with other values arises. Absent a claim of need to protect military, diplomatic, or sensitive national security secrets, we find it difficult to accept the argument that even the very important interest in confidentiality of Presidential communications is significantly

diminished by production of such material for in camera inspection with all the protection that a district court will be obliged to provide....

To read the Art. II powers of the President as providing an absolute privilege as against a subpoena essential to enforcement of criminal statutes on no more than a generalized claim of the public interest in confidentiality of nonmilitary and nondiplomatic discussions would upset the constitutional balance of "a workable government" and gravely impair the role of the courts under Art. III.

When did **Nixon resign**?

The House of Representatives had initiated impeachment proceedings against Nixon in May 1974, voting to impeach twenty-seven to eleven on a charge of obstruction of justice. He then lost the U.S. Supreme Court case in July 1974. Facing full impeachment in the Senate, Nixon resigned on August 9, 1974. Nixon told the American public: "I have concluded that because of the Watergate matter I might not have the support of Congress that I would consider necessary to back the very difficult decisions and carry out the duties of this office in the way I believe the interests of this nation require." He added that "the nation needs a full-time President."

Did Nixon face any **jail time**?

No, President Gerald R. Ford gave a full pardon to Nixon for any offenses he may have committed.

Who were his **U.S. Supreme Court appointees**?

Nixon appointed four men to the U.S. Supreme Court—one as Chief Justice and three as associate justices. In 1969, he appointed D.C. Circuit Court of Appeals judge Warren E. Burger to chief justice of the Court to replace Earl Warren. Burger served until his retirement in 1986. He crafted many important First Amendment decisions, including the Court's decisions in *Lemon v. Kurtzman* (1971) and *Miller v. California* (1973).

Nixon appointed Harry Blackmun, a close friend of Burger's, as an associate justice in 1970, where he served until 1994. Burger and Blackmun originally were known as the "Minnesota Twins" because they were both from the Gopher State and originally voted the same way in many cases. Over time, Blackmun—who had been a judge on the U.S. Court of Appeals for the 8th Circuit—moved to the left in his judicial philosophy. He later renounced capital punishment in his last year on the Court.

Nixon also appointed Lewis F. Powell Jr. to the Court, where he served from 1972 to 1987. Powell was a distinguished attorney who had been a former president of the American Bar Association. He tended to vote as a moderate on the Court and was the key swing vote in many cases.

Nixon's last appointment was Arizona-based William H. Rehnquist, who had never been a judge before his Supreme Court appointment. Rehnquist worked in the Justice Department, as assistant attorney general to the Office of Legal Counsel. He came to the Court in 1972 and did not leave until his death in 2005. In 1986, President Ronald Reagan elevated him to Chief Justice as Burger's replacement.

POST PRESIDENCY

What **books did Nixon write** in his post-presidential period?

Nixon wrote several books during his retirement years, including: *The Memoirs of Richard Nixon* (1978); *The Real War* (1980); *Leaders* (1982); *Real Peace: Strategy for the West* (1984); *No More Vietnams* (1985); and *Victory without War* (1988).

When did he **die**?

Nixon died on April 22, 1994, four days after suffering a stroke, at a Manhattan hospital in New York.

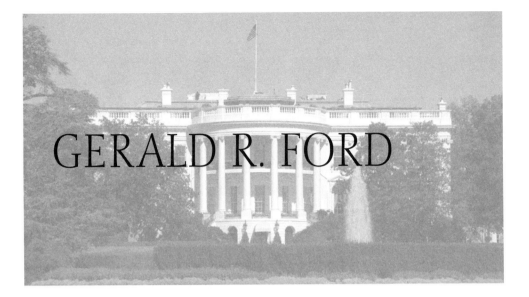

GERALD R. FORD

(1913–2006)
38th President, 1974–1977
Party Affiliation: Republican
Chief Opponent: None

EARLY LIFE AND FAMILY

Where and when was he **born**?

Gerald Ford was born as Leslie Lynch King Jr. in Omaha, Nebraska, to Leslie Lynch King Sr. and Dorothy Gardner King on July 14, 1913.

What were the **occupations** of Ford's **biological and adoptive fathers**?

Ford's biological father, Leslie King, worked as a wool merchant. His adoptive father, Gerald Ford, owned a painting store. Ford did not have a relationship with his biological father, who died when his son graduated law school.

Did Ford have any **siblings**?

He had no full siblings. His biological father remarried and had three children, who were Ford's half-siblings. They were named Leslie, Marjorie, and Patricia. From his mother's marriage to his adoptive father, he had three half brothers: Thomas, Richard, and James.

391

President Gerald R. Ford.

When did he take the name of Ford?

Dorothy Gardner left her abusive husband Leslie Lynch King only sixteen days after the birth of her son. She left Nebraska and moved to Grand Rapids, Michigan. In 1916, she married Gerald Rudolph Ford, who adopted her son. The couple renamed the boy Gerald R. Ford Jr.

What was his **early education**?

Ford attended various public schools in Grand Rapids, Michigan: Madison Elementary School for kindergarten, East Grand Rapids Elementary School for grades one through six, and then South High School for junior high and high school. He starred on the offensive line for the football team.

Who was his **wife**?

Gerald Ford married Elizabeth Anne Bloomer on October 15, 1948. Known as Betty, she became a beloved First Lady for the country. She battled alcoholism for many years and created the Betty Ford Clinic for those struggling with chemical dependency.

Did he have any **children**?

Gerald and Betty Ford had four children: Michael, John, Steven, and Susan. Michael became a minister. John worked in business and journalism, founding a company and a magazine. Steven became an actor with a recurring role on the daytime soap opera *The Young and the Restless.* Susan worked in photography.

Where did he **attend college**?

Ford went to the University of Michigan, where he majored in economics and political science. He starred on the football team, though he had to sit on the bench for a couple years behind All-American center Chuck Bernard. Ford had an outstanding senior year, and earned the opportunity to play professional football in the National Football League.

Why did Ford decide against **playing professional football**?

Ford turned down offers from the Chicago Bears and the Green Bay Packers because he wanted to study law. He applied repeatedly to Yale Law School. Though rejected, Ford kept applying and eventually gained admission in 1938. Before gaining admission to Yale Law School, he worked at Yale as an assistant football coach and a boxing

President Ford with First Lady Betty Ford and daughter Susan Ford at a Christmas Party at the White House.

coach. He graduated from Yale Law School in January 1941 and gained admission to the Michigan bar in June 1941.

EARLY CAREER

After graduating law school, what did Ford do?

He practiced law with Philip Buchen, who was a University of Michigan classmate. Buchen later served as White House counsel for Ford.

What was his military service record?

Ford enlisted in the navy following the attack on Pearl Harbor by Japanese forces. Ford served in the navy from 1942 to 1946, rising from ensign to lieutenant commander. He worked as a gunnery officer aboard the USS *Monterey*, which saw action in the South Pacific. During his career, he garnered numerous medals for his combat service. He also coached football and boxing during his navy tenure.

What did he do after leaving the military?

He joined the law firm of Butterfield, Keeney, and Amberg. This was the firm that his good friend and former law partner Philip Buchen had joined. Ford soon turned his attention from law to politics.

POLITICAL OFFICES

When did he become a member of the **U.S. House of Representatives**?

Gerald Ford won election to the U.S. House of Representatives in 1948, and he served in the House until 1973 when he became President Richard Nixon's vice president. During his early years he became friendly with both Richard Nixon and John F. Kennedy. He admired Nixon's debating talents. He nearly became Nixon's running mate when Nixon ran for president against Kennedy in 1960. President Johnson later appointed Ford to serve on the Warren Commission investigating the circumstances of Kennedy's assassination.

What **key position** did Ford take in the U.S. **House of Representatives** in 1965?

Ford became House minority leader in 1965 for the Republicans. He proved to be an able spokesman for his party. Once after Ford had upset President Johnson, the president famously said: "He's a nice fellow but he spent too much time playing football without a helmet."

Whom did Ford **seek to impeach** while a member of the House?

Ford sought the impeachment of sitting U.S. Supreme Court Justice William O. Douglas. Ford charged that Douglas was "unfit and should be removed." He criticized Douglas for his connections with Ralph Ginsberg, the publisher of girlie magazines, and Albert Parvin, who had an ownership interest in a Las Vegas casino.

When did he **become vice president**?

President Nixon offered Ford the position when his first vice president, Spiro Agnew, was facing corruption charges. After Agnew resigned, President Nixon announced Ford as his choice. Pursuant to the Twenty-fifth Amendment, a president could fill a vice presidency vacancy. The Senate confirmed Ford by a vote of 92 to 3 and the House by a vote of 387 to 35. When sworn in as vice president on December 6, 1973, he humbly said: "I am a Ford, not a Lincoln."

PRESIDENCY

When did he **become president**?

Ford became president after Richard Nixon resigned from office on August 9, 1974. U.S. Supreme Court Justice Warren Burger swore in Ford as the thirty-eighth president of the United States. The *Chicago Tribune* reported that he was a "lineman in a quarterback's city."

Who was his **vice president**?

After Ford moved to the presidency, he asked former New York governor Nelson Rockefeller to serve as his vice president. Many Democrats questioned Rockefeller's extreme wealth, but the Senate confirmed him by a vote of ninety to seven.

Why did **Ford pardon Nixon**?

President Ford gave a "full, free, and complete pardon" to former President Nixon on September 8, 1974. "After years of bitter controversy and divisive national debate, I have been advised, and I am compelled to conclude that many months and perhaps more years will have to pass before Richard Nixon could obtain a fair trial by jury in any jurisdiction of the United States under governing decisions of the Supreme Court," Ford said. He concluded:

> Now, therefore, I, Gerald R. Ford, President of the United States, pursuant to the pardon power conferred upon me by Article II, Section 2, of the Constitution, have granted and by these presents do grant a full, free, and absolute pardon unto Richard Nixon for all offenses against the United States which he, Richard Nixon, has committed or may have committed or taken part in during the period from January 20, 1969 through August 9, 1974.

What did **Ford accomplish** in the **Middle East**?

The Ford administration, primarily through the efforts of Secretary of State Henry Kissinger, managed to maintain an uneasy peace between Israel and surrounding Arabic countries through two Egyptian-Israeli Disengagement Treaties. Egypt and Israel signed pacts in 1974 and 1975 that created a twenty-mile buffer near the Suez Canal. The 1975 pact enlarged the U.N. buffer zone between the two nations. Between 1973 and 1975, Kissinger exercised his "shuttle diplomacy" by making eleven trips to the Middle East to work on the Egyptian-Israel Disengagement Treaties.

What was the **Helsinki Agreement**?

The Helsinki Agreement or Helsinki Accords was an international agreement signed by more than thirty-five countries, including the Soviet Union. The United States and other Western countries agreed to recognize the territorial boundaries created by the Soviet Union in the wake of World War II. In exchange, the Soviet Union and other Eastern countries agreed to observe human rights principles. The act's ten major principles included: recognizing territorial boundaries; preserving peace, equal rights, and self-determination for people; and refraining from the use of force.

What two women tried to assassinate President Ford?

In two different instances, women shot at President Ford in September 1975. On September 5, Lynette "Squeaky" Fromme, a follower of imprisoned cult leader Charles Manson, pointed her gun at Ford in Sacramento, California, but Secret Service agent Larry Buendorf quickly intervened. Fromme was given a life sentence for her attempted assassination of Ford. She finally received parole in August 2009.

On September 22, Sara Jane Moore fired a shot at President Ford that missed. As she was about to take a second shot, ex-Marine Oliver Sipple heroically dived toward her and knocked her arm. Moore was a left-wing sympathizer and former FBI informant who was hoping to gain acceptance in radical revolutionary circles. She was given a life sentence, but was paroled in 2007—after President Ford had died.

Some critics charged that the Ford administration caved to the Soviets, but Ford and Secretary of State Henry Kissinger believed that by formally recognizing the Soviet control in Eastern Europe, there would be expanded cultural and diplomatic exchanges.

Who was President Ford's only U.S. **Supreme Court appointee**?

President Ford had the opportunity to choose a justice after William Douglas suffered a stroke in late 1974 and retired in 1975. Ford selected U.S. Court of Appeals judge John Paul Stevens, who was easily confirmed. Stevens served until 2010 on the Court, writing many important decisions.

What was **unique** about Ford with respect to his **tenure as vice president and president**?

Gerald R. Ford is the only person in American history to be vice president and president without being elected to either office. He was appointed vice president after Spiro Agnew resigned and he was appointed president after Richard Nixon resigned.

POST PRESIDENCY

Did Ford try to **keep his presidency**?

Yes, President Ford ran in 1976 to stay in the White House. Robert Dole, a U.S. Senator from Kansas, was his running mate. First, he survived a very tough challenge

President Ford at the House Judiciary Subcommittee hearing concerning Richard Nixon's pardon. At the time, many Americans were irate at Ford's decision, but more recently historians have felt that Ford did the right thing to help restore a sense of normalcy to a long-troubled nation.

from California governor Ronald Reagan in the Republican primary. Ford narrowly captured the nomination by a vote of 1,187 to 1,070. However, he lost the general election to Democrat Jimmy Carter from Georgia. Ford was way behind in the polls—as much as 30 percent in some—but managed to close the gap by emphasizing Carter's lack of experience.

Carter won the election in an electoral vote count of 297 to 240. Ford actually won more states (27 to Carter's 23) but lost the key states of New York, Texas, and Ohio.

What **book** did he **write** in his post-presidential period?

Ford wrote the book *A Time to Heal: An Autobiography of Gerald R. Ford* (1979) in his post-presidential days.

Did he ever consider **another run for the presidency** after losing to Carter?

Yes, Ford seriously considered running for president in 1980. He feared that Republican Ronald Reagan might be too conservative and not able to defeat Carter. However, he decided against running. Reagan talked with Ford about having the former president be his vice presidential candidate, but no agreement could be reached.

What was Ford's **relationship** with his former rival **Jimmy Carter**?

Ford maintained a friendly relationship with Carter in later years. In 2001, he and Carter were honorary co-chairs of the National Commission on Federal Election Reform. The group held four public hearings and released a report in July 2001.

What famous **awards** did he win in his later days?

Ford won the Presidential Medal of Freedom from President Bill Clinton in 1999 and the Kennedy Profiles in Courage award in 2001 for helping the country heal in the post-Watergate period.

When did he **die**?

Ford died on December 26, 2006, in Rancho Mirage, California, at the age of ninety-three.

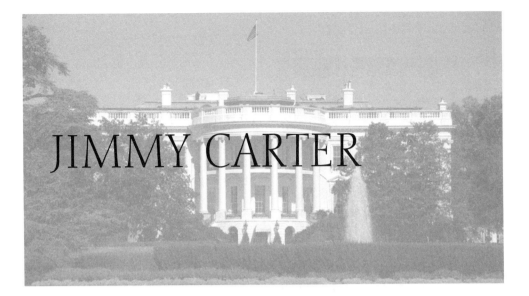

JIMMY CARTER

(1924–)
39th President, 1977–1981
Party Affiliation: Democrat
Chief 1976 Opponent: Gerald Ford (Republican)

EARLY LIFE AND FAMILY

Where and when was Carter **born**?

James Earl Carter Jr. was born in Plains, Georgia, to James Earl and Lillian Gordy Carter on October 1, 1924.

What did his **parents do** for a living?

James Earl Carter Sr. worked as a farmer and the owner of a store. James Sr. owned a sizeable amount of land, and his son learned the value of hard work picking cotton. His mother, Lillian, worked as a registered nurse.

Did he have any **siblings**?

Yes, Jimmy Carter had three younger siblings: Gloria, Ruth Carter, and Billy. His youngest sibling—brother Billy—was a controversial figure who sometimes embarrassed the president with his odd behavior. He signed as lobbyist for the Libyan government and also drank heavily. He even promoted his own "Billy Beer," trying to cap-

President Jimmy Carter.

italize on his image of someone who loved to party.

What was his **early education**?

Carter attended segregated public schools in Plains, Georgia. He graduated from Plains High School, where he excelled in both academics and athletics when he had time to participate.

Did he **marry**?

Carter married Eleanor Rosalynn Smith on July 7, 1946, in Plains, Georgia. She became one of the most politically active and visible first ladies in U.S. history.

Does he have any **children**?

Yes, Jimmy and Rosalynn Carter have four children: John William, James Earl, Donnel Jeffrey, and Amy.

EARLY CAREER

Where did he go to **college**?

Carter first attended Southwestern Junior College for one year and then Georgia Tech University for another year. He then attended where he really wanted to go all along—the U.S. Naval Academy. He graduated in the top ten percent of his class.

What was his **naval career**?

After Carter graduated from the Naval Academy, he was assigned to the U.S.S. *Wyoming* and then the U.S.S. *Mississippi*. In July 1947, he transferred to the navy's submarine unit, working on the U.S.S. *Pomfret* in Pearl Harbor, Hawaii. When the Korean War began, Carter received another submarine ship assignment aboard the U.S.S. *K-1*. He then worked under the direction of Admiral Hyman Rickover, who was in charge of the navy's nuclear submarine program. He also studied nuclear physics at Union College in New York. In 1998, he received the ultimate honor for a veteran when a U.S. Navy submarine was named after him.

Why did he **leave the navy**?

He left the navy for family reasons. His father died and his mother asked him to come home to manage the family's farming and warehouse business. His father had a large farm and a peanut warehouse business. It was this fact about his family business that led people to describe Carter as a peanut farmer.

POLITICAL OFFICES

When did he get **involved in politics**?

Carter was civic minded and looked for ways to improve his community. He became elected to the county board of education and then became president of the Georgia Planning Association.

When did he become a **state senator**?

Carter ran for a seat in the Georgia State Senate in 1962. He lost the election by a close margin. He was able to prove that his opponent's campaign involved voter fraud and the election was overturned in his favor. He served a second term.

What was the **next political position** that Carter sought?

Carter took a shot at the gubernatorial election in Georgia. He lost the Democratic primary election, but finished in a strong third place showing considering the fact that he was a virtual unknown in some areas of his state..

When did he become **Georgia's governor**?

A revitalized Carter who had become a born-again Christian ran again for governor and won in 1970. He became a leader of the "New South" movement, calling for an end to racial discrimination and segregation. He improved government efficiency by merging various bureaucracies. He introduced a system where certain government officials—such as judges—were selected based on merit rather than political connections.

PRESIDENCY

Whom did **Carter beat** to win the **Democratic nomination** in 1976?

Carter defeated Alabama governor George Wallace, California governor Jerry Brown, and U.S. senator Harold Jackson from Washington. Carter successfully ran as the political outsider and captured the nomination.

President Carter celebrates his victory with Vice President Walter Mondale

Whom did **Carter defeat** in the **general presidential election**?

Carter defeated incumbent Republican Gerald Ford in a very close election. Carter seized upon the fact that Ford had pardoned former President Richard Nixon; he also emphasized the fact that he was a Washington outsider who could change the political system for the better.

Who was his **vice president**?

Walter Mondale served as Carter's vice president. Mondale had been a U.S. senator from Minnesota since 1964. Mondale also had been the attorney general for his home state before a twelve-year-career in the Senate. Mondale would be Carter's running mate in their failed 1980 reelection campaign. Mondale later captured the Democratic presidential nomination in 1984, but lost badly to popular Republican incumbent Ronald Reagan.

What **economic phenomenon plagued** Carter's years in the White House?

Inflation peaked during the Carter years, creating an unstable economic environment. Carter had been a harsh critic of Ford's economic policies, but the economy worsened during his residency. Both inflation and unemployment rose in Carter's tenure, because the lessening value of the U.S. dollar caused in part by greater dependence on foreign oil.

Who was Carter's **national security advisor**?

Polish-born Zbigniew Brzezinski served as Carter's national security advisor. A former professor at Harvard University and then Columbia University, Brzezinski specialized in knowledge about the Soviet Union, its various nationalities, and its totalitarian government. In 1981, Carter awarded his advisor the Presidential Medal of Freedom. A highly respected advisor, Brzezinski won a place on the Chemical Warfare Commission during the Reagan Administration. He is the author of numerous books on foreign policy.

What was the **high point** of Carter's **foreign policy**?

Carter's coup—and perhaps the high point of his entire presidency—was negotiating peace between Egypt and Israel. Carter brought Egyptian President Anwar Sadat and Israeli Prime Minister Menachem Begin to Camp David. The three leaders crafted the so-called Camp David Accords, named after the location where the three met in secret over a twelve-day period in September 1978.

The Camp David Accords consisted of two agreements: (1) A Framework for Peace in the Middle East and (2) A Framework for the Conclusion of a Peace Treaty between Egypt and Israel. They later led to the formal peace agreement, the Israel-Egypt Peace Treaty, signed in March 1979. For their efforts, Sadat and Begin received the Nobel Peace Prize.

What **major agreement** did Carter sign with **Soviet Union leader Leonid Brezhnev**?

In June 1979, Carter and Brezhnev signed the SALT II Treaty, which sought to reduce the dangerous arms race between the world's two nuclear superpowers. Many members of the Senate believed that the treaty was too favorable to the Soviets. Also, the Soviet Union invaded Afghanistan, leading to even greater strain between the two countries. Because of this, the Senate never formally ratified the treaty. However, the two countries acted as if the treaty went into effect. In 1986, President Reagan withdrew the United States from the SALT II agreement, alleging that the Soviets were violating the agreement.

The newly elected President Carter with his wife, Rosalynn, and daughter, Amy.

What did Carter do when the **Soviet Union invaded Afghanistan**?

He protested the invasion and attempted to enlist support from other countries to condemn the Soviet's action. He also boycotted the 1980 Olympic Games, which were held in Moscow. That led to the Soviets boycotting the 1984 Olympic Games in Los Angeles.

What was the **Carter Doctrine**?

The Carter Doctrine was President Carter's declaration that the United States would not tolerate Soviet attempts to gain control of the Persian Gulf region. Carter proclaimed in his January 1980 State of the Union address: "Let our position be absolutely clear: An attempt by any outside force to gain control of the Persian Gulf region will be regarded as an assault on the vital interests of the United States of America, and such an assault will be repelled by any means necessary, including military force."

What diplomatic and **international nightmare** haunted the end of the Carter presidency?

An Islamic revolution occurred in Iran that forced the shah of Iran to flee the country. The religious leader Ayatollah Ruhollah Khomeini ordered the storming of the American embassy and took hostage more than sixty Americans. The Iran hostage crisis doomed Carter's presidency, as he was unsuccessful in negotiating with the Ayatollah and a rescue attempt failed miserably. Fifty-two of the hostages were not released until President Ronald Reagan took office.

What did Carter do with the **Panama Canal**?

Carter signed two treaties that relinquished American control over the Panama Canal to Panama. Carter said his objective was "fairness, not force" in turning over the canal to Panama. The U.S. Senate passed the treaties by a vote of sixty-eight to thirty-two.

President Carter meets then-Chinese Vice Premier Deng Xiaoping.

Did he try to **retain the presidency**?

Yes, Carter held off a strong challenge by Ted Kennedy, the brother of slain former president John F. Kennedy and presidential contender Robert F. Kennedy, to win the Democratic Party nomination. However, he lost badly to Republican challenger Ronald Reagan, who outperformed Carter in the televised debates.

POST PRESIDENCY

What center did Carter establish to further **human rights causes**?

In 1982, Jimmy and Rosalynn established the Carter Center, which is designed to address human rights concerns around the world. It advocates for democracy and peaceful solutions to conflict. It has spearheaded attempts to provide better health and welfare to people in various countries. In 2002, Carter received the Nobel Peace Prize in part for his efforts to promote democracy and human rights in the world.

What other **philanthropic group** is Carter well known for helping?

Carter has taken an active and leading role in Habitat for Humanity, a group that helps provide housing for low-income people. He became involved in the organization

407

The 1978 Camp David Accords were the crowning achievement of President Carter's career. He met with Egyptian President Anwar Sadat (shown here at left) and Israeli Prime Minister Menachem Begin to hash out a successful peace agreement between the two nations.

in 1984 and hosts an annual event that raises money for the worthy causes of the group.

What has Carter done with respect to **North Korea**?

President Bill Clinton sent Carter on a secret diplomatic mission to try to negotiate with North Korean leaders on their continued nuclear testing facilities. Carter secured an agreement that led to a treaty between the two countries. He also traveled to North Korea on his own to secure the release of U.S. citizen and Christian missionary Aijalon Mahli Gomes. Carter was successful in his venture.

For his humanitarian efforts what **award** named after a former president did **Carter win**?

In 1998 Carter won the Hoover Medal, named after President Herbert Hoover, who did great humanitarian and relief work during the time of World War I and beyond. Carter won for "promoting peace and goodwill among peoples and nations; resolving conflict, promoting democracy and protecting human rights; advancing health in the developing world; and attacking social problems in the United States." Hoover, Eisenhower, and Carter are the only presidents to win this award.

What **books** has **Carter written** in his post-presidential period?

Carter has written more than twenty books since he left the White House. Some of the more prominent include: *Keeping Faith: Memoirs of a President* (1982 and 1995); *Talking Peace: A Vision for the Next Generation* (1993); *Our Endangered Values: America's Moral Crisis* (2005); *Beyond the White House: Waging Peace, Fighting Disease, Building Hope* (2008); and *We Can Have Peace in the Holy Land: A Plan That Will Work* (2009).

RONALD REAGAN

(1911–2004)
40th President, 1981–89
Party Affiliation: Republican
Chief 1980 Opponent: Jimmy Carter (Democrat)
Chief 1984 Opponent: Walter Mondale (Democrat)

EARLY LIFE AND FAMILY

Where and when was Reagan **born**?

Ronald Wilson Reagan was born in Tampico, Illinois, to John Edward and Nelle Wilson Reagan on February 6, 1911.

What did his **father do** for a living?

John Edward Reagan worked a shoe salesman, a boot store operator, and a director of public works projects in Dixon, Illinois. He had some success with his boot store until the Great Depression forced him to close it.

What was Reagan's **early education**?

Reagan attended local grade schools in Illinois. His family moved to Dixon, Illinois, when he was nine, where he also attended public schools. He graduated from Dixon High School in 1928. At Dixon, he served as president of the student body and played football, basketball, and track.

411

President Ronald Reagan.

Did he have any **siblings**?

Yes, Reagan had one older brother named John Neil Reagan. He worked in the advertising business in California.

Did he **marry**?

Yes, Reagan had two marriages. He married actress Jane Wyman on January 26, 1940, in Hollywood, California. The couple divorced in 1948. Reagan married a second time to actress Nancy Davis on March 4, 1952, in San Fernando Valley, California.

Did he have any **children**?

Yes, Reagan had two children—one biological and one adoptive—with Jane Wyman. He also had two children with Nancy Davis. From his first marriage, he had a biological daughter named Maureen and an adoptive son named Michael. Maureen, who died in 2001, was active in Republican politics just like her famous father. Michael Reagan worked in business and as a radio talk show host. He also appeared on Fox News as a political consultant.

From his second marriage, Reagan had a daughter named Patti and a son named Ronald Jr. Patti worked as an actress and has written several books. She created controversy when she posed in *Playboy* in 1994. Ronald Reagan Jr. dropped out of Yale University to become a ballet dancer. He later became involved in journalism and politics, serving as a political pundit for MSNC News, and had his own radio show. Ronald advocates liberal political views that are opposite to his famous father.

EARLY CAREER

Where did he go to **college**?

Reagan attended Eureka College in Eureka, Illinois. He earned a partial scholarship for football. He played for the Eureka Golden Tornadoes football, swimming, and track teams. He also served on the debating team and joined the drama club. He performed in school plays and reported for the school newspaper. He graduated in June 1932.

After graduating college, what did he do?

Reagan worked as a radio announcer. He worked for WOC in Davenport, Iowa, and then WHO radio in Des Moines, Iowa, where he broadcast Chicago Cubs baseball games and Big Ten football games. He became a popular regional announcer.

What was his **acting career** like?

Reagan decided to use his radio broadcasting career as a launching pad into acting. While covering spring training for a baseball team in California, he auditioned for a screen test and was signed as an actor. He appeared in more than fifty movies in his career, which lasted for nearly thirty years from 1937 to 1965. He starred as football player George Gipp in the popular film of Notre Dame football *Knute Rockne: All American*. He also starred in the comedy *Bedtime for Bonzo* with a chimpanzee as his leading costar. He appeared in the movie *Hellcats of the Navy* with his wife Nancy. He served as president of the Screen Actors Guild for six years.

What **interrupted** Reagan's **acting career**?

He served in the U.S. Army from April 1942 to July 1945, starting as a second lieutenant and finishing as a captain. Because of his poor eyesight, he did not see combat duty.

When did he become **interested in politics**?

He became more interested in politics in the early 1960s. Previously, he was a registered Democrat, but he gradually moved to the right. He served as a co-chairman for California Republicans for Goldwater, supporting Republican 1964 presidential candidate Barry Goldwater. He gave a rousing speech for Goldwater that was televised. People began to take notice of Reagan as a possible political force.

POLITICAL OFFICES

What was his **first political office**?

Reagan's first political office was as governor of California. He won his first term in 1966 with a win over Democratic incumbent Pat Brown. He won reelection in 1970 with a win over Jesse "Big Daddy" Unruh, who had sparred with Reagan from his position in the California legislature. He declined to seek a third term, leaving the office in 1975. Reagan cracked down on student protestors in his first term and pushed through welfare reform in his second term.

What **other races** did he enter?

Reagan sought the presidency in both 1968 and 1976. In 1968, he presented himself as a compromise candidate between Richard Nixon and Nelson Rockefeller. He finished third. In 1976, he nearly pulled an upset, almost unseating incumbent Gerald Ford. He carried out a strong campaign and told his supporters after the race: "I shall rise and fight again."

PRESIDENCY

Whom did **Reagan defeat** to win the **1980 Republican presidential nomination**?

Reagan won the 1980 Republican presidential nomination over his future vice president George H. W. Bush. There were other contenders initially, including Bob Dole, U.S. senator from Kansas; Howard Baker, U.S. Senator from Tennessee; and John Anderson, a U.S. Representative from Illinois, who later ran as an independent. Bush won a few primaries, but Reagan dominated and the field had dropped out of the race by the time of the convention.

Whom did **Reagan defeat** in the 1980 **general presidential election**?

Reagan defeated incumbent Democrat Jimmy Carter, who was beset with a struggling economy, hostages in Iran, and other problems. During one of the debates, Reagan famously asked Americans to consider something before they voted for their next president: "I think when you make that decision it might be well if you could ask yourself, are you better off now than you were four years ago?" Many Americans were worse off and it showed at the polls. In a landslide, Reagan tallied 489 electoral votes to only 9 for Carter.

Whom did Reagan **defeat** in **1984** to win reelection?

Reagan defeated Walter Mondale, Carter's former vice president. Mondale made history by announcing that he had chosen a woman as his vice presidential candidate— Geraldine Ferraro of New York, a U.S. representative. Reagan dominated the election, winning 525 electoral votes to only 13 for Mondale. Reagan's 525 electoral votes remains a record in American presidential election history.

Who was his **vice president**?

Reagan chose as his vice president his former rival from the primaries, George H. W. Bush, who served as his second-in-command for all eight years. Reagan initially considered former president Gerald Ford as his running mate, but Ford wanted an arrangement similar to a co-presidency. Bush loyally served as Reagan's vice president and then later became Reagan's ultimate successor.

Who were his U.S. **attorneys general**?

Reagan had three U.S. attorneys general: William French Smith, who served from 1981-85; Edwin Meese, who served from 1985 to 1988; and Richard Thornburgh, who

415

served from 1988 to 1989. Smith opposed affirmative action and aggressively fought crime. Meese was the most controversial of the three attorneys general. A strong advocate for interpreting the Constitution pursuant to the Founders' original intent, he was not bashful about criticizing Supreme Court justices when he thought they interpreted the Constitution according to their personal preferences. He resigned after a report cleared him of wrongdoing in the Iran-Contra affair—something for which he took much criticism. Richard Thornburgh, a former Pennsylvania governor, stayed on when George H. W. Bush became president.

First Lady Nancy Reagan was the president's second wife. Instrumental in supporting her husband's career, she was very active in the White House and especially in social campaigns such as the "War on Drugs."

What was the **"War on Drugs"**?

The War on Drugs was the catchphrase used by the Reagan administration to define their efforts to combat what many saw as a crack epidemic in the country—a drug that devastating many urban communities particularly. Reagan signed into law a 1986 criminal law that imposed mandatory minimums and created greater sentences for drug traffickers. First Lady Nancy Reagan participated actively in the fight against drugs with her national campaign: "Just Say No."

What **assassination attempt** did Reagan survive?

On March 30, 1981, John Hinckley Jr. shot President Reagan at the Washington Hilton Hotel in Washington, D.C. Reagan—who had been in office only a short time—suffered an injured arm and a punctured lung, but survived the attack. Hinckley shot White House Press Secretary James Brady in the head, leaving him disabled. He also shot Secret Service agent Timothy McCarthy and District of Columbia Metropolitan police officer Tom Delahanty.

Hinckley, who came from a wealthy family, acted irrationally out of an obsession for actress Jodie Foster, who had starred in the film Taxi Driver as a child prostitute. Hinckley identified with the protagonist in the movie, Travis Bickle, who tries to assassinate a United States senator; Bickle is convinced that violence is the answer to the social ills he

What was Reaganomics?

Reaganomics is the name given to Ronald Reagan's economic policies, which included broad tax cuts, cuts in social programs, and increases in defense spending. Reagan came into office with the mantra: "government isn't the solution to our problems, government is the problem." He believed in supply-side economics, reducing government taxes on business that would allow the private sector to grow the economy. Critics charged that Reaganomics favored the rich to the detriment of the poor and constituted a form of "trickle down" economics.

feels have caused the downfall of Foster's character. A jury found Hinckley not guilty by reason of insanity and he remains confined in a mental hospital to this day.

What small **military action** did the United States win in **1983**?

Reagan ordered the deployment of American troops to the island of Grenada. Reagan deployed more than seven thousand troops to support the government from a left-wing military coup by a Cuban-supported regime. It was the United States's first major military operation since Vietnam and led to an easy American victory. President Reagan kept his promise to remove American troops by the end of the year.

What was the **Iran–Contra Affair**?

This was a scandal that plagued the later years of the Reagan administration. It was alleged that, despite an embargo, the American government traded arms to Iran. It was conjectured that Reagan was motivated by a desire to secure the release of American hostages in Lebanon, even though he publicly denied an arms-for-hostage agreement. In addition, it became known that some of the funds from the arms sales in Iran were funneled to an insurgent group in Nicaragua called the Contras, which the United States supported over the Communist Sandanista government despite the fact that further funding of the Contras had been prohibited by Congress. The plan was carried out by National Security Advisor John Poindexter and Lieutenant Colonel Oliver North.

Reagan appointed a commission headed by U.S. Senator John Tower to investigate. The Tower Commission found no evidence that Reagan knew of the diversion of the funds, but criticized him for failing to be more involved.

Who were Reagan's **U.S. Supreme Court appointees**?

Reagan elevated one associate justice to chief justice and named three individuals as associate justices to the Supreme Court. In 1981, Reagan made history by nominating

417

the first woman to the U.S. Supreme Court—Sandra Day O'Connor. Reagan had pledged during the campaign to nominate a woman to the Court and he kept his word. A former Arizona state legislator, O'Connor served on the Court from 1981 to 2006. She crafted many important decisions on religious freedom and served as a key swing vote on many cases. She supported the right of abortion for women.

In 1986, Reagan pulled a coup for conservatives when he elevated sitting associate justice William H. Rehnquist to chief justice. That left an open spot for an associate justice, and Reagan nominated Antonin Scalia, a firebrand conservative serving as a judge on the D.C. Circuit Court of Appeals. The Senate focused on the nomination of Rehnquist, allowing Scalia to skate through with a ninety-eight to zero confirmation vote. Rehnquist served on the Court until his death in 2005. He was regarded as an excellent administrator of the Court. Scalia, who is still on the Court, changed the culture of oral argument, asking more questions of attorneys than any previous justice. He is a powerful voice on the Court.

In 1988, Reagan nominated Justice Anthony Kennedy, who is still on the Court. Reagan originally chose former Nixon solicitor general Robert Bork as his nominee, but the Senate rejected (or "borked") him because of his ultraconservative views. Reagan then nominated Douglas Ginsburg, who withdrew after allegations surfaced of past marijuana usage.

What **terrorist leader** did the Reagan administration **target**?

Reagan targeted Libyan leader Muammar al-Gaddafi for his sponsorship of terrorists who attacked the United States. Reagan referred to Gaddafi, who became the leader of Libya in 1969, as the "mad dog of the Middle East." U.S. air forces targeted several areas near Tripoli, Libya's capital, on April 15, 1986. Reagan justified the attack after learning that Gaddafi was responsible for the bombing of a West Berlin disco that left two Americans dead. Reagan also believed that Gaddafi had sponsored attacks on the airports in Rome and Vienna in 1985.

What was Reagan's **policy on abortion**?

Reagan publicly stated his opposition to the U.S. Supreme Court decision in *Roe v. Wade,* which protected a woman's right to an abortion. He issued an executive order that prohibited the use of federal funds to advocate on behalf of abortion.

POST PRESIDENCY

What **disease afflicted Reagan** in his retirement period?

In 1994, the eighty-three-year-old Reagan was diagnosed with Alzheimer's disease, a neurological disorder that has no known cure. Reagan's last public appearance was at former President Nixon's funeral in April 1994.

When did he **die**?

Reagan died at the age of ninety-three on June 5, 2004.

GEORGE H. W. BUSH

(1924–)
41st President, 1989–1993
Party Affiliation: Republican
Chief 1988 Opponent: Michael Dukakis (Democrat)

EARLY LIFE AND FAMILY

Where and when was he **born**?

George H. W. Bush was born in Milton, Massachusetts, to Prescott S. and Dorothy Walker Bush on June 24, 1924.

What did his **parents do** for a living?

Prescott S. Bush was a successful Wall Street banker who later went into politics. He served as a U.S. senator for Connecticut from 1952 to 1963. Dorothy Walker Bush, a great tennis player in her youth, reared the couple's children and, while Prescott served in the Senate, wrote a column entitled "Washington Life of a Senator's Wife."

What was his **early education**?

George H. W. Bush attended exclusive private schools. First he attended Greenwich (Connecticut) Country Day School, and then at age thirteen he entered Phillips Academy in Andover, Massachusetts. He served as president of his senior class, captained the

421

President George H. W. Bush.

baseball team, and managed the school's basketball team. He graduated from Phillips Academy in 1942.

Did he have any **siblings**?

Yes, George H. W. Bush had four siblings: Prescott Jr., who died as an infant, Nancy, Jonathan, and William.

Did he **marry**?

Yes, George H. W. Bush married Barbara Pierce on January 6, 1945, in Rye, New York. He was twenty and she was nineteen at the time of their marriage. Barbara Bush later became a very respected first lady.

Does he have any **children**?

George and Barbara Bush have six children, including five that lived to adulthood. Daughter Pauline Robinson ("Robin") died of leukemia at age four in 1953. The five children are: George W. Bush, who later became the forty-third president of the United States; John E. "Jeb," who became governor of Florida; Neil, who became an oil executive; Marvin, who became an investment consultant; and Dorothy, who has been a successful businesswoman.

EARLY CAREER

What did he do **after** his **high school graduation**?

After the attack on Pearl Harbor in December 1941, Bush decided to join the navy when he finished high school. He became the navy's youngest aviator at age eighteen. He flew more than fifty combat missions—including at least one from which he barely survived—and earned numerous medals, including the Distinguished Flying Cross and several Air Medals.

What did he do **after leaving** the **military**?

Bush attended his father's alma mater, Yale University, where he had been accepted before he had joined the military. He entered an accelerated program that allowed individuals to graduate in two and a half years instead of the traditional four years. He captained the baseball team and participated in two College World Series. He was considered an exceptional fielder, but only decent hitter. He graduated with honors in 1948.

What did he do **after graduating** from **Yale**?

He decided to strike out on his own and enter the oil business in Texas. He first landed a job with Dresser Industries, as the president of the company was a family friend. A couple years later, he left Dresser to form his own company—the Bush-Overby Oil Development Company in Midland, Texas. Bush and John Overby then merged their company with Bill and Hugh Liedtke to form Zapata Petroleum Corporation. Bush became a wealthy man in the oil business. He gradually developed more and more of an itch to enter politics.

POLITICAL OFFICES

What **office** did Bush **first seek**?

In 1964, Bush served as chairman of the Republican Party for Harris County, Texas, and attended the 1964 Republican National Convention. He ambitiously ran for a seat in the U.S. Senate. He captured the Republican nomination but lost to Democrat incumbent Ralph Yarbrough.

When did he first become a **member of Congress**?

Bush first joined Congress after winning a 1966 election for the U.S. House of Representatives. He served in the House until 1971. He served on the prestigious House Ways and Means Committee.

Why did Bush **receive threatening letters** from his constituents when he was serving in the House?

Bush voted for the 1968 Fair Housing Act, which was very unpopular in his Texas district. It was considered a courageous vote given the unpopularity of the bill.

What **race** did Bush **lose in 1970**?

Bush again sought a seat in the U.S. Senate, thinking that he could defeat Yarbrough this time. However, Yarbrough lost to former congressmen Lloyd Bentsen. Bush lost to Bentsen in the general election. He nearly quit politics after the loss. As an interesting side note, Bentsen later served as the vice presidential nominee for Bush's 1988 presidential opponent Michael Dukakis.

What was Bush's **next political position** after the failed Senate race?

President Richard Nixon appointed Bush as U.S. ambassador to the United Nations, a position he held from 1971 to 1973. This position gave Bush keen insight into numerous foreign countries.

What was the **next political position** that **Nixon gave to Bush**?

President Nixon talked Bush into taking the job of chair of the Republican National Committee in 1973. This was a most difficult time for this job, as the Watergate scandal continued to mushroom out of control. Bush steadfastly defended the Republican Party.

What **position** did **President Ford** appoint Bush to?

Bush had wanted to be President Gerald Ford's vice president, but he was the president's second choice behind Nelson

President George H. W. Bush received the 2010 Medal of Freedom from President Barack Obama.

Rockefeller. However, President Ford designated Bush as chief U.S. liaison or envoy in China, a position in which Bush excelled. He improved U.S.-Sino relations significantly during his time.

What was the **next position** that **Ford assigned** to him?

President Ford then asked Bush to take the position of director of the Central Intelligence Agency—a position that Bush did not want, but accepted nonetheless. Bush improved the morale of the agency and even briefed President-elect Jimmy Carter on various affairs. He hoped to stay in the position, but Carter wanted a Democrat for the job.

What did Bush do for the several years **before he became vice president**?

Bush became a chairperson of a bank in Houston and taught part-time at Rice University's business school. After this, he served as a director for the Council on Foreign Relations, and decided that he wanted to run for president. He won key primaries in Iowa, Michigan, and Pennsylvania, but lost the presidential candidacy to the popular Ronald Reagan, who later asked Bush to be his running mate.

What did Bush do **as vice president**?

Bush was a very loyal vice president to Reagan, particularly during the time when Reagan was recuperating from the assassination attempt by John Hinckley Jr. He had weekly lunches with the president and worked on key task forces. He traveled to many foreign countries and further developed an expertise in foreign policy.

PRESIDENCY

Whom did **Bush defeat** to win the **1988 Republican primary**?

Bush defeated some formidable challengers, including Bob Dole, U.S. senator from Kansas; Jack Kemp, a popular U.S. representative from New York; former secretary of state Alexander Haig; and wildcard candidate Reverend Pat Robertson.

Whom did **Bush defeat** in the **general election**?

Bush defeated Michael Dukakis, the governor of Massachusetts. Dukakis had an early lead in the polls, but the Bush campaign team did an effective job of attacking their opponent as soft on crime and too liberal for much of middle America. The Bush team ran the infamous "Willie Horton" ad, linking Dukakis's support of weekend passes for felons with the story of a Massachusetts inmate who had committed a violent crime while on a weekend furlough. The ad was effective, and Bush won the election in an electoral vote landslide, 426 to 111.

Who was **Bush's vice president**?

Bush chose conservative Dan Quayle, a U.S. senator from Indiana. Quayle had managed to defeat the longtime Democratic senator Birch Bayh, even though there was a popular conception that Quayle was not the brightest politician. He went on to make some memorable gaffes in spelling and speaking during his time as vice president.

Who was Bush's **secretary of defense**?

Bush chose Richard Cheney, a longtime congressman from Wyoming as his secretary of defense. Cheney later served as vice president to Bush's son during his presidency. Bush had actually wanted former senator John Tower of Texas as his secretary of defense, but Tower was rejected by the Senate, the first time the Senate had rejected a cabinet appointment in more than twenty years.

What foreign policy occurrences led to Bush having a really **high popularity rating** early in his presidency?

Several factors contributed to Bush's high approval rating. First, the Berlin Wall fell, Communism collapsed, and the Cold War ended. Then, Bush successfully waged the First Persian Gulf War, soundly defeating Iraq after its leader, Sadaam Hussein, invaded Kuwait. These events gave Bush a popularly rating of nearly 90 percent—an unprecedented amount for a president.

What presidential campaign pledge later came back to haunt Bush?

During his nominating speech, Bush emphatically stated: "Read my lips. No new taxes." When he did raise taxes during his presidency, his veracity was called into question and, in part, led to his fate as a one-term president.

What **treaty** did Bush sign with **Soviet president Mikhail Gorbachev**?

Bush and Gorbachev signed the Strategic Arms Reduction Treaty, in which both countries pledged to reduce their nuclear arms. Bush called the treaty a "significant step forward in dispelling half a century of mistrust." It was these two leaders—Bush and Gorbachev—who played a key role in the historic ending of the Cold War, a truly remarkable accomplishment between the two superpowers.

What **Panamanian leader** did the Bush administration take **out of power**?

U.S. forces invaded Panama and removed dictator Manuel Noriega from power. Noriega had defied the results of a democratic election in his country in which he had been ousted. The U.S. faced charges of "American imperialism" for its intervention. Bush referred to the U.S. deployment of more than twenty thousand troops as "Operation Just Cause."

What fellow member of the Reagan administration did **Bush pardon**?

Bush pardoned Reagan's secretary of defense Caspar Weinberger, who faced criminal charges arising out of the Iran-Contra scandal. Bush called Weinberger a "true American patriot."

What **trade agreement** did Bush sign with the leaders of **Canada and Mexico**?

Bush signed the North American Free Trade Agreement (NAFTA) with the leaders of Canada and Mexico. This measure greatly reduced tariffs on the countries' goods and many believed that it had positive impacts on the economy.

What major **anti-discrimination law** did Bush sign into law?

On September 25, 1990, Bush signed into law the Americans with Disabilities Act of 1990, a law that provided protection to those with disabilities in employment, public accommodations, and other areas of life. Title I of the ADA provides protections for those employees or applicants who are qualified individuals with a disability. The law, a bi-partisan effort, made a tremendous difference in the lives of those with physical and mental disabilities.

Former presidents George H. W. Bush and Bill Clinton have established foundations and worked as a team to pull together funding for relief efforts following natural disasters. In 2004, at the request of President George W. Bush, they led efforts to raise funds for humanitarian aid when a devastating tsunami hit Indonesia. They worked together again in 2005—once more by request of President George W. Bush—to help victims of Hurricane Katrina in the Gulf Coast. Past rivals, the two seem to have become close friends in their post-presidential years.

Who were his U.S. **Supreme Court appointees**?

Bush had two appointments to the U.S. Supreme Court: David Souter and Clarence Thomas. Souter, a relatively little known jurist from New Hampshire, was expected to be a conservative. Bush's chief of staff John Sununu referred to him as a "home run for conservatives." He turned out to be a single—if that— for conservatives, as Souter proved himself to be an independent and often liberal jurist on the Court. Souter retired from the Court in 2009.

With his next selection, Bush chose Clarence Thomas, an African-American conservative, to replace the great liberal giant Thurgood Marshall, the nation's first African American Supreme Court justice. Thomas barely won Senate confirmation—fifty-two to forty-eight—after former co-worker Anita Hill, a law professor from Oklahoma, alleged that Thomas sexually harassed her while both worked for the Equal Employment Opportunity Commission. Thomas, who was Hill's boss at two different jobs, vehemently denied the charges and famously referred to the Democrats' interrogation as a "high-tech lynching."

POST PRESIDENCY

Did Bush seek a **second term**?

Yes, Bush sought a second term, but the failing economy led to challenges for the Bush campaign. The Democratic challenger Bill Clinton proved to be an effective and resilient campaigner. Bush was harmed further by the entrance into the race of Independent candidate Ross Perot, who drew more votes away from Bush.

BILL CLINTON

(1946–)
42nd President, 1993–2001
Party Affiliation: Democrat
Chief 1992 Opponents: George H. W. Bush (Republican), Ross Perot (Independent)
Chief 1996 Opponent: Bob Dole (Republican)

EARLY LIFE AND FAMILY

Where and when was he **born**?

Bill Clinton was born in Hope, Arkansas, to William Jefferson Blythe Jr. and Virginia Dell Cassidy on August 19, 1946. His birth name was William Jefferson Blythe III. He formally took the last name of his stepfather, Roger Clinton, when was a teenager.

What did his **biological parents do** for a living?

William Jefferson Blythe Jr. was a traveling salesman who died in an automobile accident several months before Bill Clinton was born. His mother, Virginia, worked as a nurse.

How many **times** did Clinton's **mother marry**?

Bill Clinton's mother married five times (twice to the same man). Her first husband was William Jefferson Blythe Jr. Her second husband was Roger Clinton, whom she married, divorced, and then married again. Her third husband was Jeff Dwire. Her fourth husband was Richard Kelley.

429

President Bill Clinton.

What was Clinton's life like with his stepfather Roger Clinton?

It was trying, as Roger Clinton abused Bill's mother and drank too much. Bill Clinton had to intervene to protect his mother from physical abuse. Clinton has said that dealing with such a chaotic environment helped prepare him for the rough-and-tumble world of politics.

Did he have any **siblings**?

He had a younger half-brother, Roger Clinton Jr. His younger brother had a checkered past, including drug charges. Clinton later pardoned his brother when he was president. Roger Clinton Jr. has had some success as an actor in recent years.

What was Clinton's **early education**?

He attended St. John's Catholic School and Ramble Elementary School for his elementary education. He then attended Hot Springs High School in Hot Springs, Arkansas. He excelled in academics and as a musician, showing promise playing the saxophone. He even contemplated a career in music for a time.

Did he **marry**?

Yes, Bill Clinton married Hillary Rodham on October 11, 1975. They met when they both were students at Yale Law School. She was a year ahead of Bill at Yale. She later became a political force in her own right; she served as U.S. senator from New York, and almost won the 2008 Democratic nomination for president. When the nomination and the presidency went to Barack Obama, she went on to become his secretary of state.

Does he have any **children**?

Yes, Bill and Hillary Clinton have one daughter, Chelsea. She graduated from Stanford University, and then acquired several master's degrees. She married in 2010.

EARLY CAREER

Where did Clinton go to **college**?

He attended the Edward A. Walsh School of Foreign Service at Georgetown University, where he graduated in 1968. After college, he won a prestigious Rhodes Scholarship to study at Oxford in England. He is the only president to be a Rhodes Scholar.

First Lady Hillary Rodham Clinton.

What **famous senator** did Clinton **intern for** during his college years?

The summer before his senior year, he interned for James William Fulbright, a U.S. senator from Clinton's home state of Arkansas. Fulbright served thirty years in the Senate.

Did he serve in the **military**?

No, Clinton did not serve in the military. He was of military age during the Vietnam War, but traveled to England for his Rhodes Scholarship program. Critics charge that he used his connections with Senator Fulbright to claim that he was going in an ROTC program to avoid being drafted.

Where did he go to **law school**?

Clinton went to Yale Law School, where he graduated in 1973. It was at Yale that Bill Clinton met his future wife, Hillary.

Did Clinton ever **practice law**?

Clinton practiced law with the firm Wright, Lindsey, and Jennings. His friend Bruce Lindsey got Clinton the job. Clinton later returned the favor, enlisting Lindsey as his deputy White House counsel and senior advisor.

POLITICAL OFFICES

To whom did Clinton **lose** his **first political race**?

In 1974, the twenty-eight-year-old Clinton lost to Roger Paul Hammerschmidt in a race for the U.S. House of Representatives. Hammerschmidt was a formidable foe, as he had already served four terms. Hammerschmidt went on to serve thirteen terms in the House, from 1967 until his retirement in 1993.

What **two positions** did **Clinton win**?

In 1976, he became Arkansas's attorney general, and then in 1978 the thirty-two-year-old Clinton became the youngest governor in the country. He lost his position after only one term to Republican challenger Frank D. White. After that defeat, Clinton worked in his friend Bruce Lindsey's law firm, while working on his reelection. Clinton later regained the governorship, defeating White in 1982 and 1986.

Who gave Clinton the nickname **"Slick Willie"**?

Paul Greenberg, a newspaper editorial writer for the *Pine Bluff Commercial* and later for the *Arkansas Democrat-Gazette,* called Clinton "Slick Willie" when Clinton was governor. The nickname was used to describe Clinton's ability to change positions to suit his political need.

PRESIDENCY

Whom did **he defeat** to win the **1992 Democratic presidential primary**?

Clinton defeated a formidable array of challengers in the primaries, including Tom Harkin, a U.S. senator from Iowa; Paul Tsongas, a former U.S. senator from Massachusetts; former California governor Jerry Brown; and Bob Kerrey, a U.S. senator from Nebraska. Clinton lost the primary in Iowa to Harkin and the New Hampshire primary to Tsongas. But he became the "Comeback Kid," even overcoming allegations of a long-term affair with a woman named Gennifer Flowers. Clinton ended up dominating the primary with more than three thousand delegates—far more than second-place finisher Brown.

Whom did **he defeat** to win the **1992 general presidential election**?

Clinton defeated Republican incumbent George H. W. Bush and Texas billionaire Ross Perot, who ran as an Independent. Clinton seized upon the flagging economy, Bush's dropping popularity numbers, and the fact that Bush broke his 1988 campaign promise of "no new taxes." Clinton garnered 370 electoral votes to 168 for Bush. Perot did not win a single electoral vote, though he did capture nearly 20 percent of the popular vote. Clinton garnered 43 percent of the popular vote and Bush won 37.5 percent.

What was the **"two for the price of one"** campaign slogan?

Clinton used this slogan to promote his wife, Hillary, who had an impressive legal career. He encouraged the American voters to put him in the White House because Hillary would benefit the country as first lady.

433

Who called Clinton "the first black president"?

Toni Morrison, the acclaimed African American novelist, wrote a piece for the *New Yorker* magazine in which she called Clinton "the first black president." She explained: "Clinton displays almost every trope of blackness: single-parent household, born poor, working-class, saxophone-playing, McDonald's-and-junk-food-loving boy from Arkansas."

Whom did Clinton **defeat** to win **reelection** in the **1996 presidential election**?

Clinton defeated Robert Dole, a longtime U.S. senator from Kansas, to win reelection in 1996. Dole had served in the U.S. House of Representatives in the 1960s before winning a seat in the U.S. Senate in 1968. He was reelected to that seat four more times. He resigned from the Senate while running for president in 1996. As a former war hero—he was wounded in World War II—with plenty of experience, it seemed that Dole presented a formidable challenge to Clinton. But Clinton easily defeated him with an electoral vote count of 359 to 179.

Who was his **vice president**?

Clinton selected Albert Gore Jr., a U.S. senator from Tennessee, as his running mate. Gore was young and from the South, but gave the campaign ticket credibility on environmental issues and on family values. Gore served as Clinton's vice president for two full terms. He went on to run for the presidency, but lost a hotly contested race to George W. Bush.

What Clinton **cabinet members** were the **first women** to hold **such positions** in American history?

Madeleine Albright and Janet Reno were the first women to serve as secretary of state and U.S. attorney general, respectively, in American history. Born in Czechoslovakia, Albright served as U.S. ambassador to the United Nations in 1993 before Clinton elevated her as to secretary of state in 1997, replacing Warren Christopher. The Senate confirmed her by a vote of ninety-nine to zero. She later published her memoir titled *Madam Secretary* (2003).

Janet Reno became the first female U.S. attorney general in U.S. history in 1993. Clinton had actually chosen Zoe Baird and Kimba Wood, but both of them withdrew their names from consideration after both admitted they had employed an illegal alien as nannies. Reno, a graduate of Harvard law school, had served as state attorney for Miami-Dade County for many years. She helped to create the nation's first drug court during her tenure. She served as Clinton's only attorney general.

What **foreign policy mistake** led to the death of nearly a million people?

The Clinton Administration failed to act quickly in Rwanda. Because of that inaction, the Rwanda Genocide occurred, in which the Hutu militants, including some in the government, slaughtered more than 800,000 Tutsis and more moderate Hutus. Many believe that if the United Nations and the United States had intervened more quickly, the bloodshed would have been much less. To his credit, in 1998, during a visit to Rwanda, Clinton apologized for not acting sooner.

What major piece of **employment legislation** did Clinton sign early in his presidency?

Clinton signed into law the Family and Medical Leave Act of 1993, which provided that employees working for larger employers (employers who have fifty or more employees) can take a three-month period of paid or unpaid leave (at the employer's discretion) for pregnancy or a serious medical condition.

What major **legislative goal** did **Clinton fail** to get through Congress?

Clinton supported health care reform, an issue that his wife, Hillary, spearheaded for the administration. However, the Republicans, the health insurance agencies, and the American Medical Association fought the measure with vigor. Ultimately, Hillary Clinton's health care plan failed to get through Congress.

What **federal law** related to the **veto power** was signed by Clinton, but later **invalidated** by the **U.S. Supreme Court**?

President Clinton signed into law the Line Item Veto Act of 1996, which gave the president the power to veto specific budgetary provisions of a bill without impacting the rest of the legislation. The measure had been introduced by Senator Robert Dole. The U.S. Supreme Court invalidated the measure in *Clinton v. City of New York* (1998) by a six to three vote. Writing for the majority, Justice John Paul Stevens wrote: "this Act gives the President the unilateral power to change the text of duly enacted statutes." He concluded: "If there is to be a new procedure in which the President will play a different role in determining the final text of what may 'become a law,' such change must come not by legislation but through the amendment procedures set forth in Article V of the Constitution."

What initiative did Clinton establish to **improve race relations**?

In June 1997, Clinton issued an executive order establishing his One America in the 21st Century: The President's Initiative on Race. The initiative sought to encourage

435

During his campaign the future President Clinton raised eyebrows by fostering a hip image as a saxophone player.

community discussion about race and diversity, bringing people together and healing divisions based on race and culture. Clinton named Dr. John Hope Franklin, a leading African American historian, as chairman of the advisory board for the initiative. The initiative led to two reports: *One America in the 21st Century: Forging a New Future* and *Pathways to One America in the 21st Century: Promising Practices for Racial Reconciliation.*

What **major terrorist attacks** occurred on U.S. soil during Clinton's presidency?

In February 1993, a bomb in a car went off in the bottom parking lot of the North Tower of the World Trade Center in New York City. It killed six people and injured more than one thousand. Ramzi Yousef —who had received some training from the terrorist group al-Qaeda—and several others planned and implemented the attack. Pakistani authorities captured Yousef in February 1995, and he later received a life sentence from a federal judge in New York. He exclaimed in federal court: "Yes, I am a terrorist, and proud of it as long as it is against the U.S. government and against Israel, because you are more than terrorists; you are the one who invented terrorism and [are] using it every day. You are butchers, liars and hypocrites."

In April 1995, former U.S. military members and right-wing extremists Timothy McVeigh and Terry Nichols carried out the Oklahoma City bombing—the bombing of a federal building that led to the death of 168 people and more than 600 injuries. It was the worst act of terrorism on U.S. soil until the September 11,

Who was Monica Lewinsky?

Monica Lewinsky was a twenty-two-year-old White House intern who had a sexual affair with Clinton. Extra-marital affair allegations had dogged Clinton for years, but this one was more problematic. Clinton testified under oath in a deposition that he never had sex with Lewinsky in a case brought by Paula Jones. Jones was suing Clinton for sexual harassment for conduct when he was governor of Arkansas.

Independent counsel Ken Starr—who was investigating Clinton for other White House scandals—found out about the Lewinsky matter and cited it in detail in his report. The alleged lies in Clinton's testimony in the Paula Jones case led to impeachment charges for perjury and obstruction of justice.

2001, attack in New York City. McVeigh and Nichols had been upset over the U.S. invasion at the Branch Davidian compound in Waco, Texas, in 1993 and the U.S. actions in Ruby Ridge, Idaho, where F.B.I. snipers killed some of white separatist's Randy Weaver's children. In fact, McVeigh planned to carry out the attack on April 19, 1995, two years to the date of the Waco invasion. McVeigh was convicted and later executed in June 1997, the first execution of a federal prisoner in thirty-eight years. Nichols was sentenced to multiple life sentences and will remain incarcerated for the rest of his life.

What happened during the Clinton **impeachment process**?

The Republican-controlled House voted to impeach Clinton on perjury and obstruction of justice in December 1998. However, in a twenty-one-day trial presided over by U.S. Supreme Court Justice William Rehnquist, the U.S. Senate acquitted Clinton on both counts. The Senate voted fifty to fifty and forty-five to fifty-five on the two counts, far short of the necessary sixty-seven votes needed for conviction.

What did **Hillary Clinton call** the **impeachment process** against her husband?

Hillary Clinton famously referred to the impeachment process as a "vast right wing conspiracy."

What was **controversial** about Clinton's **pardons**?

Clinton issued more than 140 pardons on his last day in office. Some of them were not very controversial, but the Marc Rich pardon was a notable exception. Rich was a billionaire commodities trader who made a fortune selling and trading in oil with coun-

437

tries such as Iran and Iraq. Prosecutors had charged Rich back in the 1980s with insider trading with Iran and tax evasion. Because his former wife, Denise Rich, had made very sizeable donations to the Clinton Library and the U.S. Democratic Party, it was alleged by some critics that the pardon was bought. Others alleged that Hugh Rodham, Hillary Clinton's brother, had received money from those seeking pardons.

What was **TrooperGate**?

TrooperGate refers to allegations by two former Arkansas state troopers about then-governor Bill Clinton. The troopers—Larry Patterson and Roger Perry—alleged that they arranged sexual meetings with several women for Clinton when he was Arkansas governor.

What was **Whitewater**?

Whitewater refers to a failed land deal by Jim and Susan McDougal and Bill and Hillary Clinton. McDougal convinced Clinton to invest money in a land development project. The four agreed to buy more than 230 acres of land in the Ozark Mountains in Arkansas, which they hoped they would sell for a handsome profit. Pursuant to that plan, the four formed the Whitewater Development Corporation. The Clintons claimed that McDougal was the active partner and that they were passive silent partners. James and Susan McDougal faced criminal charges, but the Clintons were never charged with a crime. James McDougal faced many criminal charges for fraud for allegedly using proceeds from federally insured savings and loans to pay for the land.

Who were Clinton's U.S. **Supreme Court appointees**?

Clinton appointed Ruth Bader Ginsburg and Stephen Breyer as associate justices to the U.S. Supreme Court. Ginsburg, who had been called the "Thurgood Marshall of gender equality," had successfully argued women's rights cases before the Supreme Court in the early 1970s. She had a distinguished career in academia and served on the U.S. Court of Appeals for the Second Circuit. Breyer had served for many years on the U.S. Court of Appeals for the First Circuit. After graduating from Harvard Law School, he served as a law clerk for U.S. Supreme Court justice Arthur Goldberg.

POST PRESIDENCY

What **books** did **Clinton write** in his post-presidential period?

Clinton wrote a lengthy autobiography titled *My Life* (2004). He received a whopping $15 million-dollar advance for the book. It has sold millions of copies. He also authored *Giving: How Each of Us Can Change the World* (2007), which was also well received critically and commercially.

What **humanitarian efforts** has he engaged in with his former rival **George H. W. Bush**?

Former presidents Bill Clinton and George H. W. Bush have established foundations and worked as a team to pull together funding for relief efforts following natural disasters. In 2004, at the request of President George W. Bush, they led efforts to raise funds for humanitarian aid when a devastating tsunami hit Indonesia. They worked together again in 2005—once more by request of President George W. Bush—to help victims of Hurricane Katrina in the Gulf Coast. Past rivals, the two seem to have become close friends in their post-presidential years.

In what **campaign** did Bill Clinton take an **active role**?

Clinton took an active role in campaigning for his wife, Hillary's run for the presidency in 2008. Bill vigorously campaigned for his wife, but some of his critical statements about her rival Barrack Obama and other seemingly insensitive comments led some to think that he may have harmed her campaign more than helped it.

What roles has he had with respect to **Haiti**?

Clinton was named the United Nations Special Envoy to Haiti in 2009. He traveled to Haiti in 2010 to discuss ways to help the country after a devastating earthquake. Along with former president George W. Bush, he worked on relief efforts for the ravaged island.

GEORGE W. BUSH

(1946–)
43rd President, 2001–2009
Party Affiliation: Republican
Chief 2000 Opponent: Al Gore (Democrat)
Chief 2004 Opponent: John Kerry (Democrat)

EARLY LIFE AND FAMILY

Where and when was he **born**?

George W. Bush was born in New Haven, Connecticut, to George H. W. and Barbara Bush on July 6, 1946.

What did his **father do** for a living?

His father, George H. W. Bush, was a success in both private and public life. He is most famous for serving as the forty-first president of the United States—from 1989 to 1993, before losing a reelection bid to Bill Clinton. The Bushes join John Adams and John Quincy Adams as the only fathers and sons to hold the title of chief executive.

Did he have any **siblings**?

Yes, George W. Bush had five siblings, four of whom are still living. A sister died from leukemia at age three in 1953. His four living siblings are Jeb, Neil, Marvin, and Dorothy. John E. "Jeb" became governor of Florida, Neil became an oil executive, Marvin became an investment consultant, and Dorothy became a successful businesswoman. 441

From 1968 to 1972, President Bush served in the National Guard, where he trained as an F-102 pilot and achieved the rank of first lieutenant.

What was Bush's **early education**?

He attended public schools in Midland, Texas. Then, he attended a private school in Houston, The Kinkaid School. After this, he attended Phillips Academy in Andover, Massachusetts, where he played baseball.

Did he **marry**?

Bush married Laura Lane Welch on November 5, 1977, in Midland, Texas. Laura Bush became a popular first lady; during her tenure she encouraged education and reading for children and adults.

Does he have any **children**?

George and Laura Bush have twin daughters: Barbara Pierce and Jenna Welch. Barbara Pierce Bush graduated from Yale and Jenna Welch Bush Hager graduated from the University of Texas.

EARLY CAREER

Where did he go to **college**?

Like his father and grandfather, Bush attended Yale University, graduating in 1968. He earned a bachelor's degree, majoring in history. He was president of his fraternity.

What did he do **after college**?

He joined the Texas Air National Guard in May 1968. He served in that capacity for several years before transferring to the Air Force Reserves on inactive duty. He received an honorable discharge in 1974.

What was his career in the **oil business**?

Beginning in the late 1970s, Bush created an oil company called Arbusto Energy. He later changed the name to Bush Exploration. He then expanded his company by merging with the larger Spectrum 7.

When did Bush become intimately **involved** with **major league baseball**?

In 1989, Bush became part owner of the Texas Rangers, a major league baseball team. He served as managing general partner of the team for several years. He attended games regularly, but sat with the regular fans, not far removed in boxes like some owners. He sold his shares of the team in 1998 for $15 million, a nice profit from his initial investment of less than $1 million.

POLITICAL OFFICES

When did Bush **first run** for **political office**?

In 1978 George W. Bush ran for a seat in the U.S. House of Representatives in Texas against Kent Hance, who was able to gain traction by pointing out that Bush had not been a Texas resident for very long. Hance, a lawyer who also had taught law at Texas Tech, said that Bush was "not a real Texan." This argument worked especially well in rural Texas, and Bush lost the election. It was this loss that propelled Bush into the private sector for some time. But this was the only election that George W. Bush ever lost.

What **political work** did Bush do in **1988 and 1991**?

Bush moved from Texas to Washington, D.C., to work as a key advisor on his father's initial presidential campaign and reelection campaign. While doing this, George W. made important contacts that proved to be beneficial to his own political future.

When did Bush become **governor of Texas**?

Bush won election as Texas governor in 1994 over Democratic incumbent Ann Richards. Bush emphasized during his campaign several major themes, including education, tort reform and crime. Richards had given a speech at the 1988 Democratic National Convention in which she attacked Bush's father, George H. W. Bush, as having been born with a "silver spoon" in his mouth. This gave George W. Bush even more incentive to win the election, which he did by a percentage of 53 to 46.

PRESIDENCY

Whom did **Bush defeat** to win the **2000 Republican primary** for president?

Bush defeated a large array of contenders to capture the 2000 Republican nomination, including John McCain, U.S. senator from Arizona; Steve Forbes, editor of *Forbes*

443

What made the 2000 presidential election so controversial?

The election was controversial because Bush was awarded the twenty-five electoral votes from Florida by a decision of the U.S. Supreme Court.

Gore was initially predicted the winner due to exit polling by the media but that was retracted, as poll results showed Bush pulling ahead. The networks then declared Bush the winner, but vote results were still coming from three counties—Miami-Dade, Broward, and Palm Beach ñand these counties were expected to vote for Gore. The gap shrunk to just two thousand votes statewide—enough to force a recount. Gore asked for manual hand recounts in four counties—the three mentioned earlier and Volusia county.

Florida's secretary of state Katherine Harris—a Republican—certified the results on November 14, declaring Bush the winner. Lawsuits erupted over the recounting. Gore wanted the recounting process to continue and the deadline extended; Bush wanted the result declared official.

The Florida Supreme Court ruled in favor of Gore, saying that the recount process deadline should be extended. However, the U.S. Supreme Court effectively decided the election in *Bush v. Gore* (2000), ruling that the Florida system of counting votes differently in different counties violated the Equal Protection Clause. The result was deemed largely political, as it was decided by a vote of five to four with the five more conservative justices—Chief Justice William Rehnquist, Justice Antonin Scalia, Justice Anthony Kennedy, Justice Sandra Day O'Connor, and Justice Clarence Thomas—voting for Bush. The four more liberal judges—Justice John Paul Stevens, and Associate Justices Ruth Bader Ginsburg, Stephen Breyer, and David Souter—voted for Gore.

magazine; Gary Bauer of the Family Research Council; Orrin Hatch, U.S. senator from Utah; and Allan Keyes, former United Nations diplomat. The most serious challenge came from McCain, who prevailed in the initial New Hampshire primary. But Bush ended up dominating the race.

Whom did **he defeat** to win the **2000 presidential election**?

Bush defeated Democrat Al Gore. Gore had served in the U.S. House of Representatives and U.S. Senate for Tennessee before serving two terms as Clinton's vice president. The 2000 presidential election turned out to be arguably the most controversial election in American history. Gore won the popular vote and some networks actually named Gore the winner. However, Bush ended up capturing the electoral vote—and the presidency—by a vote of 271 to 266.

What **state could Gore have won**—aside from Florida—that would have **avoided the ultimate controversy**?

While political pundits and much of the country obsessed about the controversy in Florida, the sad reality for Gore was that he failed to carry his home state of Tennessee. He is the only presidential candidate from a major party to lose his home state in a presidential election. If Gore had won Tennessee's eight electoral votes, he would have won the presidency.

What **revelation** nearly led to **Bush's defeat** in the presidential election?

Close to the 2000 presidential election, it was revealed that Bush had been arrested for a driving under the influence charge on September 4, 1976, near his family's vacation home in Kennebunkport, Maine. Bush pled guilty to the misdemeanor charge, paid a fine, and had his drivers'

President Bush appeared on the *Jay Leno Show* on November 18, 2010.

license in Maine suspended for two years. A radio station in Maine reported the news of the arrest only one week before the presidential election. In response, Bush admitted that he drank too much earlier in his life. He said that he gave up drinking on his fortieth birthday after waking up with a hangover.

Whom did **Bush defeat** to win the **2004 presidential election**?

Bush defeated U.S. senator John Kerry of Massachusetts to win a second term in office. The election was close: Bush won 286 electoral votes to 251 for Kerry. Bush carried thirty-one states, while Kerry took nineteen states and the District of Columbia. The key state was Ohio with twenty electoral votes. Some charged that there were some voting irregularities in Ohio, but Kerry did not make it a protracted legal matter as Gore had in 2000.

Who was Bush's **vice president**?

Richard "Dick" Cheney served as Bush's vice president for his two terms in office. Cheney previously had served as secretary of state for Bush's father, George H. W. Bush. Cheney was known for his strong defense of conservative positions and his unwillingness to back down from political opponents. One example occurred when cameras caught Cheney using some choice words in an argument with Democratic senator Patrick Leahy.

Who were Bush's choices for **secretaries of state**?

For the first time in history, an African American was chosen as secretary of state when President Bush appointed Colin Powell to his cabinet. Powell, a respected four-star general, had been national security advisor to President Ronald Reagan and chairman of the Joint Chiefs of Staff under President George H. W. Bush. He served as Bush's secretary of state from 2001 to 2005.

After Powell left office, President Bush chose another African American, Condoleezza Rice, to fill the post. Rice had been Bush's national security advisor from 2001 to 2005. Previously, she had been provost at Stanford University, her alma mater, and a key member of President George H. W. Bush's national security team.

Who was Bush's **key advisor** for many years and later his **deputy chief of staff**?

Karl Rove served as Bush's key advisor for several of his political campaigns. Some critics referred to him as "Bush's Brain," referring to Rove's craftiness and intelligence. Bush himself referred to Rove as "The Architect." Without a doubt, Rove was one of the persons most responsible for Bush's two election victories for Texas governor in 1994 and 1998 and for president in 2000 and 2004. Rove is now a political pundit for Fox News.

What awful **terrorist strikes** occurred that defined the early years of the Bush administration?

On September 11, 2001, nineteen Islamic radicals conducted the worst terrorist strike on American soil. They hijacked four commercial airliner jets and crashed two airplanes into the Twin Towers of the World Trade Center in New York City, killing more than three thousand people. They crashed another plane into the Pentagon, killing nearly two hundred people. A fourth plane crashed in Pennsylvania due to the heroic efforts of the passengers who lost their lives when they stormed the attackers, diverted the plane from its probable destination of Washington, D.C., and saved an untold number of lives in the process.

The hijackers were all members of the terrorist group al-Qaeda, led by Osama Bin Laden. The United States and others responded with a global War on Terror and sought to cripple al-Qaeda. Bin Laden was finally located hiding in a fortified Pakistan hideout in May 2011. U.S. Navy Seals shot him to death.

What did **Bush** say in his **speech** to the country **after the terrorist attacks**?

Bush gave an inspired speech to the American public following the attack. He said things such as:

Terrorist attacks can shake the foundations of our biggest buildings, but they cannot touch the foundation of America. These acts shatter steel, but they cannot dent the steel of American resolve.

The search is underway for those who are behind these evil acts. I've directed the full resources for our intelligence and law enforcement communities to find those responsible and bring them to justice. We will make no distinction between the terrorists who committed these acts and those who harbor them.

None of us will ever forget this day, yet we go forward to defend freedom and all that is good and just in our world.

What **country** and regime did **Bush order invaded** after the 9/11 terrorist attack?

Bush, with Congressional approval, authorized the attack on Afghanistan, which began on October 7, 2001. "Operation Enduring Freedom" sought to crush the Taliban government in Afghanistan, which had given safe haven to the al-Qaeda regime. Initially, the war in Afghanistan was successful in the sense that the Taliban regime was toppled and some members of al-Qaeda captured. However, the war has dragged on and its popularity has waned, as U.S. casualties have risen.

What **federal law** did Congress pass and President Bush sign shortly **after the September 11 attacks**?

In October 2001, Congress passed a law known as Providing Appropriate Tools Required to Intercept and Obstruct Terrorism, better known by its acronym the PATRIOT Act. President Bush signed the measure into law on October 26, 2001. The law served as a lightning rod for controversy and for the debate over what is the proper balance between national security and civil liberties. Supporters contend that the Patriot Act was necessary to protect the country from future terrorist attacks to help prevent another 9/11 attack. Critics charged that the Patriot Act violated constitutional rights and gave government too much power.

Part of the problem when discussing the Patriot Act is confusion over the vast number of provisions in the law. It consisted of more than three hundred pages and amended more than fifteen different federal laws. The law approved of roving wiretaps, sneak-and-peak warrants, and national security letters, and it sought to bridge the gap between foreign and domestic intelligence in the U.S.

Some provisions of the law arguably were necessary to bring surveillance laws up to speed in the newer technological age. Other provisions seemed to unnecessarily

447

What happened to Saddam Hussein?

U.S. forces captured Hussein on December 13, 2003. The U.S. turned him over to the new Iraqi government, which tried Hussein for various crimes in November 2006. He was found guilty and executed in December 2006.

encroach upon the Fourth Amendment right to be free from unreasonable searches and seizures.

President Bush adamantly believed that the Patriot Act was necessary to fight the War on Terror and to prevent future terrorist attacks on American soil. Supporters contend that the act helped American law enforcement to break up terror cells and to prevent another 9/11 for the rest of the Bush presidency.

What **treaty** did President Bush and **Russian leader Vladimir Putin** sign that limited nuclear weapons?

President Bush and Russian leader Vladimir Putin signed the Moscow Treaty, or the Strategic Offensive Reductions Treaty (SORT), on May 24, 2002, in Moscow. Under the measure, each country agreed to keep its level of operational nuclear warheads at a number between 1700 and 2200. SORT is an extension of earlier treaties between the two countries, such as SALT I and II and START I, II, and III.

What major **federal law** did Bush sign with regard to **education**?

On January 8, 2002, President Bush signed into law the No Child Left Behind law, often known by its acronym NCLB. Bush had sought to improve education mightily as Texas governor and called for national educational reform during his presidential campaign. NCLB requires school districts to meet specific state standards and testing to ensure that children are learning. The federal law does not set national standards, but allows states to set their own level of standards to measure student competency. The law also has led to increased funding for education in the country. But NCLB is not without its critics. They charge that the law has distorted education by focusing too much on standardized tests and not teaching enough about civic education and other subjects. It is a controversial law with many educators.

What **dictator** met the **end of his reign** during the Bush presidency?

President Bush called for the invasion of Iraq in 2003, which he called a necessary extension of the War on Terror. Bush believed that Iraqi dictator Saddam Hussein was harboring and creating "weapons of mass destruction" and not adhering to United Nations sanctions with regard to weapons and testing of facilities. The invasion, which included a multinational force of troops from the U.S. and other countries, began in March 2003 and led to the fall of Baghdad and Hussein's regime. The U.S. military led a military campaign of bombing called "Shock and Awe." The attack ended Hussein's twenty-four-year-old stranglehold of control in Iraq.

Who were Bush's U.S. **Supreme Court appointees**?

President George W. Bush made two appointments to the U.S. Supreme Court: Chief Justice John G. Roberts Jr. and Associate Justice Samuel A. Alito Jr. When Justice Sandra Day O'Connor announced her intention to retire, President Bush nominated Roberts—who was then a judge on the U.S. Court of Appeals for the D.C. Circuit— as an associate justice to take her place. However, shortly after that, Chief Justice William Rehnquist died and Bush renominated Roberts as chief justice. Congress confirmed Roberts by a vote of seventy-eight to twenty-two.

Bush had asked Justice O'Connor to stay on the Court until another justice would be confirmed. Bush originally submitted the name of Harriet Miers, White House counsel, as his nominee for associate justice. Miers received widespread criticism on her qualifications, so she decided to withdraw her name. Bush then nominated Justice Alito, who had been serving for many years as a judge on the U.S. Court of Appeals for the Third Circuit. The Senate confirmed Roberts by a vote of fifty-eight to forty-two.

POST PRESIDENCY

Has **Bush criticized his successor**, President Barack Obama?

No, President George W. Bush has not criticized his successor, saying that President Obama "deserves my silence." Many view that as a classy move, as Obama has been vocal about criticizing President Bush for past decisions.

What **fund** has Bush worked on **with former President Clinton**?

President Barack Obama asked former Presidents George W. Bush and Bill Clinton to jointly work on promoting a fund for relief to victims of the earthquake in Haiti. The former presidents formed the Clinton Bush Haiti Fund in early 2010.

What **memoir** did Bush publish in his post-presidential years?

Bush published a memoir titled *Decision Points* (2010), which examines key personal and political decisions he had to make in his life.

449

BARACK OBAMA

(1961–)
44th President, 2009–
Party Affiliation: Democrat
Chief 2008 Opponent: John McCain (Republican)

EARLY LIFE AND FAMILY

Where and when was he **born**?

Barack Hussein Obama was born in Honolulu, Hawaii, to Stanley Ann Durham (so named because her father wanted a son) and Barack Obama Sr. of Kenya on August 4, 1961.

Why was his **mother's first name** Stanley?

His mother's first name was Stanley because her father, Stanley Armour Dunham, had hoped to have a son. According to Obama biographer David Remnick in his book *The Bridge* (2009), she would say to people when they asked about her name: "Hi, I'm Stanley. My dad wanted a boy."

What did his **parents do** for a living?

Barack Obama Sr. was a foreign student studying at the University of Hawaii, where he met a young Ann Dunham, who also was a student at the university. He and Dunham

451

President Barack Obama.

What is the controversy over Obama's birth?

Some Obama critics insist that Obama may have been born in Kenya, which would disqualify him for the office of the presidency. The so-called "Birthers" believe that Obama's proof of birth in Hawaii is uncertain. President Obama finally put all doubts to rest in 2011, when he released the long form of his birth certificate.

married, even though—unbeknownst to her—he still had a wife back home in Kenya. Obama left Dunham to pursue his doctorate degree at Harvard. He later worked in the Kenyan government as an economist. Ann Dunham worked as an anthropologist; she studied and lived extensively in Indonesia.

Where did **Obama live** as a **youngster**?

Obama lived in Hawaii for his first few years. However, his mother married an Indonesian student named Lolo Soetoro, who was studying geology. The couple moved to Indonesia, so young Barry—as he was known then—spent several years in Jakarta. In 1971, he returned to Hawaii to live with his maternal grandparents—Stanley and Madelyn Dunham.

Does Barack have any **siblings**?

He does not have any full siblings, but he does have half-siblings. They are: Maya Soetoro-Ng, George Obama, David Ndesandjo (who died in a motorcycle accident), Mark Ndesandjo, Bernard Obama, Auma Obama, and Roy Obama.

What was his **early education**?

Barack Obama attended local public and private schools in Indonesia as a youngster, including St. Francis of Assisi School and then the Model Primary School Menteng I. When he moved back to Hawaii to live with his grandparents, he attended Punahou School—an exclusive private school. Obama played on his high school basketball team at Punahou, but did not crack the starting lineup, as his state-winning championship team featured several college prospects.

Did he **marry**?

He married Michelle Robinson on October 3, 1992, in Chicago, Illinois.

Does he have any **children**?

Yes, Barack and Michelle Obama have two daughters: Malia Ann and Natasha.

President Obama spent much of his youth in his birthplace of Hawaii. He played basketball in high school, a sport he continues to enjoy.

EARLY CAREER

Where did he go to **college**?

Obama first attended Occidental College in Los Angeles, California. He then transferred to Columbia University in 1981, where he majored in political science. He graduated in 1983.

After graduating college, what did he do?

After college, he first worked at Business International Corporation, a company that did research for American firms conducting business overseas. Obama worked in the financial-services division. He then went to the New York Public Research Interest Group, an organization that works on college campuses to engage young people in activism and social justice. Obama met with students at City College and got them engaged in many public issues, ranging from public transportation to voter registration.

What did Obama do when he **moved to Chicago**?

After working in New York, Obama moved to Chicago to work for a community activist-organizer named Jerry Kellman, who became one of Obama's mentors. Kellman led a group called the Calumet Community Religious Conference, which consisted of several churches working to improve surrounding neighborhoods. Kellman started the Developing Communities Project to do community activism. He realized he needed an African American community activist to help with his projects and he saw great potential in Obama.

Obama worked under Kellman for three years from 1985 to 1988. He tried to improve public housing and help create a job training program.

Who was Obama's **first political hero** in Chicago?

Obama's political hero in Chicago was Harold Washington, who became the city's first African American mayor in 1983 with a hard-fought victory over Richard Daley in the Democratic primary and Republican candidate Bernard Epton in the primary. Obama first lived in Chicago in 1985 when Washington was still mayor.

He **left Chicago in 1988** to do what?

Obama left Chicago to attend Harvard Law School. Obama excelled at Harvard, an academic career that culminated in being named editor in chief of the *Harvard Law Review,* the most exclusive student legal publication in the nation. He made a favorable impression on many leading law professors, including Laurence Tribe, Martha Minow, and Charles Ogletree. He worked as a research assistant for Tribe.

At what **law firm** did Obama **meet his future wife**?

During one summer, Obama worked at the Chicago law firm Sidley Austin. There he worked with a young associate attorney named Michelle Robinson—his future wife.

At what university did he **teach law** classes?

Obama accepted a position at the University of Chicago Law School, first as a visiting fellow and then as a lecturer of law. He taught constitutional law at the school from 1992 until 2004, the last eight years as a senior lecturer. He also taught a seminar entitled "Current Issues in Racism and the Law."

At what **law firm** did Obama work in **civil rights**?

Obama accepted a position with Davis, Miner, Barnhill & Galland, a smaller firm specializing in civil rights law. Judson Miner, who had worked for Mayor Harold Washington, wanted Obama to come to the firm. Obama worked as an associate attorney for several years and then took an "of counsel" position.

What **other project** did Obama work on while an **attorney** at Davis, Miner?

He worked for Project Vote, a nonprofit group established in 1982 by Sandy Newman that sought to increase voter registration. Obama accepted Newman's offer to run Project Vote in Illinois. He helped Project Vote register nearly 150,000 new voters.

What **book** did he publish in 1995?

Obama published *Dreams from My Father: A Story of Race and Inheritance* in July 1995, before he launched his political career. A literary agent in New York named Jane Dystel had contacted Obama in 1990, after reading about his editorship of the *Harvard Law Review* in a *New York Times* article. Dystel sold Obama's book to Poseidon Press, a branch of Simon & Schuster, for an advance of $100,000. Obama received $50,000 on signing the contract.

It took him several years to the write the book. A new edition of the book was published after Obama hit the national political stage at the 2004 Democratic National Convention.

POLITICAL OFFICES

What was his **first political position**?

Obama won election as Illinois state senator in 1996 under unusual circumstances. The incumbent, Alice Palmer, had initially decided not to seek reelection, choosing instead to run for a seat in the U.S. Congress. After losing to Jesse Jackson Jr., she applied to run for reelection for her State Senate seat. Obama's campaign challenged whether Palmer and the other candidates had met the legal requirements, questioning whether they had acquired

President Obama successfully nominated Judge Sonia Sotomayor to the U.S. Supreme Court in 2009. Justice Sotomayor is the first Hispanic American woman to serve on the nation's highest court.

enough legitimate signatures. Election authorities determined that Palmer and other candidates did not have enough petition signatures, leaving Obama as the only candidate remaining. Palmer later endorsed Hillary Clinton for president in 2008.

Obama won reelection to the Illinois State Senate in 1998 and 2002. He remained in the Illinois State Senate until winning a seat to the U.S. Senate.

What election did **Obama lose** in **2000**?

Obama challenged four-term incumbent Bobby Lee Rush for the Democratic primary. He lost badly to the popular Rush, as Rush garnered 61percent of the vote to only 30 percent for Obama. Rush said during the campaign: "Barack is a person who read about the civil-rights protests and thinks he knows all about it." Rush, who had served on the Chicago City Council when Harold Washington was the mayor, remains the only person to have defeated Obama in a public election.

Whom did **he defeat** to win a **U.S. Senate seat** in 2004?

Obama won the Democratic primary over numerous challengers. He was set to face Republican Jack Ryan. However, Ryan withdrew from the race after his divorce records became public. His ex-wife, actress Jeri Ryan, alleged that her husband made her have sex with him in sex clubs in New York, New Orleans, and Paris. Ryan withdrew and Alan Keyes accepted the Republican nomination. Obama won easily, capturing 70 percent of the vote.

PRESIDENCY

When did **Obama announce** his run for the presidency?

Obama announced that he was running for president on February 10, 2007, in front of the Old State Capital Building in Springfield, Illinois. It was at this location that Abraham Lincoln gave his "House Divided" speech when he ran for the Senate in 1858.

Whom did **Obama defeat** for the **2008 Democratic primary**?

Obama defeated several candidates in the Democratic primary: Hillary Clinton, senator from New York and wife of former president Bill Clinton; John Edwards, former U.S. senator from North Carolina; Joe Biden, U.S. senator from Delaware; Chris Dodd, U.S. senator from Connecticut; Mike Gravel, former U.S. senator from Alaska; Dennis Kucinich, U.S. representative from Ohio; and Bill Richardson, governor of New Mexico.

It turned out to be a contest between Obama and Clinton. He defeated her by garnering more than 2,300 delegates—more than the necessary 2,117. Clinton ran a tough race and obtained nearly 2,000 delegates herself.

Whom did **Obama defeat** to win the **2008 presidential election**?

Obama defeated Republican John McCain. A longtime U.S. senator from Arizona, McCain presented a formidable foe. He survived nearly six years as a prisoner of war in Vietnam and had served in the U.S. Senate since 1987. Nonetheless, Obama won the electoral vote count 365 to 173.

457

Which former **Democratic primary challengers** did Obama name to his **cabinet**?

Obama named Joe Biden as his vice president and Hillary Clinton as his secretary of state.

What was the **first measure** that Barack Obama signed into **law**?

The first bill that Obama signed into law was the Lily Ledbetter Fair Pay Act, which extends the time period an individual has to file a suit under the Equal Pay Act. Congress had passed the law in response to the U.S. Supreme Court's decision in *Ledbetter v. Goodyear Tire & Rubber Co.* (2007), when the Court ruled that Lily Ledbetter did not file her Equal Pay Act lawsuit in time. The Court had reasoned that the limitations period began when the pay agreement was made, not at each new paycheck.

With Ms. Ledbetter present, Obama signed the measure, and stated: "It is fitting that with the very first bill I sign—the Lilly Ledbetter Fair Pay Restoration Act—we are upholding one of this nation's first principles: that we are all created equal and each deserve a chance to pursue our own version of happiness."

What law did he sign to try to **stimulate the economy**?

Obama signed into law the American Recovery and Reinvestment Act of 2009, colloquially called "the stimulus bill." The law was designed to create jobs, pump money into the economy, and increase consumer spending. The law contains provisions on infrastructure investing, aid to the unemployed and low-income persons, and housing. Obama said upon signing the measure: "The American Recovery and Reinvestment Act that I will sign today—a plan that meets the principles I laid out in January—is the most sweeping economic recovery package in our history."

What **hate crimes law** did Obama sign?

In October 2009, Obama signed into law the Matthew Shepard and James Byrd Jr. Hate Crimes Prevention Act of 2009. It expanded the existing federal hate-crimes law to include crimes motivated by a victim's actual or perceived gender, sexual orientation, gender identity, or disability.

"You understood that we must stand against crimes that are meant not only to break bones, but to break spirits—not only to inflict harm, but to instill fear," Obama said, "You understand that the rights afforded every citizen under our Constitution mean nothing if we do not protect those rights—both from unjust laws and violent acts. And you understand how necessary this law continues to be."

What **major health care law** has President Obama signed into law?

He signed into law the Patient Protection Affordable Care Act, which expands Medicaid coverage, prohibits insurance companies from denying care based on pre-existing illnesses, and supports medical research. There is a four-year window on the implementation of many of the law's major measures.

"[The] bill I'm signing will set in motion reforms that generations of Americans have fought for and marched for and hungered to see," Obama said upon signing the measure into law. "It will take four years to implement fully many of these reforms, because we need to implement them responsibly."

Who were his U.S. **Supreme Court appointees**?

Obama has nominated two associate justices to the U.S. Supreme Court: Sonia Sotomayor and Elena Kagan. Sotomayor, who served on the U.S. Court of Appeals for the Second Circuit and on a federal district court in New York, became the nation's first Latino justice in Court history. The Senate confirmed her by a vote of sixty-eight to thirty-one.

Kagan, formerly Obama's solicitor general, became the fourth woman in Supreme Court history, following after Sandra Day O'Connor, Ruth Bader Ginsburg, and Sotomayor. The Senate confirmed her by a vote of sixty-three to thirty-seven.

PRESIDENTIAL TRIVIA

AGE, BIRTH, AND DEATH

Who was the **youngest president**?

Theodore Roosevelt was forty-two years old when he became president in September 1901, following the death of William McKinley.

Who was the **oldest president** at inauguration?

Ronald Reagan was nearly seventy years old at his inauguration on January 20, 1981.

Which presidents lived to be in their **nineties**?

John Adams, Herbert Hoover, Gerald Ford, and Ronald Reagan all lived until they were at least ninety years of age.

Which **four presidents** were **fifty-seven years old** when they were **inaugurated**?

George Washington, Thomas Jefferson, James Madison, and John Quincy Adams were all fifty-seven when they were inaugurated.

Which presidents were **in their forties** when they became president?

James K. Polk (49), Franklin Pierce (48), Ulysses S. Grant (46), James A. Garfield (49), Grover Cleveland (47), Theodore Roosevelt (42), John F. Kennedy (43), Bill Clinton (46), and Barack Obama (47) were in their forties when they first became president.

Which presidents **died** on the **Fourth of July**?

John Adams, Thomas Jefferson, and James Monroe all died on the Fourth of July. Adams and Jefferson—great political rivals—actually died on the same day, July 4, 1826. Monroe died on July 4, 1831.

In what **month** have **no presidents died**?

No presidents have died in the month of May.

Were any presidents **born** on the **Fourth of July**?

Yes, Calvin Coolidge was born on July 4, 1872.

Which two presidents **died** on the **day after Christmas**—December 26?

Harry Truman and Gerald Ford both died on December 26.

Which two presidents **died** on **March 8**?

Millard Fillmore and William Howard Taft both died on March 8.

Who is the only president to **die before both of his parents**?

Both of his parents were still alive when John F. Kennedy died at age forty-six.

STATES OF BIRTH

More presidents have been born in what state?

Eight Presidents have been born in Virginia: George Washington, Thomas Jefferson, James Madison, James Monroe, William Henry Harrison, John Tyler, Zachary Taylor, and Woodrow Wilson.

What state has been called **"The Mother of Presidents"**?

Ohio has been called The Mother of Presidents because seven presidents have been born there: Ulysses S. Grant, Rutherford B. Hayes, James Garfield, Benjamin Harrison, William McKinley, William Howard Taft, and Warren G. Harding.

Which two presidents were **born in Vermont**?

Chester A. Arthur and Calvin Coolidge were born in Vermont.

Who was the only president **born in New Jersey**?

Grover Cleveland was the only president born in New Jersey.

Which presidents were born in **Tennessee**?

None, but three presidents spent much of their political lives in Tennessee: Andrew Jackson, James K. Polk, and Andrew Johnson.

Who was the only president born in **Missouri**?

Harry Truman was born in Missouri.

Who is the only president born in **Hawaii**?

Barack Obama is the only president born in Hawaii.

FAMILY

Which president had the **most children**?

President John Tyler had fifteen children—eight from his first marriage and seven from his second.

Which presidents had **no children**?

Presidents James K. Polk and James Buchanan never had children. Polk was married but was sterile from an operation as a teen. Buchanan was the only bachelor President.

Who is the **only president** to be **divorced**?

President Ronald Reagan was divorced from Jane Wyman in 1948. He later married Nancy Davis.

President John Tyler was the father of fifteen children, the most of any president.

463

Who is the only president to **have twins**?

President George W. Bush has twin daughters, Barbara and Jenna.

Which three presidents **married while** they were **in office**?

John Tyler, Grover Cleveland, and Woodrow Wilson all married while they were president.

Which **two presidents had sons** who later **became president**?

John Adams's son John Quincy Adams became president. George H. W. Bush's son, George W. Bush, also became president.

Which president's **grandson** also **became president**?

William Henry Harrison was the grandfather of Benjamin Harrison.

APPEARANCE

Who was the **biggest president** in terms of **weight**?

William Howard Taft weighed well over three hundred pounds during his presidency. He is the only president to weigh more than three hundred pounds.

At over three hundred pounds, President Howard Taft (second from left) was America's heftiest president.

Who was the **tallest president**?

Abraham Lincoln was the tallest president in history at six feet, four inches tall.

Who was the **shortest president**?

James Madison was the shortest president, standing only five feet, four inches tall.

Who were the **next shortest presidents**?

Martin Van Buren and Benjamin Harrison were both only five feet, six inches.

Which presidents were **left-handed**?

Eight presidents have been lefties: James A. Garfield, Herbert Hoover, Harry Truman, Gerald Ford, Ronald Reagan, George H.W. Bush, Bill Clinton, and Barack Obama.

Who was the first president to have a **full beard**?

Abraham Lincoln was the first—but certainly not the last—president to have a beard.

EDUCATION

Who was the first president to **graduate from Harvard University**?

John Adams, the second president, graduated from Harvard.

Which two presidents graduated from the **U.S. Military Academy**?

Ulysses S. Grant and Dwight D. Eisenhower both graduated from the U.S. Military Academy.

Who is the **only president** to graduate from the **U.S. Naval Academy**?

Jimmy Carter is the only president to graduate from the U.S. Naval Academy.

Which two presidents graduated from **Harvard Law School**?

Rutherford B. Hayes and Barack Obama are the only two presidents to earn a law degree from Harvard.

Which two presidents graduated from **Yale Law School**?

Gerald Ford and Bill Clinton both graduated from Yale Law School.

Who is the only president to **earn a Ph.D.**?

Woodrow Wilson, the nation's twenty-eighth president, earned a Ph.D. in history and political science from John Hopkins University.

Who is the only president to have an **M.B.A.**?

George W. Bush, the nation's forty-third president, is the only president to earn an M.B.A, which he obtained from Harvard Business School.

Which **other president attended business school** but did not finish his studies?

John F. Kennedy enrolled in Stanford's business school but withdrew.

Which president attended **medical school**?

William Henry Harrison attended medical school at the University of Pennsylvania, but left before finishing.

Who is the only president to have been a **Rhodes Scholar**?

Bill Clinton earned a Rhodes Scholarship to Oxford after graduating from college.

OCCUPATIONS

How many presidents previously **served as vice presidents**?

JAMES BUCHANAN
SECRETARY OF STATE

The last time a secretary of state became president it was James Buchanan, who served in the Polk administration and became the nation's fifteenth president. Some have speculated that Hilary Rodham Clinton, the secretary of state under President Barack Obama, could run for the office.

There were fourteen vice presidents who later became president: John Adams, Thomas Jefferson, Martin Van Buren, John Tyler, Millard Fillmore, Andrew Johnson, Chester A. Arthur, Theodore Roosevelt, Calvin Coolidge, Harry Truman, Richard Nixon, Lyndon B. Johnson, Gerald Ford, and George H.W. Bush.

Who was the last **secretary of state** to later **become president**?

James Buchanan served as secretary of state to James K. Polk, the eleventh president. Buchanan later became the fifteenth president.

Which two presidents previously had **served as secretaries of war**?

James Monroe briefly served as James Madison's secretary of war and William Howard Taft served as Theodore Roosevelt's secretary of war.

Who was the last president to have **served as an ambassador**?

George H. W. Bush served as ambassador to the United Nations before becoming president.

Which presidents **served in U.S. Congress after** they served as the **chief executive officer**?

John Quincy Adams served in the House of Representatives after he was president. Andrew Johnson served in the United States Senate after he was president.

Who was the **only Speaker of the House** to later become **president**?

James K. Polk, former Speaker of the House, later became the eleventh president of the United States.

Which four **former New York governors** later became president?

Martin Van Buren, Grover Cleveland, Theodore Roosevelt, and Franklin D. Roosevelt were governors of New York before becoming president.

Which three **Ohio state senators** later became president?

William Henry Harrison, James A. Garfield, and Warren G. Harding all served in the Ohio State Senate prior to becoming president.

Which two presidents were **formerly state attorneys general**?

Martin Van Buren and Bill Clinton were state attorneys general for New York and Arkansas, respectively, before becoming president.

Which two presidents were **formerly in law enforcement**?

Grover Cleveland was sheriff of Erie County, and Theodore Roosevelt was police commissioner of New York.

Which three presidents had **no prior political experience** or political appointments before becoming president?

Zachary Taylor, Ulysses S. Grant, and Dwight D. Eisenhower were all career military officers who later became president.

SPORTS

Which president had a **chance** to play in the **National Football League**?

President Gerald Ford, a star offensive lineman at the University of Michigan, had a chance to play in the National Football League. He declined and went to law school instead.

Which president had the sports-based nickname of **"The Kansas Cyclone"**?

Dwight D. Eisenhower was known as The Kansas Cyclone for his abilities as a halfback at West Point.

Which president played in the **College World Series** twice?

President George H.W. Bush played for Yale in the college world series on two occasions.

Which presidents were involved in the sport of **boxing**?

President Theodore Roosevelt loved to box, and participated in the sport at Harvard. He later boxed under the tutelage of Mike Donovan. Gerald Ford coached boxing at Yale University.

Which president played **movie roles** about famous **sport figures**?

Ronald Reagan played the part of Grover Alexander in the movie *The Winning Team*. He also played the role of the gifted Notre Dame football player George Gipp in *Knute Rockne: All American*.

Which presidents have hit **holes-in-one in golf**?

President Dwight D. Eisenhower scored a hole-in-one in 1968 at the age of seventy-seven. Gerald Ford hit a hole-in-one at a Celebrity Pro-Am event in Memphis, Tennessee. It was later called the "Shot Heard Round the World."

Which president was **part-owner** of a **major league baseball team**?

President George W. Bush was part-owner and managing general partner of the Texas Rangers.

MILITARY

Which presidents were **former full generals**?

George Washington, Andrew Jackson, Ulysses S. Grant, and Dwight D. Eisenhower were all generals before becoming presidents.

Which presidents were **major generals**?

William Henry Harrison, Zachary Taylor, and James Garfield achieved the rank of major general.

Which presidents achieved the rank of **brigadier general**?

Franklin Pierce, Andrew Johnson, Chester A. Arthur, and Benjamin Harrison were brigadier generals.

Which presidents were considered genuine **war heroes** before becoming president?

George Washington was a hero from the Revolutionary War. Andrew Jackson was a war hero from the War of 1812, the War with the Creek Indians, and the war with the Seminole Indians. William Henry Harrison was a hero from the Northwest Indian War. Zachary Taylor was a war hero from the Mexican–American War, though he served in numerous other wars in his illustrious military career. Ulysses S. Grant was a war hero from the Civil War. Dwight D. Eisenhower was a war hero from World War II. John F. Kennedy was considered a war hero, but never rose higher than the rank of lieutenant.

ELECTIONS

Which president won the **most electoral votes** in a single election?

President Ronald Reagan won reelection in 1984 with 525 electoral votes to only 13 for his Democratic opponent Walter Mondale.

Which president initially **tied** for the **most electoral votes** with someone else?

In the election of 1800, Thomas Jefferson and his vice presidential candidate Aaron Burr each received seventy-three electoral votes. That led to the Twelfth Amendment and separate electoral vote counts for the president and vice president.

Which president won by a **single electoral vote**?

Rutherford B. Hayes defeated Samuel Tilden by an electoral vote count of 185 to184 in the Election of 1876.

Which presidents **never won a presidential election**?

John Tyler, Millard Fillmore, Andrew Johnson, Chester A. Arthur, and Gerald Ford never won a presidential election. They all assumed the presidency while they were vice presidents.

Which president was **never elected president or vice president**?

Gerald Ford served in both capacities but was never elected to either position.

Which presidents **won the election** to president even though they **didn't win the popular vote**?

Presidents Rutherford B. Hayes, Benjamin Harrison, and George W. Bush won the presidency even though they lost the popular vote to Andrew Jackson, Samuel Tilden, Grover Cleveland, and Al Gore, respectively. President John Quincy Adams probably also lost the popular vote—even though there wasn't a popular vote at the time— because he finished behind Andrew Jackson in the number of electoral votes in 1824.

Which **third-party candidate finished second** in a presidential election?

Former President Theodore Roosevelt finished second in the 1912 presidential election, running as a member of the Progressive Party. He finished ahead of third-place finisher, Republican incumbent William Howard Taft. However, he still lost to Democrat Woodrow Wilson.

CABINET

Which president appointed the **first woman** to a cabinet position?

President Franklin D. Roosevelt appointed Frances D. Perkins as his secretary of labor in 1933.

Which president appointed the **first African American** to a cabinet position?

President Lyndon B. Johnson appointed Robert C. Weaver as secretary of housing and urban development in 1966.

President Gerald Ford—shown here (second from right with First Lady Betty Ford, Vice President Nelson Rockefeller (far left) and Bob Dole) after winning the Republican nomination—has the distinction of being the only president who was never elected to high office, not even as vice president.

Which president appointed the **first African American female** to a cabinet position?

President Jimmy Carter appointed Patricia Roberts-Harris as secretary of housing and urban development in 1977.

Which president appointed **more African Americans** to his cabinet **than any other**?

President Bill Clinton appointed seven African Americans to his cabinet: Mike Espy, Ron Brown, Alexis Herman, Rodney Slater, Hazel O'Leary, Jesse Brown, and Togo West.

Which presidents named their **chief primary opponents** as their **secretary of state**?

President Abraham Lincoln named William Seward as his secretary of state when they competed for the 1860 Republican nomination. John Quincy Adams named Henry Clay as his secretary of state after they competed for the 1824 presidential election. James K. Polk named James Buchanan as his secretary of state after they competed for

471

the 1844 Democratic nomination. James Garfield named James Blaine as his secretary of state after they competed for the 1880 Republican nomination. Barack Obama named Hillary Clinton as his secretary of state after they competed for the 2008 Democratic nomination.

Which president **appointed his own brother** to a cabinet position?

President John F. Kennedy appointed his brother Robert as U.S. attorney general. That precedent later led to a federal law that prohibits presidents from naming family members to cabinet posts.

Democratic president Barack Obama **named which Republican** as his **secretary of defense**?

Obama named Robert Gates as his secretary of defense—a position he had held under President George W. Bush.

SUPREME COURT

Who is the **only president** to serve on the **U.S. Supreme Court**?

William Howard Taft served as both president and later as chief justice of the U.S. Supreme Court.

Which presidents **never appointed** someone to the **U.S. Supreme Court**?

William Henry Harrison, Zachary Taylor, Andrew Johnson, and Jimmy Carter never appointed anyone to the Supreme Court.

Which president **appointed more people** to the **U.S. Supreme Court** than any other?

President George Washington appointed nine men to the U.S. Supreme Court and ten appointments in all because he appointed John Rutledge as both associate justice and chief justice. President Franklin D. Roosevelt appointed eight men to the Court.

Who appointed the **first person of the Jewish faith** to the U.S. Supreme Court?

Woodrow Wilson appointed Louis Brandeis to the Court in 1916.

Who appointed the **first African American** to the U.S. Supreme Court?

President Lyndon Johnson appointed Thurgood Marshall to the Court in 1967.

Who appointed the **first female** to the **U.S. Supreme Court**?

Ronald Reagan appointed Sandra Day O'Connor to the Court in 1981.

Who appointed the **first Hispanic** to the U.S. Supreme Court?

President Barack Obama appointed Sonia Sotomayor to the Court in 2009.

Louis Brandeis was the first person of the Jewish faith to be appointed a member of the U.S. Supreme Court. President Woodrow Wilson selected him.

NAMES AND NICKNAMES

Which presidents **changed their last names**?

Gerald Ford was born Leslie Lynch King Jr. He later took the name of his adoptive father, Gerald Ford. William Clinton was originally named William Jefferson Blythe, but changed his name to William Jefferson Clinton to take his stepfather's last name.

Which president **switched** his **first and middle names**?

President Dwight David Eisenhower was born David Dwight Eisenhower. He switched when he went to West Point.

Which president was **named after a reverend**?

Grover Cleveland was named after the Reverend Stephen Grover, a mentor to Cleveland's father.

Which president was **named** in part **after the physician** who delivered him?

Chester A. Arthur was named after Dr. Chester Abell, the physician who delivered him.

473

Which president had his **mother's maiden name** as his **first name**?

Millard Fillmore was named after his mother, Phoebe Millard.

What is the **most common first name** of the presidents?

There have been six presidents named James: James Madison, James Monroe, James K. Polk, James Buchanan, James Garfield, and James Earl Carter Jr.

Who was called **"Dubya"**?

George W. Bush was called "Dubya" after his middle initial.

Who was called **"The Great Communicator"**?

Ronald Reagan was called The Great Communicator for his great public speaking ability and penchant for connecting with audiences.

Who was called **"The Great Humanitarian"**?

Herbert Hoover was known by this nickname for his humanitarian efforts around the time of World War I.

Who was called **"The Great Emancipator"**?

Abraham Lincoln was called The Great Emancipator for his role in freeing the slaves with the issuance of the Emancipation Proclamation.

Who was called **"The Great Manager"**?

Martin Van Buren was called The Great Manager for his skill in politics.

Who was called **"The Napoleon of Protection"**?

William McKinley was called The Napoleon of Protection because of his sponsorship of an extremely high tariff law.

Who was called **"The King of Camelot"**?

John F. Kennedy was called The King of Camelot after his wife revealed that his favorite musical was the play *Camelot*.

ASSASSINATIONS

Who was the **first president killed** by an **assassin**?

President Abraham Lincoln was killed by John Wilkes Booth in 1865.

How many presidents have been **assassinated**?

Abraham Lincoln, James Garfield, William McKinley, and John F. Kennedy were all murdered.

Who were **the assassins**?

John Wilkes Booth killed Lincoln; Charles Guiteau killed Garfield; Leon Csolgosz killed McKinley; and Lee Harvey Oswald killed John F. Kennedy.

Which presidents **survived assassination attempts**?

Andrew Jackson, Theodore Roosevelt, Franklin D. Roosevelt, Harry Truman, Gerald Ford, and Ronald Reagan all survived assassination attempts.

Index

Note: (ill.) indicates photos and illustrations.

499